Peter Altmann
Festive Meals in Ancient Israel

Beihefte zur Zeitschrift für die alttestamentliche Wissenschaft

Herausgegeben von
John Barton · F. W. Dobbs-Allsopp
Reinhard G. Kratz · Markus Witte

Band 424

De Gruyter

Peter Altmann

Festive Meals in Ancient Israel

Deuteronomy's Identity Politics
in Their Ancient Near Eastern Context

De Gruyter

ISBN 978-3-11-025536-2
e-ISBN 978-3-11-025537-9
ISSN 0934-2575

Library of Congress Cataloging-in-Publication Data

Altmann, Peter.
    Festive meals in ancient israel : Deuteronomy's identity in their ancient
Near Eastern context / Peter Altmann.
        p. cm. — (Beihefte zur zeitschrift für die alttestamentliche Wissen-
schaft ; Bd. 424)
    Includes bibliographical references and index.
    ISBN 978-3-11-025536-2 (hardcover 23 × 15,5 : alk. paper)
    1. Dinners and dining — Biblical teaching.   2. Fasts and feasts —
Biblical teaching.   3. Bible. O.T. Deuteronomy — Criticism, interpreta-
tion, etc.   4. Food habits — Israel.   5. Food habits — Middle East.
I. Title.
    BS1275.6.D55A48   2011
    222'.15083942 — dc22

                                                            2011006107

Bibliographic information published by the Deutsche Nationalbibliothek

The Deutsche Nationalbibliothek lists this publication in the Deutsche
Nationalbibliografie; detailed bibliographic data are available in the Internet
at http://dnb.d-nb.de.

Acknowledgements

This monograph represents a revised version of my dissertation completed for Princeton Theological Seminary in 2010. My advisor, Dennis Olson, stepped in to offer assistance while allowing space to develop both the thought represented here and as a young scholar in general. Thanks to Chip Dobbs-Allsopp and Jeremy Hutton, members of my doctoral committee, whose doors and minds were open for dialogue both on the dissertation and throughout my time at Princeton. They, as well as Tremper Longman have seen me through from the early stages of Old Testament study and continue to offer their expertise.

I am grateful for the many other people who have been willing to read a draft or a section and provide feedback along the way, including various SBL sessions and University of Zürich and PTS Old Testament Colloquiums, as well as Nathan MacDonald, Konrad Schmid, Simi Chavel, Daniel Fleming, Christoph Uehlinger, Billie-Jean Collins, Beate Pongratz-Leisten, Dan Pioske, Elaine James, Janling Fu, and Jonathan Greer. In addition, Jürg Hutzli, Safwat Marzouk, Sarah Zhang, Blake Couey, Micah Kiel, and Matt Novenson provided intellectual and needed social support. The faults in the monograph remain my own, but they are far fewer as a result of the many cooks in the kitchen.

Thanks to the editors of BZAW for accepting the monograph and for their helpful suggestions for revisions. The de Gruyter staff have provided excellent support for turning a dissertation into a book.

Without the financial support of the Green Fellowship from PTS, grants from the Swiss National Science Foundation and Zürcher Universitätsverien, the University of Zürich, and my parents, I cannot imagine I would have had the means to finish this project.

My early theological interactions at Mars Hill Graduate School in Seattle birthed the desire for Old Testament study: thanks to the early dreamers of this dream with me. Andy McCoy and Safwat Marzouk have been two hearty and hardy companions along the way.

Reu and Eli, my children, continue to wonder how it can take so long to write one book. Thanks to Birgit for her unflagging support of me as I shaped this book and it me, and moreso for her repeated nudges to be about more than a book.

Zürich, April 2011   Peter Altmann

Table of Contents

Abbreviations

The following abbreviations are in addition to those found in Patrick H. Alexander et al., eds., *The SBL Handbook of Style: For Ancient Near Eastern, Biblical, and Early Christian Studies* (Peabody, Mass.: Hendrickson, 1999).

Akk.	Akkadian
BF	Baghdader Forschungen
BH	Biblical Hebrew
BM	*Beit Miqra'*
BM	British Museum
BZABR	Beihefte zur Zeitschrift für altorientalische und biblische Rechtsgeschichte
CC	Covenant Code of Exodus 20:22–23:31.
CHANE	Culture and history of the ancient Near East
DC	Deuteronomic Code of Deuteronomy 12:1–26:19
DtrH	Deuteronomistic History: Deuteronomy – 2 Kings
DUL	*A Dictionary of the Ugaritic Language in the alphabetic Tradition.* 2d ed. G. del Olmo Lete and J. Sanmartín. 2 vols. Edited and translated by W. G. E. Watson. Leiden, 2004
HANES	History of Ancient Near East Studies
HAV	*Hilprecht Anniversary Volume.* Leipzig, 1909
HBS	Herders biblische Studien
HC	Holiness Code of Leviticus 17:1–26:46
JHebS	*Journal of Hebrew Scriptures*
K	Tablets of the Kuyunjik Collection of the British Museum
l., ll.	Line, lines
Msk	Texts from (Tell) Meskene, Emar
ND	Field numbers of the tablets excavated at Nimrud
OB	Old Babylonian
OG	Old Greek: the reconstructed original Greek translation of the Hebrew and Aramaic scriptures (LXX).
SamP	Samaritan Pentateuch
SFEG	Schriften der Finnischen Exegetischen Gesellschaft
STT	O. R. Gurney and J. J. Finkelstein. *The Sultantepe Tablets I/II.* London, 1957/64.

TAD   B. Porten and A. Yardeni. *Textbook of Aramaic Documents from Ancient Egypt.* 4 Volumes. Jerusalem, 1986–1999
VAS   *Vorderasiatische Schriftdenkmäler der Staatlichen Museen zu Berlin.* Berlin, 1971–
VTE   Vassal Treaties of Esarhaddon
VWGT   Veröffentlichungen der Wissenschaftlichen Gesellschaft für Theologie

Introduction

"Food as communication finds most of its applications in the process of defining one's individuality and one's place in society. Food communicates class, ethnic group, lifestyle affiliation, and other social positions. Eating is usually a social matter, and people eat every day. Thus, food is available for management as a way of showing the world many things about the eater. It naturally takes on much of the role of communicating everything. Indeed, it may be second only to language as a social communication system."[1]

Since the beginning of human society meals in general and feasts in particular have served as defining moments in the construction of human individual and group identity. The French literary critic and philosopher Roland Barthes notes,

No doubt, food is, anthropologically speaking (though very much in the abstract), the first need; but ever since man has ceased living off wild berries, this need has been highly structured. … food permits a person (and I am here speaking of French themes) to partake each day of the national past. In this case, the historical quality is obviously linked to food techniques (preparation and cooking). These have long roots, reaching back to the depth of the French past.[2]

The Old Testament book of Deuteronomy projects a similar notion, prescribing ritual festive celebrations as a primary place for the implementation of its vision of Israelite society.[3] Food in centralized festive

---

1   Eugene N. Anderson, *Everyone Eats: Understanding Food and Culture* (New York: New York Press, 2005), 124.

2   Roland Barthes, "A Psychosociology of Contemporary Food Consumption," in *European Diet from Pre-Industrial to Modern Times*, (ed. R. Forster and O. Ranum; trans. E. Forster and P. M. Ranum; vol. 5 of *Food and Drink in History: Selections from the Annales: Economies, Sociétés, Civilisations*; Baltimore: Johns Hopkins University Press, 1979), 168, 170.

3   I understand Deuteronomy as first directed to a Judahite audience, making *Israelite* primarily an ideological construct in the book. Juha Pakkala, "The Date of the Oldest Edition of Deuteronomy," *ZAW* 121 (2009): 394, notes that 6:4 at least "... refers to a religious community rather than to the inhabitants of a state." I do not find it necessary to date such a conception to the exile as Pakkala does, however, and it may also be that state and religious community need not be separated (i.e., theocracy). It could also easily fit the efforts reflected in Hezekiah's attempts to incorporate refugees from the north after the (repeated) destruction of the northern kingdom by the

celebrations, as well as in localized meals, is a literary *topos* for the construction and maintenance of the common Israelite story and shared identity in Deuteronomy.

The book of Deuteronomy as a whole focuses on the creation of a cohesive communal identity for the people of God, the Israelites.[4] The rhetoric of the book moves toward a unified (though not completely undifferentiated) picture of ONE YHWH, ONE PEOPLE, worshipping at ONE SANCTUARY.[5] This rhetoric promotes common identity among the Israelites by continually referring to a repeated storyline— "remember that you were slaves in Egypt" or "remember that Yhwh has brought you forth from the land of Egypt."[6] Yet in the older layers of the book this function was primarily carried out by prescribing a common set of laws and rituals for the structuring of civil, familial, and ritual life.[7]

Assyrians, such as naming his heir "Manasseh" (cf. Suee-Yan Yu, "Tithes and Firstlings in Deuteronomy" [Ph.D. diss., Union Theological Seminary in Virginia, 1997], 200, n. 80).

4   Mark E. Biddle, *Deuteronomy* (Macon, Ga.: Smyth and Helwys, 2003), 197, for instance states, "Like the prefatory exhortations (chs. 4–11), the [Deuteronomic] Code focuses on transmitting, engaging, and actualizing the fundamental principles of YHWH's covenant with Israel."

5   E. Theodore Mullen Jr., *Narrative History and Ethnic Boundaries: the Deuteronomistic Historian and the Creation of Israelite National Identity* (Atlanta: Scholars Press, 1993), 58.

6   Deut 5:6, 15; 6:12, 21; 13:5, 10 (Heb. 6, 11); 15:15; 16:1, 6, 12; 20:1; 24:18, 22; 26:8. Mark Leuchter, "'The Levite in Your Gates': The Deuteronomic Redefinition of Levitical Authority," *JBL* 126 (2007): 491, observes, "The rhetoric of Deuteronomy evidences a desire to appeal to public memory." Siegfried Kreuzer, "Die Exodustradition im Deuteronomium," in *Das Deuteronomium und seine Querbeziehungen* (ed. T. Veijola; SFEG 62; Helsinki: Finnische Exegetische Gesellschaft and Göttingen: Vandenhoeck & Ruprecht, 1996), 84–87, 101, notes that there is no sign of the exodus tradition in the earliest version of Deuteronomy's centralization law outside of its reception of the Passover-Mazzot traditions in Deut 16.

7   Ronald S. Hendel, *Remembering Abraham: Culture, Memory, and History in the Hebrew Bible* (Oxford: Oxford University Press, 2005), 19, notes four ways in which common identity was marked and built: "Although the varying internal boundaries in Israelite religion and culture suggest a real cultural pluralism, there were also external boundaries that demarcated, more or less clearly, where Israelite culture began and ended ... one such common cultural ground was, of course, language, though there is evidence of dialectal variation within Hebrew. Another source of shared identity was the recitation of traditional stories of the past, such as the Exodus story discussed previously. A third source was the web of genealogies, in which one's family and clan were explicitly related to everyone else in the lineages of Israel. And fourth was the body of shared rituals. In the practices of everyday life, Israelites enacted their cultural identity in symbolic actions, whether offering animal sacrifice at local shrines, making pilgrimages on the major festivals, or undergoing rites of healing or

The shared story appears prominently in the paranetic (exhortative) rhetoric of chapters 5–11 and in the retelling of the common journey up out of Egypt in chapters 1–3. However, the narrative is also enshrined in the law corpus itself (chapters 12–26), especially as part of the motivational clauses within the laws, such as 24:17–18: "Do not deprive the alien or the fatherless of justice... Remember that you were slaves in Egypt and Yhwh your God redeemed you from there. That is why I command you to do this."

In addition to—and perhaps historically prior to—the use of this broad narrative as motivation for keeping the laws, the rhetoric of the Deuteronomic law corpus positions the prescribed feasts to enact a unified common identity. The Deuteronomic law corpus (DC) makes cultic meals a central part of Israelite religious practice, thereby employing an image both earthy and powerful for early "Israelite" and later audiences. The rhetorical potential of the Deuteronomic meal texts (Deut 12:13–27; 14:22–29; 16:1–17; 26:1–15)[8] takes shape from their interplay with the socio-religious and political-economic circumstances of the period—for example, the symbolic importance of meat compared with its increased rarity reflected in the faunal (archaeozoological) record, and the description of meals in relation to the various iconographic and literary portrayals of banquets used both in the local (Israelite and "Canaanite") and Mesopotamian religio-political spheres.

Much like the DC's use of the loyalty-oath or covenant genre, the DC adoption of the cultic meal *topos* exhibits a certain hybrid character: the DC uses tradition-historical elements appearing in the literature and iconography of the wider ancient Near Eastern and the narrower Levantine traditions, adapting them to its particular setting, perhaps fitting best in view of Neo-Assyrian imperialism. The resulting literary formation of cultic meals proposes the participation of all Israel as a conglomeration of household units, first at a singular sanctuary and

---

passage." While all four play a general role in my analysis, the second and especially the fourth receive special attention.

8   I will omit discussion of Deut 26:1–15 in this monograph, as it is as an example of later Deuteronomistic development of the DC cultic meal. I hope to argue elsewhere that the view of meals and food in Dtr Deuteronomy shifts slightly from a focus on identity building through communal remembrance and enjoyment through consumption. In these Dtr texts the focus becomes both 1) remembrance through eating *and* words (26:5–10) and 2) eating and satisfaction (26:13). I characterize this conception of eating as an "eating towards home," targeting a community under the shadow of possible exile or in actual exile. The picture presented in Deut 26:1–15 calls for the community to only experience fullness when consuming cultic meals provided by Yhwh and living in Yhwh's land.

then throughout the land. They are unified by communal consumption in celebration of their shared deity and by their place of worship rather than being unified in their identification with a shared king. The use of communal ritual meals as a central image also taps into broader human tendencies pointed out by modern research in the anthropology and biology of eating that heighten the rhetorical potential of the DC text. In its milieu, the image of cultic meals portrays a pro-Yhwh and subversively anti-imperial, most likely anti-Assyrian "Israel."

This study uses a wide variety of available material and theoretical tools to describe the rhetorical possibilities of the cultic meal texts of the early Deuteronomic law corpus among its ancient audiences. Following the methodology of recent anthropological studies of food and meals, I will unpack various levels of meaning (social, political, religious, and economic) implied in these texts.

My investigation offers a wide range of *potentially* important factors for the construction of meaning by an implied audience. Such an approach to the construction of meaning depends in part on both broadly cultural and specifically individual factors variable with each reception. My study—also dependant on the factors from my own setting—seeks to offer an enriching and persuasive construction of meaning for these DC cultic meal texts.[9]

---

9   I wish here simply to recognize that both my place as a Christian Caucasian male who grew up in the western United States, now living in Europe, married, etc.—as well as very particular and idiosyncratic experiences—play a necessarily important role in my approach to, formulation of, and answer to my question in this monograph.

1. Overview of the History of Scholarship of Deuteronomy

Interpretation of the Deuteronomic meal texts has centered largely on the relationships between the DC and the other biblical law treatments of the various celebrations and sacrifices. One primary axis of discussion revolves around the question of which text(s) from Exodus that the DC uses as *Vorlage(n)*.[1] This general approach appears in a large number of scholarly works since 1990.[2] While there is general agreement

---

1   John Van Seters is an exception to this trend. A short summary of his treatment of the CC (Covenant Code) and its relationship to the DC festivals can be found in "Cultic Laws in the Covenant Code and Their Relationship to Deuteronomy and the Holiness Code," in *Studies in the Book of Exodus: Redaction — Reception — Interpretation* (ed. M. Vervenne; BETL 126; Leuven: Leuven University Press and Peeters, 1996), 319–34. He argues that Deuteronomy precedes the CC. Bernard Levinson, "Is the Covenant Code an Exilic Composition? A Response to John Van Seters," in *In Search of Pre-exilic Israel: Proceedings of the Oxford Old Testament Seminar* (ed. J. Day; JSOTSup 406: London: T & T Clark, 2006), 272–325, reinforces the redactional nature of the CC in its context, which leaves open the possibility of a preexilic date. See further critic of Van Seters' position below. A second exception in recent scholarship is Christoph Levin, "Das Deuteronomium und der Jahwist," in *Liebe und Gebot: Studien zum Deuteronomium* (ed. R. G. Kratz and H. Spieckermann; FRLANT 190; Göttingen: Vandenhoeck & Ruprecht, 2000), 121–36, who sees the CC as an exilic polemic responding to the DC altar law, but as Thomas C. Römer, "Cult Centralization in Deuteronomy 12: Between Deuteronomistic History and Pentateuch," in *Das Deuteronomium zwischen Pentateuch und Deuteronomistischen Geschichtswerk* (ed. E. Otto and R. Achenbach; FRLANT 206; Göttingen: Vandenhoek & Ruprecht, 2004), 179, notes, just because the CC might have been used this way during the exile does not mean that it was written then.

2   These include Timo Veijola, *Das 5. Buch Mose: Deuteronomium: Kapitel 1,1–16,17* (ATD 8,1; Göttingen: Vandenhoeck & Ruprecht, 2004); Shimon Gesundheit, "Intertextualität und literarhistorische Analyse der Festkalender in Exodus und im Deuteronomium," in *Festtraditionen in Israel und im Alten Orient* (ed. E. Blum and R. Lux; VWGT 28; Gütersloh: Gütersloher Verlag, 2006), 190–220; Eleanore Reuter, *Kultzentralisation: Entstehung und Theologie von Dtn 12* (BBB 87; Frankfurt am Main: Hain, 1993); Martin Rose, *5. Mose Teilband 1: 5. Mose 12–25: Einführung und Gesetze* (ZBK 5; Zurich: Theologischer Verlag, 1994); Richard Nelson, *Deuteronomy* (OTL; Louisville: Westminster John Knox, 2002); Eckart Otto, *Das Deuteronomium: politische Theologie und Rechtsreform in Juda und Assyrien* (BZAW 284; Berlin: de Gruyter, 1999); Norbert Lohfink, "Kultzentralisation und Deuteronomium" (Review of Eleanore Reuter, *Kultzentralisation: Entstehung und Theologie von Dtn 12*), ZABR 1 (1995): 117–48; Berhard M. Levinson, *Deuteronomy and the Hermeneutics of Legal Innovation* (Oxford: Oxford Uni-

that DC had the CC text of Exod 20–23 at its disposal, commentators disagree about the status of the "Cultic Code" of Exod 34.[3] Those rejecting the Documentary Hypothesis increasingly view Exod 34 as a later combination of the CC and DC, and perhaps also P,[4] while classic Documentary analysis attributed Exod 34 to J (making it the oldest law code) and the CC to E.

Weinfeld and Milgrom offer a modified approach, assuming not only the Exodus "Covenant Code" (CC) and possibly the "Cultic Code" (or *Privilegrecht*, Exod 34:18–26) texts as *Vorlagen*, but also possibly a preexilic Priestly corpus (P; for Weinfeld, Exod 13 as well).[5] As a result of this major difference in methodological assumptions, these two re-

---

versity Press, 2002); Reinhart G. Kratz, *The Composition of the Narrative Books of the Old Testament* (trans. J. Bowden; London: T & T Clark, 2005); trans. of *Komposition der erzählenden Bücher des Alten Testaments: Grundwissen der Bibelkritik* (Göttingen: Vandenhoeck & Ruprecht, 2000), 117–18; and Jan C. Gertz, "Tora und Vordere Propheten," in *Grundinformation Altes Testament* (3d ed.; ed. idem; Göttingen: Vandenhoeck & Ruprecht, 2008).

3   For a more comprehensive history of scholarship and opposing views, see Reuter, *Kultzentralisation*, 14–42; Otto, *Das Deuteronomium*, 324–40; Gesundheit, "Intertextualität und literarhistorische Analyse der Festkalender in Exodus und im Deuteronomium," 190–220; and Levinson, *Deuteronomy and the Hermeneutics of Legal Innovation*, 8–9, 69–70. Instead of providing a fuller history of scholarship here, I will address concerns as they arise, both in this introductory section and throughout the monograph.

4   Shimon Bar-On (Gesundheit), "The Festival Calendars in Exodus XXIII 14–19 und XXXIV 18–26," *VT* 48 (1998): 166–68; Bernard M. Levinson, "The Revelation of Redaction: Exodus 34:10–26 as a Challenge to the Standard Documentary Hypothesis," paper delivered at "The Pentateuch: International Perspectives on Current Research," Zurich, 11 January, 2010; also Kratz, *Composition*, 149, for a graphic display; David M. Carr, "Method in Determination of Direction of Dependence: An Empirical Test of Criteria Applied to Exodus 34,11–26 and its Parallels," in *Gottes Volk am Sinai: Untersuchungen zu Ex 32–34 und Dtn 9–10* (ed. M. Köckert and E. Blum; VWGT 18; Gütersloh: Gütersloher Verlaghaus, 2001), 107–40. Erhard Blum, *Studien zur Komposition des Pentateuchs* (BZAW 189; Berlin: de Gruyter, 1990), 369–70, attributes it to his KD; Frank Crüsemann, *Die Tora: Theologie und Soizialgeschichte des alttestamentlichen Gesetzes* (Munich: Kaiser, 1992), 139–69, rejects Blum's position because there are too many differences in the details, arguing instead that the earliest layer of Exod 34 comes from the 9th–8th century on the basis of its similarities with Hosea and the Elijah/Elisha narratives.

5   Moshe Weinfeld, *Deuteronomy and the Deuteronomistic School* (Oxford: Clarendon, 1972); idem, *Deuteronomy 1–11: A New Translation with Introduction and Commentary* (AB 5; New York: Doubleday, 1991); and idem, *The Place of the Law in the Religion of Ancient Israel* (VTSup 100; Leiden: E. J. Brill, 2004), 20–33. Jacob Milgrom, *Leviticus: A New Translation with Introduction and Commentary* (3 vols.; AB 3–3B; New York: Doubleday, 1991–2001). They argue that the differences between the DC and P stem from different interests and sociological locations rather than different periods of composition (generally postulated as preexilic for D versus exilic or postexilic for P).

cent approaches provide different conclusions about the importance that P has for explaining the rhetorical and theological emphases of the DC.[6]

The second primary (and related) discussion topic in recent scholarship is the date of composition for Deuteronomy and the different layers of the Deuteronomic law corpus. Classic historical-critical interpretation has concluded that the DC in its earliest form was written between the late eighth and late seventh century. The classic foundation for this determination was de Wette's study, which reintroduced interpretation to the "re-discovery" of the Deuteronomic law in Josiah's time (2 Kgs 23), which de Wette posited as the time of the DC's composition.[7] On the one hand, I do find it important to note that a number of the DC laws likely go back to an earlier period as noted by Jeffrey Tigay.[8] On the other hand, there have always been voices of dissent arguing for a later date.[9]

These discussions of the DC's relationship to particular biblical *Vorlagen* prove vital for the implied historical meaning of the Deuteronomic meal texts. However, while incorporating these concerns, my study extends the discussion to include other important historical, an-

---

6   Alfred Cholewinski, *Heiligkeitsgesetz und Deuteronomium: Eine vergleichende Studie* (AnBib 66; Rome: Biblical Institute Press, 1976); Georg Braulik, "Die dekalogische Redaktion der deuteronomischen Gesetze: Ihre Abhängigkeit von Levitikus 19 am Beispiel von Deuteronomium 22,1–12; 24,10–22; 25,13–16," in *Bundesdokument und Gesetz: Studien zum Deuteronomium* (ed. idem; HBS 4; Freiburg: Herder 1995), 1–25; Weinfeld, *The Place of the Law in the Religion of Ancient Israel*, 80–94; Eckart Otto, *Gottes Recht als Menschenrecht: Rechts- und literaturhistorische Studien zum Deuteronomium* (BZABR 2; Wiesbaden: Harrassowitz, 2002), 35–38; and Jeffrey Stackert, *Rewriting the Torah: Literary Revision in Deuteronomy and the Holiness Legislation* (FAT 52; Tübingen: Mohr Siebeck, 2007) all discuss the relationship between the Holiness Code (HC) and DC with divergent conclusions as to literary priority. Weinfeld asserts that P might have been an essential background text that underlies the DC, while for interpreters dating P to the exilic or postexilic period, P plays little or no role in the exegesis of the DC. Stackert tries to secure an early date for P by relegating all texts that refer to Deut to later H layers.

7   *Dissertatio qua Deuteronomium a priorbus Pentateuchi libris diversum alius cuiusdam recentioris autoris opus esse demonstratur* (1805). For a superb history of scholarship on this point see Cees Houtman, *Der Pentateuch: Die Geschichte seiner Erforschung neben einer Auswertung* (Contributions to Biblical Theology 9; Kampen: Kok Pharos, 1994), 279–332.

8   *Deuteronomy* (Philadelphia: Jewish Publication Society, 1996), xxi.

9   Interpreters since Gustav Hölscher, "Komposition und Ursprung des Deuteronomiums," *ZAW* 40 (1922): 227–30, have dated even the original layer of Deuteronomy to the exilic period (cf. below, i.e., pp. 15–16).

thropological, and human-biological factors.[10] Accordingly, I plan to investigate the DC cultic meal texts and their relationships with the diets of the ancient Levant, with ancient Near Eastern ritual and literary texts, as well as with anthropological theory. To lay the foundation for my study, Deuteronomy's compositional history will be explored briefly to postulate the historical and sociological location for the texts and the extent of the text encountered by the early audiences.

1.1. Compositional History

1.1.1. Deuteronomy, Hezekiah, and Josiah

The now somewhat fragmented scholarly consensus chose the period of the late eighth–late seventh century period for the writing of the DC based on the historical situation described in 2 Kings (and possibly 2 Chronicles), when Hezekiah begins a process of cult centralization continued by Josiah.[11] The "Scroll of the Torah" found in the Temple ac-

---

10   The highlighting of the question of *Vorlagen* is not to suggest that many of these authors have ignored outside factors. Otto's comparison (*Das Deuteronomium*, 59–73) between the Assyrian vassal treaties of Esarhaddon (VTE) and Middle Assyrian Laws is exemplary of such analysis. See also Hans Ulrich Steymans, *Deuteronomium 28 und die adê zur Thronfolgeregelung Asarhaddons: Segen und Fluch im Alten Orient und in Israel* (OBO 145; Freiburg, Switz.: Universitätsverlag and Göttingen: Vandenhoeck & Ruprecht, 1995). Several classic studies in this regard include Weinfeld, *Deuteronomy and the Deuteronomistic School* and Meredith G. Kline, *Treaty of the Great King: the Covenant Structure of Deuteronomy, Studies and Commentary* (Grand Rapids: Eerdmans, 1963). Christoph Koch, *Vertrag, Treueid und Bund: Studien zur Rezeption des altorientalischen Vertragrechts im Deuteronomium und zur Ausbildung der Bundestheologie im Alten Testament* (BZAW 383; Berlin: de Gruyter, 2008) has recently critiqued the direct link between the VTE and the DC promoted by both Steymans and Otto. See below.

11   For a general reconstruction of the history of Hezekiah's reign see Nadav Na'aman, "Hezekiah and the Kings of Assyria," in *Ancient Israel and Its Neighbors: Interaction and Counteraction* (vol. 1 of *Collected Essays*; Winona Lake, Ind.: Eisenbrauns, 2005), 98–117; repr. from *TA* 21 (1994). Many scholars now doubt the historicity of Hezekiah's centralization. Juha Pakkala, "Why the Cult Reforms in Judah Probably Did Not Happen," in *One God - One Cult - One Nation: Archaeological and Biblical Perspectives* (ed. R. G. Kratz and H. Spieckermann, BZAW 405; Berlin: de Gruyter, 2010), 229, for example concludes, "It is more probable that they are literary inventions and projections of later ideals into the monarchic period," and sees some sort of cult purification by Josiah as the maximum. However, see the counter arguments of Menahem Haran, *Temples and Temple Service in Israel: An Inquiry Into the Character of Cult Phenomena and the Historical Setting of the Priestly School* (Oxford: Clarendon Press, 1978), 126–47, and Israel Finkelstein and David Silbermann, "Temple and Dynasty: Hezekiah, the Remaking of Judah and the Rise of the Pan-Israelite Ideology," *JSOT*

cording to 2 Kgs 22–23 is usually equated with the DC in some form, though disagreement continues about how long before its discovery this document was written.[12] Because Josiah's reforms as reported in 2 Kings do not totally follow the DC prescriptions, a legitimate question arises as to the particular form of the DC "Book of the Torah" at his, or his literary embellisher's, disposal.[13] Some scholars have responded to

---

30 (2006): 259–85, esp. 269–75. The nature and extent of Josiah's reform and centralization have produced an unending number of studies. In addition to general scholarship on Deuteronomy, important studies include Christoph Uehlinger, "Gab es eine joschijanische Kultreform? Plädoyer für ein begründetes Minimum," in *Jeremia und die »deuteronomistische Bewegung«* (ed. W. Gross; BBB 98; Winheim: Beltz Athenäum, 1995), 57–89; Norbert Lohfink, "Zur neueren Diskussion über 2 Kön 22–23," in *Das Deuteronomium: Entstehung, Gestalt und Botschaft* (ed. N. Lohfink; BETL 68; Leuven: Peeters Press, 1985), 24–48, translated as "Recent Discussion on 2 Kings 22–23: The State of the Question," in *A Song of Power and the Power of Song: Essays on the Book of Deuteronomy* (ed. D. L. Christensen; Winona Lake, Ind.: Eisenbrauns, 1993), 36–61; and Bernd Gieselmann, "Die sogenannte josianische Reform in der gegenwärtigen Forschung," *ZAW* 106 (1994): 223–42.

12 Some interpreters understand the book "finding" instead to be a cover for a book "writing," meaning that the book was simply created by Josiah and his colleagues to support their reform efforts. While other fraudulent book findings occur in the ancient Near East, the differences between the DC and Josiah's reforms—such as the difference between the provisions set for the Levites in Deut 18:1–8 and the actual rations reported in 2 Kgs 23:8–9 (see Christoph Bultmann, *Die Fremde im antiken Juda: Eine Untersuchung zum sozialen Typenbegriff »ger« und seinem Bedeutungswandel in der alttestamentlichen Gesetzgebung* [FRLANT 153; Göttingen: Vandenhoeck & Ruprecht, 1992], 48–52) and the Passover ordinances in Deut 16:1–8 and the Passover celebration reported in 2 Kgs 23:31–23 (see following note)—reveal sufficient dissonance to support the argument that an *older* book could have been unearthed. Cf. Hermann Spieckermann, *Juda unter Assur in der Sargonidenzeit* (FRLANT 129; Göttingen: Vandenhoeck & Ruprecht, 1982), 156–57; and Bernard M. Levinson, "The Reconceptualization of Kingship in Deuteronomy and the Deuteronomistic History's Transformation of Torah," *VT* 51 (2001): 512–34. The latter points out the evisceration of the king's powers in the judicial, military, and cultic arenas. Reuter, *Kultzentralisation,* 251–58, argues that the Josianic reforms are instead based on the Covenant Code. Otto, *Gottes Recht als Menschenrecht,* 46, details the problems with this view. Thomas C. Römer, *The So-called Deuteronomistic History* (London: T & T Clark, 2007), 49–56, dates the book finding of 2 Kgs 22 to the Persian period. Kratz, *Composition,* 169, sees the starting point for the material in 2 Kings as an annalistic framework (2 Kgs 22:1–2, 4–7, 9, 23:4a, 11–12, 28–30), thereby excluding not only the bookfinding, but also the covenant, the law based reform, and the Passover.

13 Spieckermann, *Juda unter Assur in der Sargonidenzeit,* 136–37, argues that 2 Kgs 23:21–23, which relates the Passover observance, was constructed by DtrN to show that Josiah follows the Deuteronomic ordinances in Deut 16:1–7 completely. One striking difference between the narrative in 2 Kgs 23 and Deut 16 is the central role Josiah plays in the Passover celebration, while the Passover regulations of Deut 16:1–7 promote a decidedly non-royal event. Gary Knoppers, "Rethinking the Relationship between Deuteronomy and the Deuteronomistic History: The Case of Kings," *CBQ* 63 (2001) 408, persuasively argues, "The contrast with the many limitations placed

the difficulties with identifying the layers of 2 Kgs 22–23 to a time near
the seventh century by discounting the importance of 2 Kgs 22–23 and
the reported reform's reliance on the DC as the starting point for dating
the DC to the seventh century. Relinquishing this "Archimedean point"
has raised numerous methodological issues on dating the texts, some of
which I will address below.

The archaeological records of the proposed sanctuaries at Arad and
Beer-sheba around 700 B.C.E. deserve mention at this point, however.
Excavations at these two sites found remains of altars at each site that
were dismantled but not destroyed.[14] There has been considerable discussion as to how, if at all, these finds might be related to the biblical
reports of Hezekiah's reform, especially in 2 Kgs 18:4. While the description of events in the biblical passage does not closely match those
of the archaeological record, there is good reason to conclude that the
centers of worship in Arad and Beer-sheba were carefully dismantled
prior to Sennacherib's invasion.[15] Israel Finkelstein concludes

> Excavations at three sites, Arad, Beer-sheba, and Lachish, seem to have un-
> earthed evidence for eighth-century shrines, or cult places, that were abol-
> ished before the end of the century. It is no less important to note that none
> of the many seventh and early sixth-century B.C.E. sites excavated in Judah
> produced evidence for the existence of a sanctuary.[16]

---

on royal authority in Deuteronomy is startling. As we have seen, the legislation in
Deuteronomy imposes a series of important constraints upon kingship and does not
explicitly accord to the king any role of leadership in the campaign for centralization
(Deut 12:1-31), in the enforcement of the punishments for oneiromancy and seditious
agitation (13:2–19), in the reform of the three major feasts (16:1–17) , in the reorgani-
zation of the judiciary (16:18–20; 17:2–13), or in the restructuring of the military
(20:1–9) Over against this reforming legislation, the Deuteronomist assumes that
monarchs are to enforce centralization, appoint priests, serve in some judicial capacity (at least as a final court of appeals), lead major feasts, and head the military. In
the one literature royal powers are stringently delimited, while in the other formida-
ble royal powers are mandated. In one work the royal role is that of a figurehead,
bereft of traditional kingly authority, while it is assumed in the other that the king
leads the nation and exercises substantial authority in implementing specific Deuteronomic legislation."

14   Early publications are Yohanan Aharoni "Arad: Its Inscriptions and Temple," *BA* 31
     (1967): 2–32 and idem, "The Horned Altar of Beer-sheba," *BA* 37 (1974): 2–6.

15   Ze'ev Herzog, "Perspectives on Southern Israel's Cult Centralization: Arad and
     Beer-sheba," in Kratz and Spieckermann, *One God - One Cult - One Nation: Archaeo-
     logical and Biblical Perspectives.*

16   *The Quest for the Historical Israel: Debating Archaeology and the History of Early Israel:
     Lectures Delivered at the Annual Colloquium of the Institute for Secular Humanistic Juda-
     ism, Detroit, October 2005* (ed. B. B. Schmitt; SBLABS 17; Atlanta: SBL, 2007), 155. Fur-
     thermore, for some sort of implementation of Deuteronomy one merely needs to ar-
     gue for some sort of sacrificial centralization, not comprehensive cultic centrali-

Exactly how this relates to Hezekiah's or Josiah's cultic actions rests on one's methodological approach to the biblical texts, though the congruence is striking.[17]

1.1.2. Streams of Scholarly Analysis

Theories about the compositional history of the DC are manifold, but one might distinguish between two main camps largely separated by language and methodology. The various approaches are not necessarily affected by religious confession, and there are some constants across the groups. With few exceptions the priority of the CC as a *Vorlage* for the DC and the importance of cult centralization for the DC are shared presuppositions for all parties.

On one pole, North American and Israeli scholars tend to formulate positions similar to North American scholar Richard Nelson, who argues that the main portion of Deuteronomy (5–28, minus 27 and other smaller additions) was written and "micro-redacted" in a short period of time before public presentation in the seventh century.[18] These schol-

---

zation. This follows Norbert Lohfink, "Opferzentralisation, Säkularisierungsthese und mimeische Theorie," in *Studien zum Deuteronomium und zur deuteronomistischen Literatur III* (SBAB 20; Stuttgart: Verlag Katholisches Bibelwerk, 1995), 220: "Aber das deuteronomische Gesetz spricht nirgends von der Abschaffung von israelitischen Heiligtümern. Seine sogenannten Zentralisationsgesetze, vor allem die Zentralisationsgesetze in Dtn 12, handeln nur von der Zentralisation bestimmter Akte, vor allem der Opfer. Dtn 12 in seinem Hauptstück ist Opfer-, nicht Heiligtumsgesetzgebung." [But the Deuteronomistic Law never mentions the abolition of Israelite sanctuaries. Its so-called centralization laws, especially the centralization laws of Deut 12, only deal with the centralization of specific actions, primarily sacrifice. Deut 12 focuses chiefly on sacrificial and not sanctuary law.]

17 Nadav Na'aman, "The Debated Historicity of Hezekiah's Reform in Light of Historical and Archaeological Reserach," in *Ancient Israel's History and Historiography: The First Temple Period* (vol. 3 of *Collected Essays*; Winona Lake, Ind.: Eisenbrauns, 2005), 274–90; repr. from *ZAW* 107 (1995): 179–95, however, calls into question the solidity of the dismantling of altars in Beersheba and Arad, partially on the basis of the cult paraphernalia depicted as booty in Sennacherib's Lachish reliefs.

18 Nelson, *Deuteronomy*, 8. Nelson does not completely avoid identification of later additions. Weinfeld, *Deuteronomy and the Deuteronomic School*, 7, also works from the standpoint that Deuteronomy (in his case most of 5–28) receives the bulk of its shaping in the seventh century. While admitting to various redactional levels, he is quite typical of this group in expressing despair about attempts to separate various redactions due to the lack of sufficient criteria: "Though the book of Deuteronomy quite probably consists of different editorial strands, no established criterion exists by which we can determine either the extent of each strand of its composition or its ideological teaching." Eckart Otto, *Das Deuteronomium*, 351–64 (chart on p. 353) pre-

ars are 1) more skeptical about modern interpreters' ability to identify and date particular editorial redactions and additions; 2) more confident in the general completeness of the "original" preexilic version of Deuteronomy; and 3) more reliant on external archaeological or non-biblical comparative texts for the absolute dating of the DC.[19] Their basis for the interpretation of the early DC is generally chapters (4:45) 5–28. This conclusion allows for the identification of the original form of the DC as some combination of a covenant treaty and "law code" (more on this below).

At another pole Veijola—like other Continental European and especially German-speaking scholars such as Gesundheit, Gertz, and Rose—argues for multiple redactional levels between the time of Josiah (or Hezekiah for Rose and Braulik) and post-Priestly redactions in the DC.[20] This observation leads to two conclusions: 1) These scholars put more confidence and weight on the successful separation of layers in the text of Deuteronomy itself; and 2) They are less convinced by ancient Near Eastern comparative texts when it comes to absolute dating for the biblical texts. For example, they argue for a relatively late (exilic or postexilic) date for the covenantal structure of Deuteronomy.[21] Veijola argues that references to covenant cannot be preexilic because they

---

sents an exception as a German scholar who contends for a seventh-century date for Ur-Deuteronomy consisting of chapters 5–28*. However, like his German-speaking colleagues he locates most redactional insertions in the exilic and postexilic periods and expresses more confidence in modern scholarly abilities to identify later additions. Otto's distinctive argument is that Deuteronomy is literarily dependent upon and reacting against the Succession Treaty of Esarhaddon (VTE) .

19   A fourth category may be the heavier reliance on a political-historical approach to dating in the American-Israeli camp versus the more thematic approach to redaction criticism found in Continental European scholarship.

20   Timo Veijola, 5. Mose, 2–5. See also idem, "Bundestheologisches Redaktion im Deuteronomium," in Deuteronomium und seine Querbeziehungen (ed. idem; SFEG 62; Helsininki: Finnische Exegetische Gesellschaft and Göttingen: Vandenhoeck & Ruprecht, 1996), 257. Each scholar has their own particular story and much cross-pollination occurs, which certainly qualifies my general categorization, but I still find it helpful in providing a general overview. One such example of cross-pollination is Shimon Gesundheit (Bar-On), who teaches in Israel but has a significant German-speaking background.

21   Veijola (ibid.), for instance, dates this layer, DtrB: "Deuteronomistische Bundesredaktion" or "Deuteronomistic covenantal redaction," to the postexilic period. Compare Koch, Vertrag, Treueid und Bund, 11–12, who also follows many tenets of Germanic interpretation but critiques Veijola's postulation of a DtrB (which follows the Göttingen model for the DtrH) since it cannot be firmly connected with the postexilic period.

are dependent on the First Commandment.[22] This issue has significant consequences for determining whether the (posited) DC comes from the seventh century and contains significant anti-Assyrian polemics.

Braulik, and Otto (and Gesundheit for later stages of Deuteronomy's textual growth) consider both the Covenant Code and the so-called "Cultic Code" (Exod 34:10–26) as the most important *Vorlagen* for the DC, and especially Deut 16.[23] Braulik also contends that the basic text of the DC comes from the time of the *sacrificial* centralization under Hezekiah based on the biblical narrative of 2 Kgs 18:4, 22, as well as on the archaeological finds related to the altars found at Arad and Beersheba. He finds evidence of centralization in the "Cultic Code" and argues that this code likely served as the impetus for Hezekiah's cultic centralization reforms.[24]

---

22 Veijola, "Bundestheologisches Redaktion," 273–74; also Koch, *Vertrag, Treueid und Bund*. See the earlier critique in Jon D. Levenson, *Sinai to Zion: An Entry into the Jewish Bible, New Voices in Biblical Studies* (San Francisco: Harper, 1985), 25–26 n. 10, of this line of reasoning. Psalms 50, 74, 78, 81 are noted in Stephen L. Cook, *The Social Roots of Biblical Yahwism* (Studies in Biblical Literature 8; Atlanta: Society of Biblical Literature, 2004), 24–26, and further discussion of ancient covenant in the ancient Near East, ibid., 26–27. See the more detailed discussion of covenant below.

23 Georg Braulik, *Deuteronomium*, (vol. 1; NEchtB 15; Würzburg: Echter Verlag, 1986), 10; Otto, *Das Deuteronomium*, 325–35. Gesundheit, "Intertextualität und literarhistorische Analyse der Festkalender in Exodus und im Deuteronomium," 198, 205, argues for a complex redaktional intermingling of the various festival calendars, which carries further implications for Deuteronomy as a whole. For example, he argues that Deut 16:1–17 has Exod 23:14–19, and Exod 34:18–26 as *Vorlagen* because it takes their language into account and then changes their order, bringing Massot and Passover together. To date Gesundheit has not published a thoroughgoing compositional history for Deuteronomy, but his analysis for the "festival calendars," such as Deut 16, is exemplary for its attention to detail. Like Gesundheit, Jan C. Gertz, "Die Passa-Massot-Ordnung im deuteronomischen Festkalender," in *Das Deuteronomium und seine Querbeziehungen* (ed. T. Veijola; SFEG; Helsinki: Finnische Exegetische Gesellschaft and Göttingen: Vandenhoek & Ruprecht, 1996), 56–80, argues that while a few minor details stem from a later time period, the section as a whole comes from the hand of the Deuteronomic author. Gertz, then, does not necessarily see the DC as the work of a committee from various backgrounds as Nelson does; however, he does argue that the core of Deut 12–25 stems on the most part from the late preexilic period. A summary of Gertz's view of 16:1–8 is found on ibid., 69: "Bis auf den Nachtrag in V.5bβ stammen somit alle Passagen in den V.1–8, das sich mit dem Passa beschäftigen, vom dt Gesetzgeber." ["Except for the addition in v. 5bβ all sections of vv.1–8 dealing with the Passover originate with the Deuteronomic lawgiver."] As ibid., 69, n. 44 explains, this does not mean the Deuteronomic writer constructed it, but that nothing comes later. For an overview of his determination of the original layer of Deuteronomy, see idem, "Tora und Vordere Propheten," 255.

24 Braulik, *Deuteronomium*, 10. As an important side note to Braulik's heavy reliance on the "Cultic Code" (Exod 34), he dates Deut 16:18–18:22 to the exilic period. In effect this separates the laws regarding the cult (and meals) not only thematically but his-

Braulik (like Rose) sees 12:13–19, for example, as the oldest layer in chapter 12, and he dates this earliest layer to the time of Hezekiah,[25] which contrasts with dates proposed by Veijola and Gesundheit. Like many European interpreters, Braulik detects a "Decalogue redaction" that adds the Decalogue of Deut 5 and serves to order the laws of the DC loosely according to the Ten Commandments.[26]

An exception or mediated view might be seen in Mayes, an Irish scholar, who postulates a process of growth in which the DC began as a law code like other ancient Near Eastern law codes, meaning that especially the Decalogue (ch. 5), the exposition of the first commandment (chs. 6–11), and the blessings and curses (ch. 28) were added during the exilic period.[27] His stance also proposes an ongoing and complicated redactional process: "It is, of course, not to be denied that additions were made to the book ... However, these are to be seen as unconnected, isolated additions which do not constitute a systematic editing and reworking of the content."[28] Mayes thus parallels Continental European scholarship in determining that the DC was originally a law corpus void of a covenantal structure until Deuteronomistic editing during the exile, but his work bears similarities to the North American and Israeli tendencies that remain more skeptical about the possibility of precisely identifying the time, place, and connectedness of various redactional levels (beyond his identification of exilic Deuteronomistic editing). He also identifies the late preexilic context as decisive for the formation of the basic thematic trajectory of Deuteronomy as a whole.[29]

---

torically from those laws for governing (ibid., 12). This can be contrasted with the positions of Otto, *Das Deuteronomium*; Levinson, *Deuteronomy and the Hermeneutics of Legal Innovation*; and William S. Morrow, *Scribing the Center: Organization and Redaction in Deuteronomy 14:1-17:13* (SBLMS 49; Atlanta: Scholars, 1995). Braulik's determination that the Cultic Code brought on Hezekiah's reform is too hypothetical and speculative to be given much weight.

25 Braulik, *Deuteronomium*, 93.

26 Georg Braulik, *Die deuteronomischen Gesetze und der Dekalog: Studien zum Aufbau von Deuteronomium 12–26* (SBS 145; Stuttgart: Verlag Katholisches Bibelwerk, 1991). This position is also accepted by Otto, *Das Deuteronomium*, 233. In addition to reconstructing the compositional history of Deuteronomy, Braulik's writings are also important for my project for a second reason: he has devoted several essays to the meaning of the Deuteronomic feasts. Interaction with these essays will feature prominently below.

27 Andrew D. H. Mayes, *Deuteronomy* (NCB; London: Marshall, Morgan & Scott, 1979), 54, argues, "It is with the deuteronomistic editing of Deuteronomy, particularly in its second stage, that the treaty elements are introduced."

28 Ibid., 47.

29 Mayes, "On Describing the Purpose of Deuteronomy," *JSOT* 58 (1993): 30.

A development within the Continental European and German-speaking conversation has resulted in a return to dating the earliest layers of the DC after 586 B.C.E. Kratz's prominent *The Composition of the Narrative Books of the Old Testament* follows in the lines of much Germanic scholarship in its reliance on text-internal methods for dating: "So there is nothing for it but to date Deuteronomy according to the criterion given by the basic text itself, the theological programme of centralization of the cult. This notion is so special and singular in the world of the ancient Near East that there must be special reason for it."[30] Yet this does not mean that Kratz disregards archaeological and other external factors (he proposes two possible dates—late eighth century directed against the various manifestations of Yhwh and post 586 directed against the fragmentation of Judahite society).[31] Pakkala issues a more confident challenge to those who date *Urdeuteronomium* to the preexilic period, suggesting ten problems with the majority position from the lack of a monarch in *Urdeuteronomium*, no reference to a temple or Judah or Jerusalem, the Elephantine papyri, and Deuteronomy's supposed idealism.[32] These arguments do call for a reexamination of the reasons for dating Deuteronomy to the late preexilic period. Of special importance for the methodological discussion is Pakkala and Kratz's (also Otto) denial of the connection between Josiah's reform and the DC generally taken for granted since de Wette and Wellhausen.

1.2. Methodology for Dating Texts

If the connection to 2 Kings cannot be trusted as a basic point of reference—of course this point is still up for debate—what might be a different basis for dating the earliest layer of the DC?

Otto opened this line of questioning in recent scholarship and turned specifically to the DC's similarities to the VTE (Vassal Treaty of Esarhaddon), especially in Deut 13 and 28 and tied the date of Deuter-

---

30   Kratz, *Composition*, 132, cf. 118.
31   Ibid. He has backed away from the later date somewhat in "The Idea of Cultic Centralization and Its Supposed Ancient Near Eastern Analogies," in Kratz and Spieckermann, *One God - One Cult - One Nation: Archaeological and Biblical Perspectives.*, 137.
32   Pakkala, "The Date of the Oldest Edition of Deuteronomy," 388–401. He summarizes them conveniently in "Cult Reforms in Judah," 210–11. Strong rebuttals of an exilic or postexilic dating are found in Frank Crüsemann, *Die Tora: Theologie und Sozialgeschichte des alttestamentlichen Gesetzes* (Munich: Kaiser, 1992), 243–46,. For the problems with Pakkala's view see Nathan MacDonald, "Issues in the Dating of Deuteronomy: A Response to Juha Pakkala," *ZAW* 122 (2010): 431–35.

onomy directly to this connection.[33] His turn to the Neo-Assyrian text also represents skepticism with regard to dating based on inner-biblical data.[34]

Kratz offers a strong critique, however:

> Similarities to the Assyrian state treaties and especially to the much-quoted vassal treaty of Esardaddon [sic!] with the princes of Media occur at various literary levels which are recognized as being late, so that the Neo-Assyrian period gives us a *terminus a quo* for Deuteronomy, but no more than that. If we went only by the parallels from the Near East, we would have to date Ps. 104; Prov. 22.17-23.11 or the Job poem towards the end of the second millennium BC.[35]

Kratz instead returns to inner-biblical criteria: the so-called *Numeruswechsel*,[36] the relationship with the CC, and "tendency criticism" (*Tendenzkritik*) dominated by the centralization idea:

> Therefore what belongs to Ur-Deuteronomy and what does not is not decided either by reconstructed pre-Deuteronomistic collections in Deut. 12–26 or by the supposed external evidence from Hittite and Assyrian treaty texts, which can always have had an influence everywhere, but by these three criteria: the change of number, the relationship to the Book of the Covenant, and the law of the centralization of the cult.[37]

This approach leads him to conclude, "Everything else in Deut. 12-25 falls outside the framework in terms of style, composition and theme and therefore proves to be secondary."[38] All three criteria must be met simultaneously for him to consider the text part of the earliest Deuteronomy. One might question whether texts, authors, and readers are truly so single minded? Perhaps sometimes an author has one criterion more in view than another? Kratz's complete discounting of the importance of identifying "pre-Deuteronomistic" layers and of comparative ancient Near Eastern texts in this statement are somewhat mitigated by his own analysis elsewhere, but they stand as important challenges. I would contend that the identification of Deuteronomistic additions can

---

33   Otto, *Das Deuteronomium*, 6, 14, 32–33, etc.
34   Ibid., 14. See also Houtman, *Der Pentateuch,* 323.
35   Kratz, *Composition*, 132.
36   See especially Georges Minette de Tillesse, "Sections 'tu' et sections 'vous' dans le Deutéronome," *VT* 12 (1962): 29–87.
37   Kratz, *Composition*, 118. Bar-On (Gesundheit), "The Festival Calendars in Exodus XXIII 14-19 and XXXIV 18-26," 187, makes a similar methodological statement for the Sinai pericopes: "As least so far as the first stages of critical study and its point of departure are concerned, the literary and textual analysis must certainly precede the typological and comparative study."
38   Ibid., 119. In detail (ibid., 133: 6:4–5; 12:13–14a, 15–18; 14:22, 25–26; 15:19–23; 16:16–18; 17:8–9aα, 9b–10a; 19:2a, 3b–7, 11–12, 15–17a, 18bα; 21:1–4, 6–7; 8b; 26:1–4, 11, 16).

certainly be helpful, and comparative treaty texts or law codes carry the most weight in times when these texts are important in and of themselves. There is, however, significant skepticism towards internal historical-critical criteria such as those stated by Kratz. For example, the so-called *Numeruswechsel* between 2nd person masculine singular and 2nd person masculine plural pronouns is helpful in the move from 2nd person plural pronouns in 12:2–12 to 2nd person singular pronouns in 12:13–27. However, the use of the *Numeruswechsel* as a criterion can only be taken so far. As Hillers noted decades ago, changes in pronouns between 2nd singular and 2nd plural also occurs in the Sefire Treaties, which raises the question of their absolute effectiveness as a criterion.[39]

Unfortunately the methodology cannot be delimited quite as clearly as one might hope, and multiple factors must be taken into consideration in order to form grounded hypotheses in the dating of these texts. In the sections that follow I will highlight several important factors for dating — the relationship with the CC, covenantal and law corpora form-critical concerns, the historical situation in the Neo-Assyrian period — while readily admitting that none of these factors are determinate.[40] One secondary criterion I employ are the possible separation between *pre*-Deuteronomistic layers and Deuteronomistic texts in Deuteronomy based on their verbal similarities with other biblical texts, but especially the so-called DtrH and similarities with texts that Erhard Blum has also attributed to his KD in the rest of the Pentateuch.[41]

Finally, in terms of my project, the interpretive power of meals cannot be limited to one historical period. Feasts are in part important precisely because of their trans-historical relevance. Nonetheless, positing the early exigency for the construction of these texts and their implications remain important.

---

39   Delbert R. Hillers, *Treaty Curses and the Old Testament Prophets* (BibOr 16; Rome: Pontifical Bible Institute, 1964), 32–33. My chapter on Deut 12 will discuss this feature further.

40   Gertz, "Tora und Vordere Propheten," 253–55, provides similar criteria.

41   Blum, *Studien Zur Komposition Des Pentateuch*, 202–203, for texts in Deut (i.e., 6:20–25) that, along with Exod 12:24–27; 13 exemplify similarities that suggest shared authorship. See also below in my discussion of the inner-biblical parallels to Deut 16, 4.4.2. Exodus 23 and Source-Critical Analysis of Deuteronomy 16.

1.2.1. The Relationship Between the
Deuteronomic and the Covenant Codes

I begin with perhaps the most widely accepted criterion, the notion that the CC forms an essential *Vorlage* for the early version of Deuteronomy. In accepting this position I maintain that the centralization theme of Deut 12–21 (26) is a primary goal within the DC text.[42] While I disagree with proposals such as von Rad's that see centralization as a later redactional addition,[43] these theories are not without ancient support: the covenantal ceremony in Deut 27 including sacrificial elements, showing that cult centralization could be relativized even within the redactional history of Deuteronomy itself,[44] and the Elephantine correspondence (TAD A4.7 [*COS* 3.51] , TAD A4.8 [*COS* 3.52] , and TAD A4.10 [*COS* 3.53]) concerning the rebuilding of a temple in Elephantine shows that the possibility of building a temple outside Jerusalem complete with burnt (*'ōlāh*) and festive (*zebaḥ*) sacrifices existed in the fifth century B.C.E. or earlier.[45] Yet even this early evidence is not decisive for the interpretation of Deut 12:13–19 itself: a counter-example within the so-called DtrH *and* Deut 12:8–12 is the notion of periodization (Israel can sacrifice outside the central sanctuary *until* the period of rest is reached), which is introduced in

---

42 Levinson, *Deuteronomy and the Hermeneutics of Legal Innovation*, 27–28; Alexander Rofé, "The Strata of the Law about the Centralization of Worship in Deuteronomy and the History of the Deuteronomic Movement" in *Deuteronomy: Issues and Interpretation* (London: T & T Clark, 2002): 97–101.

43 Gerhard von Rad, *Das fünfte Buch Mose: Deuteronomium* (ATD 8; Göttingen: Vandenhoeck & Ruprecht, 1964), 63; also Baruch Halpern, "The Centralization Formula in Deuteronomy," *VT* 31 (1981): 20–28. Peter T. Vogt, *Deuteronomic Theology and the Significance of Torah: a Reappraisal* (Winona Lake, Ind.: Eisenbrauns, 2006), 167–78, makes a similar argument without considering the *māqôm* formula as a later edition. Vogt, however, rejects all source- and redactional-critical analysis of the book.

44 I find the argument placing this complex of texts (Deut 11:26–30; 27; Josh 8:30–35; 24) in the postexilic period convincing as argued in Nadav Na'aman, "The Law of the Altar in Deuteronomy and the Cultic Site Near Shechem," in *Rethinking the Foundations: Historiography in the Ancient World and in the Bible* (ed. S. L. McKenzie and T. Römer; BZAW 294; Berlin: de Gruyter, 2001), 141–61; repr. in *Ancient Israel's History and Historiography: The First Temple Period* (vol. 3 of *Collected Essays*; Winona Lake: Eisenbrauns, 2006).

45 Pakkala, "The Date of the Oldest Edition of Deuteronomy," 397–98, sees the Elephantine texts as evidence pointing to the non-existence of Deuteronomy at this time. His logic does not hold up, however, as seen by the very inclusion of Deut 27 within the book of Deuteronomy itself.

order to explain why sacrificial centralization only begins after the completion of the first temple.[46]

Because centralization is one of the major changes from the CC, I read the DC diachronically with regard to its location of sacrifice at the central place. As such, the DC envisions a significant change in the way that ritual festivals take place in ancient Israel. Several lines of argumentation support the general connection between the DC and CC: 1) The sacrificial cultic ordinances of Deut 12:13–19 take up and reuse the language and themes found in Exod 20:24–26.[47] 2) The reception of the slave laws of Deut 15:12–18 displays the incorporation and revision of the CC slave law of Exod 21:2–11 in light of the Deuteronomic "brother" ethic.[48] 3) Deuteronomy's "festive calendar" in 16:1–17 displays significant correspondence with the shorter calendar in Exod 23:14–19.

Establishing the DC's dependence on the CC is an important scholarly milestone, yet probing the nature of this dependence is also important: in what way does the DC use this earlier source? Biddle argues that the DC attempts a reformulation of the earlier agrarian code for an

---

46 Halpern, "The Centralization Formula in Deuteronomy," 26, concludes that centralization really comes with a later, likely Dtr layer of Deuteronomy. Morrow, *Scribing the Center,* 54, critiques Halpern's position: "There is no reason to believe that the contrast in 12:14–15 means something different than these clearer references to a single (central) cult place [cf. 17:8 and 18:6]." I am also unconvinced by Van Seters, "Cultic Laws in the Covenant Code and Their Relationship to Deuteronomy and the Holiness Code," 330–32, where he argues that the CC is a reworking of the DC. He reads Exod 20:24 with the Syriac Peshitta ("Everywhere you invoke my name"), but there is little reason to conclude that the text of the Peshitta offers a better reading than the wealth of other ancient readings. The Peshitta is more likely updating the text for its own era, while the MT (and others) implies an ancient (pre-Deuteronomistic) context. Furthermore, it is much easier to explain Deut 16:16a as quoting from Exod 23:17 than the reverse because *kol-zĕkûrĕkā* ("each of your males") in Deut 16:16a does not work well with the theology of the DC, which emphasizes the inclusion of the whole people. This focus simply on the males is less problematic for the CC. See also the critique found in William S. Morrow, "'To Set the Name' in the Deuteronomic Centralization Formula: A Case of Cultural Hybridity," *JSS* 55 (2010): 379 n. 62.

47 Levinson, *Deuteronomy and the Hermeneutics of Legal Innovation,* 28–36.

48 Otto, *Das Deuteronomium,* 125–60. Otto, in his essay "The Pre-exilic Deuteronomy as a Revision of the Covenant Code," in *Kontinuum und Proprium: Studien zur Sozial- und Rechtsgeschichte des Alten Orients und des Alten Testaments* (Orientalia Biblica et Chrstiana 8; Wiesbaden: Harrassowitz, 1996 [rev. paper from 1993 SBL Annual Meeting in Washington D.C.]), 112–22, goes so far as to understand all of the CC as received or revised in the DC.

urban monarchial period.[49] Levinson, on the other hand, not only sees the DC as an update, but he goes a step further:

> The point is that the authors of Deuteronomy used the Covenant Code dialectically. On the one hand, the Covenant Code was known to and used by the authors of the legal corpus of Deuteronomy, even if not in its present compass or yet redacted into the Sinai pericope; thus, textual dependence exists … The authors of Deuteronomy used the Covenant Code as a textual resource in order to pursue their own very different religious and legal agenda. The authors of Deuteronomy employed the garb of dependence to purchase profound hermeneutical independence.[50]

Levinson, whose argument has been widely accepted, sees the reception of the CC by the DC as essentially subversive: "In the end, however, inner biblical exegesis does not provide a satisfactory model to describe the achievements of the authors of Deuteronomy. The concern of the authors of Deuteronomy was not to explicate older texts but to transform them."[51]

Levinson's conclusions have not gone unchallenged. Vogt notes that Levinson's argument is based on an unnecessary premise.[52] In order for the DC to use CC language to bolster its credentials, the audience must be quite aware of the contents and wording of the CC. However, any such audience, being so aware, would then likely be able to detect the "Deuteronomic wolf in Covenant Code clothing." Otto also counters Levinson's argument: "If the laws of the Covenant Code were supplemented in Deuteronomy, this did not mean that the Covenant Code was no longer valid."[53] The difficulty with Otto's perspective, as Hutzli notes, is that Otto's argument does not account for the wider societal transformation involved in the Deuteronomic formation, such as the oft-noted increase in offerings to the central sanctuary at the expense of regional cult places. Hutzli also points out that just because

---

49　Biddle, *Deuteronomy*, 199.

50　Levinson, *Deuteronomy and the Hermeneutics of Legal Innovation*, 149.

51　Ibid., 15; also Jürg Hutzli, *Die Erzählung von Hanna und Samuel: Textkritische- und literarische Analyse von 1. Samuel 1–2 unter Berücksichtigung des Kontextes* (ATANT 89; Zurich; Theologischer Verlag Zürich, 2007), 250–52.

52　Vogt, *Deuteronomic Theology and the Significance of Torah*, 68: "The program [Levinson] envisions is based on careful reworking of existing legal texts, using even the lemmas of the earlier works. This seems to presuppose great familiarity with the existing texts … Thus the texts being modified were, in some instances, familiar only to the scribes, so it is this audience (initially, at least) to which Deuteronomy addresses its hermeneutical and legal innovation." He goes on to note that the DC in fact seems directed eventually at an assembly of the people, rather than only the Deuteronomic scribes.

53　Otto, "The Pre-exilic Deuteronomy as a Revision of the Covenant Code," 115.

the CC continued to maintain an authoritative status does not mean that the DC does not intend subversive revision of the CC. The later inclusion of both law corpora in the Torah merely implies that later readers were able and willing to include the variations within one work.[54]

Schaper attempts to rebut Levinson's argument differently, suggesting the CC and DC altar laws (Exod 20:24b–26 and Deut 12:13–19) can be read non-contradictorily through a reinterpretation of the definite article in Exod 20:24b (*bĕkol ḥammāqôm 'ăšer 'azkîr šĕmî*) so that the phrase is rendered "in the whole place where I cause my name to be remembered." This move, which could be defended on the grounds that it eliminated an earlier ambiguity in the text, allowed for the DC innovation to continue appearing in line with tradition.[55] Schaper's conclusion suggests an improvement to Levinson's judgment of the DC author's moves as subversive ideology:

> Sie entstehen aus einer Schriftkultur heraus, deren Priester und Schreiber die Notwendigkeit der beständigen Aktualisierung normativer Texte klar erkennen und Möglichkeiten der Abhilfe entwickeln, ohne die Tradition *so* radikal in Frage zu stellen, dass die von ihnen vorangetriebenen Neuerungen sich destruktiv ausgewirkt hätten. Im Gegenteil: Sie wirkten stabilisierend, und so waren sich auch gedacht. Die Abfassung des vorexilischen Deuteronomiums und die Zentralisation des Kultes antworteten auf die sozialen und politischen Veränderungen in Juda und nicht zuletzt auch auf die neuassyrische Krise.[56]

Nonetheless, the intention of the DC's authors themselves is certainly beyond modern scholarly reach. Yet at minimum, the DC formulation of Israelite law grounds the tradition in a later era.

---

54   Hutzli, *Die Erzählung von Hanna und Samuel*, 251–52.
55   Joachim Schaper, "Schriftauslegung und Schriftwerdung im alten Israel: Eine vergleichende Exegese von Ex 20,24–26 und Dtn 12,13–19," *ZABR* 5 (1999): 125–26. He goes on (ibid., 127) to argue that the use of *bḥr* is an attempt to increase the precision of *zkr* in Exod 20, calling on the tradition of Zion theology in Ps 132, such as the use of *mqwm* for sanctuary. Schaper at times connects the DC too closely to Zion theology, however, which does not account for the tension between Zion theology and the emphasis on the people of the land in the formulation of the tithe law in Deut 14:22–29 or the emphasis on the periphery in the DC.
56   Ibid., 129. [ET: They come from a scribal culture in which priests and scribes clearly recognize the necessity of ongoing actualization of normative texts and [therefore] develop possible remedies that do not question the tradition so radically that their innovations have destructive effects. On the contrary, they (the changes) added stability, and this is how they were intended. The composition of the preexilic Deuteronomy and the centralization of the cult answer the social and political changes in Judah and more significantly the Neo-Assyrian crisis.]

The DC reformulates the CC not only to reaffirm it, but it also attempts to redefine what it means to act as or to be "Israel," and the DC incorporates rhetoric about ritual in order to envision this change.[57] The DC, in its reconfiguration of Israel's worship and identity, speaks to the social, religious, and political situation as it has developed in the time between the composition of the CC and its own moment. The situation created by the Assyrian crisis, with the dual exclamation points of the fall of Samaria in 722 and perhaps also the invasion of the Southern Kingdom of Judah in 701, may have led to profound soul searching and return to roots in Jerusalem and its environs.[58]

1.2.2. The Form of Deuteronomy and the Deuteronomic "Code"

In addition to considering the texts or traditions that the writers of the DC had at their disposal, a second necessary question is the overall form or genre of the Book of Deuteronomy, and especially the generic implications of the DC's form, which set the audience expectations for the work. This appears to go beyond Kratz's three criteria, yet he also notes that an important question for finding the historical location of the DC is identifying the beginning and end of *Urdeuteronomium*.[59] While the final form of Deuteronomy, read especially in light of its ending may be understood as a testament,[60] most interpretations of

---

57   It is different than ritual because it is not the practice itself, but rather speech about practice that attempts to inscribe a reordering of the world and new creation of what the "common sense" (or accepted meaning) of the Israelite ritual festival is. This brief glance at ritual theory (more discussion below, 2.4. The Use of Ritual Theory) allows for the distinction between the theoretical (and textual) meaning, which the DC grants to the cultic meals, without needing to suggest that there ever was *one* meaning for these ritual practices. The practices themselves remain open to various emic and etic explanations.

58   Crüsemann, *Die Tora*, 250, notes, "Orte wie Mamre/Hebron, Beerseba, Arad u.a. liegen damit im Einflußbereich der feindlichen und andersgläubigen Nachbarn … so ist nach 701 eine Lage eingetreten, in der sich eine Radikalisierung dieser Sicht (Exod 20:24–26) geradezu aufdrängt: Nur mehr an einem einzigen Ort läßt der Gott Israels seinen Namen wohnen bzw. ausrufen." [ET: Places such as Mamre/Hebron, Beersheba, Arad, etc. now belonged to the spheres of influence of antagonistic neighbors with different deities … so after 701 a situation ensued in which a radicalization of this perspective (Exod 20:24–26) arose: the God of Israel now only allowed his name to dwell, that is be called upon, at one single location].

59   Kratz, *Composition*, 123–25.

60   Many early Egyptian wisdom texts also appear in the form of a last testament from king or vizier to the reigning or following king. Interpreting Deuteronomy as testament works especially well, as Braulik, *Deuteronomium*, 5–6, suggests, when viewing

Deuteronomy in its earliest form rightly focus on its relationship to covenant treaties and law corpora.[61]

Before addressing the question of the DC's relationship to covenant treaties and law codes, one should note that outside the biblical material, extant ancient Near Eastern law corpora do not address religious festivals in the manner of the DC. This difference suggests that—as was common for ancient Near Eastern scribes—the biblical authors incorporate features from various genres, allowing for generic combination.[62] The cultic meals of Deuteronomy, especially their detailed descriptions of the participants and joyful celebration, again require that one look beyond both the law corpus (both biblical and otherwise) and covenant treaty genres to understand their background and significance.

From the perspective of ancient Near Eastern literature, the combination of narrative and ritual in a law corpus as found in the cultic meals of the DC is an anomaly. Even the search for texts intermixing a legal code with narrative goes substantially unfulfilled.[63] This intermingling appears most strikingly in the Deuteronomistic passage of Deut 26 where the bringer of produce in fact repeats the Israelite story

---

the book from its narratival ending (except 32:48–52 or ch. 34), but he notes: "Doch aus ihm allein läßt sich die konkrete Struktur des Buches nicht ableiten." [ET: But the concrete structure of the book cannot be determined from this alone.]

61 Even before the significant discoveries of Hittite, Aramaic, and Neo-Assyrian covenant treaties in the middle of the twentieth century, Gerhard von Rad (*Deuteronomium-studien*, [FRLANT, II/40; Gottingen: Vandenhoeck & Ruprecht, 1947], 8 = *Studies in Deuteronomy* [trans. D. Stalker; London: SCM Press, 1961], 11) argued for a cultic ceremonial setting for Deuteronomy. The subsequent discoveries support his claim by filling out the nature of the ceremony as covenant ratification or renewal.

62 Alastair Fowler, *Kinds of Literature: An Introduction to the Theory of Genres and Modes* (Cambridge, Mass.: Harvard University Press, 1982), 152–59, discusses the idea of generic mixture or hybrid.

63 Baruch J. Schwartz, "The Priestly Account of the Theophany and Lawgiving at Sinai," in *Texts, Temples, and Traditions: A Tribute to Menahem Haran* (ed. M. V. Fox et al.; Winona Lake, Ind.: Eisenbrauns, 1996), 121, finds a comparison of the DC within the Pentateuch, arguing that all the pentateuchal sources consist of a law code that the narratives seek to help the audience accept as binding. In the Ugaritic corpus there are two such texts, one being *CTU* 1.119, which combine an offering list and ritual with accompanying prayer for the occasion when the city is besieged, and the other 1.23 ("The Birth of the Goodly Gods"). Non-Israelite cuneiform law collections are both devoid of underlying narrative (except in the separate prologues and epilogues) and of cultic and moral rules. For this point, see the discussion of Shalom Paul, *Studies in the Book of the Covenant in the Light of Cuneiform and Biblical Law* (VTSup 18; Leiden: E. J. Brill, 1970), 5–9, 36–37. This fact has led a number of scholars to conclude that the narrative allusions within the DC must be later additions. I generally concur, but it would be problematic to use this as an indication of lateness.

when offering his produce.[64] After reciting the credo, the bearer then consumes at least part of the produce. This paradigm of the Deuteronomic festivals with its connection between ritual prescriptions and narrative content, stands out against the texts of Israel's neighbors, even if more implicit in the pre-Deuteronomistic layers.

When considering Deuteronomy's relationship to the covenant genre, interpreters first considered whether Deuteronomy seems more similar to the second-millennium Hittite treaties or the eighth-century Aramaic Sefire treaties (*KAI* 200–202) and eighth to seventh-century Neo-Assyrian treaties. Most recent interpreters have opted for the later Neo-Assyrian option because, like Deuteronomy, these covenants are sealed with an oath rather than a ritual sacrifice (compare Deut 26:16–19 and the vassal treaty of Esarhaddon).[65] Furthermore, the treaties from the first millennium from Assyria and Sefire contain elaborate curses instead of the short and generic blessings and curses found in the Hittite corpus. The Hittite treaties contain an historical prologue like Deuteronomy (either 1–3 or 5–11), which does not occur in any extant Neo-Assyrian version, but most interpreters see at least chapters 1–4 if not most of 1–11 as significantly later, perhaps as an attempt to negotiate the relationship to the placing of the CC at Sinai. Within the DC proper, Weinfeld notes that the form of the sedition laws (ch. 13), while containing ancient material, could not have been written before the seventh century.[66]

---

64   Jan C. Gertz, "Die Stellung des kleinen geschichtlichen Credos in der Redaktions-geschichte von Deuteronomium und Pentateuch," in *Liebe und Gebot: Studien zum Deuteronomium* (ed. R. G. Kratz and H. Spieckermann; FRLANT 140; Göttingen: Vandenhoeck & Ruprecht, 2000), 36, concludes that the entire passage 26:1–15 is Dtr at the earliest; however, (ibid., 33) he allows the possibility that some portions (vv. 2*, 5a*, 10–13 as identified by E. Otto) could be pre-Dtr, since they could instead depend on the *Privilegrecht* from earlier law corpuses. Both of Gertz' scenarios conclude that the short historical credo is a Dtr addition. Gertz bases his argument on the conception of the earliest Deuteronomy as a legal corpus like the CC, thus generally non-narrative, which is also problematic.

65   Weinfeld, *Deuteronomy and the Deuteronomic School*, 103. As mentioned above, these are especially important for Otto, *Das Deuteronomium*, since he links the first edition of Deuteronomy to a reworking of VTE in chapters 13 and 28.

66   Weinfeld, *Deuteronomy and the Deuteronomic School*, 100. Centralization also maintains a singular purpose from this perspective because periodic appearances before the great king were important throughout the extant vassal treaty corpus. Otto, *Gottes Recht als Menschenrecht*, 116, sees a similar perspective with regard to the tribute brought by vassals: "Ziel der Institution des Jahrestributs ist nicht primär die Ausbeutung des Vasalles, sondern die kontinuierliche symbolische Darstellung seiner Vertragstreue" [ET: The goal of the institution of the yearly tribute is not primarily the exploitation of the vassal, but rather the continual symbolic display of his loyalty

Christoph Koch has proposed an updated solution to the debate between the Hittite and Neo-Assyrian background, suggesting that the Hittite material was mediated through the remnants of Hittite culture in Syria (especially Carchemish), where it was then taken up in the Sefire Treaties (eighth century).[67] Koch argues that the traditions then received in the Old Testament literature constitute a mix of Hittite and Neo-Assyrian traditions. I see this reconstruction as the most probable option in the current discussion since it is able to account for both the Mesopotamian traditions of the Neo-Assyrian overlords *and* more locally-rooted Syro-Palestinian traditions.[68]

The discussion of covenant in Deuteronomy encounters a further problem in that Deuteronomy only exhibits covenantal character in its substructure.[69] No known covenant contains a similar array of the vast legal material found in Deut 12–26 (28). Furthermore, the book of Deuteronomy as a whole contains not one, but rather two covenants (cf. Deut 28:69 [ET 29:1]). Regardless of how one approaches the book source-critically, it is difficult to imagine a plausible form of the earliest Deuteronomy simply following the form generally encountered in either a second or a first-millennium covenant treaty. So while relating the DC to covenant treaties is valuable, it is also helpful to note similarities to other literary forms and to consider how genres are extended and changed, for "the character of genres is that they change."[70]

---

to the covenant]. The depiction of Jehu bowing before Shalmaneser III on the Black Obelisk coincides with this interpretation.

67   Koch, *Vertrag, Treueid und Bund*, 28–29.

68   Lorenzo d'Alfonso, "Die hethitische Vertragstradition in Syrien (14.–12. Jh. v. Chr.)," in *Die deuteronomistischen Geschichtswerke: Redaktions- und religionsgeschichtliche Perspektiven zur "Deuteronomismus"-Diskussion in Tora und Vorderen Propheten* (ed. M. Witte et al.; BZAW 365; Berlin: de Gruyter, 2006), 303–29, esp. 325–29, argues for an ongoing use of the Hittite treaty form in the thirteenth-century treaty between Carchemish and Ugarit (SAA II 5), showing an initial reuse of the Hittite treaty form in Syria after the fall of the Hittite Empire. Cf. Billie Jean Collins, *The Hittites and Their World* (SBLABS 7; Atlanta: SBL, 2007), 80–90, who shows continuity between the Hittite Empire through these Neo-Hittite states; however, she (ibid., 109–111, 222) favors the possibility of a direct link to the Hittite covenants in the Late Bronze Age carried down to the eighth or seventh century by oral scribal tradition. Othmar Keel, *Die Geschichte Jerusalems und die Entstehung des Monotheismus* (Orte und Landschaften der Bibel IV, 1; Göttingen: Vandenhoeck & Ruprecht, 2007), 1:116–18, 222–23, shows possible connections between Jerusalem and a Hittite-Hurrian elite from the LBA and IA I.

69   Patrick D. Miller Jr., *Deuteronomy* (Interpretation; Louisville: Westminster John Knox, 1991), 10.

70   Fowler, *Kinds of Literature*, 18.

One of the key aspects that the law corpus genre brings to the interpretation of the DC is the emphasis on the inner workings of the society, in opposition to the focus of the vassal treaties or loyalty oaths focus on the general loyalty of the vassal and his country to the foreign sovereign.[71] Weinfeld's standard contention is that the DC in its most ancient form reflects the vassal treaties of the ninth to seventh centuries, and the author(s) of Deuteronomy were part of a tradition that combined the two genres so that a covenant of law served the purpose not of promoting the acceptance of a new sovereign but the acceptance of a new system of laws.[72]

Mayes and others counter with an alternate approach. He suggests that the DC only received its covenantal dressing when the Deuteronomistic Historian later constructed 2 Kgs 22–23 and at the same time created the treaty format of Deuteronomy to match the narrative of Josiah.[73] Koch argues similarly that the covenant dress only arises redactionally to shape the DC in accordance with the Decalogue, now placed at the beginning of the work in chapter 5. He maintains that this dependence on the Decalogue—in keeping with much Continental European scholarship—points towards an exilic date for the covenant material found especially in chapters 13 and 28, but also throughout the DC.[74]

---

71 Weinfeld, *Deuteronomy and the Deuteronomic School*, 148, comments, "The most important deviation of Deuteronomy from the treaty form is that its central part is dedicated to civil, cultic, and criminal law. While we may regard this section as functionally equivalent to the stipulatory section of a treaty, it is very different in substance."

72 Ibid., 156–57. He summarizes (ibid., 157), "[The author] enriched the covenant theme by introducing all the elements of the vassal treaty, and he blurred the covenantal pattern by putting it into a homiletic setting."

73 Mayes, *Deuteronomy*, 81. Christoph Levin, "Über den 'Color Hieremianus' des Deuteronomiums," in *Das Deuteronomium und seine Querbeziehungen* (ed. T. Veijola; SFEG 62; Helsinki: Finnische Exegetische Gessellschaft and Göttingen: Vandenhoeck & Ruprecht, 1996), 112, sees Jer 7 (exilic) as the first example of covenant theology in the OT, but he does not see the related covenant tradition in Deuteronomy as growing from the First Commandment, but rather from the Shema.

74 Koch, *Vertrag, Treueid und Bund*, 141–42, states: "Den entscheidenden Hinweis für die literarhistorische Verortung von Dtn 13* liefert die Beobachtung, dass das Kapitel den Dekalog und vor allem das Erste Gebot in Dtn 5,6f. 9a voraussetzt. Da der Textabschnitt Dtn 5,1–6,3* einer kompositions- und theologiegeschichtlich jüngeren Phase in der Entstehung des Deuteronomiums angehört, kann auch Dtn 13* nicht Teil des Urdeuteronomiums gewesen sein," [ET: The decisive evidence for the historical location of Deut 13* is the observation that the chapter assumes knowledge of the Decalogue, especially the First Commandment of Deut 5:6f., 9a. Because the section Deut 5:1–6:3* belongs to a later compositional and theological phase of the development of Deuteronomy, then neither can Deut 13* belong to Ur-Deutero-

This line of reasoning does not consider the similarities between Hosea and Deuteronomy important for pre-Deuteronomistic Deuteronomy, connections which make the covenantal portions of the eighth-century prophet key for understanding the underlying covenantal metaphor of Deut 5–28 and arguing in support of Weinfeld's comparisons with the Neo-Assyrian documents.[75] Furthermore, while Koch rightly critiques Eckart Otto's claim for direct dependence by the DC on the Loyalty Oath of Esarhaddon (VTE),[76] I am not convinced by Koch's argument that the covenantal language in the DC is dependent on the Decalogue or a Decalogue redaction.[77] It could rather be that the notions of covenant and centralization are both related to the unifica-

---

nomy]. See also Kratz, *Composition,* 131; and Pakkala, most recently in "The Date of the Oldest Edition of Deuteronomy," 389, but also "Der literar- und religionsgeschichtliche Ort von Deuteronomium 13" in *Die deuteronomistischen Geschichtswerke: Redaktions- und religionsgeschichtliche Perspektiven zur "Deuteronomismus"-Diskussion in Tora und Vorderen Propheten* (ed. M. Witte et al; BZAW 365; Berlin: de Gruyter, 2006), 125–37.

75   See Cook, *The Social Roots of Biblical Yahwism,* 74–75. Many reject Hosea's influence on Deuteronomy, suggesting instead that the language of "love" stems exclusively from the Neo-Assyrian treaties. I do not see the need for such exclusivity, especially given Hosea's acquaintance with the covenant metaphor as seen in the use of *bĕrît* in Hos 6:7; 8:1 (contra Lothar Perlitt, *Bundestheologie im Alten Testament* [WMANT 36; Neukirchen-Vluyn: Neukirchner, 1969], 139–52, who explains away all Hosea covenant references as later). Konrad Schmid, *Literaturgeschichte des Alten Testaments: Eine Einführung* (Darmstadt: WBG, 2008), 95, posits a post-720 date for the composition of Hos 4–9 as a unity that was then readdressed to the Judahite audience in the seventh and sixth centuries; however, he assumes that this composition grew from a group of smaller entities. Brad E. Kelle, *Metaphor and Rhetoric in Historical Perspective* (Academia Biblica 20; Atlanta: SBL, 2005), 156–66, shows that the use of Baal and love in Hosea corresponds to the use of similar language in the political discourse found in Neo-Assyrian treaty documents.

76   ND 4336. A recent translation may be found in Simo Parpola and Kazuko Watanabe, eds., *Neo-Assyrian Treaties and Loyalty Oaths* (SAA 2; Helsinki: Helsinki University Press, 1988), 28–58. Morrow, "'To Set the Name' in the Deuteronomic Centralization Formula," 377–78, notes the preference for Aramaic in the Levant during the Neo-Assyrian period, thus reducing the possibility of direct contact of Judahite scribes with an Akkadian version of the VTE.

77   Koch also more or less assumes that a Dtr redaction must be exilic at the earliest, which of course continues to be contentious, especially outside of Continental European circles (though also within: see Norbert Lohfink, "Deuteronomium und Pentateuch: Zum Stand der Forschung," in *Studien zum Deuteronomium und zur deuteronomistischen Literatur III* [SBAB 20; Stuttgart: Verlag Katholisches Bibelwerk, 1995], 17–23; Hutzli, *Die Erzählung von Hanna und Samuel,* 222–45); and Konrad Schmid, "Hatte Wellhausen recht? Das Problem der literarhistorischen Anfänge des Deuteronomismus in den Königebüchern," in *Die deuteronomistischen Geschichtswerke: Redaktions- und religionsgeschichtliche Perspektiven zur Deuteronomismusdiskussion in Tora und Vorderen Propheten* (ed. M. Witte et al.; BZAW 365; Berlin: de Gruyter, 2006), 23–47.

tion of Yhwh implied in Deut 6:4.[78] Furthermore, as Childs has argued, the simple fact that the covenant tradition does not appear in full blossom in the eighth century does not mean its absence until this point: "To summarize, even though the Deuteronomic formulation of covenant dominates whenever the topic arises, this theology consistently rests on earlier tradition which, though far from identical, has a very strong theological continuity in its earliest witnesses to a relationship between God and his people."[79]

The close relationship between the curses in Deut 28:20–44 and the Neo-Assyrian loyalty oaths does suggest the downfall of the Neo-Assyrian Empire (ca. 612 B.C.E.) as a relative date before which the early versions of the DC as covenant would have been written (*terminus ante quem*).[80] Koch rejects this argument since there are some indications that the treaty tradition continued into the Neo-Babylonian period and even the Persian period, though the evidence is scant.[81]

---

78 Thomas Römer, "Cult Centralization in Deuteronomy 12: Between Deuteronomistic History and Pentateuch," 170. Also Kratz, "The Idea of Cultic Centralization and Its Supposed Ancient Near Eastern Analogies," 126, "A rivalry between the YHWH of Jerusalem (Judah) and the YHWH of Samaria (Israel) and other manifestations of the same god at other places may have formed the background of the idea of cultic centralization (see Deut. 6:4–5)."

79 Brevard S. Childs, "On Covenant, Election, People of God," in *Biblical Theology of the Old and New Testaments: Theological Reflection on the Christian Bible* (Minneapolis: Fortress, 1992), 418.

80 Christoph Uehlinger, "Cult, Ritual and Monotheism: Considering the Rise of Judahite/Samarian Monotheism in Practical Terms" (paper presented at the "Reconsidering the Concept of 'Revolutionary Monotheism,'" Princeton, N.J., 11 February, 2007), argues that at least elites would have taken part in public readings of loyalty oaths, so the Israelite and Judahite elites were exposed to Assyrian practices.

81 Koch, *Vertrag, Treueid und Bund*, 49–50, refers to Kazuko Watanabe, *Die adê-Vereidigung Anlässlich der Thronfolgeregelung Asarhaddons* (BaghM Beiheft 3; Berlin: Mann, 1987), 21–23, who lists a number of appearances of the term *adê* in neo-Babylonian and Persian period legal texts, without any further discussion. Mark S. Smith, *God in Translation Deities in Cross-Cultural Discourse in the Biblical World* (FAT 57; Tübingen: Mohr Siebeck, 2008), 161 n. 111 (here in response to Pakkala) writes, "It is reasonable to suppose that this would have taken place during the late Judean monarchy, probably prior to the impact of the Neo-Babylonian expansion to the west. Pakkala (*Intolerant Monolatry*, 44) would assume instead that neo-Babylonian rulers continued the neo-Assyrian treaty forms, but this approach based on silence is *ad hoc* and arguably unpersuasive." What I find striking about this discussion is that since this point is so central for Koch's (and Pakkala's) position, then it would seem to behoove them to explain these texts in more depth. Kratz, "The Idea of Cultic Centralization and Its Supposed Ancient Near Eastern Analogies," 129, argues, "Since Hittite traditions were handed down via Syro-Hittite and Aramaic transmission to the 1st millennium BCE, one could assume the same for the Assyrian traditions which were handed down to Persian times via Median and Urartian transmis-

Koch and Kratz put forth an important corrective for the blind use of comparative texts for dating. Simply because a genre was used in an earlier period does not mean that all texts in that genre come from the same period. The notion of simply providing a *terminus a quo*—if it is the sole *Vorlage*—is correct. However, Koch's argument is problematic with regard to the rhetorical potency that the use of largely preexilic traditions—both Neo-Assyrian and Aramaean (from the *eighth* century!)—would have *prior to* the fall of the Neo-Assyrian Empire because these traditions constituted a central political vehicle primarily in the preexilic period. The reuse of language by Deuteronomy from the Neo-Assyrian tradition, which Koch accepts throughout, implies—though certainly does not limit—a date for the Deuteronomic material in the Neo-Assyrian period.[82]

I am also hesitant to follow the conclusion that the literary levels using covenant themes and terminology are all late. Kratz argues that because Deut 13 and 28 do not rely directly on VTE, "…it is, however, not recommended to accept the hypothesis that a composition of Deuteronomy 13 and 28 is the predecessor and literary frame of the idea of cultic centralization within the original form of Deuteronomy."[83] However, Levinson shows the close connection between VTE and Deut 13, which increases the likelihood that the preexilic DC included covenantal language and ideas from Neo-Assyrian sources, if not the VTE itself.[84] The VTE and Sefire treaties also include feasting language ("set-

---

sion." While this is quite possible, it seems like over-reliance on a particular approach to the data available.

82 It may to some degree come back to an interpreter's particular methodology and level of confidence or skepticism about biblical scholars' attempts to separate the various compositional layers within Deuteronomy. Koch (ibid., 248–49), explicitly relies on the separation of compositional layers of the biblical text, stating: "Datierungen aufgrund altorientalischer Parallelen [sind] prinzipiell problematisch, da die Vergleichstexte in aller Regel auch später eingewirkt haben können und folglich bloß für die Bestimmung eines *terminus a quo* geeignet erscheinen … überzeugender ist es demgegenüber, die biblischen Texte zunächst nach textimmanenten Gesichtspunkten zu datieren." [ET: Dating on the basis of ancient Near Eastern parallels is problematic in principle since the comparative texts could also have been worked in later, thus the parallels are only able to provide a determination of the *terminus a quo* … in contrast, it is more convincing to date the biblical text first on the basis of text-internal perspectives]. Yet Koch does not account for the relatively long span of time, especially between the Sefire treaties and his proposed exilic date for the covenant material in Deuteronomy.

83 Kratz, "The Idea of Cultic Centralization and Its Supposed Ancient Near Eastern Analogies," 125.

84 Bernhard M. Levinson, "The Neo-Assyrian Origins of the Canon Formula in Deuteronomy 13:1," in *Scriptural Exegesis: The Shapes of Culture and the Religious Imagination*

ting up a table" and "drinking the cup" in §13), which point to the importance of this *topos* in relation to ratification of a treaty, as has long been noted.[85]

Koch's methodological starting point may also be critiqued because it does not adequately place the biblical text in its wider political setting. Since, as Koch argues, Deuteronomy used curses found throughout Neo-Assyrian treaties *and* letters, this points me towards identifying the Neo-Assyrian period as a good potential setting for Deuteronomy as a covenant with covenant curses.[86]

So in terms of genre, the DC itself combines various genres that were available in the Neo-Assyrian period for its own purposes: the

---

(ed. D. A. Green and L. S. Lieber; Oxford: Oxford University Press, 2009), 25–45; cf. idem, "But You Shall Surely Kill Him! The Text-Critical and Neo-Assyrian Evidence for MT Deuteronomy 13:10*," in *Bundesdokument und Gesetz: Studien zum Deuteronomium* (Ed. G. Braulik; Freiburg: Herder, 1995), 37–63. Karen Radner, "Assyrische *ṭuppr adê* als Vorbild für Deuteronomium," in *Die deuteronomistischen Geschichtswerke: Redaktions- und religionsgeschichtliche Perspektiven zur "Deuteronomismus"-Diskussion in Tora und Vorderen Propheten* (ed. M. Witte et al; BZAW 365; Berlin: de Gruyter, 2006), 274–75, notes that the similarity between VTE and Esarhaddon's treaty with Baal of Tyre (SAA II 5) shows a consistency in the tradition, meaning that VTE need not be the direct *Vorlage*. William S. Morrow, "The Paradox of Deuteronomy 13: A Post-Colonial Reading," in *"Gerechtigkeit und Recht zu üben" (Gen. 18:19): Studien zur altorientalischen und biblischen Rechtsgeschichte, zur Religionsgeschichte Israels und zur Religionssoziologie* (ed. R. Achenbach and M. Arneth; BZARB 13; Wiesbaden: Harrassowitz, 2009), 231, states, "For my part, I remain impressed by the number of parallels between Deuteronomy 13; 28 and the VTE; no other extant Assyrian treaty has as many. It is difficult to believe that correspondences with the VTE are merely coincidental."

85 This connection has recently been noted by Smith, *God in Translation*, 58–59, along with various other appearances of this trope throughout the ancient Near East in Amarna (EA 162), biblical texts, and other Neo-Assyrian texts.

86 Perhaps decisive, and again hypothetical and controversial, is where one judges the early text of Deuteronomy to have begun. If one follows Lohfink, "'d(w)t im Deuteronomium und in den Königsbüchern," in *Studien zum Deuteronomium und zur deuteronomistischen Literatur III* (SBAB 20; Stuttgart: Verlag Katholisches Bibelwerk, 1995), 172–75; repr. from *BZ* 35 (1991), and sees the beginning of the earliest text at 4:45, especially including *hā'ēdōt* (translated as "decrees" in NRSV, but more likely originally related to Aramaic *'dy* and Akkadian *adê* meaning "treaty" or "loyalty oath"), then there are strong covenant overtures in the early text. Hillers, *Treaty Curses and the Old Testament Prophets*, 32, states, "Whatever the date of composition of Deut 28, it is clear that the author intended it to represent part of a covenant." In contrast, Kratz, *Composition*, 130, argues, "Deuteronomy 6.4–5 and 26.16 formed a more or less independent framework around Ur-Deuteronomy. Through the historicization of the Deuteronomic law in the formula about election and the gift of the land, the heading 5.1aα1 and the first person used by Moses in 6.6, the concluding paraenesis in 26.1f. , 11 and the transition in 34.1a, from the start, or very soon, Deuteronomy was included in the earlier narrative, which runs from Num. 25.1a through Deut. 34.5f. to Josh. 2.1; 3.1."

law corpus genre of the CC and the vassal treaty genre underlying Hosea and found in Assyria and Sefire provided the author(s) of the DC with ample material for the fusion of genres in order to project an image of a unified "Israel"—following its own ideals in subservience to its singular deity who is to be worshipped in one central sanctuary.[87] The DC takes the notion of the ordering of internal society in praise of the lawgiver found in the law corpus genre—the parade example being the prelude of Hammurabi's Code—and combines it with the loyalty oath, which generically projects a speech act between parties. The covenant places Yhwh in the position as sovereign as law-giver[88] and treaty overlord. Yhwh calls for obedience and promises beneficence to the community that "loves" him.

1.2.3. Deuteronomy's Relationship to Assyrian Imperialism?

The thorny question of the wider political situation raised in discussion of the date of Deuteronomy's covenant structure can be addressed further with reference to the Neo-Assyrian Empire. As I have hinted at already, I see the ongoing Neo-Assyrian threat as the most likely context for Deuteronomy.[89]

---

87 This melding of genres continues to work within the so-called "horizon of expectation" propounded by Tzetan Todorov and adapted by John Frow, *Genre* (London: Routledge, 2005), 69, as follows "The mode of existence of genres is social: 'In a given society the recurrence of certain discursive properties is institutionalised, and individual texts are produced and perceived in relation to the norm constituted by that codification.' … It is because they have this institutional existence that they can work as a '**horizon of expectation**' for readers as 'models of writing' for authors" [bold original].

88 The question of the DC as "law of Yhwh" or the "law of Moses" in the earliest layers is a difficult. Moses presence in the law code of 12–26 is very minimal, even in the received form of the text (only in ch. 18), but discerning a beginning and end without Moses' presence is difficult.

89 Schmid, *Literaturgeschichte des Alten Testaments*, 113–14, notes, "Von besonderer Bedeutung dürfte dabei die politische Theologie des Jesajabuchs und des Deuteronomiums gewesen sein: Vorstellungen wie diejenige aus Jes 10, dass Assur der Stock des göttlichen Zorns sei, und zwar des Zorns des Gottes Israels, sind wohl nicht erst nachassyrisch formuliert worden, und die Gestaltung des Deuteronomiums als eines exklusiven Treueeides Gott – und nicht dem assyrischen Großkönig – gegenüber mit Dtn 6,4 als programmatischer Eröffnungsaussage, zeigen bereits elementare Elemente einer universalen, politische determinierten Gottesvorstellung…" [ET: Of special importance is the political theology of the book of Isaiah and Deuteronomy: conceptions such as that found in Isa 10, where Assur is the rod of divine anger, that is the anger of the God of Israel, certainly were not first formulated after the fall of Assyria, and the formulation of Deuteronomy as an ex-

Assyria began to apply pressure to the Levant as early as the ninth century, and its hold on the region became tenacious through the incursions of Tiglath-Pileser III in the 740s and 730s according to Assyrian and biblical records. The destruction of the Northern Kingdom in 722, and then the desolation of Judah but the deliverance of Jerusalem in 701, which changed the economic, political, and social make-up of Judahite society, provided important impetuses for the reformulation of Judahite society and law.[90] Just such a reformulation takes place in the promulgation of the DC. It is imaginable that such a reformulation came about in response to the great destruction and loss of people taken captive by Sennacherib.[91] Because much of the country but not Jerusalem was destroyed, centralization therefore became something of a natural response. There were few villages to go back to, thereby making Jerusalem the *de facto* cultic and material centerpiece in Judah.[92] Na'aman argues,

> The centrality of Jerusalem in the Kingdom of Judah in the seventh century BCE was so remarkable that we can speak of the kingdom as being a kind of city-state, in which the great capital city dominated a large territory that supplied all the needs of its population and elite. The political, demographic, administrative, social, cultic and cultural situation in seventh cen-

---

clusive loyalty oath with God—and not with the Assyrian great king—placed with Deut 6:4 as the programmatic opening statement, show that elementary elements of a universal, politically determined notion of the divine already existed...]

90   Stephen Stohlmann, "The Judaean Exile After 701 b.c.e." in *Scripture in Context II: More Essays on the Comparative Method* (ed. W. W. Hallo, J. C. Moyer, and L. G. Perdue; Winona Lake, Ind.: Eisenbrauns, 1983), 174–75, concludes that this Assyrian exile of Judahites shaped prophetic understanding and made interpretation of the Babylonian exile possible in the received form. Baruch Halpern, "Jerusalem and the Lineages in the Seventh Century BCE: Kinship and the Rise of Individual Moral Liability," in *Law and Ideology in Monarchic Israel* (ed. B. Halpern and D. W. Hobson; JSOTSup 124; Sheffield: JSOT Press, 1991), 48, attributes the beginnings of the change in the demographics of Judah to a Hezekian reform in anticipation of Sennacherib's attack, which is then further accentuated by the attack itself.

91   Contra Kratz, *Composition,* 131, necessity can easily become the midwife to creative solutions. See, i.e., from an archaeological perspective, Elizabeth Bloch-Smith, "Assyrians Abet Israelite Cultic Reforms: Sennacherib and the Centralization of the Israelite Cult," in *Exploring the* Longue Durèe: *Essays in Honor of Lawrence E. Stager* (ed. J. D. Schloen; Winona Lake, Ind.: Eisenbrauns, 2009), 41: "That the Judahite capital city of Jerusalem managed to survive the Assyrian campaigns even after Hezekiah's treasonous behavior (2 Kgs 18:7–8) in rebelling against Assyria, annexing Philistine territory, and holding hostage the loyal Assyrian vassal Padi of Ekron, served to enhance Jerusalem's status as Yhwh's chosen city. As an unintended consequence of Assyrian imperial policy, therefore, their campaign facilitated Hezekiah's efforts to centralize the cult in Jerusalem."

92   See the similar conclusions in Nelson, *Deuteronomy,* 148–49.

tury BCE Judah, coupled with the belief in the divine immunity of Jerusalem that developed after its deliverance from the 701 BCE Assyrian campaign, and the great sanctity attributed to its ancient temple—all these explain the emergence of the concentration law in the Book of Deuteronomy and the efforts to implement it in the time of king Josiah.[93]

He insightfully combines the factors of *de facto* centralization and the ongoing and ancient traditions surrounding the Jerusalem temple.[94] Together these factors suggest this period as a fruitful season for the composition of the centralization portions of the DC. These broad societal events also affected the individual families: as a result of the Neo-Assyrian crisis from 723–700, the rural populace from Israel and Judah relocated to urban Jerusalem, having lost their land and graves, as well as the ancestor cults which were tied to these physical sites.[95] This change likely brought about a severe erosion of the ways in which a solidarity ethos could be constructed.[96]

The drastic consequences of these societal-changing events offered the potential for backlash against both the Neo-Assyrian overlords and perhaps also their loyal vassals, such as Ahaz, perhaps the later Hezekiah, or Manasseh of Judah.[97] Otto notes the connection between Deuteronomy and Assyrian rhetoric, "Das Deuteronomium als Mitte von Theologie und Literaturgeschichte des Alten Testaments entsteht

---

93 Nadav Na'aman, "The Distribution of Messages in the Kingdom of Judah in Light of the Lachish Ostraca," *VT* 53 (2003): 172. Cf. the expression "Jerusalem and Judah" (2 Kgs 21:21; Jer 52:3), which reflects this situation.

94 Keel, *Die Geschichte Jerusalems und die Entstehung des Monotheismus*, 1:470, also notes a *de facto* centralization, that he views as being made *de jure* during Josiah's time, which is a bit later than I imagine it to have taken place.

95 Francesca Stavrakopoulou, *Land of Our Fathers: the Roles of Ancestor Veneration in Biblical Land Claims* (LHBOTS 473; London: T & T Clark, 2010), 5, argues "In particular, the ancestors played an important dual role within the lives of their descendents; they bore some responsibility for the fertility and perpetuation of the family line and household, and they acted as guardians and guarantors of inheritable property and places, including the plots of land upon which many ancient West Asian families depended, and upon which they themselves would likely be buried." Joseph Blenkinsopp, "Deuteronomy and the Politics of Post-Mortem Existence," *VT* 45 (1995): 1–16, notices the same dichotomy between the centralized worship of Deuteronomy and the ancestor cults. He reads Deuteronomy as an official state document of the seventh century that attempts to wrest power from the periphery. I wonder if such a grab for power needs to be posited, given that the Assyrians had destroyed much of the periphery.

96 Otto, *Das Deuteronomium*, 365–66. This situation could provide fertile ground for the creation of a new form of collective identity as imagined in Seth Sanders, *The Invention of Hebrew* (Champagne, Ill.: University of Illinois Press, 2009), 170.

97 While the portrayals of these kings in the book of 2 Kgs are of course polemic, they nonetheless present important insights on their foreign policy.

mit assyrischer Geburtshilfe, im sich mit dem ersten Atemzug gegen diesen Geburtshelfer zu wenden. "[98]

As Otto argues for the reception of the covenant idea and form, so also the cultic meal texts of Deuteronomy seem to play off of the central religious festival of the Neo-Assyrian Empire, the *akītu* and the related *Enuma Elish*. The celebration of the *akītu* was particularly important for Sennacherib and is featured in his inscriptions more than all other religious festivals. Under his reign the Assyrian practice of the *akītu* in Assyria proper also changed by incorporating significant Babylonian elements, especially the ritual meal. Esarhaddon rebuilt Marduk's temple in Babylon where the *akītu* was celebrated, underlining the ongoing importance of this feast.

Outside of Assyria and Babylonia proper the Assyrian rulers supported some regional cults, such as the worship of the moon god Sin at Harran.[99] Pongratz-Leisten notes, "With the exception of the city of Aššur, it is not the national god Aššur who is the central figure of the cultic events. Rather, the Assyrian king is at the centre, accompanied by the respective patron-god whose blessing the king receives after the *akītu*-festival."[100] From this perspective, Assyria showed significant flexibility in its incorporation and appropriation of regional religion and religious forms, though always with the point of placing the Neo-Assyrian king at the center. In the biblical text, Ahaz is quite impressed

---

98 Otto, *Das Deuteronomium*, 74, all italicized in original. [ET: "Deuteronomy, as the center of the theology and compositional history of the Old Testament, was born with the help of Assyrian midwifery and used its first breath to turn against this midwife"]. Similarly, Sanders, *The Invention of Hebrew*, 149: "But if the Assyrian texts were a paradigm for constructing empires, they were also a paradigm for challenging them. Assyrian rhetoric was so susceptible to pirating precisely because of its success: if its discourse was an icon of imperial power, then to use it was to claim to be the equal of the Assyrians."

99 Christoph Uehlinger, "*Figurative Policy*, Propaganda und Prophetie" in *Congress Volume, Cambridge 1995* (ed. J.A. Emerton; VTSup 66; Leiden: E. J. Brill, 1997), 320, concludes that the Old Testament texts of the Assyrian period could have been responding against Assyrian use of the Sin cult of Harran because he concludes that Sin functioned as the high god of the West under Assyria. Similarly, Steven W. Halloway, *Aššur is King! Aššur is King!: Religion in the Exercise of Power in the Neo-Assyrian Empire* (CHANE 10; Leiden: E. J. Brill, 2002), 58, 211–13.

100 Beate Pongratz-Leisten, "The Interplay of Military Strategy and Cultic Practice in Assyrian Politics," in *Assyria 1995: Proceedings of the 10th Anniversary Symposium of the Neo-Assyrian Text Corpus Project Helsinki, September 7-11, 1995* (ed. S. Parpola and R. M. Whiting; Helsinki: University of Helsinki, 1997), 252. Cf. Maria Grazia Masetti-Rouault, "Le roi, la fête et le sacrifice dans les inscriptions Royales assyriennes jusqu'au VIIIe siècle Av. J.-C.," in *Fêtes et Festivités* (Cahiers Kubaba 4:1. Paris: L'Harmattan, 2002), 74.

by the altar of Damascus he saw when appearing before Tiglath-pileser (2 Kgs 16:10–19). The altar itself appears to have been of Aramaic style.[101] The fact that the Judahite king has his temple furniture rearranged and a new altar built based on a foreign design is reminiscent of Sennacherib's temple renovations in Assur. This text also points to the conflation of the Assyrian king and religious practice outside the Assyrian heartland.

Deuteronomy similarly receives and reforms the genres and rhetorical symbols used in the Levant and Mesopotamia during the Assyrian period. The DC accepts the *topos* of the cultic meal as important politically and socially, but as a tool to promote an anti-Assyrian program. As Kuhrt has concluded for Assyria, "The king was the fulcrum of the empire, the hub around which the whole system was organised. Like all autocratic rulers, his power was absolute and unchallengeable."[102] The central location of the Assyrian king thus makes him the target of the DC program: "Man entzieht dem assyrischen König die religiöse Legitimation seiner Herrschaft, indem man den Loyalitätseid, der ihm geschworen wurde, direkt zitierend auf JHWH überträgt… *Dies ist die Geburtsstunde der Bundestheologie im Deuteronomium.*"[103]

As such, the DC receives and reuses the metaphors, symbols, and rhetoric of the empire and is inextricably linked to the projections of power and reality emanating from Nineveh. The DC depends upon, speaks in, and reacts through the genres used in Assyrian rhetoric. As a caveat, however, the date of Deuteronomy's use of these metaphors, symbols, and rhetoric cannot be determined by the suggestion of the connection itself. So none of these factors—possible agreement between

---

101 Keel, *Die Geschichte Jerusalems und die Entstehung des Monotheismus*, 1:381.

102 Amélie Kuhrt, *The Ancient Near East c. 3000-330 BC* (London: Routledge, 1995), 505.

103 Otto, *Das Deuteronomium*, 74, italics original. [ET: One removes the religious legitimization for the authority of the Assyrian king by taking the loyalty oath sworn directly to him and transferring it to YHWH. *This was the birth hour for the covenant theology in Deuteronomy*]; cf. Levinson, "The Reconceptualization of Kingship," 527–28. Koch, *Vertrag, Treueid und Bund*, 259 n. 56, counters for Deuteronomy that "Wahrscheinlicher ist aber, dass der König übergangen wird, weil es schlicht und ergreifend kein Königtum mehr gab, als die Bundestheologie in Juda konzipiert worden ist." [ET: It is more probable, however, that the king was passed over because there simply was no longer a monarchy when covenant theology was conceptualized in Judah]. Yet while Koch's theory is certainly also a possibility, the central importance of the king during the Assyrian hegemony makes his idea unnecessary, since the DC could easily be responding to the centrality of the monarchy (in Judahite and Assyrian forms). Furthermore, the relative absence of the king, detailed by Sanders, *The Invention of Hebrew*, 58–66, from several West Semitic ritual texts from scenarios were kings were in existence (Mari, Emar, Ugarit, and Lev 16) weakens Koch's reconstruction.

text and archaeology with regard to cult centralization, the historical developments between Judah and Assyria, loyalty oath language, or any others mentioned here—can be said to function as a smoking gun. Nonetheless, each set of data can be profitably incorporated into a unified reconstruction of the situation into which the DC was received.

2. Treatment of the Deuteronomic Cultic Meals

A significant lacuna arises with regard to the biblical scholarship I have discussed so far: these treatments of cultic meal texts focus (primarily) on the DC's use of previous biblical material and Assyrian loyalty-oaths. However, zeroing in on the particular *topos* of the cultic meal, both the numerous articles of Georg Braulik as well as the recent works of Nathan MacDonald and Walter Houston draw nearer to the rhetorical potential of the ritual meals portrayed in the DC.[1] After surveying their work, this section will then introduce recent developments in the anthropology of meals and the biblical appropriations of this dialogue. This latter discussion provides some help when considering the construction of the texts themselves. It's main payoff, however, comes in considering the reception of texts.

Braulik's ongoing reflections prove quite helpful.[2] He interprets the festive meals in light of the socio-political and religious currents at play in the eighth and seventh centuries in Judah. In his reading, the covenant treaty in Deuteronomy replaces the Assyrian vassal treaty, picking

---

1   Nathan MacDonald, *What Did the Ancient Israelites Eat? Diet in Biblical Times* (Grand Rapids, Mich.: Eerdmans, 2008); idem, *Not Bread Alone: The Uses of Food in the Old Testament* (Oxford: Oxford University Press, 2008); and idem, "Ancient Israelite Diet: Problems and Prospects," Paper presented at the annual meeting of SBL, Philadelphia, 21 November, 2005; Walter J. Houston, "Rejoicing Before the Lord: the Function of the Festal Gathering in Deuteronomy," in *Feasts and Festivals* (ed. C. Tuckett; CBET 53; Leuven: Peeters, 2009), 1–13.

2   He has published a number of related articles: "Commemoration of Passion and Feast of Joy: Popular Liturgy According to the Festival Calendar of the Book of Deuteronomy (Deut 16:1–17)," in *The Theology of Deuteronomy: Collected Essays of Georg Braulik, O.S.B.* (trans. U. Lindblad; N. Richland Hills, Tex.: BIBAL Press, 1994), 67–85; idem, "The Joy of the Feast: The Conception of the Cult in Deuteronomy," in *The Theology of Deuteronomy*, 27–65; idem, "Von der Lust Israels vor seinem Gott: Warum Kirche aus dem Fest lebt," in *Studien zum Deuteronomium und seine Nachgeschichte* (SBAB 33; Stuttgart: Verlag Katholisches Bibelwerk, 2001), 91–112, repr. from *Den Himmel offen halten: ein Plädoyer für Kirchenentwicklung in Europe* (ed. I. Baumgartner, C. Riesl and A. Mate-Toth; Innsbruck: Tyrolia, 1992), 113–22; idem, "Die Politische Kraft des Festes: Biblische Aussagen," *Liturgie Zwischen Mystik und Politik: Österreichische Pastoraltagung 27. bis 29. Dezember 1990* (ed. H. Erharter; Vienna: Herder, 1991), 65–79; idem, "Deuteronomy and the Commemorative Culture of Israel," *The Theology of Deuteronomy*, 183–98.

up on an old Judahite tradition.[3] He sees the consistent allusions to the exodus narrative serving the political purpose of filling the political vacuum left by Assyria with a dependence on Yhwh instead of Egypt.[4] The cultic meals then become a ritual method for establishing an "Israelite" identity to counter the Canaanite, Assyrian, Egyptian, and Aramaic influences overwhelming the small Judahite kingdom from the time of Hezekiah until after Assyria had abandoned Palestine.[5]

He considers each of the cultic meals as a response to these larger tendencies as well as particular concerns. On a larger scale, he views the DC prescription for all offerings to end up in the centralized sanctuary as working to include the people in a ritual move from slavery in Egypt to possession of their own land: a ritual gathering that focuses on Yhwh worship in the land instead of service to Egypt or a Canaanite deity.[6] Furthermore, he sees the tithe laws of 14:22–29 as formulated to counteract Canaanite fertility rituals in service of Baal.[7] Likewise, he views the feasts of Weeks and Booths as taking significant elements of the "Canaanite" harvest festivals and transferring them to Yahwistic practices at the central sanctuary in order to deemphasize the cultic meal and emphasize the symbolism of the Yahwistic liturgy.[8] Mean-

---

3   Braulik, "Commemoration of Passion and Feast of Joy," 69 (cf. the covenant of Joash in 2 Kgs 11:17–18). It is of course also possible to see Joash's covenant as a retrojection from a later period.

4   Ibid., 70. Hendel, *Remembering Abraham: Culture, Memory, and History in the Hebrew Bible,* 35–62, provides a lengthier discussion of the same topic. Further comparison with the Egyptian Sed or Opel festivals might be worth investigation in this regard.

5   In "The Joy of the Feast," 29–30, Braulik gives a general overview of his understanding: "For over a century, Judah was subjected to strong influences from the superior Assyrian culture. The identity of the small satellite state was deeply affected. The traditional faith in YHWH was no longer socially credible. Simple people were more impressed by military successes, celebrated as victories of the god Assur. True, it seems probable that the new rulers did not oblige their Judean vassals to accept the Assyrian state cultus. Nevertheless, political tactics alone made it desirable to take into account the world view of the new overlords. ... Judah had suffered a cultural shock. The world had become pluralist. A complex process of defense and adaptation began."

6   Ibid., 51. Note that this move from slavery to the land is especially relevant for the redactional texts of Deut 12:8–12 and 26:11. See also below, p. 110.

7   Ibid., 56–57.

8   Ibid., 60. Also idem, "Von der Lust Israels vor seinem Gott: Warum Kirche aus dem Fest lebt," 103–104. A helpful statement of Braulik's perspective is found in ibid., "Commemoration of Passion and Feast of Joy," 70–71: "Now rural life is fashioned mainly by the natural cycle of seasons. And thus, from the very beginning of Israel's history as a people, the Canaanite fertility cults held considerable fascination for Israel's pious. ... However, this [Deuteronomic] theory also removed all characteristics which were contrary to the authentic tradition of YHWH's blessing. In view of the

while, Passover's conflation with Unleavened Bread becomes a step in constituting Israel's way of being as a people coming out of Egypt.[9]

While Braulik certainly offers the most in-depth and persuasive readings of these cultic meal texts to date, the following chapters will argue for a modified field of meaning for the Deuteronomic vision of these festivals. Firstly, Braulik overemphasizes the dichotomy between the fertility religion of the Canaanites and the DC's subsequent response to this fertility religion.[10] Secondly, Braulik fails to highlight the ubiquity and importance of the cultic meal as a political, social, and religious *topos* in the ancient Near East at large and particularly in the Neo-Assyrian Empire and Ugaritic traditions. Thirdly, the growing availability of the zooarchaeological data (study of animal bones) allows for more specific connection with the material and existential situation in ancient Judah and Israel, thereby providing more depth for reading the DC in this context. Finally, cultural anthropology and human biology provide tools to illuminate additional dimensions of the DC cultic meal texts.

MacDonald's work goes a considerable distance in providing the groundwork for just such an investigation. Firstly, his monograph on the Israelite diet, *What Did the Israelites Eat? Diet in Biblical Times*, summarizes the currently available data on the variety in the diets of the region based on climate zone, socio-economic situation, and political situation in ancient Israel. He has tracked the various archaeological reports that analyze human and animal bones among other data to arrive at a variegated picture of the foodways (the acquiring of food and eating habits) in ancient Israel and Judah.[11] In addition to his investigation of the material diets in ancient Israel, MacDonald has also conducted a number of literary readings of texts that highlight the role of food in his *Not Bread Alone: The Uses of Food in the Old Testament*, with one chapter devoted to Deuteronomy.[12] This monograph is particularly helpful in its exemplary use of cultural anthropology, showing how

---

seductive alternatives provided by the social environment, the harvest festivals in particular had become confessions of faith. Their centralization secured the integrity of the YHWH cult and was thus principally religiously motivated."

9   Idem, "Commemoration of Passion and Feast of Joy," 76.

10   Houston, "Rejoicing Before the Lord," 3, makes a similar critique. Houston's article provides a very insightful reading of Deut 16, bringing together many of the perspectives I discuss at length below.

11   The analyses of human and animal remains to determine diet has only recently become a standard part of the archaeological report, so the data remains fairly limited but is being continually augmented.

12   MacDonald, *Not Bread Alone*, 70–99.

food and meals play significant roles in manifold human societies. However, as the title suggests, MacDonald's work encompasses readings of many texts from across the Old Testament (including Deutero-Canonical texts), which highlights the potential that exists in bringing together the methodologies on display in each of his monographs—a comparison with material culture and cultural anthropology—and applying them to a narrower range of texts as will be done in this study.[13] Furthermore, MacDonald's work does not include detailed reflection on the role of food, meals, and feasts in the wider ancient Near Eastern context in his readings of the biblical texts. Thirdly, I delve more deeply into the question of the historical-critical dating of Deuteronomic texts than the approach taken in *Not Bread Alone*. While MacDonald generally places the DC in the seventh century, I attempt to go a step further in proposing in more detail what the early form of the DC may have included for a more nuanced understanding of the rhetorical potential of these texts in that particular context.

Finally, mention should be made of Walter Houston's article, "Rejoicing Before the Lord." This short article also marks much of the territory to be covered in the rest of my study. He combines solid textual observations with an updated understanding of Israelite religious history to critique Braulik's contrast between Canaanites and Israelites. More specifically than in MacDonald's work, Houston also applies the various types of feasts suggested in the anthropological literature to the DC meal texts.[14] Houston concludes that "Deuteronomy implicitly offers its hearers national *communitas*, national solidarity in place of local *communitas* and solidarity," and also that "Even more than the solidarity of Israel, what the Deuteronomists want to put across is the total dependence of Israel on the grace of YHWH their God, and the necessity of the response of exclusive loyalty and absolute obedience."[15]

---

13 MacDonald's work will also be incorporated and discussed more thoroughly below, 2.3.4. MacDonald: *Not Bread Alone*.

14 See especially my summary of Dietler's categories below in 2.3.2 Belnap: "Filets of Fatling and Goblets of Gold."

15 Houston, "Rejoice Before the Lord," 9, 12–13.

2.1. Methodological Note: Interpretation of the DC Meals Texts as *Texts* About Meals

My study attempts to bring together broad tools for the meaning of the DC meal texts for its implied audience. As such, my investigation veers away from 1) the determination of a real author or audience, though the historical features of ancient Judah and its cultural milieu are highly important; 2) the determination of a *single* meaning of these texts because such a determination depends on the internal (conscious and unconscious) intentions of an unknown and, more importantly, unreconstructable author and his/her hopes for an implied audience; 3) the determination of the actual construction of the text's meaning by particular preexilic Judahite or later audiences because such a determination also requires irrecoverable data; and 4) the meaning of an actual historical celebration (a ritual practice) of the ritual meals posited by the Deuteronomic Code (a *text* concerned with ritual meals).

Let me take up these concerns in reverse order. Concerning the relationship between actual ritual practice and the DC texts, it is important to distinguish between the *actual events* of the meals and the DC *texts* that speak of them. Watts, in his discussion of Leviticus, articulates a helpful distinction: because the rituals themselves cannot be recreated from the texts, interpretation should instead focus on the actual contents of the text in contrast to other possible descriptions of the ritual meals.[16] Yet, to address the other three points together, the interpretation of ritual texts, including Leviticus and Deut 12:13–19; 14:22–29; and 15:19–16:17, must also take place with an understanding of ritual practice in mind. This means that the textual "reality" must be compared to the actual human ritual movements and corresponding human reflections upon those rituals.[17]

---

16   James W. Watts, *Ritual and Rhetoric in Leviticus: From Sacrifice to Scripture* (Cambridge: Cambridge University Press, 2007), 31–34.

17   Thomas W. Overholt, *Cultural Anthropology and the Old Testament* (GBS; Minneapolis: Augsburg Fortress, 1996), 17–18, states, "The objective is not to establish 'reality' in some positivistic sense—this or that actually happened—but to suggest a broader social reality that was a part of the context in which the texts were produced and that continues to be reflected in the texts, despite their subsequent literary history," and (ibid., 21), "In other words, texts are shaped by the interplay of authors, who have particular mindsets, with the social realities of their time and place and the rules of their language. Texts do not mirror social reality directly, but to the extent that we can discover their 'determinate and particular' meaning, they need not leave us entirely in the dark." One should note that the DC texts bear distinct similarities to other ritual texts. With regard to Deut 16, Lohfink, "Opferzentralisation, Säkularisierungsthese und mimeische Theorie," 233, states: "Sie wird ganze gewisser

2.2. The Anthropology of Meals

In order to unpack the richness of the meal *topos*, I will first note recent developments in anthropology, specifically the anthropology of meals. MacDonald's recent work has begun to incorporate these insights, and an in-depth survey of their developments both within the field of anthropology itself and their appropriations in biblical studies allow for new perspectives in understanding Deuteronomy's meals. However, a challenge arises when applying methods normally employed for understanding human functioning to the textualized feasts.[18] This presents a potential difficulty when moving from human societal functioning to textual analysis. However, texts are produced by actual people and based in part on their actual experience. Similarly, texts are received by actual people and interpreted according to their actual experience.

As mentioned above, this section helps explain—from a general human perspective—why feasts and food play an important role in ancient texts and the cultural situations they are speaking to. Behind ancient and modern debates about when and how to celebrate feasts are basic anthropological realities. This section highlights several such underlying reasons from cultural anthropology and human biology.

---

maßen im Stil eines Ritus präsentiert, in ihrer Darstellung tritt so etwas wie Typik von Ritualsprache auf." And in the corresponding note: "Trotzdem liegt eine textliche Realität vor, die Analogien zu Ritualtexten hat." [ET: They are presented to a certain degree as a ritual, in their portrayal there is something akin to a type of ritual language ... Nevertheless, there is a textual reality that has analogies to ritual texts."] (233, n. 49). Catherine M. Bell, *Ritual: Perspectives and Dimensions* (Oxford: Oxford University Press, 1997), 66, notes the connection between rituals or texts and social reality, for example, in the thought of the anthropologist Clifford Geertz: "Geertz attempted to describe how the symbols and activities of ritual can project idealized images that reflect the actual social situation, on the one hand, yet also act as a template for reshaping or redirecting the social situation on the other. Hence, for Geertz, the symbolic system that constitutes culture is neither a mere reflection of the social structure nor totally independent of it. It always exists in response to the problems of meaning that arise in real human experiences."

18   Rolf Knierim, "The Concept of the Text, not of the Performance," in *Text and Concept in Leviticus 1:1-9: a Case in Exegetical Method* (FAT 2; Tübingen: J.C.B. Mohr, 1992), 19–20, suggests three difficulties: "1) the prescription of a ritual in a text is not identical with the description of an observed ritual, let alone with a performed ritual itself; 2) that a hermeneutical system or a 'culture's private universe' of ritual is not everywhere and at all times the same; and 3) that different types of rituals have their respectively different systems and significance." Watts, *Ritual and Rhetoric in Leviticus*, 17, 28–35, and Robert P. Carroll, "Prophecy and Society," in *The World of Ancient Israel* (ed. R. E. Clements; Cambridge: Cambridge University Press, 1989), 203–25, express similar concerns.

These insights engage the interpretive categories of the *how* of audiences' reception and the *why* of authors' choice of meals as a motif.

James Brown approaches meals in texts from the perspective of "meal-as-sign," moving the focus from the text itself to the text as embedded in a "dynamic interaction with history."[19] Brown suggests two particular matrices, which he calls the psycho-genetic and the socio-genetic.[20] The psycho-genetic matrix relates to the basics and "universals" of eating, which begin as pre- or extra-linguistic. This perspective will be taken up in my discussion of the biological relationship between memory and the senses of taste and smell. His socio-genetic code relates to specific cultures and the sociology of their idiosyncratic meal codes. There is significant overlap between the two:

> In terms of social psychology the table symbolizes maternal affection and physical contact with the environment. Just as the mother serves as the infant's first introduction to the world, so the table becomes the locus of his initiation into society. By extension the table represents the mother-country, and eating figures as an act of identification with one's compatriots and adherences to their values.[21]

While this statement focuses on the anthropological, per se, Brown continues, "In fiction [or a political-religious text, in the case presented here] the table appropriates the social structure of a nation, its geographical diversity, and even a larger world-space. ... This metonymical appropriation of the world serves as the fundamental device whereby novelists transpose the socio-cultural phenomena of the *hors-texte* into fictional structures ..."[22]

In other words, the meal text subsumes and sublimates the biological and anthropological codes for meals. Like the case of the nineteenth century French novels analyzed by Brown, Deuteronomy incorporates the ancient Israelite *hors-texte* [that reality found outside the text] into

---

19 James W. Brown, "On the Semiogenesis of Fictional Meals," *Romanic Review* 69:4 (1978): 322–35. He (ibid., 322) contrasts "meal-as-sign" with the structuralist view of "meals-as-phenomenon." For an interpretation of "meals-as-phenomenon" in biblical studies, see Diane M. Sharon, *Patterns of Destiny: Narrative Structures of Foundation and Doom in the Hebrew Bible* (Winona Lake, Ind.: Eisenbrauns, 2002). I am grateful for the work of Eleanore Schmitt, *Das Essen in der Bibel: literaturethnologische Aspekte des Alltäglichen* (Studien zur Kulturanthropologie 2; Münster: Lit, 1994), which pointed me to Brown's article.

20 Ibid., 326.

21 Ibid., 332.

22 Ibid. In this aspect Brown imagines his analysis of fictional texts to function much like Clifford Geertz sees the Balinese cockfight: the singular cultural or textual event is a salient single manifestation of Balinese cultural themes, see below, 2.4. The Use of Ritual Theory.

its legal structures. The meals texts of Deuteronomy use a cultural *topos* that is embedded in the culture and human situation of their origin. Similarly, these texts are caught up in a very similar *hors-texte* on the part of its early audiences. Not only are they caught up in this *hors-texte*, but the Deuteronomic meal texts thereby contain significant rhetorical potential to engage the similar culture outside the text.

The subsequent sections follow Brown's methodology and look into anthropological analyses of the social-cultural functioning of meals. After this analysis is a discussion of the biological conditions of human taste and smell with regard to food.

2.2.1. The "Socio-Genetic" Code: Sociological and Anthropological Perspectives

Since the 1980s numerous social scientists have studied the importance of food (and drink) and meals, noticing that food is a powerful and condensed sociological artifact. Introductions to the work of three figures will provide an overview of the field and some of its major insights. Goody stands at the beginning of the movement; Sutton takes particular interest in the relationship between food and memory; and Montanari provides a recent crystallization of the field.

2.2.1.1. Goody

Jack Goody inaugurated the change in the sociology of food from interest primarily in its production and distribution to the inclusion of the further categories of consumption and symbolic value.[23] This development highlights food not merely for its nutritional value, but also for its culturally symbolic import. For, as many have recognized, every culture goes beyond the medically necessary distinction between edible and inedible to distinguish between non-food and food.[24] Goody notes that certain cultural values, or symbolic capital, permeate the process of

---

23　Jack Goody, *Cooking, Cuisine and Class: A Study in Comparative Sociology* (Cambridge: Cambridge University Press, 1982).
24　One might take the example of horse meat, which can be found on the menu in several European cultures, but rarely in the U.S.A.

obtaining and consuming food and drink, from production to distribution to preparation to consumption.[25]

One of Goody's conclusions is that there need not be an *haute cuisine* for a culture to use food and meals as a means of symbolic communication. He supports this claim by setting analysis of the nonmodern LoDagaa and Gonja tribes of northern Ghana alongside analyses of medieval Western Europe and various Asian cultures (China, India during the time of Ghandi, and Abbassid Arabia). He shows that whether one was in China (or ancient Egypt[26]) with a well-differentiated *haute cuisine* or in Ghana without such differentiation, food and meals remain socio-religious and political symbols. He observes that festival meals among the Gonja of Ghana consist of the same dishes as the meals of everyday life, just in more plentiful quantity. The amounts of food are greater, but there is no special menu,[27] similar to ancient Israel, which did not generally possess the differentiated menu items appearing in Old Babylonian recipe texts.[28] What Goody's work demonstrates, however, is that these extensive cultural developments, complexities, and interactions are not necessary for food and meals to play central roles in maintaining and determining social structures.

Goody also recognizes the importance of meals for maintaining or adjusting a culture's hierarchy: "Since its preparation and consumption had such important implications for hierarchy, food tended to be the subject of competition between those of similar status as well as the subject of regulation between those of different rank."[29]

---

25 Goody, *Cooking, Cuisine and Class*, 37. His system includes production phases (i.e., breeding, herding, slaughtering, husbandry) and aspects (items, labor force, resources, technology, quantities and qualities produced); distribution types (within the unit of production [family], gift, reciprocal exchange, market, obligatory transfer, destruction) and aspects (nature of transactions, equality, technologies of storage and transport, periodicity of distribution); preparation phases (butchering/ shelling, cooking, dishing up) and aspects (who cooks for whom, technology); and consumption phases (assembling participants, serving, eating, clearing away) and aspects (distribution in time, structure of meal, way of eating, technology, who eats with whom, differentiation of the cuisine).

26 Goody (ibid., 99) comments that in ancient Egypt, "There was a great gulf between the frugal diet of the peasantry, consisting of dates, vegetables and occasionally fish, and the elaborate tables of the ruling classes—a gulf that was not simply a matter of quantity but of quality, of complexity and of ingredients."

27 Ibid., 92.

28 Lucio Milano, "Food and Identity in Mesopotamia," in *Food and Identity in the Ancient World* (HANES 9; ed. C. Grottanelli and L. Milano; Padua: Sargon, 2004), 245.

29 Goody, *Cooking, Cuisine and Class*, 140.

Displays of elitism guarded the status quo, while attempts to move up the ladder included showing that one's cuisine followed the traditions of the upper class. This is balanced, however, by the general approach taken by revolutionary, or stasis-overthrowing movements. In Oliver Cromwell's England, for instance, "since differences in cuisine parallel class distinctions, egalitarian and revolutionary regimes tend, at least in the initial phases, to do away with the division between the *haute* and the *basse cuisine*."[30] Such an observation opens up the choices of local food in, i.e., Deut 14:23, 26, in contrast to Solomon's exotic choices in 1 Kgs 5:2–3 [ET 4:22–23]. Yet even this attempted break with the past does not eliminate significant continuity with the past. Much like Lévi-Strauss' *bricolage*, even a culture-changing movement uses the elements of the former language (in this case, meal ingredients and practices) to construct a new entity.[31] This point reveals the temporal and transitional overlap in the symbolic meaning of meals—functioning much like verbal language.

2.2.1.2. Sutton

David Sutton, writing two decades later, is able to take Goody's conclusions for granted in his approach to the relationship between food and memory. He focuses on the Mediterranean culture of the (Greek) Kalymnian islanders and describes the power of eating and drinking for the creation and maintenance of shared experience (a form of communal identity) through memory.[32] It is worth noting that Sutton's book discusses one particular culture, which assumes—correctly—that food, which carries symbolic import in every culture, does not necessarily symbolize the same things in each culture. Thus the particular meanings of food in one particular culture may or may not carry the same meanings in another culture.

Three insights from Sutton's work are helpful for my study of meals in Deuteronomy. The first insight relates to the interplay of food and

---

30 Ibid., 147.

31 Ibid., 151: "The conservative nature of these actions is partly due to the fact that they are learnt by direct experience, at an early age, at home, in the domestic group. As a consequence, their staying power is great." The importance of eating culture (foodways) is an intricate part of the enculturation process of maturity that determines lifelong attitudes and values.

32 David E. Sutton, *Remembrance of Repasts*, 102, "Food does not simply symbolize social bonds and divisions; it participates in their creation and recreation."

memory. For the Kalymnians, food is particularly powerful in its ability to trigger past experiences of consumption, and in the structure of desire looking forward to similar consumption.[33] Sutton sums up this phenomenon by quoting a Kalymnian folklorist: "At least for us old folks we don't just long for them [the foods] for their delicious taste but because they awaken in us, unconsciously, a series of rare scenes which are being constantly lost and remain only memories."[34] Desire for special foods relates not only to their (culturally-developed!) pleasant taste, but also to their connections with important past and future social experiences. Past social experiences serve as the primary stories from which Kalymnians construct their communal identity and also their individual place within the group. This connection with the past thus carries important implications for identity formation, showing the special role that feasts and festive ordinances could play in a texts such as Deuteronomy in its attempts to reorganize the society.

A second contribution from Sutton is his observation of the interpenetration between ritual and mundane meals. Special and common meals often mutually strengthen the messages symbolized in each because they are variations of a theme that repeats itself: "The basic similarity of meal structure means that one meal *calls others to mind*, other meals that share many similarities, but are worth narrating for their differences, their divergences from the recognizable pattern."[35] This interpenetration supports the connections made between meals eaten in various local villages and meals eaten at the central sanctuary in Deuteronomy, such as Deut 12:13–14 with 12:15; 16:1–6 with 16:4, 7; or 14:22–27 with 14:28–29. Especially when speaking of festive meals, each instance adds more weight to the symbolic message: "Yhwh as beneficent lord provides us with lavish food throughout our land."[36]

---

33 Ibid., 109. Also ibid., 28, where food is not just mnemonic, "because food is equally important in creating *prospective memories,* that is, in orienting people toward future memories that will be created in the consumption of food."

34 Ibid., 33. Quoted and translated by Sutton from Themelina Kapella, *Kalymnian Echoes* (Athens: press unknown, 1981), 26.

35 Sutton, *Remembrance of Repasts,* 108 (italics original). He also argues that this is implicit in the overlap between the ritual and mundane meal (ibid., 19): "… ritual is a key site where food and memory come together, but this should not blind us to the importance of everyday contexts of memory… Indeed, in many cases ritual and everyday memory are mutually reinforcing." See also Mary Douglas, "Deciphering a Meal," in *Myth, Symbol, and Culture* (ed. C. Geertz; New York: Norton & Co, 1971), 67.

36 Cf. Sutton, *Remembrance of Repasts,* 160: "I argue that ritual feasting or mundane food exchanges can create lasting memory impressions, particularly when cultivated through narratives of past exchanges. Further, unlike solid objects, food *internalizes*

A third helpful insight concerns the role of food for the construction and maintenance of culture. Sutton notes the power of food to provide an experience of wholeness or sense of self in the midst of fragmented circumstances. He shows that eating a known meal can serve to combat feelings of *xenita*, or estrangement from home, whether spatial or temporal.[37] Identity, or human experience of wholeness and integrity, is confirmed and strengthened through consumption: "Integrity is restored through a remembered coherence, or structural repetition between domains. This restoration occurs because the food event evokes a whole world of family, agricultural associations, place names and other 'local knowledge.'"[38] Sutton's research confirms the potential for festive meals as an important cultural symbol available to the authors of the DC if they were attempting to foster an unified "Israelite" identity.

2.2.1.3. Montanari

In *Food as Culture,* Massimo Montanari begins from the premise that food is *always* "culture" in the sense that it is manipulated by humans at every stage of its production and consumption. Food is "culture" when it is produced and harvested because humans do not simply use what is found in nature. Food is "culture" when prepared because humans use means such as cooking. Finally, food is "culture" when consumed because humans do not eat everything that is edible but instead choose particular items for consumption.[39] The last contention, that humans choose from among the edible possibilities when defining what is "food," highlights the importance of distinct cultures and the possibilities for symbolic importance. Just as horse meat is taboo in some modern cultures but not others, and as swine is called taboo in the Torah, cultural strategies define the boundaries of the "acceptable" and of the "desired."[40]

In his discussion of medieval recipe books (geared for the elite), Montanari notes that the written sources, upon closer analysis, provide

debt, once again calling for verbal and non-verbal acts of remembrance and reciprocity" (italics original).

37   Ibid., 76–84.
38   Ibid., 83. Cf. ibid., 84–85.
39   Massimo Montanari, *Food is Culture* (trans. A. Sonnenfeld; New York: Columbia University Press, 2006), xi–xii.
40   Montanari, (ibid., 61) comments, "The organ of taste is not the tongue, but the brain, a culturally (and therefore historically) determined organ through which are transmitted and learned the criteria for evaluations."

an important resource for understanding the foodways of popular (non-elite) culture as well: "… one can perceive a network of continuity between the cuisine of the elites—one that is *explicitly* portrayed [in the cookbooks]—and a different kind of cuisine that can be traced back through popular culture."[41] While elites attempt to differentiate themselves from lower groups by means of food choices, they continue to share tastes, habits, and traditions. Specifically,

> the rigidity of the symbolic patterns or grids opposing the lifestyle of the peasantry to that of its lords and masters … coexists peacefully with the presence of country produce and peasant flavors in the cuisine of the elite classes. In fact, to some extent it presupposes it. The real contamination between the two cultures somehow renders indispensable the erection of ideological barriers, and the symbols of differentiation and separation.[42]

It is the very similarity between the two that *compels* elites to find some means of separation. Yet the very separation must take place both with the available ingredients, and, more decisively, within the same symbolic and linguistic continuum so that the difference can be understood by the various members of the society.

Montanari's analysis is also helpful in a further direction, namely, incorporating diachronic change and the instability of human identity: "… every culture, every tradition, every identity is a dynamic, unstable product of history, one born of complex phenomena of exchange, interaction, and contamination."[43] Humans are ever in the process of eating and drinking their way towards meaning and towards group and individual identities.[44] Montenari's conclusions imply that Deuteronomy's description of the cultic meal has the potential to project and qualify the "actual" practice and experience of worship and sacrifice in each unique historical and cultural system. The DC meals propose a particular form of eating as an act of participation in the corporate identity as "Israelites" against their surroundings.[45] The potential of the DC text

---

41   Ibid., 36.
42   Ibid., 37.
43   Ibid., 139.
44   Ibid., 130, "Within this intricate system of relationships and exchanges, it is not the roots but ourselves who are the fixed point: identity does not exist at the outset but rather at the end of the trajectory."
45   Jon D. Holtzman, "Food and Memory," *Annual Review of Anthropology* 35 (2006): 368, notes that one may not even need to have had the actual experience oneself, but can create an identity through imagined consumption ("nostalgic remembering of comfort foods need not be linked to a happy childhood but can serve to create the fiction of one").

lies in its offer of a particular sense of "being Israelite" *if* one partakes in centralized feasts and the corresponding local meals.

This short survey demonstrates how meals work towards differentiations between groups and group unity. Goody's work shows that a particular menu need not be utilized, but it is instead more important that those partaking in the consumption (whether of food itself or of the image of food projected by the text) understand the symbolic meanings of the meal signs. Sutton demonstrates the power of food for maintaining an ongoing sense of self within a particular culture, while Montenari highlights the process by which meals and foodstuffs signify difference. First and foremost, this survey shows that meals are culturally-defined concepts and events that function similarly across a wide variety of cultures, and therefore must be understood in light of this reality.

2.2.2. The "Psycho-genetic" Code: Biology of Smell and Taste

In the English language one typically speaks about "tasting" food, and not about "smelling" food.[46] Nevertheless, most "tastes" are actually smells: "the actual taste receptors on the tongue detect salt, sweet, bitter, and sour. ... Everything else—meatiness, rose and saffron flavors, scorched tastes, yeasty and fermented notes, and all—is processed by scent receptors in the nose."[47]

Surprisingly, when turning to the biology of smell and taste, the discussion also moves fairly quickly from the "pure biology" to inclusion of sociological concerns. Recent research theorizes that the human sense of smell, which forms the essential basis for food preferences,[48] requires years of training, unlike visual and auditory senses, often lasting at least until adolescence.[49] "One cannot predict a child's response

---

46 There is certainly no hard boundary between the two in English usage, but the connection between the two terms is less apparent than in German, for instance, where the verb "schmecken" is used to encompass both "smell" and "taste" with regard to food.

47 Anderson, *Everyone Eats*, 70.

48 Richard J. Stevenson and Robert A. Boakes, "A Mnemonic Theory of Odor Perception," in *Psychological Review* 110:2 (1993): 340, explain, "Chemical stimuli can be transported to the olfactory receptors via the nose through sniffing (orthonasal perception) or via the release of volatile chemicals in the mouth during eating and drinking ... These volatiles then ascend via the posterior nares of the nasopharynx to stimulate the olfactory receptors (retronasal perception)."

49 Ibid., 358.

to an odour knowing only the nature of the stimulus. One must know the age and experimental factors affecting the child's acquisition of the meaning and description of odours."[50] Repetition (experience) is vital for the shaping of odor and food preferences. Experiments have also shown that while humans have a very difficult time identifying smells, they are able to remember smells best when the smells are combined with linguistic labels: thus "language shapes perception."[51] Furthermore, since tastes are experienced as a part of meals, it is the social context of meals that provides the boundaries for the development of individual tastes, as will be seen below.

The experiential and social factors result, as Elizabeth Capaldi notes, because "... in omnivores such as rats and people, most food preferences are produced by experience."[52] In fact, Pavlov realized much earlier that the stomach releases more acidic secretions for meat, but this happens before the meat arrives, which means that the physiological process has been triggered by the psychological expectation based on past experiences with meat. From this Capaldi concludes, "The fact that physiological responses are subject to learning is not part of commonsense mentality."[53] From a biological perspective, Birch and Fisher conclude, "associative conditioning contributes to the formation of children's food likes and dislikes through associations of food cues with social contexts in which ingestion occurs. Evidence suggests that children learn to prefer foods associated with positive contexts and dislike foods presented in negative ones."[54] One poignant example has

---

50   Trygg Engen, "The Acquisition of Odour Hedonics," in *Perfumery: the Psychology and Biology of Fragrance* (ed. S. Van Toller and G. H. Dodd; London: Chapman & Hall, 1988), 90. This position has since been nuanced (cf. Stevenson and Boakes, "A Mnemonic Theory of Odor Perception," 358), but the general argument still holds true.

51   Ibid., 345. See also Frank R. Schab and William S. Cain, "Memory for Odors" in *The Human Sense of Smell* (ed. D. G. Laing et al.; Berlin: Springer-Verlag, 1991), 223–24.

52   Elizabeth D. Capaldi, "Conditioned Food Preferences," in *Why We Eat What We Eat: The Psychology of Eating* (ed. eadem; Washington D.C.: American Psychological Association, 1996), 53.

53   Eadem, "Introduction," in *Why We Eat What We Eat: The Psychology of Eating* (ed. idem; Washington D.C.: American Psychological Association, 1996), 5. These conclusions highlight the importance of cultural context, *a la* Gadamer's *Bildung*, a concept that highlights the important social role in the development of "taste" (Hans-Georg Gadamer, *Truth and Method* [trans. J. Weinsheimer and D. Marshall; rev. ed.; New York: Continuum, 2004], 9–19).

54   Leann L. Birch and Jennifer A. Fisher, "The Role of Experience in the Development of Children's Eating Behavior," in *Why We Eat What We Eat: The Psychology of Eating* (ed. E. D. Capaldi; Washington D.C.: American Psychological Association, 1996), 130. This data is further confirmed by Stevenson and Boakes, "A Mnemonic Theory

been cross-cultural research done with German and Japanese participants that measured their responses to culturally specific items (like
aniseed, which is typical in German culture and dried fish, common
among Japanese). "Judgments of liking revealed, as expected, that culturally specific odors were more preferred by their respective
groups."[55]

One possible difficulty that grows out of current olfactory research
is the posited lack of imagery for the sense of smell. For while humans
can often imagine complex sounds (i.e., music) and images (paintings
or movies), this is more difficult with smells. Specifically, smell typically needs *physically present stimuli* to activate smell memories.[56] However, as Stevenson and Boakes note, one type of study disagrees with
this conclusion: "Lyman and McDaniel ... found that a condition in
which participants imagined smelling items from a word list produced
better subsequent recognition of those actual odors than did a condition in which participants were asked to visualize the list items."[57]
What this suggests is that verbal reminders of foods and beverages can
lead to better recognition and enjoyment of those particular items.[58]

These conclusions provide an important implication for the formation of the Deuteronomic meal texts and also for their potential recep-
tions. Since festive meals (according to the description of Deut 14:26—
"for whatever you desire") often allow the worshiper to choose their
meal, the particular meals envisioned in this text can become the meals
most desired by the audience.[59] This step into the desires of the audience taps into *communal* and *individual* positive associations with foods

---

of Odor Perception," 345–48. They suggest that the human sense of smell is essentially a *tabula rasa*.

55   Stevenson and Boakes, "A Mnemonic Theory of Odor Perception," 345–46. Many
Germans thought that fermented soya beans smelled like "cheesy smelly feet," while
Japanese evaluated aniseed as "disinfectant-like." See also Anderson, *Everyone Eats*,
78: "Learning, of course, greatly influences scent and taste preferences. ... cultural
learning leads to highly culture-limited appeal, such as local tastes for particular regional plant foods, or highly localized cultural fondnesses for cheese, fish sauce,
pickled cabbage, and hung game."

56   Stevenson and Boakes, "A Mnemonic Theory of Odor Perception," 352.

57   Ibid.

58   Sutton, *Remembrance of Repasts*, 90, supports this analysis with a personal anecdote:
"In other words, apricots evoke the Second World War for Yiannis, but they just give
me hives. But *say the words* [italics mine] 'Chinese Pressed Duck' and I am sent into
reveries of early college years and love in bloom."

59   Or at least the heads of households to whom this text is addressed. This must be
somewhat modified to recognize that those living close to the sanctuary did not have
the same freedom according to Deut 14:23.

and beverages. Allowing for this individualization provides the rhetorical potential for members in the community receiving this text to imagine it in their own way, maneuvering away from potential individual pitfalls based on individual, family, or clan differences.

This psycho-biological research also provides further support for the symbolic importance of meat in Deut 12:13–27. While not the only valued commodity, meat looms large in the list of culinary treats in the ancient Near East. This strong desire likely develops—especially for the non-elites—out of their urge to move up the hierarchy (symbolized in the more common meat consumption habits of the elites) and out of their own positive experiences with meat consumption, occurring largely during cultic meals.

Furthermore, by focusing repeatedly on specific items, especially meat but also wine, oil, fruit, and to some degree grains, these verbal cues—whether intended as descriptive or prescriptive—strengthen the audience's orientation towards these items. In other words, the verbal mention of these foods and drinks allows for psychosomatic effects in the reception of the texts.

Another set of insights that proves important for understanding the role of smell and taste in Deuteronomic meals is the particular connection between smell and memory. Perhaps the best insight into this phenomenon can be found in Proust's *Remembrance of Things Past*, where he describes a specific memory that floods his mind as a result of eating a particular cookie. To reference another literary text, Eugene Marlitt writes, "Nichts in der Welt macht Vergangenes so lebendig wie der Geruch."[60]

These literary remarks coincide with recent biological research into the connection. Schab and Cain remark, "When an odor triggers memory in everyday experience, the odor occurs within a context that often has personal significance and an emotional component for the perceiver."[61] Stottart argues further, " … odours are processed in the part of the brain which is thought to be the seat of emotional response,"[62] which provides a scientific explanation for the reality which earlier

---

60 Eugenie Marlitt, *Das Eulenhaus* in *hinterlassener Roman* in *Gesammelte Romane und Novellen* (vol. 9; Leipzig: Keil 1888), 118 [ET: Nothing in the world can make the past come alive like smell.]

61 Schab and Cain, "Memory for Odors," 220.

62 D. Michael Stoddart, "Human Odour Culture: a Zoological Perspective," in *Perfumery: The Psychology and Biology of Fragrance* (ed. S. Van Toller and G. H. Dodd; London: Chapman & Hall, 1988), 16. Anderson, *Everyone Eats,* 72, notes that more than one percent of human genes are devoted to smell, making it the largest gene family thus far identified in mammals.

literary authors had perceived intuitively. Generally speaking, the sensuality of eating experienced through taste and smell appear to be the primary impetus for food's connection with memory.[63] Important for this connection are the simultaneously *individual* and *subjective* as well as *communal* natures of food and drink consumption. The subjectivity "destabilizes truth through a concern with the subjective ways that the past is recalled, memorialized, and used to construct the present."[64] This subjectivity, however, exists within the limited and culturally constructed *topos* of the meal, as Montanari has demonstrated.

2.3. Recent Uses of Anthropology in Ancient Near Eastern and Biblical Studies on Commensality

2.3.1. Schmitt: *Das Essen in der Bibel*

Eleanore Schmitt, in her revised dissertation, *Das Essen in der Bibel*, employs Goody's methodology in an attempt to understand the role of food in biblical texts. She connects the food in the Bible with the role of food outside the Bible.[65] She recognizes that the various symbolic meanings of food and meals are inextricably tied to food's biological role, and this biological role creates the foundation for cultural, psychological, social, and literary meanings.[66] Her analysis of the feasts of ancient Israel is more problematic. Firstly, she more or less sticks to an analysis of the feasts as found in the Holiness Code, which is of course legitimate in and of itself, but her conclusions conflate the various legal traditions, and she generalizes the understandings of food and festivals in the HC as representative of the other biblical law corpora. Her analysis does not fit for the DC, which does not have all the same feasts or issues in mind (at least explicitly) as the HC. Her analysis also omits matters of social class and hierarchy.[67]

---

63 Holtzmann, "Food and Memory," 373.
64 Ibid., 363.
65 Ibid., 65: "Bevor die Bedeutung des Essens in einem Text verstanden werden kann, muß die Bedeutung des Essens außerhalb des Textes, also innerhalb der im Text dargestellten Gesellschaft geklärt werden." [ET: Before the meaning of eating in a text can be understood, the meaning of eating outside the text, that is inside the society portrayed in the texts, must be explained.]
66 Schmitt, *Das Essen in der Bibel*, 7. Cf. Barthes, "A Psychosociology of Contemporary Food Consumption," 168 (cited above, p. 1).
67 She comments (ibid., 45), "Betrachtet man den israelitischen Festkalender, so muß man feststellen, dass auch hier eine gewisse Kontinuität von Opfern für eine

2.3.2. Belnap: "Filets of Fatling and Goblets of Gold"

Daniel Belnap's dissertation on meal events in the Ugaritic corpus[68] provides both a helpful overview of ritual studies and their application to Ugaritic and biblical studies as well as a detailed analysis of the feasts in the Baal Cycle and other important Ugaritic texts. He identifies three basic types of feasts in the Ugaritic and biblical texts investigated that strive towards divergent goals:[69] 1) The entrepreneurial feast is given to acquire symbolic capital. In this feast one gives the feast in order to move up the social ladder. 2) The patron-role feast is given for reiterating and legitimizing institutionalized relations of unequal social power. The patron gives the feast in order to rally his clients to his side. And, 3) the diacritical feast, which is also given to legitimize inequality, is instead an intra-class meal. In this meal the host invites those on the same hierarchical level in order to consolidate their place over against those of other classes (who also may eat somewhat different foods). Belnap's use of these categories reveals that there is a necessary step beyond merely stating that commensality is a powerful sociological and historical event. One should ask to what end the host and attendees intend to "use" the particular feast. The purpose of a feast need not clearly fit into one or the other, however. Provisions of hospitality could simply cut across all three. Sutton notes that in Kalymnos, the return expected for providing food is a continued narrative of the

---

ausreichende Proteinzufuhr gesorgt haben dürfte: Jeder Neumond, der zugleich den Beginn des Monats markiert, wird mit umfangreichen Opfern gefeiert. Hinzu kommen Feste in der Mitte der aufeinanderfolgenden Frühjahrsmonates Nisan, Ijar und Siwan…" [ET: Viewing the Israelite festival calendar allows one to conclude that there is a certain continuity from the sacrifices for the sufficient intake of protein. Every new moon, which also marks the beginning of the month, was celebrated with extensive sacrifices. In addition are the festivals in the middle of the consecutive spring months Nisan, Iyyar, and Sivan…]. This statement that the sacrifices provided a sufficient amount of protein assumes that individuals could all generally partake in these meals. Ibid., 97–99, gives her analysis of Lev 23.

68 Daniel L. Belnap, "Fillets of Fatling and Goblets of Gold: The Use of Meat Events in the Ritual Imagery of the Ugaritic Mythological and Epic Texts" (Ph.D. diss., The University of Chicago, 2007).

69 Ibid., 50–52. Cf. Michael Dietler, "Feasts and the Commensal Politics in the Political Economy: Food, Power, and Status in Prehistoric Europe," in *Food and the Status Quest* (ed. P. Wiessner and W. Schiefenhövel; Providence: Berghahn Books, 1996), 87–125, esp. 90–117; idem, "Theorizing the Feast: Rituals of Consumption, Commensal Politics, and Power in African Contexts," in *Feasts: Archaeological and Ethnographic Perspectives on Food, Politics, and Power* (ed. M. Dietler and B. Hayden; Washington: Smithsonian Institution Press, 2001), 76, has reformulated his category of "entrepreneurial feast" as "empowering feast."

giver's hospitality.[70] This aspect corresponds well with the rhetorical aim of the DC to create the impression of Yhwh as lavish host: the Israelites are to retell the narrative of Yhwh's goodness (in a likely later text, Deut 6:20–25). This festal picture also corresponds well with the notion of Yhwh as patron to the Israelite clients; however, there is no good candidate (in the singular) for the role of human patron.

Belnap's project, with its detailed considerations of Ugaritic narrative material fits in most directly with my chapter on Deut 16 in relation to the Ugaritic feasts; however, his overall approach also provides an example of the resources that recent studies in commensality from an anthropological and sociological angle can offer ancient Near Eastern and biblical studies.

2.3.3. Janzen: *The Social Meaning of Sacrifice*

David Janzen undertakes an analysis of the various social meanings that sacrifice can have in narrative texts of the Hebrew Bible. His study provides important methodological guidelines for understanding the DC meals, which are also sacrificial in some respects.[71] Especially insightful is his argument that "... sacrifice can have different meanings for different biblical authors."[72] Building on this point, he determines that the social space in which the ritual—whether ritual event or ritual text—is found proves decisive for its meaning.[73] So Janzen, like Belnap, asks what a particular ritual communicates in its particular literary context, rather than extracting the ritual from its surrounding text and analyzing it in some theoretical empty space. This approach also con-

---

70 Sutton, *Remembrance of Repasts,* 48. The informed reader will notice the overlap with Mauss' classic analysis of gift-giving, which Sutton (ibid., 46) also notes.

71 Some caution should be noted here depending on how one understands "sacrifice." Deuteronomy uses the normal classical Hebrew terms for sacrifices, *zebaḥ, 'ōlāh, nēder, nidbāh, běkōrāh, tērûmāh,* and *ma'ăśar.* Yet the DC does not interpret "sacrifice" with the same propitiatory lens as P, for example, but instead leans more towards the sense of "gift" or "communion."

72 David Janzen, *The Social Meaning of Sacrifice: A Study of Four Writings* (BZAW 344; Berlin: de Gruyter, 2004), 3.

73 Ibid., 4, "Even the same kinds of rituals, I will show, can communicate very different social meanings depending upon the social contexts in which they are located." Janzen speaks specifically of the social meanings of sacrifice here, albeit as represented in the biblical texts. In contrast I lay more emphasis on the literary context, seeing the texts themselves less as windows (or at least as less transparent windows) to the social context behind them. Cf. Wright's and Watts' cautions (see above p. 41 and below, p. 168).

trasts with attempts that specifically focus on Israelite practice behind the texts.

As a general answer to the social function of the ritual of sacrifice, Janzen states that his analyses "… show ritual to function as an expression of social meaning, which informs participants of the way in which they should conceive of the world and, therefore, the ways in which they should rightly act."[74] So Janzen sees sacrifice as a method of *Bildung* (enculturation), contributing to the manner in which the receivers of the text might potentially construct their understanding of the world.[75] While competing or complementary views and uses of sacrifice occur both synchronically and diachronically in the biblical text, Janzen's conclusions generally hold true: the stories and prescriptions of rituals of sacrifice (including the cultic meals of the DC) imagine situations in which the people act in unison in order to create unified understandings of reality. This point of view articulates a reason why the DC might imagine ritual meals as a primary location for the creation and implementation of its social vision: the DC ordains cultic meals as a vehicle for the construction of a unified understanding of reality, a vehicle whose power is based in specific cultural practices that link in with basic human functioning.

2.3.4. MacDonald: *Not Bread Alone*

As mentioned above, the most recent and most significant contribution to the understanding of meals as an important *topos* for Deuteronomy appears in Nathan MacDonald's *Not Bread Alone*.[76] He follows the theoretical work of David Sutton, for whom the relationship between food and memory (whether "real" or "imagined") is particularly important. He examines how "food is the vehicle through which Deuteronomy envisages Israel expressing her remembrance of YHWH."[77] My project

---

74 Ibid., 5. He continues (ibid., 5–6), "Ritual … attempts to ritualize morality, which is to say that it attempts to persuade its participants to carry out their quotidian activities in a way that reflects the worldview and moral systems that rituals themselves express."

75 Ibid., 68.

76 My comments on MacDonald here can be read in conjunction with my general response to his work on food, see above, pp. 39–40. As mentioned above, Houston's recent essay, "Rejoicing Before the Lord," builds on and contains many similar insights.

77 MacDonald, *Not Bread Alone*, 75. He is here quoting an earlier book, idem, *Deuteronomy and the Meaning of 'Monotheism'* (FAT, II/1; Tübingen: Mohr Siebeck, 2003), 139.

is in some sense a furthering of MacDonald's analysis, since Israel's memory (or memorializing) in Deuteronomy, as he notes for Deut 26:1–15, occurs through the offering of food.[78] He recognizes the centrality of communal consumption, which is the locus for celebration of the past actions of Yhwh on the part of the Israelites as well as Yhwh's present provision.[79]

My approach expands on that of MacDonald in two ways. First, in his argument dealing with the whole of Deuteronomy, he synchronizes the various layers of the text. While he notes the origins of Deuteronomy as mid-seventh century,[80] MacDonald does not chronicle the importance of food in the historical development of the text. This approach limits the analysis of meals texts as texts from a particular setting, lessening the potential connection to a specific audience.[81] So, bringing forward Dietler's concern for the particular function of a meal, I find it important to ask how the cultic meals in the DC function in their pre-Dtr context before moving on to consider their meaning in the later and fuller perspective of the whole book of Deuteronomy.[82]

A second way in which I try to further develop MacDonald's work "in the text" is with regard to his reliance on Connerton's matrix of "inscribed" and "incorporated" memory.[83] MacDonald approaches the

---

78   Ibid., 77.
79   Ibid., 79: "The Deuteronomic cult is centred around communal acts of eating which connect the memory of the past actions of YHWH with the present experience of divine generosity in the Promised Land. The memory of the past and the experience of the present are united in acts of joyful celebration, which are central to the Deuteronomic concept of worship."
80   Ibid., 75.
81   He also does notes (ibid., 79) the common view that Deuteronomy's designation "Canaanite" refers to other forms of Israelite worship in the seventh century, a view I would locate more closely connected with the Dtr portions of the text, yet well in keeping with the epigraphic evidence from Khirbet el-Qom and Kuntillit Ajrud. In MacDonald's defense, his methodology is not uninformed: his comments in "Review of Sven Petry, *Die Entgrenzung JHWHs: Monolatrie, Bilderverbot und Monotheismus im Deuteronomium, in Deuterojesaja und im Ezechielbuch*. JHebS 9 (2009). Cited 10 January, 2010. Online: http://www.arts.ualberta.ca/ JHS/ reviews/ reviews_new/ review385.htm, note the problems with the approach I take here.
82   MacDonald's broader question is also very valuable, and I would suggest that it can best be answered by considering the various levels of Deuteronomy as history of reception, looking to see how they incorporate and exegete the earlier text to create a fuller "whole."
83   Paul Connerton, *How Societies Remember* (Cambridge: Cambridge University Press, 1989). MacDonald, *Not Bread Alone*, 96, summarizes the difference as follows: "Incorporated memories are embodied experience, whilst inscribed memories are those that are held on physical devices." He is quite similar to Sutton, *Remembrance of Repasts*, 19–30, in this regard.

question of how Deuteronomy textualizes an incorporative memory process (eating) as follows:

> … food and communal meals are the basic means by which Deuteronomy establishes its particular memory of the past amongst the Israelites …

> Yet it is also an essential component of Deuteronomy's strategy of memorialization, for in Deuteronomy it appears inscribed memories only truly become possessed as memories when they are incorporated. The most apt example is the *Shema* in Deut. 6.4–9 whose words are to be placed as amulets on the hands and forehead, and written on the door-frames of houses and on the city gates. The purpose of these actions is to impress the commandment in the memories of the Israelites. Food is also an incorporated memory that furthers Deuteronomy's inscribed memory. This is true of the feasts, which embody a memory about exodus, wilderness and the Promised Land, that can also be expressed in textual form (e.g. Deut 26.5–11) … Nevertheless, it is clear for the strategy of Deuteronomy that inscription is not sufficient on its own.[84]

MacDonald's analysis is helpful in that it recognizes that Deuteronomy (in every layer of the text) uses the inscribed written text—which is a form of memorialization itself—to prescribe an alternate and incorporated form of memorization. However, his analysis might benefit by explaining more explicitly the connection between text and practice. Deuteronomy is *only* a text, meaning that the meals described and prescribed take place first and foremost in the *imaginations* of the hearers and readers. This kind of experience is markedly void of any "incorporation" in the literal sense. MacDonald states, "Food is also an incorporated memory that furthers Deuteronomy's inscribed memory."[85] This is a definite possibility, but it depends on if and how a particular audience of the text then puts it into practice. Deuteronomy may project this sort of practice, but this need not be the way the text is received and appropriated.[86] Therefore, MacDonald's analysis comes up against the same question with which I started this chapter: how does one make or describe the connection between the text and its world and the bodily commensal experience of its audience? My answer has been to consider the connections between text and body through the psychological and sociological matrixes supplied by Brown's notion of "meal-

---

84 Ibid., 96.
85 Ibid.
86 Note that Christian communities' reception of this text does not necessitate such meal consumption. I note this merely to show that one cannot take for granted that the text will be interpreted and followed "literally."

as-sign."[87] Nonetheless, MacDonald's work provides an essential introduction into the central role of food and meals in Deuteronomy.

2.4. The Use of Ritual Theory

The study of ritual actions or ritual theory requires an introduction of its own. What is ritual and how can texts relating to ritual such as the chosen DC meal texts be understood in relation to the modern social scientific studies of ritual?

Theorists have noticed various complex relationships such as those between ritual and societal change, ritual and symbolic meaning, ritual and societal cohesion, and ritual and social power. So instead of providing a definition of ritual, it seems more appropriate to speak of what is intended to take place through the category of writings and actions that concern ritual. Catherine Bell offers the following insight:

> … ritualization is a way of acting that is designed and orchestrated to distinguish and privilege what is being done in comparison to other, usually more quotidian, activities. As such, ritualization is a matter of various culturally specific strategies for setting some activities off from others, for creating and privileging a qualitative distinction between the 'sacred' and the 'profane,' and for ascribing such distinctions to realities thought to transcend the powers of human actors.[88]

By approaching ritual from the perspective of "that which is focused on in ritual" (and thus to a certain degree "emic"), one can take into account both the overlap and the distinction between rituals as actions and rituals as textually-imagined entities. This formulation provides an approach to the DC cultic meal texts, which themselves set off certain meals as ritualized by determining a distinct time, place, and narratival background for the meals' realization and their symbolic field of meaning, both of which will be discussed in detail below.

For application to the DC discourse, Bell's approach implies that the DC as "ritual theorizing" (or ritual text) reorders the values that underlie Israelite understanding of reality, the symbolic framework that reigns as common sense. As Turner has suggested: "All rituals have this exemplary, model-displaying character, in a sense, they might

---

87   See above, pp. 42–44.
88   Catherine M. Bell, *Ritual Theory, Ritual Practice* (Oxford: Oxford University Press, 1992), 74.

be said to 'create' society."[89] Correspondingly, the DC's ritualized focus proposes a particular vision of Israelite society. I will argue that the DC presents ritual meals "as part of a historical process in which past patterns are reproduced but also reinterpreted or transformed."[90]

There are four specific aspects from discussions of ritual theory that will prove helpful for my investigation: 1) Robertson Smith's focus on eating to establish kinship bonds; 2) Geertz's concept of the ritual as "deep play"; 3) Turner's insight into rituals as potential societal change agents; and 4) de Certeau's analysis of the use by marginal members in society of ideology broadcast from the center.

The modern study of ancient Israelite cultic meals began no later than the epoch-making anthropological studies of William Robertson Smith, whose view of meat consumption—which continues to be widely accepted—consists of the notion that sacrifice worked not only vertically between deity and worshippers, but also horizontally to strengthen community bonds: "According to antique ideas, those who eat and drink together are by this very act tied to one another by a bond of friendship and mutual obligation."[91] He imagines, "The law of the feast was open-handed hospitality; no sacrifice was complete without guests, and portions were freely distributed to rich and poor within the circle of a man's acquaintance. Universal hilarity prevailed, men ate, drank and were merry together, rejoicing before their God."[92] For Robertson Smith, as for Braulik much later, this law is at work in both Israelite and Canaanite worship, and all primitive religion.[93] Therefore, Robertson Smith concludes that to be able to eat together, one must *be* kin or one *becomes* kin. This kinship bond is signified by commensality (communal consumption) and also implies an ethical bond.[94]

Robertson Smith's conclusions do provide a helpful basis for the analysis of Deuteronomy. Deuteronomy specifically highlights the connection between the kinship bond (Deut 15:3, 7, 9) and an ethical re-

---

89 Victor Turner, *The Ritual Process: Structure and Anti-Structure* (New York: de Gruyter, 1995), 117. Note the similar perspective of Janzen above (2.3.3. Janzen: *The Social Meaning of Sacrifice*).

90 Bell, *Ritual: Perspectives and Dimensions*, 83. One might compare this statement with the debate over the DC's relationship to the CC.

91 William Robertson Smith, *Religion of the Semites: the Fundamental Institutions* (2d. ed., New York: Meridian Books, 1957 [1889]), 265.

92 Ibid., 245.

93 John W. Rogerson, *Anthropology and the Old Testament* (Growing Points in Theology; Oxford: Basil Blackwell, 1978), 28–34, critiques of Robertson Smith's evolutionary development model that assumes that societies evolve through identical stages.

94 Ibid., 273–74.

sponsibility. The cultic meal texts, especially 12:18; 14:27–29; and 16:11, 14 emphasize the connection between festive meals among kin and social provision. Furthermore, the particular relationship between *meat* consumption and connection with the divine appears forcefully in 12:13–27, which repeatedly mentions *baśar* (meat) along with the command to eat in the presence of Yhwh.[95]

Clifford Geertz offers further assistance for my analysis of the meal texts, turning the symbolic and structural analysis of Lévi-Strauss to particular ethnological and historical situations. His analysis of the Balinese cockfight notes that it, like the Deuteronomic meal, is a (not *the*) central event in his object of analysis (Balinese culture). Having highlighted what he sees as the correspondences between the cockfight and Balinese culture as a whole, he argues,

> Quartets, still lifes, and cockfights are not merely reflections of a pre-existing sensibility analogically represented; they are positive agents in the creation and maintenance of such a sensibility. … In the cockfight, then, the Balinese forms and discovers his temperament and his society's temper at the same time. Or, more exactly, he forms and discovers a particular facet of them.[96]

Similarly, according to Deuteronomy, in the cultic meals the "Israelites" discover their identity (Geertz's "sensibility" and "temper") as individuals and as a group: they both become and create their group identity and grow in their sense of belonging to the group through the textually prescribed experience.

By describing these cultic meals as one significant element of the Deuteronomic text, various features of the Deuteronomic conception of reality come to light. Geertz notes that the prescribed worldview appears most clearly in ritual: "In a ritual, the world as lived and the world as imagined, fused under the agency of a single set of symbolic forms, turn out to be the same world, producing thus that idiosyncratic transformation in one's sense of reality …"[97] Deuteronomy, especially

---

95   One difficulty for Robertson Smith's analysis is how ritual, or prescriptions for rituals such as cultic meals, function in relation to societal change. Since he generally argues that meals and religious rituals work to maintain social bonds, his theory does not provide an understanding for the notion that rituals can function as change implements. Nor does he account for the fact that one may eat and form bonds without becoming kin. See the similar analysis in Belnap, "Fillets of Fatling and Goblets of Gold, 3–4.

96   Clifford Geertz, "Deep Play," in *The Interpretation of Cultures: Selected Essays* (New York: Basic Books, 1973), 451.

97   Clifford Geertz, "Religion as a Cultural System," in *The Interpretation of Cultures: Selected Essays* (New York: Basic Books, 1973), 112.

through its portrayal of the cultic meals, prescribes an image of the community of Israel (*běnê Yiśrā'ēl*) as one cohesive unit that cares for one another as kin, exemplified in the unity of households feasting together centrally before Yhwh and providing liberally for all members of the group throughout the land. The text portrays and mandates a particular vision for Israelite identity and reality, a vision conceived to take place in ritual feasts.

Victor Turner revolutionizes thinking about ritual in terms of its relationship to societal change. While Robertson Smith and Lévi-Strauss saw ritual as either enforcing the status quo or expressing the static values of a culture, Turner suggests that rituals may in fact function as change elements. While agreeing with earlier anthropologists that ritual could function as a mode for releasing built up tension resulting from societies' iniquities by momentarily inverting societal hierarchy but inevitably leading back to supporting the traditional societal structure,[98] Turner also goes a step further. Bell sums up Turner's argument accordingly: "Rituals did not simply restore social equilibrium, they were part of the ongoing process by which the community was continually redefining and renewing itself."[99] This notion that ritual can serve as a vehicle for social change provides a key insight for the reading of Deuteronomy as responding to the crises of the late preexilic period, possibly embodying an anti-Assyrian polemic. The communal celebrations can accordingly be understood as theorizing a new formulation of society that moves beyond the king-focused structure. "Turner recognizes ritual's capacity to suspend social norms, criticize social structure for its inability to meet the need for direct and egalitarian relationships, present alternatives, and to transform the existing social

---

98   Victor Turner, *Dramas, Fields, and Metaphors: Symbolic Action in Human Society* (Ithaca: Cornell University Press, 1974), 55–56, states, "The drama of ritual action—the singing, dancing, feasting … are ennobled and the normative referents are charged with emotional significance. I call the biological referents, insofar as they constitute an organized system set off from the normative referents, the 'orectic pole,' 'relating to desire or appetite, willing and feeling,' for symbols, under optimal conditions, may reinforce the will of those exposed to them to obey moral commandments, maintain covenants, repay debts, keep up obligations, avoid illicit behavior. In these ways anomie is prevented or avoided and a milieu is created in which a society's members cannot see any fundamental conflict between themselves as individuals and society."

99   Bell, *Ritual: Perspectives and Dimensions*, 39. Bobby C. Alexander, *Victor Turner Revisited: Ritual as Social Change* (AARAC 74; Atlanta: Scholars, 1991), 27, summarizes Turner as follows, "Ritual does not simply rehearse the problems of everyday life. It is itself redressive activity."

structure."[100] Ritual need not, therefore, only describe and re-inscribe what is, but a ritual or ritual text may also theorize about a utopian vision of what can be.[101]

Michel de Certeau and his co-authors provide a final important tool for interpreting the DC meals by analyzing "ordinary life" responses to the power dynamics and rhetorical displays broadcast by the overarching powers in societies. While their analysis is limited to modern France, its applicability extends to any society where some distance—geographic or otherwise—exists between those broadcasting the symbolic meaning of events and texts, and other more marginal segments of society under their power. In the case at hand, I imagine a geographical, cultural, and political distance between the Assyrian Sargonid projections of reality—and secondarily the Judahite monarchy[102]—and the Judahite audience's experience of these projections. To distinguish between these two locations, de Certeau coins the terms "strategy" and "tactic." The former, which corresponds to the in-power Assyrians, is "the calculus of force-relationships that becomes possible when a subject of will and power (a proprietor, an enterprise, a city, a scientific institution) can be isolated from an 'environment.'"[103] A "strategy" names the symbolic meaning that can be broadcast from a place of power. The latter, the "tactic," is instead "a calculus which cannot count on a 'proper' locus of power (a spatial or institutional localization), nor thus on a borderline distinguishing the other as a visible totality."[104] "Tactics" describes the process of reception and (re)use by the marginalized of the concepts and symbolic meanings

---

100 Alexander, *Victor Turner Revisited*, 29.

101 There is a similar interplay of ideology and utopia promulgated by Paul Ricoeur, *Lectures in Ideology and Utopia* (ed. G. H. Taylor; New York: Columbia University Press, 1986). The placing of Deuteronomy both as the divine law and in the Mosaic past (either originally or in a later version of Deuteronomy) attempts to undergird the power of the theorized ritual.

102 Ephraim Stern, *Archaeology of the Land of the Bible, Volume 2: The Assyrian, Babylonian, and Persian periods, 732-332 BCE* (New York: Doubleday, 2001), 215, notes ""Assyrian influence in 7th century BCE Judah is attested in only a few finds. The most distinguished one is a small model for a wall painting from the royal Judaean palace of Ramat Rachel. It depicts a ruler sitting on his throne, imitating a style frequently used in portraying Assyrian kings." Sanders, *The Invention of Hebrew*, 170, underlines this notion in Deuteronomy as follows: "By producing the words of an otherworldly sovereign in non-state-sponsored texts, the biblical texts could act as a radical limit on the claims of the human sovereign, what Taubes called the danger of 'chaos from above.'"

103 Michel, de Certeau, *The Practice of Everyday Life* (trans. S. Rendall; Berkeley: University of California Press, 1984), xix.

104 Ibid.

projected by the center (the "strategies" of those in power). Key for de
Certeau is that those who must use "tactics" (the marginalized) should
not simply be assigned the passive role of "consumer" of ideology.
Instead, as de Certeau shows, they are also active in the construction of
meaning, and are therefore accorded the active title "users."[105] Essential
for my analysis of Deuteronomy, de Certeau's notion of tactics allows
for active and constructive Judahite reception of the projections of Assyrian ideology. De Certeau and his coauthors provide the theoretical
underpinnings for considering change, modification, and movement
between various levels of a societal power structure. Accordingly, the
composers of the Deuteronomic vision adopt various parts of the Assyrian vision and then rework them in accordance with their own values as "users" of the Assyrian strategy so that in the end the Assyrian
strategy is upended. Specifically, the Judahite "audience" of the Neo-
Assyrian projections of power—the loyalty-oaths, the festive meals in
Sennacherib's *akītu*,[106] and the appropriation of Judahite goods (such as
meat)—could in turn use these same symbols for the projection of their
own values.

In conclusion, in order to address the meaning of Deuteronomic
meal rhetoric, I plan to heuristically reconstruct the rhetorical potential
of the cultic ritual meals in late Iron Age. I will do this using a varied
methodology, incorporating both literary data from the biblical corpus
as well as relevant ancient Near Eastern texts that include or allude to
communal meals and foodstuffs. This textual data will be supplemented by discussion of the iconographic representations of meals and
archaeological conclusions about the diets of ancient Syria-Palestine. I
will attempt to map the meanings of the communal meal texts for ancient hearers to facilitate understanding of the DC texts prescribing the
rituals or ritual-like behavior of the Deuteronomic meals. In other
words, my project will be substantially interdisciplinary, bringing together conclusions from fields as diverse as current anthropological
theory and zooarchaeological analysis of faunal remains (animal bones)
from Iron Age II archaeological sites. Victor Turner's logic points out
the basis for this investigation: "Light can be shed on ritual and politi-

---

105 Ibid., 31.
106 Beate Pongratz-Leisten, "Translating Universalism into Cultic Omnipresence in
    Assyria and Babaylonia in the 7th and 6th Century BCE" (paper presented at the
    "Reconsidering the Concept of 'Revolutionary Monotheism,' Princeton, N.J., 11 Feb-
    ruary, 2007), notes that the *takultu* ritual providing meals for Aššur was a festive and
    daily cult that exercised some economic centralization by exacting offerings from
    provinces ("the four directions").

cal symbols by considering them not as atemporal abstract systems, but in their full temporality, as instigators and products of temporal sociocultural processes."[107] So, for the portrayal of the cultic meals of the DC, combining historical and cultural-anthropological analysis is essential.

2.5. Outline of the Work

The subsequent chapters build on the methodological foundations of MacDonald and Braulik: both interpret the role of meals in Deuteronomy with respect to their historical context and MacDonald additionally brings together wider interdisciplinary perspectives (anthropology and zooarchaeology) for the interpretation of biblical meal texts. Each chapter will introduce comparative material (archaeology, ancient Near Eastern texts, iconography) that is generally applicable to all the festive meals in the DC, yet certain features are most aptly discussed in relation to specific texts.

My first investigation, "Material Culture and the Symbolic Meaning of Meat in Deuteronomy 12," will consider the physical and social realities of food and drink consumption through extant archaeological and iconographic evidence from the ancient Near East.[108] These investigations will help to determine how festive meals compared to the meals of everyday life, revealing the increased physical and symbolic importance for certain foods as objects of desire based on their limited accessibility.

This section will show that meat was a rare treat for the majority of the population, and meat consumption therefore serves as a powerful symbol. This special value for meat occurred in part because meat was often reserved for royal and divine "consumption" in the ancient Near East.[109] Cultic meals differed significantly from everyday meals in terms of the type of food and drink consumed, those present, and the way the

---

107 Turner, *Dramas, Fields, and Metaphors,* 151. Also Bell, *Ritual Theory, Ritual Practice,* 81: "ritual should be analyzed and understood in its real context, which is the full spectrum of ways of acting within any given culture, not as some a priori category of action totally independent of other forms of action. Only in this context can the theorist-observer attempt to understand how and why people choose to differentiate some activities from others."

108 In conjunction with administrative and "non-literary" texts.

109 The reservation for elite consumption is apparent from the work of Jean Bottéro, "The Cuisine of Ancient Mesopotamia" *BA* 48 (1985): 36–47.

meal was consumed. For example, meat was often eaten only at ritual feasts or special occasions,[110] though some consumption of game may have been "secular."[111]

Next, iconography from the period includes numerous portrayals of the banquet scene, which appears as a type scene in ancient Near Eastern seals and other iconography from the third millennium onwards.[112] This genre of the banquet scene shows the enjoyment of drink, and also of the accompanying food. Furthermore, the portrayal of a banquet scene is often related to a victory celebration, where seated guests drink from bowls, surrounded by servants, musicians, captives, and booty. References to meat in administrative and historical texts supplement meat's role in the iconographic portrayals.

The available archaeological record of faunal remains shows a significant decline in meat consumption in Judah during the period of Deuteronomy's writing. This data suggests that the Neo-Assyrian Empire demanded that those under their control hand over such desirable items to the imperial elites.

Upon completing this survey of the wider biblical context, diet, zooarchaeology, and iconography, I will then offer an historical-critical analysis and a reading of Deut 12:13–19 in order to highlight the contribution that this archaeological and iconographic data makes for the interpretation of the festival meals, especially the symbolic importance of meat. The iconographic and zooarchaeological perspectives become especially pertinent in light of the repeated focus on meat consumption by households and their dependents both in the centralized sacred context and in the peripheral village setting within this particular section of Deuteronomy. This focus on meat suggests that meat consumption carries particular importance for socio-religious identity formation in Judah under the shadow of Neo-Assyrian domination. My reading argues that emphasis on meat results *not only* from consideration of the practical implications of sacrificial centralization.[113] Instead, authorizing

---

110 Philip J. King and Lawrence E. Stager, *Life in Ancient Israel* (Louisville: Westminster John Knox Press, 2001), 68.

111 As reflected in Deut 12:15, 23. Yet bones of game animals were found at the Iron I cultic site on Mt. Ebal, cf. Loira Kolska Horwitz, "Faunal Remains from Mount Ebal." *TA* 13–14 (1986–87): 173–87; however, game was more prominent in the north than in Judah (see MacDonald, *What Did the Ancient Israelites Eat?*, 28).

112 Dominique Collon, *First Impressions: Cylinder Seals in the Ancient Near East* (Chicago: University of Chicago, 1987), 27.

113 This has been the traditional interpretation of the appearance of meat in Deut 12. The logic runs as follows: since animals could no longer be consumed at local shrines, some other means of local consumption must be provided, though it must now be

the local consumption of a festive food such as meat, which the people by necessity (either military or economic) were mostly sending to their Assyrian or other overlords, serves to contrast the easy yoke of service to Yhwh with the heavy burdens applied by Nineveh and Aššur and other foreign powers.

The second section, "The Cultic Meals of the Deuteronomic Cultic Calendar (16:1–17) in Light of Comparative Ancient Near Eastern Texts," will nuance Braulik's presentation of the cultic background underlying these DC meal texts. He rightly considers the vassal treaties like those of Esarhaddon as providing the metaphorical underpinning for the persuasive power of Deuteronomy as a whole.[114] However, when turning to the cultic meals, Braulik points to the Canaanite fertility cults, which he argues "… held considerable fascination for Israel's pious"[115] because of their close relationship to rural life. He argues for this attraction based on the critiques of Hosea, especially 2:7, 13, which are directed against Baal worship, rather than turning to a wider range of texts for determining the background of the DC meals. I will augment Braulik's treatment by relating the DC meal texts to further key texts from the surrounding ancient Near Eastern context. These texts display the broader importance of festive consumption, providing different rhetorical potentials for the DC text.

First, presentation of Levantine ritual meal texts from Emar and Ugarit will offer comparison with the Deuteronomic texts as ritual texts. The Akkadian-language ritual texts of Emar eschew royal ideology, instead working through the citywide *zukru* festivals on both a yearly and a seven-year cycle to unite the people of the city around a common view of the divine realm (or common story). Fleming notes that "feasting by the population of Emar is recorded explicitly only for the *zukru*, and this provision adds to the inclusive character of the whole event."[116] The Ugaritic ritual text *CTU* 1.40 displays the central role both for the inclusion of foreigners and other outsiders as well as for just interactions with them, which bears significant overlap with the DC vision of social reality portrayed in its ritual meal texts.

Second, comparison between Deuteronomy and narrative texts from Ugarit and Mesopotamia will show that Deuteronomy conceives

---

some kind of secular meal which contrasts with the sacred consumption at the central sanctuary. See Veijola, *5. Mose,* 269, for a recent formulation.

114 Braulik, "The Joy of the Feast," 30.

115 Braulik, "Commemoration of Passion and Feast of Joy," 70.

116 Daniel E. Fleming, *Time at Emar: the Cultic Calendar and the Rituals from the Diviner's Archive* (Mesopotamian Civilizations 11; Winona Lake, Ind.: Eisenbrauns, 2000), 79.

of feasts based on the model of the divine-royal victory feast and temple dedication feast prevalent in surrounding cultures. The DC differs significantly, however, from the overt "royal" ideology in most ancient Near Eastern banquet texts such as the feasts of the Baal Cycle from Ugarit and the *Enuma Elish* from Mesopotamia, or the biblical feasts like 1 Kgs 5:2–4. On the political and religious levels, the Deuteronomic formulation of the festive meal uncouples the celebration from any glorification of the human monarch around whom a community's identity might coalesce, thereby propounding a different formulation of communal identity. Furthermore, these comparative banquet texts from the surrounding cultures carry powerful socio-political and religious messages, and Deuteronomy both appropriates and modifies these messages. One modification is in Deuteronomy's inclusion of diverse members of the community such as Levites, slaves, and sojourners, who are not generally highlighted in royal banquet texts but become "special insiders" in the DC feasts. These discussions will build a picture of how the ritual and narrative texts in other ancient Near Eastern cultures used meals as a primary *topos* for identity formulation.

After discussion of these comparative texts, my second reading of a DC meal text focuses on the festival calendar of Deut 16:1–17 in relation to other biblical festival calendar texts. This comparison with both the wider texts from the ancient Near East and the biblical material will highlight Deuteronomy's notion of Israelite identity made up of a multiplicity of households that together make up a unified whole, unlike the royally-focused narrative texts of Ugarit and the texts and practices of the various ancient Near Eastern empires.

I will also pursue the connections of taste and smell with memory highlighted in modern studies of food and meals and allowed for in the richest description of Deuteronomy's festive meal:

The third and final section, "Deuteronomy's Tithe (14:22–29) in Light of Ancient Near Eastern Tribute and Modern Anthropology," will compare other pentateuchal and ancient Near Eastern tithes and temple tributes in conjunction with modern food studies. This final section investigates the significance of Deuteronomy's inclusion of a tithe ordinance, the earliest historical appearance of such a law in the Pentateuch. The lack of human monarch as recipient marks an important change from the typical formulation of a tithe or tribute in the texts and images from the ancient Near East. Secondly, this tithe is in large part to be consumed by those who bring it, again an important digression from other biblical and ancient tithes.

"With the silver secure in hand, go to the place that Yhwh your God will choose; spend the silver on whatever you wish—oxen, sheep, wine, strong drink, or whatever you desire. And you shall eat there in the presence of Yhwh your God, you and your household enjoying together." (Deut 14:25b–26) .

In this regard, David Sutton summarizes the mnemonic power of the senses of taste and smell at communal meals as follows: "Through repetition in ritual and other forms, [smell] focuses the attention of the members of a single society in the same direction."[117] In other words, the constructed culture of the community is therefore decisive for the determination of which smells and tastes individuals sharing a common culture remember, and also which smells and tastes these persons associate with important moments. These culturally-determined sensual experiences become the raw material with which specific culture practices, like the cultic meals described in Deuteronomy, can bring about the real inscription and consumption of a common communal identity. In Iron Age II Judah, much like the rest of the ancient Near East, the most emphasized meals were part of the religious celebrations. These considerations are perhaps less important for the exegesis (strictly-speaking) of these texts, and they instead find their significance in considerations of how these texts—and the events implied in them— might be received and appropriated by ancient audiences.

Overall, these celebratory meals include a comparatively extravagant menu, making them powerful mnemonic symbols for identity construction in the social, religious, and political senses. Neurobiological studies have shown that the memory-triggering power of the meals also results from the specific way smell and taste work together with memory on a biological level.[118] This conclusion provides support for my claim that the stuff of meals is of particular importance for identity creation and re-affirmation (since human identity is intrinsically linked to memory) because the senses of taste and smell remind people of specific experiences when they ate similar foods (in Deuteronomy, festive consumption).

Describing this rhetorical potential will be analogous to unpacking a metaphor in order to get a better understanding of a text's meaning.

---

117 David E. Sutton, *Remembrance of Repasts*, 90.

118 Trygg Engen, *Odor Sensation and Memory* (New York: Praeger, 1991), 81, argues that "while visual and auditory memory usually decrease with time … [smell] is specialized for the ability to reinstate the past and to ignore subsequent odor experiences not associated with the formative event." See also Gabrielle Glaser, *The Nose: A Profile of Sex, Beauty, and Survival* (New York: Atria, 2002), 136. She states, "Researchers believe that the olfactory process helps explain why smell, memories, and feelings are closely intertwined."

Yet it is not a metaphor *per se*, but rather a textually-described social practice that includes psychological and biological processes.

3. Material Culture and the Symbolic Meaning of Meat in Deuteronomy 12

3.1. Introduction

Modern scholarship on Deut 12 focuses intensely on altar centralization and the resulting notion of sacred versus profane slaughter. Considered from the perspective of historical-religious development, this scholarly emphasis relates closely to the move from multiple altars in Exod 20:24b ("in every place that I cause my name to be remembered") to the focus on one particular chosen place in the Deuteronomic text ("in the place that Yhwh your God chooses").[1] This centralization is of course pivotal for much of the Deuteronomic text.

Yet the portion of the text often considered the oldest (vv. 13–19)[2] displays both movement towards a central place and centrifugal movement back to the enlarged borders of the divinely given land. The concern in both the centrifugal and centripetal commands is the offerings, particularly their consumption, which often includes their enjoyment.[3] However, while the ordinances dealing with the central sanctuary focus on offerings in general—especially burnt offerings (v. 13)[4]—the primary concern of the ordinances concerning the "gates" of Israel is meat meant for communal consumption. In addition to the scholarly interest for centralization, my specific concern is the repeated mention of meat consumption. What makes meat (*bāśār*) so significant? I will argue that Deuteronomy's narrow focus on meat consumption functions as a direct and incisive response to the felt concerns of those desiring more of the symbolically good gift of meat. I imagine that the best

---

1   Veijola, *5. Mose,* 266–67; Eduard Nielsen, *Deuteronomium* (HKAT I/6; Tübingen: Mohr, 1995), 136; and especially Levinson, *Deuteronomy and the Hermeneutics of Legal Innovation,* 30–32, show the reliance of Deut 12 on Exod 20:24–26.
2   I will address the composition history of Deut 12 below, 3.5. Deuteronomy 12: Compositional History.
3   For a similar perspective see Nelson, *Deuteronomy,* 153–55.
4   The term *'ōlōtêkā* could metonymically designate the entirety of the offerings. Similarly Norbert Lohfink, "Kultzentralisation und Deuteronomium," notes that 14b (which perhaps belonged to the seventh-century text) broadens the mention of burnt offerings into an ordinance for the whole sacrificial system.

possible situation in which to place such a focus is that of a Judah that
has experienced Assyrian hegemony in the late eighth through the seventh century B.C.E. While the dating of the text is of course heuristic, the
various threads of argumentation explore the kinds of concerns—
biological and cultural—that provide insight into its layers of meaning.
In order to work out this proposal, the chapter considers various sets of
evidence from the biblical texts, zooarchaeology, iconography, and
related texts on the role of meat and banquets in ancient Israel. Diachronic analysis of Deut 12 follows, and the chapter will conclude with
a reading of Deut 12 highlighting the symbolic importance of "meat" as
a focusing element for the concerns of the early audience.

As an opening investigation I will address various aspects of the
biblical and material culture background for feasting. Of primary important for understanding celebratory consumption in the Old Testament texts is the symbolic importance of meat in the biblical record,
given its preeminent role—along with wine—in these meals. I will focus on meat here, as it plays the most important role in Deuteronomy,
especially ch. 12. The conclusions from the biblical investigations will
then be compared with iconographic portrayals, historical texts, and
administrative records from various ancient Near Eastern cultures.
Finally, I will discuss the archaeozoological finds (the record of faunal
remains) from Iron Age II archaeological sites and the diets of ancient
Israel.

To preview my conclusions, I believe that Deut 12 keys in on the
"promise" or "acceptance" of meat consumption in local villages in
order to show that Yhwh is a good God who deserves full allegiance.
This promise becomes attractive in the face of the restricted quantity of
meat available due to the Assyrian hegemony, which embodied the
threatened curse of Deut 28:31: "Your ox will be slaughtered before
your eyes, but you will not eat of it." In contrast, the Deuteronomic
vision offers the Israelites a desirable commodity that is considerably
less available while Assyria is the dominant covenant partner. Similarly, the command to make sure that all members of the community—
regardless of social or economic status—receive a share of the meat
counteracts the normal distribution pattern of highly valued goods in
which they often end up disproportionately in the hands of the elite.

3.2. Importance of Meat as a Symbol in the Biblical Corpus

The Hebrew scriptures are stocked full with references to meals that include meat, yet according to the canon's current shape, humans begin as vegetarians.[5] Even in the Noahic covenant of Gen 9 through which meat consumption becomes acceptable, God makes the covenant with both humans and animals, unified as a collective covenant partner in the expression *kol bāśār* ("all flesh," Gen 9:15). This covenant details the parameters for meat consumption: humans may eat meat, but they may not eat the meat with its blood as the blood "is" the life (*nepeš*).

This shift from humans as herbivores to omnivores otherwise only plays an important role in eschatological images such as Isa 11:6. Instead a plentitude of animals appears available for human consumption and enjoyment, allowing meat consumption to take on further significant symbolic meanings (rather than those related to the switch from herbivore to omnivore). For example, Abraham takes a good, tender calf (*rak wāṭôb*) from his herd to prepare for his visitors (Gen 18:7–8). The gift of this animal symbolizes Abraham's warm hospitality because of the animal's significant value: maintaining young domestic animals for the purpose of slaughter instead of for traction (plowing), wool, or milk constituted a significant economic burden.

The high value placed upon meat for consumption continues throughout the biblical text. Amos criticizes those in Israel whose wealth is displayed through their eating of rams, and also calves from the stall (Amos 6:4; cf. 1 Sam 28:24). Various types of meat, namely, fattened and pasture-fed cattle, sheep, and various types of game animals graced Solomon's royal menu (1 Kgs 5:3 [ET: 4:23]). Daniel defines desirable food as wine and meat (Dan 10:3; cf. Isa 25:6), and the same value is assigned to meat through its contrast with vegetables in Prov 15:17. This proverbial use takes meat's higher comparative value for granted and employs this difference in value to emphasize the real point of the proverb (that love is better than hatred). As a whole, these references support the traditional scholarly conclusion that ancient Israelite society considered meat highly desirable for consumption,

---

5   In fact, all uses of *bāśār* in Gen 2–8 refer either to man and woman becoming one "flesh" (Gen 2:24), emphasizing kinship (a connotation is also found in Gen 29:14; 37:27; Lev 18:6; 25:49; Judg 9:2; 2 Sam 5:1; 19:12–13; 1 Chr 11:1; Neh 5:5; and Isa 58:7) or to humans and animals as a unity (Gen 6–8; this unity of animals and humans continues through much of the biblical witness; see Isa 40:5–6; Jer 12:12; 25:31; 32:27; 45:5; Ezek 20:48; 21:4–5; Joel 2:28; Zech 2:13; Job 12:10; 13:14; Pss 56:4; 65:2; 78:39; 136:25; 145:21) .

giving rise to its symbolic value as well. Notably, this significant value coincided with meat's relative scarcity.

This symbolic significance, which remains closely bound to meat's value as food, explains why animal sacrifice was an important means for worship throughout the ancient Near East.[6] Within the biblical record this importance appears both in the laws concerning sacrifice and in narratives where worship occurs.[7] Some animals were of course totally devoted to the deity through burning, while others were partially reserved for human consumption by priests or worshipers. In both practices the relative value of meat functions as a sign of the worshipers' devotion to the deity.[8]

Because meat carried such value and desirability as a commodity, the developments in Israelite politics and socio-economic conditions during the Iron Age brought on changes in the distribution of meat as well. The above-mentioned texts such as Amos 6 and 1 Kgs 5:3 demonstrate this reality. As MacDonald notes, various factors contributed to what was likely an increasingly inequitable distribution pattern. The biblical text portrays the premonarchic sacrificial system as giving preference to priestly consumption and thus displaying some level of hierarchy in meat consumption (1 Sam 2:12–17), but the move to the monarchy allowed for further socio-economic stratification.[9] Accordingly,

---

6   Joann Scurlock, "Animal Sacrifice in Ancient Mesopotamian Religion," in *A History of the Animal World in the Ancient Near East* (ed. B. J. Collins; HO 64; Leiden: E. J. Brill, 2002), 389.

7   2 Chronicles 7:5–10 reports the animals used for the Solomonic temple dedication; 2 Chr 29:21–36 for Hezekiah's Passover, and 2 Chr 35:7–16 for Josiah's Passover.

8   Specific portions of the animal also carried higher symbolic value, such as Samuel's reservation of "the thigh and its trappings" (*haššoq wĕheʿālêhû*) for Saul, who was about to be anointed as king (1 Sam 9:22–24) . This is a slightly emended reading from MT, following 4QSamᵃ as rendered in BHS. P. Kyle McCarter, Jr., *I Samuel: A New Translation With Introduction, Notes & Commentary* (AB 8; Garden City, NY: Doubleday, 1980), 170, reads the Qumran text as *hʿlynh*, meaning "upper thigh," but ultimately would rather follow LXXᴮ which omits the word altogether. The Qumran text seems the more difficult yet understandable reading, and therefore the preferable reading. The significance of this particular cut of meat is garnered from the fact that Samuel also gives Saul a seat at the head of the table. Furthermore, this piece of the sacrificial victim often belongs to the priest (i.e., Exod 29:22; Lev 7:32–33). Krijn van der Jagt, "What Did Saul Eat When He Visited Samuel?" *BT* 47 (1996): 226–30, argues that Samuel gives Saul the cut that Samuel — likely as the eldest living brother of the extended family — would himself normally receive; this action marks Saul as of higher rank than Samuel.

9   MacDonald, *What Did the Ancient Israelites Eat?*, 78–79. The Samaria Ostraca tell a similar story, distinguishing between the landowning "l-men" and those who must pay taxes from their produce.

Solomon's corvée exemplifies the difference between the royal "haves" and the rest of society: the king blesses—or shares with—those he favors. There are, of course, many more festal depictions: some common settings are royal coronations (i.e., 1 Chr 12; 1 Kgs 1), victory celebrations (i.e., Isa 25; 1 Sam 14:31–35), the completion of agricultural tasks (1 Sam 25; Ruth 3), hospitality towards travelers (Gen 18), the completion of building projects (1 Kgs 8), and regular royal patronage (1 Kgs 11; 2 Kgs 25).

Within this larger framework there are two similar but opposing stories about the desire for meat during the wilderness wandering— Exod 16 and Num 11. Because "desire for meat" takes on special significance for the interpretation of Deut 12, which expresses the value of meat partially through the rhetoric of "desire" (12:15, 20, 21), these texts are important for comparative purposes. In the wilderness narratives of Exod 16 and Num 11 the Israelites complain about their food situation. Both narratives also link the provision of meat with the display of Yhwh's power and authority (Exod 16:12; Num 11:23).[10] In the Numbers narrative the people desire (*'wh*) a diet that contains some variety as an alternative to the daily manna.[11] The story in Numbers condemns the people's desire for meat because in their desire they both reject the presence and provision of Yhwh in their midst and instead look towards Egypt as the place of provision: "Who will give us meat? ... For it was better for us in Egypt!" (Num 11:4, 18, cf. v. 20). This turn to-

---

10   The Numbers passage focuses on Moses coming to know that Yhwh's word is trustworthy, while the Exodus pericope remarks that the people recognize that Yhwh is their God.

11   Baruch Levine, *Numbers 1–20: A New Translation With Introduction and Commentary* (AB 4; New York: Doubleday, 1993), 321, points out, following Rashi, that the Israelites have flocks with them, so their desire does not make sense contextually. He also notes that they do not recall eating meat in Egypt, but rather focus on cucumbers, fish, melons, leeks, onions, and garlic. However, meat and fish are parallel expressions in 11:4–5. Cathy K. Kaufman, *Cooking in Ancient Civilizations* (Westport, Conn.: Greenwood, 2006), 62, notes, "By the first millennium B.C.E., some elite Egyptians began to consider fish taboo ... The taboo was not universally observed, as plenty of fish remains litter temple complexes." Perhaps such a taboo lies in the background of the Israelite connection to the less desirable fish rather than to the more desirable meats, such as beef, which were reserved for the elites (cf. ibid., 55). This was not the case in Judah, however, where both fresh and salt water fish bones dating to the pre-exilic period have also been found (cf. Neh 13:16; MacDonald, *What Did the Israelites Eat?*, 37–38, with bibliography). Yet these fish must have been imported, which places a premium on their value. Levine, *Numbers 1–20*, 334–37, attributes this section to a non-Priestly source, while suggesting that Exod 16 is the work of a Priestly hand that secondarily incorporated additions from Num 11, especially the desire for meat which appears extraneous to the point of Exod 16.

wards the past and a different source of provision brings on a plague from God while the people are still in the act of chewing (11:33). Levine implies that the desire itself stands condemned.[12] Perhaps the very form of the verb (*hithpa'el*) hints at the coming condemnation (it also appears in *pi'el* with more positive connotations), but the main problem with this desire lies in its longing for Egyptian life coupled with despising God's gift of the manna.[13]

The importance of the desire for meat in Exod 16 is more difficult to evaluate simply because the text relegates meat to secondary importance behind the provision of manna. The nature of the Israelites' desire emerges as a desire for meat in addition to bread.

The narrative focuses on the provision of manna, rendering the evening meat an afterthought in vv. 8, 12–13a.[14] Regardless of the compositional history of this chapter, the Israelites' desire for meat is fulfilled and not condemned as worthy of punishment.[15] Yhwh duly provides when the Israelites seem headed towards starvation (vv. 3, 13–19). Since the people are not condemned for grumbling in this situation, their grumbling and underlying desire are "givens" in the situation. Desire just "is," especially when on the brink of starvation (v. 3). In this situation it appears that Yhwh creates, or at least allows for, the awak-

---

12   Ibid., 321, states, "The *hithpa'el* stem of the verb *'āwāh* 'to desire' most often, if not always, connotes an improper or excessive desire, not a bona fide one."

13   This distinction becomes important for Deut 12 for two reasons: 1) in Deut 12 the verbal stem is *pi'el* rather than *hithpa'el*, so the desire of Deut 12 cannot be condemned through a connection with Num 11. This distinction also holds when compared with the appearance of *'wh* in the Deuteronomic version of the Ten Commandments, which is *hithpa'el*.

14   William H. C. Propp, *Exodus 1–18* (AB 2; New York: Doubleday, 1998), 588–91, sees the provision of meat as part of the original story, which he attributes to Priestly source. Brevard S. Childs, *The Book of Exodus* (OTL; Philadelphia: Westminster, 1974), 280–88, considers the absence of quail from the rest of the story a result of its oral tradition history.

15   Childs, *Exodus,* 284–85, argues that there is an implicit criticism of the desire for meat in this passage through comparison with Num 11:4, Ps 78:30, and the observation that meat was a rare delicacy. Once the Exod 16 account is read on its own, the picture changes. The cries for meat and for bread cannot be separated in Exod 16, meaning that a suggestion that the desire for meat is condemned would necessarily mean that the desire for bread should also be condemned (as Childs, ibid., 284, does as well). However, in Exod 16:4 Yhwh explains that the test for the Israelites is not whether or not they can trust in divine provision of food by not crying out for it, but rather whether or not they can follow Yhwh's instructions for collecting manna daily, thereby trusting that it would come regularly (meaning they do not need to save up manna for the days to come). This means that the problem is not the desire itself, but rather the Israelites disregard for Yhwh's method of fulfillment one day at a time when they resort to hoarding manna for tomorrow.

ening of strong hunger pangs (embodied desire) in order to contrast the manner of provision in Egypt with that of the miraculous divine provision.

Furthermore, in Exod 16:3 the Israelites ate bread in Egypt while sitting "next to" pots of meat. As a result it remains unclear whether the Israelites truly ate meat in Egypt or only smelled it because one can, of course, smell meat—thereby arousing and magnifying desire—without getting the opportunity to eat the meat and satisfy that desire. So perhaps their desire for meat went unfulfilled in Egypt (this would fit with the typical diet of slave labor). If the Israelites only saw and smelled the meat in the pots, then God's provision of meat in Exod 16 (likewise in Deut 12) dramatically displays Yhwh's concern for the Israelites. The foreign rulers (and sometimes the local ones as well), whether Assyrian, Babylonian, or Egyptian, reduce the Israelites to slaves who smell the aroma of meat but cannot eat it.

Taken as a whole, the story of meat in the Old Testament points to a highly valued, though somewhat complex symbol. The desire to consume meat is a given, but it is not without certain dangers.

3.3. Iconography and Records of Meat and Banquets in the Ancient Near East

Following on the biblical depictions of meat, this section will juxtapose iconographic presentations of banquet scenes with various written descriptions (from historical and administrative texts) of banquets in order to provide some details on the imaginative power of the meal and consumable meat. These two bodies of data will be interpreted together in part because iconographic portrayal of meat consumption is quite rare in ancient Near Eastern art.

The prolific iconographic presentations of banquets in the ancient Near East confirm the banquet's role as an important *topos* for graphic representation.[16] Dominique Collon has discerned three categories of

---

16   Karl Fr. Müller, "Das assyrische Ritual," *MVAG* 41 (1937): 59, states, "Von der Zeit der frühen sumerischen Kunst an bis in die assyrische Spätzeit hinein haben sich bildliche Darstellungen des Festmahles am Hofe gefunden. Ebenso bezeugen die Königsinschriften wiederholt das Abhalten eines Mahles zur Feier eines Sieges oder der Einweihung eines Palastes bzw. Tempels." [ET: From the time of the early Sumerian art until the late Assyrian period graphic representations of banquet meals were found in the palace. Similarly the royal inscriptions repeatedly attest to banquets in celebration of a victory or the dedication of a palace or temple.]

the banquet scene "genre" in seals that signify the enjoyment not only of drink, but also of accompanying food. She concludes, "The banquet scene [in seals] can be divided into three main types depending on whether the participants, generally male and female, drink from a large vessel through drinking tubes, or from cups, or eat from a table."[17] This point about accompanying food must often, however, be made explicit to deter the errant conclusion that the iconography only portrays drinking parties, which of course leaves out meat as an important imaginative symbol. Instead, the cup becomes the iconographic symbol for banqueting—which includes drinking and eating—in the Mesopotamian and Levantine visual portrayals. Frances Pinnock notes, "the theme [of the banquet] even when a loaded table is represented, is iconographically 'summarized' in the act of drinking, through a tube from a jar, or in a cup."[18]

The value of meat can also be deduced graphically from depictions on temple offering jars. On one early Sumerian vessel, for example, the top register shows people carrying jars to a temple, while the lower registers depict ears of grain and cattle.[19] The juxtaposition of the upper and lower registers suggests that the men bring these goods before the deity. It is important to note that if there were no animal depictions, it would be difficult to conclude that meat was part of the tribute, for unlike a jar (signifying liquid or grain) it is difficult to determine what sort of vessel meat would be delivered in.[20] However, iconographic portrayals of people leading an ox into a temple also appear on the palace walls of Zimri-lim at Mari (from the early second millennium)[21]

---

17   Dominique Collon, *First Impressions*, 27.

18   Frances Pinnock, "Considerations on the «Banquet Theme» in the Figurative Art of Mesopotamia and Syria," in *Drinking in Ancient Societies: History and Culture of Drinks in the Ancient Near East* (ed. L. Milano; HANES 6; Padua: Sargon, 1994), 24.

19   Eva Strommenger, *Fünf Jahrtausende Mesopotamien* (Munich: Hirmer, 1962), images 19–22. See also Elizabeth Douglas Van Buren, *The Fauna of Ancient Mesopotamia as Represented in Art* (AO 18; Rome: Pontifical Bible Institute, 1939), plate XIII, Fig. 59.

20   This may, of course, result mostly from temporal and cultural distance. However, Eudora J. Struble and Virginia Rimmer Hermann, "An Eternal Feast at Sam'al: The New Iron Age Mortuary Stele from Zincirli in Context," *BASOR* 356 (2009): 28, note that in Syro-Hittite mortuary reliefs that portray meat do so "either on top of a stack of curved objects—presumably loaves of bread or cakes … —or sitting in a separate vessel, usually footed … common in both ceramic and stoneware in the Syro-Hittite zone during the Iron Age."

21   The Louvre, Paris and The National Museum, Aleppo. Strommenger, *Fünf Jahrtausende Mesopotamien*, image 164, gives the following description: "wall-paintings with sacrificial scenes from the palace of Zimri-lim at Mari. Larsa Period, c. 2040–1870 BC."

corroborating with written sources that meat was viewed as an important gift to the temple, pointing to meat as a valuable gift and necessary foodstuff for the divine world. A number of scenes from Assurbanipal's North Palace in Nineveh, Sennacherib's Southwest Nineveh Palace, and from the Nimrud palaces of Assurnasirpal II, Tiglath-Pileser III, and Esarhaddon all display the value of cattle, sheep, and goats by displaying their exit from captured cities as part of the spoils, at times even linked graphically to feasting.[22]

Turning to the banquet scenes themselves, Pinnock also distinguishes between the banquet scene, in which many people are present, and the representation of the king alone, which carries a different religious ritual meaning.[23] Depictions of individual diners—though not only of royal personages—often imply funeral rites. For the Zincirli KTMW stele from the late eighth century, Struble and Hermann conclude,

> The image of KTMW seated alone at a feasting table positions his stele firmly within Bonatz's existing classification system [of Syro-Hittite funerary monuments] ... This group of mortuary reliefs comprises images of a

---

22   Examples include Louvre AO 199106+Vatican 14987, where cattle are carried away as spoils with Chaldean prisoners (Richard D. Barnett, *Sculptures From the North Palace of Ashurbanipal at Nineveh (668-627 B.C.)* [London: British Museum, 1976], Plate XXIV); BM 124916+134386, also from Ashurpanipal's North Palace, discussed below, 85 n. 36; and BM 118882 from the Central Palace at Nimrud, which depicts prisoners and their flocks and herds leaving a Babylonian city (see Richard D. Barnett and M. Falkner, *The Sculptures of Aššur-Nasir-Apli II (883-859 B.C.), Tiglath-Pileser III (745-727 B.C.), Esarhaddon (681-669 B.C.) From the Central and South-West Palaces at Nimrud* [London: British Museum, 1962], 52–53), and the depiction of Astartu—BM 118908 —from the Southwest Palace in Nimrud (ibid., 118–21).

23   Pinnock, "Considerations on the «Banquet Theme»," 24. Halet Çambel and Aslı Özyar, *Karatepe-Aslantaş: Azatiwataya: die Bildwerke* (Mainz: Philipp von Zabern, 2003), 130–34, for example, argue the cultic meal sequence on the gate complex of Karatepe (circa 700 B.C.E.), depicting a single eater in the upper panel and slaughter below, most likely displays a yearly offering connected to a dead ruler. There is an extreme amount of diversity among the depictions from Karatepe: the meal is surrounded by registers with servants [or the surviving heirs, in line with Struble and Hermann, "An Eternal Feast at Sam'al," 30, for the KTMW stele] who carry vases and a rabbit on a platter and lead a bull (presumably for slaughter), a man carrying a small game animal, and battle scenes. Following Bonatz' study, Struble and Hermann (ibid., 31) link the image of birds on the KTMW stela and elsewhere to purification rites found in Hurrian and Hittite ritual texts. Dominique Collon, "Banquets in the Art of the Ancient Near East," in *Banquets D'Orient* (ed. R. Gyselen; Res Orientales IV; Bures S/Y: Groupe pour L'Étude de la Civilisation du Moyen-Orient, 1992), 28, connects this tradition to Egyptian influence.

single figure seated in front of a feasting table seemingly representing the feeding of the deceased after death.[24]

In contrast to this group of single diner mortuary depictions, a whole series of banquets feature connections to military victories, and often show multiple guests. It is this second group that bears particular importance for the DC meals.

An early depiction of the group banquet scene comes from the "Royal Standard of Ur" from the third millennium.

"Standard of Ur: Peace Panel" (BM 121201, © Trustees of the British Museum)

The upper register of the so-called peace panel (the battle scene is on the adjacent "war" panel) depicts a victory celebration with a seated ruler and guests holding cups and listening to music while servants stand by. The lower registers show people bringing fish, cattle, and sheep, while also leading pack animals carrying grain, thereby summarizing the ingredients for the meal.[25] This vivid portrayal of the banquet

---

24   Struble and Hermann, "An Eternal Feast at Sam'al," 28.
25   BM 121201. Ibid., 72. This assembly was elucidated most recently and quite adeptly by Wright, "Commensal Politics in Ancient Western Asia," 225–26.

theme puts on display the combination of the various elements that also make up the standard type scene: a seated ruler often surrounded by guests who holds a cup while musicians entertain. The depiction of a banquet relating to a victory celebration also appears in the Megiddo ivories from the Late Bronze Age, again with a seated ruler drinking from a bowl, surrounded by servants, musicians, captives, and booty.[26]

Perhaps the first extant Assyrian portrayal with explicit links between battle, taking booty and offering to the deity, and then consumption of the booty is found in the so-called White Obelisk from Sennacherib's Nineveh Palace.

The complicated eleventh-tenth century (Middle Assyrian), though it has also been dated to the ninth century, presentation has eight panels on each of the four sides and is accompanied by an unfinished inscription.[27] Though the dating and the interpretation of the iconographic registers as a unified display remain contested, one may conclude with Pittman that the Obelisk carries a reduced copy of a narrative from one of the palace rooms originally found as far back as Tiglath-pileser I (1115–1077 B.C.E.).[28] The images are then reused in a different time period. She makes the important observation that "In Mesopotamian society, images were valued for their consistent associations and so they were retained and repeated from period to period both within and across media for as long as they remained potent."[29]

Banqueting appears in the orthothat as follows: The top three rows depict the subjugation of cities, and the booty (including cattle) being taken to a temple and then apportioned among a number of figures sitting at various banquet tables. In the third row, one register (A3)

---

26   Palestine Archaeological Museum 38.780. Cf. *ANEP*, no. 332 (Image p. 111, description, p. 288). As Collon, "Banquets in the Art of the Ancient Near East," 28, states "Banquets as a celebration of the ruler, and especially in connection with military victories and hunting are to be found at all periods."

27   BM 118807. Cf. Jutta Börker-Klähn, *Altvorderasiatische Bildstelen und vergleichbare Felsreliefs* (BF 4:1-2; Mainz: Philipp von Zabern, 1982): 2: no. 132 for images and 1:60–65 for discussion. In Assyrian inscriptions, Masetti-Rouault, "Le roi, la fête et le sacrifice," 73–74, notes that Shamshi-Adad I (1812–1780) follows up his capture of Arrapha (modern Kirkuk) with a sacrifice to important deities in that city's temple of the storm god during a seasonal feast; there is then a long break in the appearance of this *topos*, until the First Millennium. Edmond Sollberger, "The White Obelisk," *Iraq* 36 (1974): 231–34, maintains that the inscription on the monument refers to Aššurnaṣirpal II (883–849) rather than to Aššurnaṣirpal I (1050–1032), but this does not mean that the features of the iconography arose only at that time.

28   Holly Pittman, "The White Obelisk and the Problem of Historical Narrative in the Art of Assyria," in *Art Bulletin* 78 (1996): 334.

29   Ibid., 354.

Side A   Side B
White Obelisk (BM: 118807, Drawings C.D. Hodder)

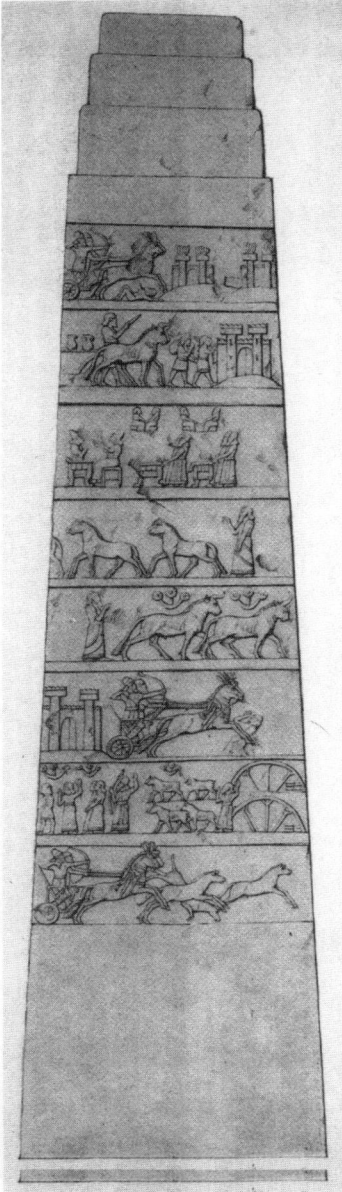

Side C   Side D

White Obelisk (Drawings C.D. Hodder)

depicts an offering scene, but the animal to be sacrificed (a bull) is partially displayed in the register next to it (B3), which is a banquet scene (also in C3). The splitting of the bull into two frames connects the divine feast (offering) with human one. The politics and religious aspects of banquets run together and overlap.[30] This is especially the case given that the priest (A3) is the king.[31] A well-attended banquet also appears in the seventh row (D7 + A7).

Pittman claims, "A monument such as the White Obelisk suggests that images were, like texts, transferred directly from monument to monument."[32] As a result, the White Obelisk broadcasts the message of an Assyrian king who is religiously observant, who easily succeeds in battle and the hunt, and who magnanimously puts on banquets for his honored guests. Furthermore, this rhetoric was put on displace beyond the eyes of visiting dignitaries or Assyrian nobles who entered the throne room: the obelisk stood outside, thereby communicating to the broader population.[33]

The connections between Assyrian depictions of royal magnanimity and power and communal banquets continue in Sargonid iconography. In Sargon's newly constructed Dur-Sharrukin palace (717–706), there are two extant banquet depictions. Both use the juxtaposition of upper and lower registers to portray their message. The first displays battle scenes both on the lower and on part of the upper register, while a meal including numerous guests attended by servants also appears in the upper register.[34] The second banquet juxtaposes not battle, but the royal hunt in the lower register with a large feast in the upper one.[35]

---

30 Masetti-Rouault, "Le roi, la fête et le sacrifice," 82–83, notes that in the inscriptions of Tikulti-Ninurta II (ninth century), it is mentioned that two-thirds of acquired booty from a certain campaign went to the deity and one-third to the palace.

31 Ursula Magen, *Assyrische Königsdarstellungen—Aspekte der Herrschaft: eine Typologie* (BF 9; Mainz: von Zabern, 1986), 65–68. Magen, (ibid., 122) lists a total of ten depictions of banqueting Assyrian kings from Tukulti-ninurta I to Ashurbanipal. The majority (7) are depicted as sitting on a throne, as found in the White Obelisk.

32 Pittman, "The White Obelisk and the Problem of Historical Narrative," 354; in this case the images were transferred from the walls of a palace to the obelisk.

33 Ibid.

34 Louvre AO 1435, 2–3, Musei e Gallerie Pontificie 14995. Pauline Albenda, *The Palace of Sargon, King of Assyria: Monumental Wall Reliefs at Dur-Sharrukin, from Original Drawings Made at the Time of Their Discovery in 1843–1844 by Botta and Flandin* (Synthèse 22; Paris: Editions Recherche sur les Civilisations, 1986), 81-82, 88; plates 109–130. Room 2, slab 14. Drawing by E. Flandin.

35 Ibid., 77–80; plates 84–90 (BM 118831, Oriental Institute Museum A 11254, A 11255, A 1125, Iraq Museum 60971/1, 60971/2, 6097/3). Room 7, slab 10. Drawing by E. Flandin.

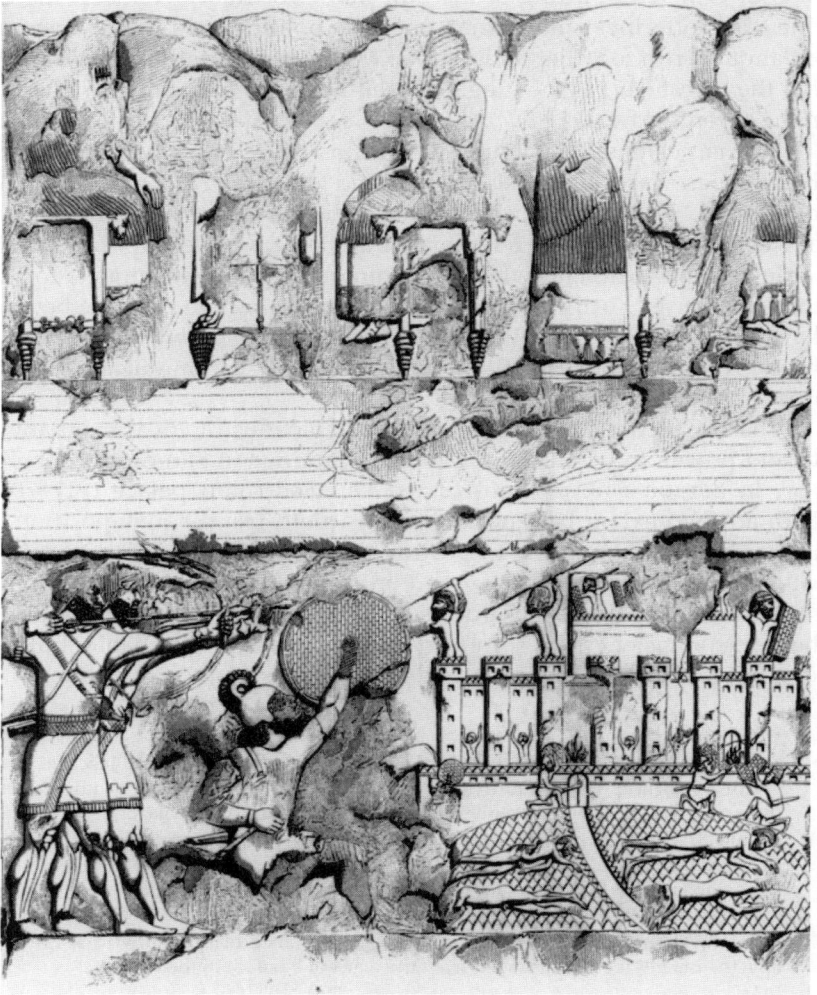

Khorsobad, Room II, 14. Drawing by Eugène Flandin.

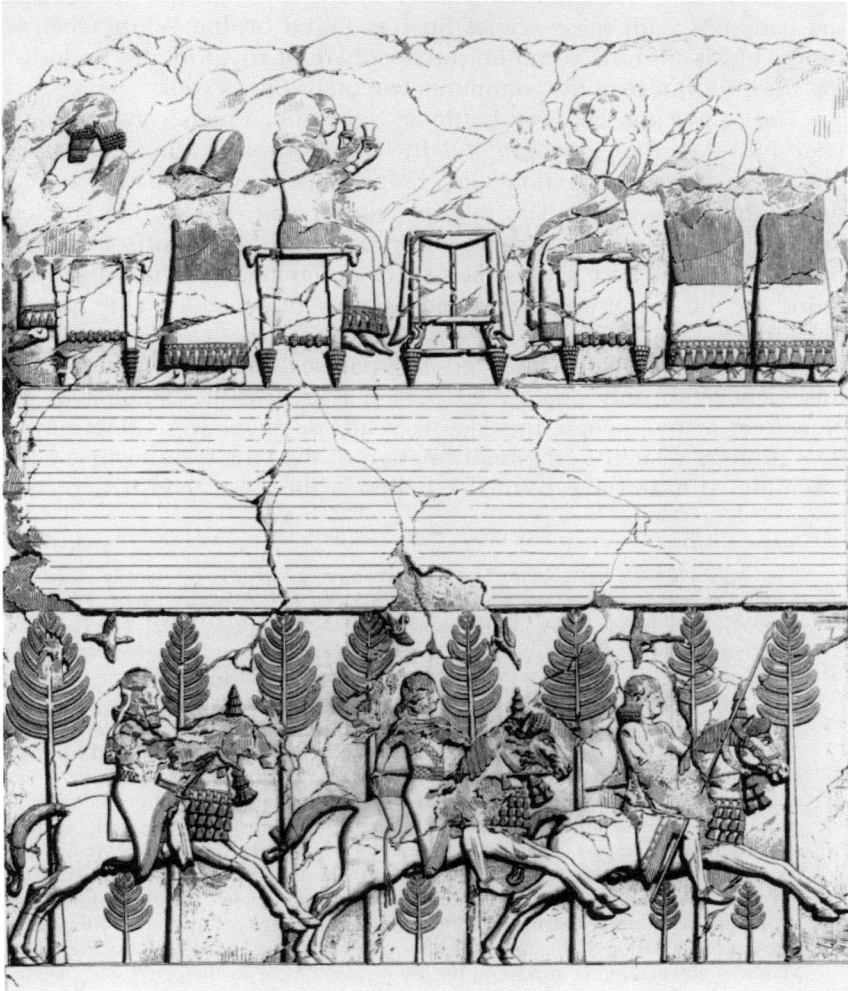

Khorsobad, Room VII, 10. Drawing by Eugène Flandin.

The activities of the hunt and battle are two of the preeminent occupations of the Neo-Assyrian kings on display in the palace art, suggesting their importance for the maintenance of the royal image. Juxtaposing the banquets with these scenes (just as found on the White Obelisk) brings meals into the communicative sphere of royal might, underlining the importance of the communal banquet *topos* as well.

The connection between battle and group banquets continues into later Neo-Assyrian iconography. In Assurbanipal's Nineveh palace, one frieze displays Assyrian soldiers, presumably on their way to battle, in the top register. The middle register shows Assyrian soldiers leading away captives carrying sheep and other foodstuffs from Hamanu in Elam. These goods then seem designated for the celebration found in the lower register, which shows three tables with people drinking.[36]

Teissier suggests that the Neo-Assyrian seals displaying versions of this scene with only one seated person represent the banquet of the New Year festival where the coming year's destinies were determined, thus directly related to the reaffirmation of the king's authority by the assembly of the divine council.[37] If this is the case, then it depicts a

---

36   BM 124916+134386, from Room S1 in Assurbanipal's North Palace (easily viewed in F.M. Fales and J. P. Postgate, eds., *Imperial Administrative Records, Part 1: Palace and Temple Administration* [SAA VII; Helsinki: Helsinki Univ. Press, 1992], 141, figure 34; otherwise found in Barnett, *Sculptures From the North Palace of Ashurbanipal at Nineveh*, Plate LXVI). Room S1 was an upper story room, and the orthostats from this room were found having fallen into Room S on the floor below.

37   Beatrice Teissier, *Ancient Near Eastern Cylinder Seals From the Marcopoli Collection* (Berkeley: University of California, 1984), 36. Michelle I. Marcus, "Art and Ideology in Ancient Western Asia," *CANE* 4:2488–89, argues for the Neo-Assyrian royal iconography, "Significantly the references are to Babylonian imagery. It provides visual support for a particularly Assyrian ideology that consciously plays upon its Babylonian foundation, especially in religious matters, but with Assyria now as the new center of Mesopotamian culture." She argues that one significant development from the earlier Mesopotamian banquet scenes is that the king takes the place of the deity sitting on the throne. Here, instead of temple functionaries presenting an offering before a representation of the deity, attendants offer the cup to the Neo-Assyrian king. Marcus's observation is intriguing for my argument (for further discussion see the subsequent chapter on the cultic calendar [Deut 16] of the DC and their reception from the view of comparative ancient Near Eastern texts) that the DC meals are reacting against the Neo-Assyrian close identification of divine and human banquet givers in the figures of Neo-Assyrian king and Neo-Assyrian deity. The earlier scene, where a deity holds a cup while receiving tribute appears on a second millennium seal, can be clearly seen in Collon, *First Impressions,* 176 (no. 833). While Marcus' conclusion seems somewhat suspect because rulers may have appeared earlier as well, Tallay Ornan, "The Godlike Semblance of a King: The Case of Sennacherib's Rock Reliefs," in *Ancient Near Eastern Art in Context* (ed. M. H. Feldman and J.

transfer of symbolic authority, attributing something of the divine authority to the Assyrian ruler through his assumption of this divine role.

The banquet scene's reuse beyond Neo-Assyrian origins can be observed in a banquet scene on a ninth century Nimrud ivory, where the
ruler sits with cup in hand, while servants bring food and play music.[38]
This scene, coming from outside the Assyrian context (West Semitic),[39]
provides an inroad into the use of a typical scene in the lands conquered by the Neo-Assyrian Empire. How the *topos* is reused on the
periphery cannot be determined from the iconography alone, though
the fact that one person—thus likely a ruler—eats alone suggests a
more central focus than the depictions in Sargon's palace. However, the
frequency of banquet iconography in the time of the Neo-Assyrian
Empire suggests that the symbolic meaning of the imagery is broadcast
widely.[40]

Finally, a prominent, though non-standard display of the genre appears in the seventh-century relief from Assurbanipal's Nineveh palace
in which King Assurbanipal and his queen feast in their garden. This
"garden banquet of Assurbanipal" portrays the royal couple celebrating the victory over the Elamites and their king Teumman, whose head
hangs from a nearby tree.[41]

In typical fashion the cups are raised, while musicians play in the
background. Servants, in this case, Elamite princes,[42] whisk away flies
and bring platters of food. In contrast to earlier forms of this type scene,

---

Cheng; Leiden: E. J. Brill, 2007), 168, also notes that Sennacherib appears as a minor
deity on the Bavian Gate.

38   BM 118179. Cf. André Parrot, *Arts of Assyria* (trans. S. Gilbert and J. Emmons; New
York: Golden, 1961), 311.

39   Jonathan S. Greer, private communication, notes that it is likely that the Nimrud
ivory was loot from elsewhere (like almost all the bowls), maybe Phoenicia, though
the hair suggests a Syrian provenance. There may also be some overlap here between the Neo-Assyrian group banquets and the Syro-Hittite funerary banquet.

40   Collon, *First Impressions*, 75. The iconography also appears in the Levant in the banquet depiction on a seal from the Transjordan, complete with seated ruler or deity
holding a cup, while bread and fish lie on a table and servants stand at attention
close by (Tell es-Sa'idiyeh, S 978, Amman, National Museum. Cf. *ANEP*, no. 859 [im-
age on p. 359, description on pp. 381–82]).

41   BM 124920; Barnett, *Sculptures From the North Palace of Ashurbanipal*, Plate LXIV Cf.
ANEP, no. 451 (images on p. 155, description on p. 301). The nature of the feast as a
victory celebration is also supported by the bow and quiver lying on a nearby table.
This relief also comes from room S1 the north palace of Nineveh.

42   Margaret Cool Root, "Elam in the Imperial Imagination: From Nineveh to Persepolis," in *Elam and Persia* (ed. J. Álvarez-Mon and M. B. Garrison; Winona Lake, Ind.
Eisenbrauns, 2011), 445.

"Garden Banquet of Assurbanipal" (BM 124920, © Trustees of the British Museum)

Assurbanipal reclines on a couch, rather then sitting on a throne. This development from other banquet scenes may attempt to emphasize his ability to relax after battle as a result of the completeness of his victory.[43] Furthermore, the appearance of the queen and lack of any fur-

---

43   Richard D. Barnett, "Assurbanibal's Feast," *ErIsr* 18 (1985): 1–6, argues that this relief constitutes conflation of Eastern and Western influences, namely of the victory and marzea⊚ themes. With Jonathan S. Greer, "A Marzeah and a Mizraq: A Prophet's Mêlée with Religious Diversity in Amos 6.4–7." *JSOT* 32 (2007): 253 n. 36, I find this identification problematic since inscriptions mentioning Teumman are instead linked to battle and even the *akītu*, which is of course also a religious connection. Note the connection made in Assurbanipal's own annals: (K 2637: translation from Daniel D. Luckenbill, *Ancient Records of Assyria and Babylonia II: Historical Records of Assyria From Sargon to the End* [Chicago: University of Chicago, 1927], 294–95): "[I] (am) Assurbanipal, king of the universe, king of Assyria. [After] I had offered sacrifices to Sheri (Kurri), the god (goddess?), [had celebrated the feast of the *bit akiti* ('House of the New Year's Feast'),] had laid hold of the reins of Ishtar, [surrounded by Dunanu], Samgunu and Apla and the decapitated head of Teumman, king of Elam, [whom Ishtar had given into my hand], I made the entrance into Arbela amid rejoicing." This final link will become of central important in the following chapter. Assurbanipal's rest may allude to the similar literary portrayal of Marduk after defeating Tiamat, where a restful banquet is enjoyed while the gods sing Marduk's praises (Enuma Elish IV.133–36) . See also Bernard Batto, "The Sleeping God: an Ancient Near Eastern Motif of Divine Sovereignty," *Bib* 68 (1987): 62. He argues with reference to Atrahasis, idem, *Slaying the Dragon: Mythmaking in the Biblical Tradition* (Louisville: Westminster John Knox, 1992), 27–28, "In the ancient Near Eastern conception one of the prerogatives or symbols of deity [*sic*] was leisure or rest."

ther guests is an anomaly for a victory banquet. Root argues that these developments play on a particular relationship between the Assurbanipal and the Elamites: their sacred groves had not been penetrated by foreigners until Ashurbanipal's soldiers accomplished the feat.

There may also be allusions to sacred sexual union with Ishtar as part of an *akitu*, such as the bed, and the combination with her pre-battle advice for the king to eat, drink, provide music, and worship Ishtar while she took care of the Elamite enemy.[44]

Taken as a whole, Jürgen Bär argues that the iconography of the Neo-Assyrian palaces reflects the changes in imperial policy.[45] The imperial policy mandating that vassals bring tribute, which was the system from the reign of Assurnasirpal II (883–859) to that of Sargon II (722–705), began breaking down with Tiglath-pileser III (745–727) because Assyria's policy towards conquered territories changed. The Neo-Assyrian Empire no longer focused on vassals bringing tribute, but rather on taking the land and its booty, while reducing the vassals to Assyrian provinces. With the change in imperial policy, the tribute

"The Destruction of Astartu" (BM 118908 © Trustees of the British Museum)

---

44   Root, "Elam in the Imperial Imagination: From Nineveh to Persepolis," 445–48. She also contends that the bed represents booty, and the erotics of the *akitu* for Ishtar.

scenes also fell by the wayside. Instead of depicting vassals bringing tribute, later iconography only shows the Assyrians leading away the "tribute goods" from a battle scene as found in the depiction in the Calah palace relief of Tiglath-pileser III's booty being lead away from Astartu (Transjordanian Ashtaroth; 733–732 B.C.E.). The various depictions of bovines and caprovids (among other animals) that do appear in Neo-Assyrian monuments and reliefs typically appear in scenes where captives are being led away from conquered cities along with their animals.[46]

Bär states, "Den Schlusspunkt dieser Entwicklung setzt die berühmte Szene, die Assurbanipal in der Gartenlaube zeigt."[47] Here, a subjected ruler does not bring tribute, but rather his head hangs on a tree while the king enjoys his food and drink.[48] This is important for Deuteronomy's cultic banquets because the tracing of these iconographic representations and imperial policies coalesce specifically around the portrayal of meals, which shows the imperial hegemony manifested through the representation of the king's relaxed ingestion of acquired booty: the depiction of the sacking of Hamanu in Elam and similar cities concludes with the Assyrian king enjoying the fruits of this military labor.[49] However, the depiction of Ashurbanipal's banquet

---

45   Jürgen Bär, *Der assyrische Tribut und seine Darstellung: Eine Untersuchung zur imperialen Ideologie im neuassyrischen Reich* (AOAT 243; Kevelaer: Butzon & Bercker and Neukirchen-Vluyn: Neukirchener Verlag, 1996), 230–31.

46   Ibid., 238.

47   Ibid., 231. [ET: The climax of this development is the famous scene that portrays Assurbanipal in the gazebo.]

48   According to Barnett, *Sculptures From the North Palace of Ashurbanipal*, 57, an accompanying inscription reads "The kings of Elam, whom with the aid of Ashur and Ninlil my hands captured ... they stood (?), and their own hands prepared their royal meal, and they brought it before me."

49   Evidence of banquets from Egypt is far more plentiful during the Old and New Kingdoms, while not offering significant parallels of banquet iconography from the Third Intermediate or Late Period (Dynasties XXI–XXVI)—the period of Neo-Assyrian dominance in the ancient Near East—according to Salima Ikram, "Banquets," in *The Oxford Encyclopedia of Ancient Egypt* (Oxford: Oxford University Press, 2001), 1:164. Nevertheless, similar conclusions can be reached with regard to the relationship between meat and power. While the entire society had at least occasional access to some form of meat, Ikram, *Choice Cuts: Meat Production in Ancient Egypt* (OLA 69; Leuven: Peeters Press & Department of Oriental Studies, 1995), 208, concludes from Papyrus Bulaq 18 of the XIIIth Dynasty, "... meat was only consumed regularly on some scale by a few people, courtesy of the Pharaoh, and was occasionally distributed by him as a special mark of favour to others." The type of meat one consumed also identified one's socio-political standing—commoners caught and ate fish from the river, while the highest nobility had access to beef (cf. ibid., 199–205). The unusual iconographic portrayal of the banquet of Horemheb (Commander-in-

is somewhat problematic for the comparison with the group feasting iconography and Deuteronomy because the banquet does not include the same communal aspect. However, in spite of the Garden Banquet's idiosyncrasies, the banquet *topos* as a whole maintains its connection to royal might on display in battle and in the hunt.

The Neo-Babylonian and Persian periods provide little in the way of graphic portrayals of meals.[50] The bearing of tribute remains a central theme for the Persian empire, if one considers the multiple depictions of delegations from throughout the empire (India, Lydia, Babylon, among many others), who bring gifts as seen on a staircase of the Apadana and from the Palace of Darius in Persepolis.[51] It is surprising, given the importance of royal banquets for the Persians—at least according to their Greek contemporaries—that no banquet iconography has been found. Sancini-Weerdenburg suggests simply that there was no reason to record in stone what was viewed in real life action. She also notes that the very foodstuffs on display in the gift-bringing delegations are also found in the Greek stories.[52] Her logic for the reason for the absence of banquet iconography is certainly open to critique, though it is difficult to come up with a intentional reason for this absence.

For its particular rhetorical goals, the DC takes up the thematic of the group banquet provided by the powerful sovereign represented in the iconographic material from ancient Mesopotamia, the Levant, and beyond. One conspicuous difference in emphasis remains. There is no question that both the Deuteronomic and ancient Near Eastern icono-

---

chief of Tutankhamun and then a pharaoh himself in the XVIIIth Dynasty; images appear in a Memphite tomb; cf. ibid., 37) shows different amounts and types of food depending on rank: the higher ranking officials (whose rank can be identified because they have more clothes and larger bellies) sit before piles of bread, meat, poultry, and a fish, while those of lower rank only have fish (and possibly one meat joint) in addition to bread.

50 On the Neo-Babylonian period Wright, "Commensal Politics in Ancient Western Asia (Part II), 343, comments, "Unfortunately we have very little information on the king's table and the role of political commensality." Jean-Marie Dentzer, *Le Motif Du Banquet Couché Dans Le Proche-Orient Et Le Monde Grec Du VIIe Au IVe Siècle Avant J.-C* (Roma: Ecole française de Rome, Palais Franèse, 1982), 47 and Figure 82.

51 See Wright, "Commensal Politics in Ancient Western Asia (Part I)," 231–32 for photo and discussion of the palace staircase. A series of plates appear in Donald N. Wilber, *Persepolis: The Archaeology of Parsa, Seat of the Persian Kings* (rev. ed.; Princeton: Darwin, 1989), Plates 18–23, Figures 48–51, and especially Figure 27, of servants carrying food on the palace staircase.

52 Heleen Sancini-Weerdenburg, "Persian Food: Stereotypes and Political Identity," in *Food in Antiquity* (ed. J. Wilkens, D. Harvey, and M. Dobson; Exeter: University of Exeter, 1995), 297–99.

graphic depictions imply both rich food and alcoholic drink. However, they differ in what is highlighted: the cup in iconography, meat in Deuteronomy. The relevance of festal symbols of power carries over throughout the region, but the portrayals differ. The similarity of the underlying symbolic value, while divergent in its portrayals, suggests that the iconography itself may not be a direct link between, for example, the Neo-Assyrian and Israelite cultures.[53] Yet the iconographic material does provide graphic evidence of the banquet theme's symbolic importance. The visual evidence also reveals the use of the symbol for political purposes, further underlying its flexibility for various symbolic purposes.

While meat usually plays a supporting role in the iconography (though an important one when understood in light of the imperial policy towards conquered states), meat headlines in Assurnasirpal II's literary descriptions of his celebratory meal that inaugurates the city of Calah, which includes 1,000[54] fattened head of cattle, 1,000 calves, 10,000 stable sheep, 15,000 lambs—for my lady Ishtar (alone), 200 head of cattle, (and) … 1,000 spring lambs, 500 stags, 500 gazelles, 1,000 ducks, 500 geese, 10,000 doves, 10,000 assorted small birds, 10,000 assorted fish, 10,000 jerboa along with large amounts of wine, beer, and other foods. These are meant for a ten-day celebration of around 70,000 people.[55] In this list, regardless of how stylized, meat weighs in as the most prominent element. The rhetorical value of this description, which would suggest that particular items were selected for their symbolic ability to communicate luxury, underscores the importance of the

---

53   Uehlinger, "Figurative Policy, Propaganda und Prophetie," 323, similarly concludes that the reception of Neo-Assyrian texts is far more common than the reception of iconographic materials: "Der Penetrationsgrad der eigentlichen Propaganda scheint im großen Ganzen gering geblieben zu sein. Die bescheidene Investition der Assyrer spiegelt sich im entsprechend dünne—wiewohl erkennbaren—Niederschlag in alttestamentlichen Texten. Es steht in keinem Verhältnis zu der viel stärkeren Rezeption textlich vermittelter assyrischer Herrschaftsrhetorik." [ET: The degree of penetration of propaganda itself appears generally to have been small. The Assyrians' modest input is mirrored in correspondingly thin—if at all recognizable—condensation in Old Testament texts. It is nothing compared to the much stronger reception of textually-mediated Assyrian imperial rhetoric.]

54   Or 100. See Andre Finet, "Le Banquet de Kalah offert par le Roi d'Assyrie Ašurnasirpal II (883–859)," in *Banquets d'Orient* (ed. R. Gyselen; Res Orientales IV; Bures S/Y: Groupe pour l'Étude de la Civilisation du Moyen-Orient, 1992), 32.

55   See the brief summary in Karen Rhea Nemet-Nejat, *Daily Life in Ancient Mesopotamia* (Peabody, Mass.: Hendrickson, 2002), 170–71. Cf. *ANET*, 558–61.

variegated description of meats.[56] Furthermore, Ashurnasirpal's banquet displays a feature absent from the iconography, the inclusion of commoners in the feast—perhaps to bring about the integration of subjugated peoples.[57] The king plays host to a joyful banquet that both adds to his prestige and supports a shared identity.

These symbolic and imaginative significations of the banquet rhetoric for the myths and historical narrative are rooted in the place of meat in everyday life.[58] Further weight is added to the imaginative power when juxtaposed with ancient recipes from ca. 1700 B.C.E.,[59] which give insights into temple and royal cuisine. Almost all the recipes discovered are meat dishes, and Bottéro also comments, "the Mesopotamians almost always added another cut of meat (possibly mutton) to vegetable dishes and, on occasion, to meat dishes."[60] While it is without question that the masses were not able to prepare the elaborate food described in these texts (which are most likely setting an example for cuisine standards rather than being used as actual didactic recipes in any case), "In any society and culture, however, imagination and taste are contagious."[61] So the consumption and display of meat by the royal and temple elites in Mesopotamia not only show their own desire for

---

56   Similarly, the early Sumerian myth of the Marriage of Sud (STT 151–54, VAS 10 177, and HAV 16; An English translation may be found in Miguel Civil, "Enlil and Ninlil: The Marriage of Sud," JAOS 103.11 [1983]: 43–66), which recounts how the goddess Sud becomes the high god Enlil's wife Ninlil, lists the food sent to Sud's parents in preparation for the wedding feast. It, like the dedication of Calah, begins with an extensive description of various animals—goats, oxen, deer, gazelles, bears, sheep, cattle, and others—followed by various dairy products, honey, and fruits (ll.104–123). Again, like the Calah celebration, the incredible variety and amount of meat describe a feast fit for the woman becoming the queen of the gods.

57   Masetti-Rouault, "Le roi, la fête et le sacrifice," 85. This importance of this feature will return below.

58   Nemet-Nejat, Daily Life in Ancient Mesopotamia, 159, gives the following description: "Meat was expensive. Mutton, beef, and goats were part of the ancient Mesopotamian diet. The gods and the king received large rations of meat."

59   YOS II 25–27. Translation and discussion can be found in Bottéro, "The Cuisine of Ancient Mesopotamia," 36–47.

60   Ibid., 42.

61   Ibid., 46. Bottéro supports this judgment by appealing to the fact that there was a chapter in a local treatise on oneiromancy devoted to dreams about food. Idem, Everyday Life in Ancient Mesopotamia (trans. A. Nevill; Edinburgh: Edinburgh University Press, 2001), 68: "And the number and variety of dishes (the majority completely real and duly attested) which the people believed they had eaten in their dreams composed an enviable menu."

these particular products, but they also may have heightened the desire for these objects throughout the society (and empire) at large.[62]

The evidence at Mari suggests a similar material and symbolic premium on consumable meat: "The amount of slaughtered animals [for consumption at the king's table], almost exclusively sheep, was staggering."[63] The lavishness of the feast at Mari continues through the Neo-Assyrian period and into the Persian period. Parpola's juxtaposition of Xenophon's *Cyropaedia* and Assurbanipal's letters[64] reveals the importance of meat distribution from the leftovers of the temple sacrifices and royal banquets.[65] The seventh-century letters show the value of these leftovers, which were primarily meat, on two levels—both for sustenance and for symbolic capital. Parpola remarks, "The [leftovers] were tokens of royal favour which could be distributed to any faithful servant."[66]

The imperial administrative records from the reigns of Esarhaddon and Ashurbanipal provide a final strand of evidence with their records of gifts and distributions of food. The distributions to various court personnel differ decidedly from the gifts brought to the crown or the Aššur Temple. The singers and other workers primarily receive bread and beer, while the royal and divine gifts consist of a richer and more variable table, which included oxen, sheep, birds, spices, truffles, and fruit.[67] Several accounts of actual banquets also appear, listing not only a sultry description of the meat cuts, but also the names of the elite

---

62   Note the analysis of Montanari above (2.2.1.3. Montanari), which makes the same argument for cuisine in medieval Europe with regard to the overlap between elite and lower class desire.

63   Jack M. Sasson, "The King's Table: Food and Fealty in Old Babylonian Mari," in *Food and Identity in the Ancient Word* (ed. C. Grottanelli and L. Milano; HANES 9; Padua: Sargon, 2004), 207–08.

64   Letters from Mari can also be mentioned here since they reveal the political importance of banquets by feeding both the stomachs and relationships of Mari's rulers and their allies.

65   Simo Parpola, "The Leftovers of God and King: On the Distribution of Meat at the Assyrian and Achaemenid Imperial Courts," *Food and Identity in the Ancient Word* (ed. C. Grottanelli and L. Milano; HANES 9; Padua: Sargon, 2004), 285–93. Parpola specifically analyzes the letters ABL 1285 and CT 53, 139.

66   Ibid., 293. Cf. Wouter F. M. Henkelman, "Parnakka's Feast: *šip* in Pārsa and Elam," in *Elam and Persia* (ed. J. Álvarez-Mon and M. B. Garrison; Winona Lake, Ind. Eisenbrauns, 2011), 106.

67   Frederico M. Fales and J. N. Postgate, *Imperial Administrative Records, Part 1: Palace and Temple Administration*, xxx–xxxvi, provide a convenient summary of the subsequent texts (found on pages 136–219). Compare also the later records from the Persian meals, a number of which are collected in Amélie Kuhrt, *The Persian Empire* (London: Routledge, 2007), 2:509, 604–13.

attendees. These records detail the primary importance that the Assyrian royal and temple leaders placed upon meat consumption. From the texts one can glean that the desire for meat among elite banqueters'—and of their god, Aššur—appears insatiable.[68]

The festive accomplishments of the Persian rulers continue to influence portrayals of the "indulgent Orient" even into the present.[69] Briant provides an overview of the Greek evidence, which shows how the Persian customs fascinated the Greek mind: "The king's table in its sumptuousness and variety was in fact considered emblematic of the political and material might of the Great King.[70] Given the dramatic descriptions of Persian feasting from contemporaneous and later Greek sources (Herodotus, Xenophon, and Polyaenus) and from late biblical texts (i.e., Esther, Judith, and Daniel), royal feasts maintained a central place in the symbolism and practice of royal authority. No narrative—iconographic or textual—of actual Persian feasts remains from a Persian perspective. Analysis of the Persian royal table from the Persepolis Fortification Tablets, however, concurs that the institution of the "king's table" was an important symbol of imperial authority and important source for the redistribution of foodstuffs, even if it did not necessarily imply consumption in the presence of the king himself.[71] Henkelman goes so far as to posit, ""In fact, a quick scan of the available livestock texts reveals that *all* animals in the Persepolis economy

---

68   Marty E. Stevens, *Temples, Tithes, and Taxes: The Temple and the Economic Life of Ancient Isarel* (Peabody, Mass.: Hendrickson, 2006), 69, notes that the Uruk priests of the Seleucid period also received various types of meat as prebends (AO 6451, translated by A. Sachs in *ANET*, 343–45: "Daily Sacrifices to the Gods of the City of Uruk").

69   I have in mind here the groundbreaking work of Edward Said, *Orientalism* (London: Routledge & Kegan Paul, 1978).

70   Pierre Briant, *From Cyrus to Alexander: a History of the Persian Empire* (Winona Lake, Ind.: Eisenbrauns, 2002), 246-47.

71   Wouter F. M. Henkelman, "'Consumed Before the King': The Table of Darius, that of Irdabama and Irtaštuna, and that of his satrap, Karkis," in *Der Achämenidenhof / The Achaemenid Court: Akten des 2. Internationalen Kolloquiums zum Thema »Vorderasien im Spannungsfeld klassischer und altorientalischer Überlieferungen« Landgut Castelen bei Basel, 23.–25. Mai 2007* (ed. B. Jacobs and R. Rollinger; Classica et Orientalia 2; Wiesbaden: Harrassowitz, 2010), 667–776. Sancini-Weerdenburg, "Persian Food," 297, instead posits, "The actual process of this sharing out is not recorded on the reliefs or anywhere else in the iconographic repertory of the Persian empire. But the Greek reports leave no doubt that much of this redistribution, if not all of it, took place during banquets."

may have been 'earmarked' as royal."[72] Distribution of meat played a central role in the giving of royal gifts and royal prestige.[73]

Therefore, while specific depictions of meat consumption are largely absent from the iconography of Mesopotamia and the Levant, the juxtaposition of the banquet scenes with the reports from Assyrian letters, Old Babylonian recipes, and historical and administrative texts provides an important backdrop for understanding the desire for meat and its communal consumption in Deut 12. Meat was an essential foodstuff for the royal and temple banquets in the Neo-Assyrian Empire, and meat's symbolic value can be observed in the report of the inauguration of the city of Calah. Feasting as a whole was a potent symbol throughout the history of the ancient Near East, from Old-Babylonian Mari to Greek (and Roman) memories and adoption of Persian opulence. Taken together, the material and symbolic values lay open the imaginative rhetorical potential carried by the symbol of meat consumption both at the sanctuary and within the villages among the early audience of the Deuteronomic text. This keeps with Bottéro's summary for ancient feasts,

> All this more spectacular largesse associated with a meal recalled both the beneficent power of the king, who provided it, and the vital importance of remaining happily subject to his advantageous authority. On another level, feasts and festivities were *eminently political acts*.[74]

Only in Deuteronomy the king is conspicuously absent, suggesting a de Certeau-like "tactical" redeployment of the imperial "strategy" of underlining royal power and shifting the focus to Yhwh's divine provision through a variety of human hands.

---

72   Henkelman, "Parnakka's Feast: šip in Pārsa and Elam," 113 (italics original).

73   "What emerges from the Fortification tablets vis-à-vis the royal earmarking of animals is in agreement with the Greco-Roman sources. Polyaenus (IV.3.32) mentions a great number of animals among the daily needs for the royal table, but he does not mention meat rations among the provisions for the royal guard. Heraclides of Cyme (apud Ath. IV.145e–f) , on the other hand, informs us that the greater part of the meat from the royal table was distributed to ordinary people, but only *via* the royal table."

74   Jean Bottéro, *The Oldest Cuisine in the World: Cooking in Mesopotamia* (trans. T. L. Fagan; Chicago: University of Chicago Press, 2004), 104–105 (italics original). Masetti-Rouault, "Le roi, la fête et le sacrifice," 90, comments that feasts, sacrifices, and writes in sum appear to be different means for celebrating royal power.

3.4. Diet and Archaeozoology

The available data concerning diets and animal usage in Israel and Judah allows for further extrapolation about the physical and symbolic importance of communal meals, and especially those meals in which meat was the main course. Towards this end I will sketch the possible and realistic diets, especially for the later Iron Age period. This sketch will then be followed by consideration of the specific evidence from Ekron, Yoqne'am, Tell Jemmeh, and Lachish, which are among the only sites with significant data on possible meat consumption patterns in the Assyrian period. This data points to the profound impact that Assyrian dominance had upon meat consumption.

The received text of Deuteronomy paints a lavish and variegated mural of the foodstuffs available in the land, summing up its description in the well-known phrase "a land flowing with milk and honey."[75] Various other ancient voices echo this sentiment, both from within the later Jewish and Christian traditions, as well as from the ancient Egyptian "Tale of Sinuhe." While sources like Josephus might be discounted because of their cultural-religious ideological motives for painting the land with this idyllic brush, the Tale of Sinuhe does not appear to have the same type of motivation for its generous description of the land of Palestine:

> It was a wonderful land called Yaa. There were cultivated figs in it and grapes, and more wine than water. Its honey was abundant, and its olive trees numerous. On its trees were all varieties of fruit. There were barley and emmer, and there was no end to all varieties of cattle.[76]

Yet in spite of even Sinuhe's report of the luxury found in Palestine, this extravagant description likely only held true for the elites, similar to the biblical presentations in Amos 6 and 1 Kgs 4. MacDonald poignantly concludes, "We cannot assume that every Israelite, especially the very poor, was able to acquire sufficient food for his or her daily nour-

---

75   For this section I am closely MacDonald, *What Did the Ancient Israelites Eat?*

76   Ll. 80–85. Translation taken from William Kelly Simpson, ed., *The Literature of Ancient Egypt: An Anthology of Stories, Instructions, Stelae, Autobiographies, and Poetry* (3d. ed.; New Haven: Yale University Press, 2003), 58. The subsequent lines go on to show the symbolic value of a good meal, specifically wine, cooked meat, roasted fowl, desert game, and sweets. This description adds to my contention that the symbolic capital of meat is significant in Deut 12.

ishment, especially if we include the vagaries of climate, the unequal distribution of goods, and the occurrence of war and famine."[77]

Despite the diversity in climates and terrains found within the geographical region associated with Judah (coastland, the Shephelah, mountainous highlands, the Dead Sea valley, and the Arabah) that further compound the sociological differences, a basic picture of the general diet will prove helpful. This is the case even if many or most of the known food options were only "real options" for the elites. MacDonald summarizes the basic diet as follows:

> In terms of generalities we can at least say that textual and archaeological evidence agree in the centrality of the so-called Mediterranean triad: bread, wine and olive oil. Fruit, vegetables, legumes, milk-products and meat made a much smaller contribution to calorific intake.[78]

A few further general notes are necessary when considering meat consumption as well. Ancient cultural realities imply that consumption of animal meat was usually a secondary, though important motivation for raising the animals of the herd and flock.[79] Borowski states, "Meat was not consumed on a daily basis for several reasons. Because killing an animal terminates its productivity, the slaughter of any animal had to be carefully calculated."[80] Yet certain scenarios arose in which meat became the primary use for the herd and flock. The Assyrian-dominated latter portion of the Iron Age provides several such examples. These isolated occurrences may be especially important given that

---

77   MacDonald, *What Did the Ancient Israelites Eat?*, 9. He goes on to state (ibid., 57), "There are good grounds for believing, then, that malnourishment was something that many Israelites would have experienced at some point during their lives." In effect, what MacDonald has done is to show that while the consensus about the ancient diet is generally correct, it is necessarily more complex than has typically been understood.

78   Ibid., 68.

79   The Iron Age inhabitants of the Levant used and categorized animals differently than current Western society. For instance, bovines were not raised primarily for their meat nor for their milk, but for plowing fields. Goats were the primary dairy providers, and — as has continued to be the case until today — sheep were valued for their wool.

80   Oded Borowski, *Every Living Thing: Daily Use of Animals in Ancient Israel* (Walnut Creek, Calif.: Altamira, 1998), 59. He goes on to claim, "Lack of means for preservation dictated that meat had to be consumed immediately after slaughter." This conclusion should be nuanced, however, since salting and other means of preservation are documented both in ancient Egyptian and Akkadian sources, as Ikram, *Choice Cuts*, 147–74, and Bottéro, *The Oldest Cuisine in the World*, 56–63, explain. Lack of preservation does not seem to be the primary reason for immediate consumption. Sociological motivations likely played a significant role.

overall "few changes are apparent in the animal economies of the high-
land area during the second part of the Iron Age (1000–550 BC)."[81]

Faunal remains (animal bones) provide archaeozoological experts
the necessary raw data for drawing conclusions about the nature of the
human society in which these animals lived and died. Archaeozoologists examine the remains to determine the following: (1) which animal
species were present, (2) the ages of the animals whose bones were
found, and (3) the relative abundance of bones.[82] The first step appears
obvious, but it is not always so straightforward because experts often
cannot distinguish between the bones of sheep and goats. Clarifying
which animals were present and in what percentages gives clues about
the nature of the society, namely whether it was more heavily agricultural or pastoral. Similarly, archaeozoologists can get some sense of the
animals' primary use by combining the second step (determining ages
of animals at their death) with theoretical models. These models determine the prime ages for killing the animals if the animals are raised
primarily for meat, and which ages are better if humans are exploiting
the animals primarily for secondary products.[83] Step three (relative
abundance) is relevant since, in the archaeological finds of Syro-
Palestine, caprovines (sheep and goats) almost always make up the
majority of bones by number, but cattle bones are heavier, therefore
implying that cattle may have supplied at least as much meat as
caprovines in spite of the fewer number of cattle bones found. A difficulty here is that bones degrade over time, thus making the determination of weights problematic. Ultimately the archaeozoological finds
must submit to the same constraints as all archaeological finds: they
rely on stratification and other identifiers for locating their temporal
and societal context, and they only "speak" when given a particular
voice by their interpreters.[84] Nonetheless, in this section I will rely on
the evidence of the finds at Tell Jemmeh (South of Gaza), Yoqne'am
(near Megiddo), Ekron (Tel Miqne), and Lachish to provide a suggestive undertone for the significance of meat in Deut 12 in its relationship

---

81 MacDonald, *What Did the Ancient Israelites Eat?*, 68.
82 A fourth step is observing any cut marks or signs of burning, which can provide
    indications of cultic use of the animals, a determination especially important for cul-
    tic sites such as Mount Ebal. See Loira Kolska Horwitz: "Faunal Remains from
    Mount Ebal," *TA* 13–14 (1986–87): 173–87, esp. 177–78.
83 One establishes the ages of the animal bones by observing the epiphyseal long bone
    fusion (i.e., in the humerus and femur) and the general wear of teeth. Brian Hesse,
    "Animal Use at Tel Miqne-Ekron in the Bronze Age and Iron Age," *BASOR* 264
    (1986): 22, gives a concise and clear explanation.
84 See ibid., 19–20.

to the historical developments of the late Iron Age.[85] Some important changes in the faunal record took place from Iron I and early Iron II to the Assyrian-dominated later Iron II period.

The first two sites (Tell Jemmeh and Yoqne'am) undoubtedly belonged to the greater Assyrian Empire in the wake of Samaria's destruction and the conversion of parts of Philistia into an Assyrian province. Ekron rose in status following Sennacherib's invasion of Judah because various portions of Judah's territory were portioned off and given to surrounding vassal states including Ekron. This political change of an increased and more immediate Assyrian presence likely carried important economic implications with it, as suggested by the archaeological conclusions from Ekron's olive presses.[86] Excavators have found a large density of these olive presses in Ekron and the nearby village of Tel Batash (Timnah),[87] which were built in the seventh century, the period of Assyrian hegemony. The Assyrian Empire appears to have provided both long-term stability as well as a large market for specialty products, like olive oil, which could not be produced easily in the rich urban centers of Assyria (and Egypt). So with the Assyrian opening of borders, the trade value of various goods increased, leading to increased production for consumption beyond the local market.

One may suspect that pastoralists encountered the same fate. Lev-Tov remarks that the percentage of sheep to goats at Tel Miqne-Ekron skyrocketed in the Assyrian period, increasing from 1:1 to 2:1 and later 3:1.[88] This suggests a specialization in wool production, rather than the

---

85   My choice of these particular sites stems from the relative lack of analysis of faunal remains from other Iron Age II sites that can demonstrate more specific conclusions for this period. Some of the data allows for further specification to the seventh century (as a result of stratification or other factors), but archaeozoological analysis generally belongs to the archaeology of longer-term social systems, rather than revealing short-term historical events.

86   With regard to the development of the export-oriented olive oil industry, see Seymour Gitin, "Tel Miqne-Ekron in the 7th Century B.C.: City Plan Development and the Oil Industry," in *Olive Oil in Antiquity: Israel and Neighbouring Countries from the Neolithic to the Early Arab Period* (ed. D. Eitam and M. Heltzer; HANES 7; Padua: Sargon, 1996), 230, who concludes, "In effect, the establishment of a new and enlarged political and economic unity created extremely favorable conditions for the development of a highly centralized industrial activity." See the similar conclusions of David Eitam, "The Olive Oil Industry at Tel Miqne-Ekron in the Late Iron Age," 183–84, in the same volume.

87   Georg Kelm and Amihai Mazar, "7th Century B.C. Oil Presses at Tel Batash, Biblical Timnah," in *Olive Oil in Antiquity*, 121–25.

88   Justin Lev-Tov, "The Social Implications of Subsistence Analysis of Faunal Remains from Tel Miqne-Ekron," *ASOR Newsletter* 49 (1999): 15.

balanced production of wool and milk (the most important secondary product of goats) expected for a sustainable local economy.

This general trend also seems to have occurred with regard to meat. During the seventh century, when Assyria repeatedly invaded and eventually subdued Egypt, Palestine served as a staging point for Assyrian armies. These large armies, as well as the Assyrian garrisons stationed in Palestine, required considerable amounts of food.[89] What the Assyrian force was unable to bring along from Mesopotamia they instead procured from the local markets. Wapnish supports this reconstruction in her comments about the animal bones recovered from Tell Jemmeh:

> Most of the faunal material was recovered in the vaulted Assyrian building which contained a sealed deposit assigned to a brief 50 year period between 679 and 630 B.C.E. ... it is probable that Esarhaddon used Tell Jemmeh and the region around it as a staging ground for his campaigns of 674, 671 and 669 B.C.E.[90]

The fact that most animal bones were recovered from an Assyrian building also suggests that the Assyrians co-opted local meat resources for their own satisfaction, which would be typical military practice.[91]

The age of the particular animals at their slaughter is also telling. Wapnish's survey of the animal ages at both Tell Jemmeh and Ekron turned up almost solely animal bones older than "market age" (which was zero to three years old), implying that the only animals consumed locally were older than three. Because a normal find includes the presence of animals of various ages, she theorizes that this constellation of faunal remains resulted from a situation where the market-age animals were sent out of the local system according to the demands of the Assyrian market (both the local garrisons and the distant urban centers)

---

89 While from an earlier time period, the Amarna Tablets reveal a similar circumstance in the Levant of the fourteenth century B.C.E. For example, EA 55:10–15 reports: "My lord, when the troops and chariots of my lord have come here, food, strong drink, oxen, sheep, and goats, honey and oil, were produced for the troops and chariots of my lord" (translation from William L. Moran, *The Amarna Letters* [Baltimore: Johns Hopkins, 1992]) Cf. EA 125:14–24; 161:11–22; 193:5–24; 226:6–16; 301:12–23; 324:10–15. The provisioning of armies was an ongoing concern in antiquity. Roman times experienced similar situations: John K. Evans, "Wheat Production and Its Social Consequences in the Roman World," *CQ* 31 (1981): 428–42, notes how important the provisioning of armies was in the Roman world for success military campaigns.

90 Paula Wapnish, "Archaeozoology: The Integration of Faunal Data with Biblical Archaeology," *Biblical Archaeology Today, 1990: Proceedings of the Second International Congress on Biblical Archaeology* (ed. A. Biran and J. Aviram; Jerusalem: Israel Exploration Society, 1993), 436.

91 Nathan MacDonald, private communication.

and the Assyrian imperial tribute.[92] Plotting the faunal remains from Ekron and Tell Jemmeh according to their age in order to show their likely use reveals an "implausible culling strategy for any production goal."[93] This suggests that there was some outside factor removing some animals from the system. Wapnish's pithy conclusion is that "producers sell what they cannot afford to eat,"[94] or in this case one might say: "producers eat the little (and less desirable) that they cannot sell,"[95] or that is not taken from them.

This constellation of finds from various agricultural and pastoral settings of Iron Age II combines to make Wapnish's theory the most plausible explanation for the Levantine territories living under the shadow of the Neo-Assyrian empire. Furthermore, while the Neo-Assyrian administrative records are rather incomplete, they nevertheless record sheep from Megiddo among those inspected by Neo-Assyrian officials and set aside specifically for the "banquet-shepherd."[96] This data points to the plausibility of exporting animals from the Levant all the way to the Assyrian heartland for festive consumption.[97]

---

92   Ibid., 439. Brian Hesse, "Review of Melinda A. Zeder, *Feeding Cities: Specialized Animal Economy in the Ancient Near East* in *American Antiquity* 59:1 (1994): 171, notes that there may be other explanations as well, such as the preference of fattier meat, which would be found on older animals. However, while ancient eaters do seem to have enjoyed fat far more than their modern Western counterparts, this conclusion does not fit with the rest of the faunal finds throughout the Levant in the Iron Age. Trade may be a possibility in place of or in addition to tribute as well, at least on a minimal scale. Wapnish's conjecture receives support from Nimrod Marom et al., "Backbone of Society: Evidence for Social and Economic Status of the Iron Age Population of Tel Rehov, Beth She'an Valley, Israel," *BASOR* 354 (2009): 71, who found that most of the faunal remains in Tel Reḥov were from more gourmet portions of animals slaughtered at ages that maximize their use as food, rather than their use in traction: "… standardization of the age and the sex of the animals consumed, and also of the portions consumed at the site, leads to the interpretation of the animal economy at Reḥov as a consumer site *sensu stricto*."

93   Wapnish, "Archaeozoology," 438; also MacDonald, *What Did the Ancient Israelites Eat?*, 69.

94   Wapnish, "Archaeozoology," 439. MacDonald, *What Did the Ancient Israelites Eat?*, 69, notes that further support comes from the evidence of Tel Harassim in the Shephelah, where cattle were exploited to a greater degree for meat in Iron Age II than Iron Age I.

95   Thanks to Nathan MacDonald for this formulation.

96   K 9996 + K 14270 + K 14309. See the translation in Frederico M. Fales and J. N. Postage, eds., *Imperial Administrative Records, Part 2: Provincial and Military Administration* (SAA XI; Helsinki: Helsinki University Press, 1995), 52–53; cf. xxiii for an overview of the data.

97   The export of meat coincides with the corresponding export of olive oil and wool from Philistia under the Neo-Assyrian Empire. Export of animals might even have been easier because the animals need not be carried.

The evidence from Judah provides a similar picture. The faunal remains from Lachish during Iron Age II reveal a large reduction in the percentage of caprovines in comparison to cattle (a drop from 78% caprovines to 65%) from Iron Age II A (1000–900) to Iron Age II B–C (900–586).[98] Furthermore, the number of young caprovines also declines, pointing to some combination of a shift to higher wool production and the removal of more of the younger and more marketable animals from the local system. Finally, cattle exploitation shifted its primary use from plowing to beef production, also supporting the notion that meat was more important in this period than before. Therefore, it appears that even though Judah did not become a full-fledged Assyrian province, the appetite of its overlord made inroads into the flocks and herds of the Lachish shepherds either directly or through the Judahite elite mirroring Assyrian practice.

Consideration of the area surrounding Samaria during Iron Age II reveals similar results. There are three sites in the same vicinity— Yoqne'am, Tell Qashish, and Tell Qiri—that yield significant data. Tell Qiri, a subsidiary of Yoqne'am located a few kilometers away, was continuously inhabited during the Iron Age. Davis, who analyzed the faunal remains, concludes that the data suggests the flock maintenance was geared heavily towards meat production.[99] The evidence also points to some form of social stratification when these finds are viewed as a constellation of one major site (Yoqne'am) with two surrounding satellites.[100] This fits with MacDonald's thesis that even if meat was more available than has been traditionally assumed, it was not available in the same amounts for the entire population. Instead, the "elite" appropriated the largest portion. Nonetheless, MacDonald also highlights that the age of slaughtered animals increases within the Iron Age

---

98   My discussion is based on the findings of Paula Croft, "Archaeozoological Studies, Section A: The Osteological Remains (Mammalian and Avian)," *The Renewed Archaeological Excavations at Lachish (1973-1994)* (ed. D. Ussishkin; vol. 5; Tel Aviv: Tel Aviv University, 2004), 2254–2348, especially 2260–79, 2316–17. The dates for Iron IIA and IIB are controversial at this point (some wanting to date them 50–100 years later), but this does not affect my argument, which deals with the later IIB–IIC period.

99   Simon Davis, "The Faunal Remains," in *Tell Qiri: A Village in the Jezreel Valley* (ed. A. Ben Tor and Y. Portugali; Jerusalem: Hebrew University, 1987), 250, remarks, "A large proportion of the sheep and goat were culled while still young … at least 26% of the caprovines were culled before the age of 5-7 months, … and 59% before two years of age."

100 MacDonald, *What Did the Ancient Israelites Eat?*, 70, notes, "The highest level [of immature slaughter] is at Yoqne'am and this may suggest that as the main urban centre a greater percentage of meat was consumed here."

at Yoqne'am, which he concludes "could suggest a shift towards wool production or the outsourcing of animals to Assyria."[101] While the Israelite elites received more meat than their brothers, Assyria still cut into the elites' best portions.

Wapnish adds one further observation: "These results suggest that the animal demands for booty and tribute found in Assyrian texts were more real than metaphoric."[102] She gives voice to the archaeozoological remains through the text of the Assyrian booty lists, effectively claiming to bring together tablet and spade. In addition, Baruch Rosen's comparison of the Assyrian accounts of booty taken from Aramaean, Anatolian, and Levantine territories notes that the Assyrian booty lists accord with the basic economic make up of each territory,[103] implying that the Assyrian booty lists were not totally scribal inventions.[104] This line of reasoning supports the contention that Judah was forced to provide animals in the form of tribute to Assyria, which thereby affected Judah's own ability to enjoy the fruit of their husbandry (cf. Deut 28:31). MacDonald's summary of the situation in Iron Age II Judah and Israel is apt:

> The incorporation of Israel into the Assyrian empire and Judah's status as an Assyrian vassal brought a new socio-political reality to bear with potential implications for food supply and distribution. … Thus, the new imperial reality brought a dimension to re-distribution that had not previously been experienced within the Israelite kingdoms. In addition, we have seen that in later periods imperial military garrisons consumed a higher level of game and beef. The reduced supply of meat would have affected [Israelite and Judahite] elites, who would have seen their access to meat severely reduced, and non-elites, who may have lost access to meat almost entirely.[105]

---

101 Ibid.

102 Wapnish, "Archaeozoology," 440. Cf. Borowski, *Every Living Thing*, 60–61.

103 Baruch Rosen, "Subsistence Economy of Stratum II," *Izbet Ṣarṭah* (ed. I. Finkelstein; BAR International Series 299; Oxford: B.A.R., 1986), 160–62. He goes on to show how this also coincides with tax and booty inventories from Ugarit, Heshbon (according to the Ammonite inscriptions), and Thutmoses III's booty from Megiddo.

104 Rosen references Moshe Elat, *Economic Relations in the Lands of the Bible c. 1000-539 B.C.* (Jerusalem: Mosad Bialik and Israel Exploration Fund, 1977), 145–54. The cattle percentages given in tribute from each group corresponds with their relative focus on either pastoral or agricultural means of production: the pastoral Aramaeans gave 5–7% of their tribute as cattle, while agricultural territories in East Anatolia, who would use cattle for plowing, gave 20% in cattle. The Levantine territories gave around 10%, suggesting a more mixed economy, which is also in line with biblical accounts of tribute.

105 MacDonald, *What Did the Ancient Israelites Eat?*, 79.

The archaeozoological data, when compared with other data related to food production and economics, accords with a general picture in which the territories and satellite states in the Levant changed their economic production and consumption of foodstuffs under the military and economic pressure of Assyria. This snapshot of the material culture with regard to faunal remains creates a suggestive hermeneutic for the consumption of meat prescribed in Deut 12.

3.5. Deuteronomy 12: Compositional History

Since the appearance of Steuernagel's revised Deuteronomy commentary in 1923, at the latest, interpreters have tied their historical-critical models of the layers in Deuteronomy to the various centralization and "secularization" laws found in chapter 12.[106] The majority conclusion has been that 12:13–19 (perhaps excluding 14b and 19) should be identified as the earliest layer.[107] Furthermore, skepticism about modern interpreters' ability to reconstruct the original version can be partially countered by the observation that the source text for Deut 12 is found in Exod 20:24b–26.[108]

---

106 Carl Steuernagel, *Das Deuteronomium: übersetzt und erklärt* (rev. ed.; HAT I.3,1; Göttingen, Vandenhoeck, 1923), 93–98.

107 Reuter, *Kultzentralization*, 29–41, gives a clear and concise overview of the past two centuries of scholarship. She basically follows this consensus (her particular reconstruction of the earliest text is vv. 13–14a, 15–18). Her delineation is accepted in Udo Rüterswörden, *Das Buch Deuteronomium* (Neuer Stuttgarter Kommentar, Altes Testament 4; Stuttgart: Verlag Katholisches Bibelwerk, 2006), 75 (with a question mark on v. 19 (ibid., 76); Lohfink argues, "Fortschreibung?: Zur Technik von Rechtsrevisionen im deuteronomischen Bereich, erörtert an Deuteronomium 12, Ex 21,2–11 und Dtn 15,12–18," in *Studien zum Deuteronomium und zur deuteronomistischen Literatur IV* (SBAB 31; Stuttgart: Verlag Katholisches Bibelwerk, 2000), 172–74; repr. from *Das Deuteronomium und seine Querbeziehungen* (ed. T. Veijola; SFEJ 62; Göttingen: Vandenhoeck & Ruprecht, 1996), that Reuter does not seem to see the need to ground this conclusion by any other means than scholarly consensus. While Lohfink ends up with the same basic seventh century text for Deut 12, he remains more skeptical, concluding that there is no reason why 13–19 must be later, but there are few positive reasons for dating it to Josiah. He concludes that one can at most say that something from this text must have come from the time of Josiah or earlier, and since none of the other laws could, then it must have been this one. This does not serve as a guarantee, however, that vv. 13–19 represent the original centralization law.

108 Skeptics include Lohfink, "Fortschreibung," 176–81, 197–98, and Steuernagel, *Deuteronomium*, 10–25. Otto, *Das Deuteronomium*, 343, provides a persuasive rebuttal.

The chapter divides most easily into four sections: vv. 2–7,[109] 8–12, 13–19, and 20–27.[110] This structure excludes 12:1, which continues a general introduction begun in 11:31.[111] The first two sections likely form later layers. This conclusion can be drawn on the basis of their "historicization" and "theologization" of the Deuteronomic law.[112] Further evidence may be found in the general *Numeruswechsel* between second masculine singular and second masculine plural pronouns (plural in vv. 1a, 1bβ, 2–7a, 8a–9a, 10–12; singular in vv. 13–15, 17–27).[113] Lohfink

---

109 While Lohfink, "Kultzentralisation und Deuteronomium," 136, argues for a clear break between vv. 2–3 and vv. 4–7, v. 4's contingency on v. 2 does not allow for this conclusion (cf. Nelson, *Deuteronomy*, 159; Rose, *5. Mose*, 1:18–19).

110 Following Gottfried Seitz, *Redaktionsgeschichtliche Studien zum Deuteronomium* (BWANT 93; Stuttgart: Kohlhammer, 1971), 106, 12:28 should be read as connecting v. 27 to v. 29. Similar connecting insertions are found in 4:1, 6:2, and 8:1.

111 See Alexander Rofé, "The Strata of the Law about the Centralization of Worship in Deuteronomy and the History of the Deuteronomic Movement," in *Deuteronomy: Issues and Interpretation* (London: T & T Clark, 2002), 98–99; repr. from VTSup 22 (1972). Reuter, *Kultzentralisation*, 43, follows his analysis. See below, n. 113 for further discussion of Rofé's position.

112 Kratz, *Composition,* 119: "If we are to describe the situation in handy formulae, in vv. 1, 8-12 we can speak of a historicization and in vv. 2-7 of a theologization of the main Deuteronomic law. Both are secondary by comparison with the simple law of the centralization of the cult itself and the differentiation between profane slaughter and sacrifice in vv. 13ff., and both are bound up in some way with the historical and paraenetic framework of Deuteronomy."

113 In the MT v. 16a is also plural. This may be a telltale sign that this verse is later, especially given its concern with blood, which could easily have only become important at a later date. However, especially in light of the surrounding verses, one may also conclude that this resulted from the loss of an energic *nun* (perhaps due to the similar shape to the next letter, *waw*, and resultant haplography). This change is suggested in footnote 16b by Hempel in BHS, with some manuscript evidence. The SamP has *t'kl* (2ms without any energic suffix), which may instead suggest that the *waw* should begin the following word, which would result in the reading "Only you shall not eat the blood, *but* you shall pour it out upon the ground like water." *Tg. Ps.-J.* reads *tyklwnyh* (2mp + 3ms suffix), and since it has leveled through the chapter with 2mp, the fact that it retains the 3ms energic suffix may point to a significant earlier tradition. OG, Peshitta, and *Tg. Onq.* agree with MT. Many of the early versions have smoothed over a number of these singular and plural differences, i.e., OG, *Tg. Neof.*, *Tg. Ps.-J.*, and Peshitta have plural suffixes in v. 1bα; Peshitta and *Tg. Neof.* have a plural suffix in v. 7b; and SamP and OG have plural suffixes in v. 9b. Morrow, *Scribing the Center,* 197 n. 1, sees the 2mp verb in v. 16a as corruption in the transmission of the text.

The recognition of the plural sections as later excludes the possibility that the chapter should be broken up as vv. 2–10 and vv. 11–27* as suggested by Horst Seebass, "Vorschlag zur Vereinfachung literarischer Analysen im dtn Gesetz," *BN* 58 (1991): 83–98. The same can be said for J. Gordon McConville, *Law and Theology in Deuteronomy* (JSOTSup 33; Sheffield: JSOT Press), 3, who argues that the *Numeruswechsel* does not signal different sources, but is instead a stylistic device. Rofé, provides a possible update to this position, suggesting that one can best explain the present overlap between the 2ms and 2mp sections by understanding the present text as an intermingling of two different formulations of a similar law.[114] This hypothesis does, however, leave open the possibility that more than one version of the DC centralization law (or the material that came to be included therein) existed simultaneously, necessitating that more than one manuscript went into the formation of the current Deuteronomy text.[115] While this point is certainly hypothetical, it does provide a possible answer to the difficulty

---

"The Strata of the Law," 98, also challenges the practice (though he separates sources at traditional points throughout Deut 12). This approach proves more persuasive for later redactional levels of Deuteronomy, such as 4:1–40 (which can be dated later for other reasons as well, such as its similarity to or dependence on Gen 1), than for earlier sections, since, as Veijola, *5. Mose*, 266, notes, this practice fits the early postexilic period. Deut 4, as heir to a longer Deuteronom(ist)ic tradition, likely had the combined text of Deut 12, and therefore a combined 2ms and 2mp text available while writing. Lohfink, "Fortschreibung," 169, notes that plural dominates in Deut 5–11, while the singular is more prevalent throughout the DC, and concludes there is little support for a stylistic understanding. Since the DC most likely chronologically precedes the paranetic sections of chapters 1–11, the singular forms in Deut 12:13–27 most likely precede 12:8–12 and 11:31–12:7.

114 Lohfink, "Kultzentralisation und Deuteronomium," 138.

115 This conclusion contrasts with the notion that scribes simply repeatedly reworked the same document. Rofé imagines various versions of the cultic unification and slaughter ordinances available at the same time; idem, "The Book of Deuteronomy: A Summary," in *Deuteronomy: Issues and Interpretation* (London: T & T Clark, 1992), 6–9, repr. from *BM* 32 (1986/7). His broader thesis argues that vv. 2–7 and vv. 8–12 form variant versions of unification of the cult, while vv. 13–19 and vv. 20–28 were different versions of profane slaughter. He understands vv. 8–12 as pre-Josianic Reform and Deut 11:31–12:7 in its wake, followed by the later halakhic midrashes of vv. 13–19 and vv. 20–28. It remains questionable if more than one copy of the scroll would have existed, especially if Deut 17:18 is read literally that the king was to write "the copy of this torah upon a scroll," which could imply one copy of a single scroll (these then being the only two in existence; note, however, GKC §126 q, which comments on the use of the article to "denote a single person or thing … as being present to the mind under given circumstances. In such cases in English the indefinite article is mostly used"). Karel van der Toorn, *Scribal Culture and the Making of the Hebrew Bible*, 154, in reliance on Na'aman ["The Distribution of Messages in the Kingdom of Judah in Light of the Lachish Ostraca,"], argues that Deut 12 consists of various royal orders about cult centralization woven together after the Josianic reform. While titillating, the position is again quite hypothetical and simply based on the possibility opened up by the letter exchanges in early sixth century Lachish. This type of letter exchange could also have been prevalent around 701, when, judging by the widespread distribution of the *lmlk* jars, a significant amount of communication likely took place in preparation for Sennacherib's invasion. However, against the highly speculative model of Na'aman and van der Toorn, a redactional model seems more appropriate for the chapter: vv. 13–19 were supplemented by much of vv. 21–27, and later with v. 20, vv. 8–12, and vv. 2–7.

of the overlap between the singular and plural sections. However, it does not explain the presence of the blood prohibition in 12:16, which does not appear intrinsic to the Deuteronomic perspective.[116]

Verses 2–3, with their connections to Deut 7:5 (cf. Exod 34:13), bear similarities to the later Deuteronomistic extension of centralized worship as a theological claim to include the destruction of foreign cults. These verses incorporate traditional language about the desecration of naturalistic sanctuaries, which approximate Canaanite altars too closely. These verses also parallel the end of the chapter, namely 12:29–13:1a.[117] This move against foreign cults and their objects radicalizes the centralization-periphery tension promulgated in the earlier layers. In fact, it stands in opposition to the centralization-periphery structure by removing everything cultic outside of the chosen place: "you shall not do thus for Yhwh your God," (v. 4). Verses 5–7 contain doublets with material found in both vv. 8–12 and 13–19: 1) go to the central place where Yhwh puts his name (v. 5, cf. vv. 11, 14), 2) bring various types of offerings there (v. 6, cf. vv. 11, 16), and 3) eat and celebrate there in wider household or village units (v. 7, cf. vv. 12, 18).

The second section, vv. 8–12, also exhibits various Deuteronomistic characteristics. The distinction between the present moment and a future time when the Israelites possess the land shows links to the Deuteronomistic periodization of history.[118] The notion of rest (12:9) corresponds with Solomon's prayer in 1 Kgs 8:56.[119] These verses, with the mention of crossing the Jordan and dwelling in the land (v. 10), fall comfortably in the wider Deuteronomistic narrative found in Deut 6–

---

116 It only appears here, in 12:23–27, and 15:23. See discussion below, 122–24.

117 J. Gordon McConville, *Deuteronomy* (Apollos Old Testament Commentary 5; Leicester, England: Apollos and Downers Grove, Ill.: InterVarsity Press, 2002), 213–16, uses this as evidence that an author produced the entire chapter at one time, but there is no reason why a later redactor might not have made the necessary additions to structure the chapter as a chiasm. See Braulik, *Die deuteronomischen Gesetze*, 23–30, who shows the balanced nature of the final form without arguing that this was the original form.

118 Levinson, *Deuteronomy and the Hermeneutics of Legal Innovation*, 44–45, contends that the Deuteronomic Historian inserted vv. 8–12 and 25:19 in order to work the DC into the history as a whole.

119 Rüterswörden, *Das Buch Deuteronomium*, 76. The Peshitta has *lbyt mšry'* ("house of dwelling") for MT *'el menuḥah*, which makes this connection explicit. The Targums make a similar move. Nelson, *Deuteronomy*, 156, argues that this section itself may have dwelling in the land rather than a particular temple's construction as its obvious *telos*. Dahmen, *Leviten und Priester im Deuteronomium*, 375, reconciles these different points in time by understanding vv. 8–10 through the reference to "everyone doing what is right in his eyes" as expanding the time of conquest to David's time, when Jerusalem is conquered.

11, suggesting their redactional nature. A further indication of this being a later layer is the use of *zibḥêkem* in the offering list of v. 11 , a term that the earlier vv. 13–19 carefully avoid in order to reflect the change in the use of the verbal form *zbḥ* there.

3.5.1. The Election Formula as a Proposed Key to Relative Dating

The various formulations of the election formula (*hmqwm 'šr ybḥr yhwh*) have also served as a source-critical starting point for many interpreters.[120] This formula can appear without any standard elaboration (12:14: *b'ḥd šbṭyk*; v.18: *bw'*; v. 26: with no elaboration at all), with one of two additional standard formulas (*lśwm šmw*: 12:21; cf. 14:24; or *lškn šmw*: 12:11, cf. 14:23; 16:2, 6, 11; 26:2), or with both additional forms in combination (12:5). There is certainly some merit to this approach, since the form with *śwm* appears closely connected with Yhwh's selection of Jerusalem in 1 Kings and generally later additions.

However, Lohfink has shown the difficulty presented by the various formations of the early versions.[121] These distinctions between formulations of the election formula do not hold in the *OG*, which translates 12:11 (+ *lškn šmw*), 12:21 (+ *lśwn šmw*), and 12:26 (no elaboration) essentially the same: τόπος, ὃν ἂν ἐκλέξηται κύριος ὁ θεὸς σου (ὑμῶν) ἐπικληθῆναι τὸ ὄνομα αὐτοῦ ἐκεῖ.[122] Furthermore, as Lohfink

---

120 Such as Rose, *5. Mose*, 1:20–21, Rosario Pius Merendino, *Das Deuteronomische Gesetz: Eine literarkritische, gattungs- und überlieferungsgeschichtliche Untersuchung zu Dt 12–26* (BBB 31; Bonn: Hanstein, 1969), 48–52. Nelson, *Deuteronomy*, 161, takes a similar approach, concluding that 12:21 is a "later clarification of the more obscure formula using *škn*" since it uses *śwm* like much of the so-called Deuteronomistic History, especially 1–2 Kings. Sandra L. Richter, *The Deuteronomistic History and the Name Theology: lᵉšakkēn šᵉmô šām in the Bible and the Ancient Near East* (BZAW 318; Berlin: de Gruyter, 2002), 207, argues for the form with *lškn šmw* as early, while Martin Keller, *Untersuchungen zur deuteronomisch–deuteronomostichen Namenstheologie* (BBB 105; Weinheim: Beltz Athenäum Verlag, 1996), 57, concludes that the short form is the earliest.

121 Lohfink, "Zur deuteronomischen Zentralisationsformel," in *Studien zum Deuteronomium und zur deuteronomistischen Literatur II* (SBAB 20; Stuttgart: Verlag Katholisches Bibelwerk, 1991) 153–161; esp. 153, where he warns that since the centralization formula was theologically explosive, there were possibly multiple textual emendations—more than normal in the book, making MT less trustworthy.

122 The distinction also breaks down in the Targums: they choose one translation formula and stick with it more or less throughout. Cf. Ibid., 153–54. Keller, *Untersuchungen zur deuteronomisch–deuteronomostichen Namenstheologie*, 15, thinks that it is more likely that *OG* and SamP are attempting to harmonize and change all forms to *lškn*. He makes this claim after stating the opposite view that the *OG* and SamP make

notes, the *OG* and SamP suggest that *lśwm* should only appear in 12:5,[123] since in 12:21 SamP reads *lškn* and *OG* ἐπικληθῆναι.[124] The *OG* translators may in fact mark the theology of their interpretation of Deut 12 through their translation of *lśwm* ("set, place") with ἐπονομαζω ("pronouncing a name") in 12:5. This translation for *śwm* only appears here in the *OG*, but Exod 20:24b (for MT *'azkîr*) reads similarly: ἐν παντὶ τόπῳ, οὗ ἐὰν ἐπονομάσω τὸ ὄνομά μου ἐκεῖ, καὶ ἥξω πρὸς σὲ καὶ εὐλογήσω σὲ. ("in every place where I will pronounce my name there, I will also enter to you and bless you"). This is also a unique translation in the *OG* for *zkr*, but the tradition of the deity placing a name stems from the *OG* reading of Gen 4:26, thereby providing continuity with the ongoing story of God's interaction with humanity.[125] The disagreements between the various early witnesses, especially the SamP, undercut attempts to provide a stable literary-historical foundation for the chapter on the basis of the various formulations of the election formula. Furthermore, this approach struggles to account for the inclusion of various texts with long forms in the original Deuteronomic text. In conclusion, I find Morrow's

---

a strong argument for being older, and without refuting their claim to being the older text.

123 Richter, *The Deuteronomistic History and the Name Theology*, 45–48, 62, argues that this form in MT is a conflation of the two long forms. She suggests that originally one stood in the text, while the other was a gloss on the side of the text that was later inserted into the text itself by a subsequent copyist. This theory is problematized if there is a theological link to Exod 20 (see below).

124 The Peshitta does differentiate, however, reading forms of *swq* in v. 21 and v. 5. This just goes one step further in showing how mixed up the various traditions are in their interpretations of the phrase. Martin Rose, *Der Ausschließlichkeitsanspruch Jahwes: Deuteronomische Schultheologie und die Volksfrömmigkeit in der späten Königszeit* (BWANT 106; Stuttgart: Kohlhammer, 1975), 70 n. 1, notes that *OG* does differentiate between *śwm* and *škn*, since it uses forms of τίθημι (for *śwm*) in 1 Kgs 9:3, 11:36, 14:21; 2 Kgs 21:4, 7.

125 This discussion generally follows the findings of Lohfink, "Zur deuteronomischen Zentralisationsformel," 159–60. Anneli Aejmelaeus, "Die Septuaginta des Deuteronomiums" in *Deuteronomium und seine Querbeziehungen* (ed. T. Veijola; SFEG 62; Helsinki: Finnische Exegetische Gesellschaft and Göttingen: Vandenhoeck & Ruprecht, 1996), 12–13, argues in line with Lohfink's position that the *OG* translator of Deuteronomy made theologically-motivated decisions to follow the general translations in the Tetrateuch. She concludes that the translator takes his cue for the *mqwm* formula for translating both long forms of the formula (like 12:21; 14:24)—with επικαλέω so that there is no presence of Yhwh there, but rather the place where Yhwh can be called upon—from Exod 29:45–46 ("I will dwell in the midst of the Israelites and I will be their God, and they will know that I am Yhwh their God, who brought them out of the land of Egypt, so I might dwell in their midst. I am Yhwh their God"). However, she makes this determination in spite of the fact, which she notes, that *OG* is supported by the SamP. Though she mentions it, her conclusion does not account for the reading in the SamP.

position the most plausible: there is some indication that *lśwm* is a marker of a later layer, but it is problematic to use the various forms of the election formula as a primary basis for dating.[126] The close connection between the formula of *lškn šmw* in Deuteronomy with the Neo-Assyrian Akkadian (and earlier in Amarna, in EA 287: 60–61) does point to some type of relationship with that found in Neo-Assyrian usage, though whether this is a loan word or an ironic imitation of Assyrian usage is debated.[127]

3.5.2. Compositional History and Reading of Deut 12:13–27

To date interpreters have not found an agreed-upon cornerstone for compositional-historical analysis within 12:13–27, which has left the determination of strata debated. Most interpreters conclude that the large majority of vv. 13–19 represents the earliest text, in part since it uses the 2ms and incorporates a clean ring structure.[128]

Scholars take a variety of positions on the date of 12:(19) 20–27: Veijola considers vv. 22–27 the latest layer, dating it to the Second Temple while Rose dates vv. 20–27 as a Josianic addition to the original stratum

---

126 Morrow, *Scribing the Center,* 52. The theory that the short form, or rather the form without either standard formula (with *lśwm* or *lškn*), as the only form present in the earliest version of Deuteronomy also cannot be accepted. This view requires that too many texts outside of chapter 12, such as 14:22–29; 15:19–23; and 16:1–17, must be severely reduced or left out of the text. This view, however, seems highly implausible because the DC appears intent on carrying thorough sacrificial centralization into such areas as the tithe, firstborn offerings, and festivals.

127 For the first position, see Richter, *Name Theology,* for the second Morrow, "'To Set the Name' in the Deuteronomic Centralization Formula," 381–83.

128 Seitz, *Redaktionsgeschichtliche Studien,* 211. Cf. Mayes, *Deuteronomium,* 222, who accepts vv. 13–19 without v. 16. Otto, *Deuteronomium,* 347, sees most of vv. 13–27 as one layer (13–19*, 21–24, 26–27). In his construction the latter two sections function as legal interpretations of vv. 13–19*. Reuter, *Kultzentralisation,* 105–106, however, argues that the presence of a ring structure does not necessitate that the whole pericope comes from the same stratum and subsequently argues that the concern for Levites only developed later; also Rüterswörden, *Das Buch Deuteronomium,* 76–78. Reuter bases this conclusion on the idea that the Levite in 12:19 belongs to the category of landless outsider, like the widow, etc. This leads her to separate this Levite from those in 17:9, 18; 18:7; 27:14, who do not fit this outsider category. In so doing she misses the connection between the Levites and the various lists of festal participants, even where the widow, orphan, and alien are missing (cf. Dahmen, *Leviten und Priester im Deuteronomium,* 363). Römer, "Cult Centralization in Deuteronomy 12: Between Deuteronomistic History and Pentateuch," 168–70, follows her dating scheme as well.

vv. 13–19 from Hezekiah's time.[129] Otto includes most of vv. 13–27 in his first layer (Josianic), while Kratz states, "Deut 12.19–28 are throughout additions to the original text in vv.13–18."[130]

Mayes, like most interpreters, considers vv. 20–21, which limit local meat slaughter to places far from the chosen place, incompatible with the regulations of vv. 13–19, which set no spatial restrictions.[131] Levinson argues that the stipulations of vv. 20–28 conform most easily to the rest envisioned for the Solomonic period, contending that the authors appropriate the Solomonic date in order to justify local slaughter by suggesting that it has been allowed since the beginning of the First Temple Period.[132] Levinson also rejects the general argument that vv. 20–28 update an earlier formulation of the ordinance during the Josianic period because the wording in 2 Kgs 23 does not correspond to Deut 12:20–27.[133] His argument expects the Deuteronom(ist)ic authors to have felt the need to reach this threshold of philological continuity with 2 Kings when they address a possible Josianic expansion. However, while such continuity might be a strong argument for the Josianic origin of these verses (but only if 2 Kgs 23 emanates from this period, which is quite controversial), as it stands, Levinson's argument makes much of the silence in 2 Kgs 23. What he is able to show, however, is that the texts of 2 Kgs 23 and Deut 12:20–27 likely stem from different authors.

Römer's short comments (in reliance on A. Rofé), prove decisive in my mind. He suggests that the most fitting situation for vv. 20–28 were the postexilic diaspora. It was in this period that a temple existed, but a considerable portion of the Jewish community (or communities) lived in Egypt or Babylon. In response to the similarly late altar law of Lev 17, the laws of Deut 12:20–28 attempt to reconcile the considerations of Deut 12:13–19 and Lev 17.[134] Rüterswörden notes the change in concerns from vv. 13–19, with its focus on the movement back and forth from the villages to the chosen place, to the section in vv. 20–27 with its cultic focus. He remarks, "Bemerkenswert ist das kultische Interesse, das von Reuter in Anschlag gebracht wird—dem deuteronomischen

---

129 Veijola, 5. Mose, 278 (also Römer, "Cult Centralization in Deuteronomy 12," 171); Rose, 5. Mose, 1:15, 1:22–26 (and Braulik, Deuteronomium 1–16,17, 94–100); Otto, Deuteronomium, 347. Interpreters almost universally view v. 20 as a later redaction.

130 Kratz, Composition, 121.

131 Mayes, Deuteronomy, 229.

132 Levinson, Deuteronomy and the Hermeneutics of Legal Innovation, 41.

133 Ibid., 40–43. Similarly Römer, "Cult Centralization in Deuteronomy 12," 171.

134 Römer, "Cult Centralization in Deuteronomy 12," 171.

Gesetz (Dtn 12–26*) ist es ansonsten fremd, auch in seinen späteren Bearbeitungsstufen."[135] Considerations of blood and the altar, as Rüterswörden notes, more likely stem from attempts to reconcile with the concerns found in Lev 17.[136]

Veijola presents a different alternative to the ring composition for the earliest stratum, dating vv. 13–14, 17–18, 21* to Josiah's reign.[137] This move allows him to remove blood manipulation from the basic Deuteronomic understanding, viewing it instead as part of a more-Priestly vocabulary.[138] Veijola's conclusion logically restricts unrestrained profane slaughter (12:15) to an exilic context because one would not want to completely forbid the enjoyment of meat everywhere except Jerusalem.[139] Most difficult for Veijola is explaining why v. 15 would be inserted in the middle of the centralization ordinances, rather than being attached to v. 21. However, even his non-traditional conclusion that first layer of vv. 13–14, 17–18, 21* concurs with the more generally accepted view in including the following elements:

---

135 Udo Rüterswörden, "Deuteronomium 12,20–28 und Leviticus 17" in "Gerechtigkeit und Recht zu üben" (Gen. 18:19): Studien zur altorientalischen und biblischen Rechtsgeschichte, zur Religionsgeschichte Israels und zur Religionssoziologie (ed. R. Achenbach and M. Arneth; BZABR 13; Wiesbaden: Harrassowitz, 2009), 218 [ET: It is noteworthy that the cultic interest observed by Reuter is foreign to the Deuteronomic law (Deut 12–26*), also in its later layers of development].

136 Ibid., 219–24.

137 Veijola, 5. Mose, 264. I find Veijola's reasoning, ibid., 273 n. 888, on the lateness of v. 15* difficult to accept: "Der Satz 'nach dem Segen, den dir Jahwe, dein Gott, beschieden hat' trennt das 'Essen des Fleisches' zu weit von der dazu gehörenden Ortsbestimmung 'in deinen Ortschaften.'" [ET: The sentence "According to the blessing that Yhwh your God has provided" separates the "eating of the meat" too far from the spatial determinant "in your localities."] Deuteronomy contains numerous subordinate clauses, so this separation seems more likely to fit the Deuteronomic style. Pakkala, "The Date of the Oldest Edition of Deuteronomy," 388, builds from Veijola's literary-critical analysis, which MacDonald, "Issues in the Dating of Deuteronomy," 432–44, shows is quite problematic.

    Veijola also concludes, ibid., 273, that vv. 15*–16 are part of a post–DtrH and pre–DtrB (bundestheologischer Deuteronomist) layer since they are unknown to the former and assumed in the latter. Mayes, Deuteronomy, 228, concurs insofar that "the original deuteronomic law made no reference to the blood." These verses do not use different vocabulary than the Priestly writings, contra Jacob Milgrom, "Profane Slaughter and a Formulaic Key to the Composition of Deuteronomy," HUCA 47 (1976): 13–14.

138 Veijola, 5. Mose, 274, n. 890.

139 Ibid., 274. He goes on to argue, ibid., 276–77, that the ordinance as formulated in 12:21 would no longer be sufficient since those living close to Jerusalem now had as little access to cultic sacrifices as those far away. From his perspective, vv. 20, 21aβ do not have some sort of historical expansion of Judah under Josiah in view, but are instead reflecting on 19:8–9a.

1. Prohibition against offering burnt offerings anywhere one sees (v. 13);

2. Positive command to offer them in the singular place (v. 14);

3. Prohibition against eating the special offerings in the local villages (v. 17);

4. Positive command to eat these offerings as a household group in the singular place (v. 18);

5. Positive command to eat meat in the local villages according to one's desire (v. 21, cf. v. 15a).

Veijola's reconstruction (and the one I offer below) omits mention of the mutual eating by clean and unclean persons. This view finds support from the following perspective: questions concerning the disposal of blood and whether the unclean could take part in the celebration would likely arise if these matters remained unarticulated at first.[140] Furthermore, matters of blood manipulation appear less important for the Deuteronomic program, rarely appearing otherwise in the cultic meal texts (only 15:23, which seems to be a similar addition). Following Rüterswörden and others' analysis of 12:20–27, these concerns for blood respond to and attempt to incorporate the concerns of Lev 17, albeit not in a fashion that would likely satisfy the authors of Lev 17:13–14, which not only forbids the consumption of blood, but also commands that the blood be covered with earth.

My main problem with Veijola's analysis is his conclusion that v. 21aαb and not v. 15a is the earliest form of the allowance for eating meat outside a sanctuary setting.[141] MacDonald notes the likelihood of the priority of v. 15 for the following reasons: 1) every word in v. 21 except the blessing is found elsewhere in *Urdeuteronomium*, and 2) it makes more sense to have the wide allowance of meat consumption restricted than to suggest that the restrictiveness was blatantly ignored without some kind of justification.[142]

---

140 A number of *OG* manuscripts (and *Tg. Ps.-J.*) provide analogous textual evidence on 12:15: both add that the clean and unclean eat *together*, like 12:22, in order to delineate how the meal should practically take place, showing the tendency of later copyists to differentiate the meals at the sanctuary from those in the villages.

141 Pakkala, "The Date of the Oldest Edition of Deuteronomy," 396–97, bases one of his arguments for an exilic date for *Urdeuteronomium* on Veijola's attribution of v. 21 to *Urdeuteronomium*. He argues that the presence of *shem*-theology in this verse poins to a time when Yhwh's Presence was no accessible in a temple. I have already noted above, 3.5.1. The Election Formula as a Proposed Key to Relative Dating, that, if any form of the election formula is late, it is this one (with *šwm*).

142 MacDonald, "Issues in the Dating of Deuteronomy," 434.

Regardless of which formulation of non-sanctuary meat consumption one views as older, some distinctions remain between the two types of meals. I would suggest that these meals also contain practical concrete differences. The simple fact of spatial separation from the chosen place implies both the obvious "absence" from the sanctuary and memory of its presence. This difference awakens desire to mark the absence ritually, implying something like the ritual regulations of vv. 15b–16 or 22–24. The fact that *zbḥ* occurs in Deut 12 outside the sanctuary[143] implies both a substantially different use of the root and a reminder of its normal usage.[144] Thus, even if Deuteronomy prescribes a new development in Israelite religion, as is often argued for its regulations of meat consumed away from the sanctuary, it cannot but textually and practically point to the sacred (sanctuary-located) meal.[145] Levinson notes,

> The verb [*zbḥ*] is given a new, secular meaning: 'to slaughter.' Its action pointedly no longer takes place in a cultic context, at an altar, but, rather, in the local settlements. The construct phrase כברכת יהוה "according to *the blessing* of Yahweh' ... thus deftly manages both to restrict the divine cultic presence to the cultic sanctuary and to maintain a mediated divine presence in the local, secular sphere: the land and its produce constitute divine gifts.[146]

I agree with Levinson's statement insofar as *zbḥ* takes on a new meaning, yet "secular" may not be the most appropriate expression. In Levinson's own words, it is preferable to see the change as a move towards "a mediated divine presence" through local meat consumption.

To return to the question of compositional history, all proposals— regardless of whether one accepts the ring structure or an analysis like

---

143 Yet contra Milgrom, "Profane Slaughter and a Formulaic Key to the Composition of Deuteronomy," especially Prov 17:1 presents a further possibility of consumption outside the sanctuary context.

144 Levinson, *Deuteronomy and the Hermeneutics of Legal Innovation*, 33–36, gives detailed arguments for the change in meaning. Noteworthy, however, is this changed use of *zbḥ* along with its use in usual sanctuary location with cultic connotations side-by-side in the earliest layer of the Deuteronomic text (15:21; 18:3).

145 Levinson, (ibid.) argues that this new usage of *zbḥ* shows the reformulation of the corresponding lemma from Exod 20:24, undermining the context and intent of the lemma in Exodus. Providing a reminder of the CC text would more likely work to strengthen the implicit authority of the CC ordinance, rather than to undermine it. This strengthening of the CC's authority argues against Levinson's thesis because even if the writers of the DC sought to appropriate the recognized authority of the CC lemmas at the expense of the CC's meaning, their actions would likely increase interest in the actual laws of the CC itself.

146 Ibid., 36 (italics original).

Veijola's on the extent of the original text—agree that the foundational layer of Deut 12 consisted of a complex set of sacrificial ordinances, focusing neither solely on the sacrificial centralization nor on consumption of "secularized" communal meat in local villages. Therefore, no "pure" centralization law existed, but rather multiple concerns arose at every layer of the text. The original layer of Deut 12 included a constellation of ordinances surrounding the following question: how should the Israelites celebrate sacred meals? The earliest Deuteronomy answers that the people must take particular choice parts of this food to the centralized place that Yhwh desires, while they should consume other portions in their villages according to their own desires. This formulation portrays the centrifugal and centripetal movements involved in the Deuteronomic vision of sacred consumption. The text of 12:13–19 coalesces around the notions of eating or enjoyment experienced both centrally and locally, thereby providing a significant overlap and interpenetration between the experiences at the central sanctuary and locally.[147]

I consider the earliest Deuteronomic stratum to have consisted of vv. 13–15a, 17–19, which divides into three sections. The first section (vv. 13–14) highlights the singular place where the Israelites should bring their offerings. The second section provides the important exception to this singularization: in spite of centralization, some festive or cultic meals may take place throughout the land (v. 15a). The third section returns the focus to the singular place of worship, providing details of the particular Deuteronomic formulations of worship and cultic celebrations (vv. 17–19).

For the most part, the ring structure suggested by Seitz[148] should be retained; however, I view vv. 15b–16 as later insertions. Kratz argues, "Deut. 12.19 begins again … and gives a special role to the levites who have been deprived of a living by the centralization of the cult but are

---

147 Cf. Braulik, *Die deuteronomischen Gesetze und der Dekalog*, 24, who also notes the pilgrimage structure underlying the whole centralization schema. It includes actions performed both at the chosen place and at home, which, "in 12,4–28 alles immer in 'essen' ('kl) und/oder 'fröhlich sein' (*śmḥ*) mündet." [ET: in 12:4–28 everything flows into 'eating' ('kl) or 'be joyful' (*śmḥ*).] Sections 5.4. Reading of Deuteronomy 14:22–29 and 5.5. Synthesis of Exegesis, Social Scientific, and Biological Evidence will explore the significance of this interpenetration from an anthropological perspective, while this section will read Deut 12:13–19 primarily in light of iconographic and archaeozoological perspectives.

148 See above, 113 n. 128.

already taken note of in v. 18."[149] It is a legitimate question whether the mention in v. 18 of the Levite ends the original text, or rather v. 19. Both could serve as a corresponding statement to the opening verse, v. 18 more in the sense that the Levites are included as the lone extra familiar element in this list of participants because they are the ones specifically impacted by the loss of multiple sanctuaries. However, v. 19 provides a better formal ring structure. Why v. 19 must be a new beginning instead of an ending corresponding to v. 13 is not clear. Nonetheless, the basic outline of my interpretation of the passage is not dependent on the status of v. 19.

This delineation creates a structure that marks the consumption of the agricultural bounty resulting from the blessing of Yhwh both throughout the land as the central element as the focal point, parallel to the Assyrian king providing a feast for his chosen guests[150] (important elements are in italics, caps, and underlined for the corresponding sections):

[1] [13]WATCH OUT, LEST YOU offer your burnt offerings in every place you see.

> [2] [14]INSTEAD, in the place Yhwh chooses from one of your tribes. There you shall offer your burnt offerings, and there you shall do everything I am commanding you.
>
>> [3] [15a]However, *in [response to] every personal desire* you may slaughter and eat meat according to the blessing of Yhwh your God, which he gives you *in all your gates.*
>>
>> [3¹] [17]You are not able to eat *in your gates*: the tithe of your grain or your wine or your oil, or the firstborn of your herd of your flock, all the vows that you vow, your free-will offerings or the contributions of your hand.

---

149 Kratz, *Composition*, 121. Otto, *Das Deuteronomium*, 346, provides a recent example of the ring structure if v. 19 is included; however, his understanding does not take v. 17 into account (though he views it as original). For an earlier version of the ring structure, see Seitz, *Redaktionsgeschichtliche Studien*, 211. Note the critique by Levinson, *Deuteronomy and the Hermeneutics of Legal Innovation*, 29 n. 14, who also omits reference to v. 17. Dahmen, *Leviten und Priester im Deuteronomium*, 377–78, provides a balanced argument and concludes that source and form-critical methods contradict each other here, which makes a decision on status of v. 19 difficult.

150 See discussion of iconography and Neo-Assyrian administrative texts above, 3.3. Iconography and Records of Meat and Banquets in the Ancient Near East.

[2¹] ¹⁸INSTEAD before Yhwh your God you shall eat them in the place which Yhwh your God chooses, you, and your son and your daughter, your male servant and your female servant, and the Levite who is in your gates. You shall enjoy before Yhwh your God [the results of] all your work.

[1¹] ¹⁹WATCH OUT, LEST YOU forget the Levite all your days *upon your ground.*

The deliberate structure highlights the rhetorically central role of Yhwh's blessing "in all your gates" juxtaposed to the people's gifts to Yhwh in the central sanctuary. The specific nature of the blessing here is the meat available in the gates for consumption, provided by the blessing "in your gates." This bi-directional giving, especially of valuable products—locally on the one hand and the centralized offerings on the other, underscores the building of social and religious bonds through food production and consumption. Both [2] and [2¹] begin with "instead" (*kî 'im*) and share a triple emphasis on the chosen sanctuary. Finally, the outermost elements share the terms "watch out, lest" (*hiššāmer lĕkā pen* + imperfect verb) and focus on dispersed local action.

This structure is not without its difficulties. The corresponding sections of [2] are not at all equal in length, but this phenomenon can be explained by the fact that [2¹] includes standard Deuteronomic lists of offerings, which underlines everything that the festive community can enjoy.

This first verse (12:13) highlights the quintessential offering that is set aside completely for the deity. Unlike the later offerings list (v. 17), Deut 12:13 takes the offering first mentioned by Exod 20:24 and uses it as a metonym for offerings in general.¹⁵¹ Deuteronomy 12:14b, if original, adds to the burnt offerings, summarizing the remainder of the cultic gifts with "and there you shall do everything I am commanding

---

151 It may be the case that Deuteronomy does not mention the second offering type from Exod 20:24, *šĕlamîm*, because these are too closely identified with the *zebaḥ*. Deuteronomy also changes the verb of Exod 20:24 from *zbḥ* to *'lh*, likely in line with its decree that one may now slaughter (*zbḥ*) throughout the land, but one may only make smoke go up (*'lh*) in the singular sanctuary. On the other hand, Christian A. Eberhart, *Studien zur Bedeutung der Opfer im Alten Testament: Die Signifikanz von Blut- und Verbrennungsriten im kultischen Rahmen* (WMANT 94; Neukirchen-Vluyn: Neukirchener Verlag, 2002), 313, notes that not only is *'lh* the most common sacrificial term, but in later texts (Chronicles, Ezra, Nehemiah) it can become a catch all term for sacrifices. He argues (idem, 317–18) that *qĕṭōret* plays this role in preexilic texts based on 1 Sam 2:28, Isa 1:13, and Ps 66:15. The first two passages do support this conclusion, while the third is less clear.

you."[152] This clause receives further explanation in 12:17. Highlighting burnt offerings in v. 14 both picks up on their presence in Exod 20:24 and the fact that they are the only meat offering not communally consumed by the people in the Deuteronomic vision. All other offering types remain with or are returned to the people for their enjoyment. But, as the following verses show, this meat consumption takes place in a variety of locations, relativizing the essential focus of 12:13–14 on the singular sanctuary.

The middle section of vv. 15–17 removes the focus from the single sanctuary and sets it upon the land as a whole. Just as burnt offerings are the quintessential action in the earlier section [2], here the text highlights eating meat. The text stands in direct contrast to the previous verses, set off by the adversative *raq* (best translated here as "however"). The section begins with the basic ordinance: "in [response to] every individual desire you may slaughter and eat meat." This ordinance is then unfolded in the rest of the section, explaining when and where it may take place, who may take part, and how it shall be carried out.

The first stipulation answers the questions of when and where: "according to the blessing of Yhwh your God in all your gates." This clause upends the practice of the CC in a wide-reaching manner. The previous verses consolidated all sanctuaries into one particular place, narrowing the possible locations for meat consumption. However, as noted above, by only mentioning the burnt offerings and the enigmatic "everything that I am commanding you," specific mention of communally consumed offerings goes missing. This particular omission allows v. 15a to explain that the DC vision does not in fact limit meat consumption so drastically. The DC instead promulgates new regulations for meat consumption based on an alternative logic.

---

152 A number of recent interpreters view this clause as secondary because it changes from third to first person. While jarring to a modern audience, it does not necessarily mark a later insertion. This kind of person change occurs in both the CC and Exod 34:11–26, and also in other genres across the ancient Near East, i.e., in the historical annals of Sennacherib (Bavian inscription, § 338). See Luckenbill, *Ancient Records of Assyria and Babylon*, 151, where the narrative report of Sennacherib's first campaign shifts unexpectedly from first to third person and back again to first person. It also takes place throughout the current text of Deuteronomy, i.e., 12:21; 15:4–5, 10–11. The suggestion that 12:14b must be late because of the change in person follows standard source-critical procedure if Moses was not present as the law promulgator in the original version of the DC (if it was Yhwh's law not Moses' law). Such a conclusion remains possible.

The text names meat, turning the focus to a symbolically rich, culti-cally specific food product as indicated by the comparative evidence for the given historical context. In this setting v. 15a links meat consump-tion to two factors: personal desire and divine blessing. These two fac-tors together determine when one may eat. I take it for granted that the people desired to eat meat far more than they could afford to eat it, making it a daily craving. The second factor, divine blessing, solidifies the presence of the deity in all the villages. So divine presence in Yah-wistic meat consumption is not only experienced in the central sanctu-ary. This divine blessing may not appear as a temporal designation, but it essentially functions this way: meat consumption occurs "in agree-ment with the manner in which Yhwh provides this blessing."[153] This clause therefore sets the Deuteronomic program against the Assyrian or any other hegemony that deprives the Judahite people of their animals in order to feed army and treasury.

The following clause of v. 15b, "the unclean and the clean may eat it like the gazelle and the deer," answers who may eat and also begins to answer how. The designation of the clean and unclean has appeared to many interpreters as a foreign element to the Deuteronomic rhetorical style and vision. While *ṭāmē'* ("unclean") appears more often than its counterpart *ṭāhôr* ("clean"), neither appears often in the book, leading many to conclude that this verse, like the food laws, come from a later Priestly hand.[154]

One might argue for the inclusion of vv. 15b–16 in the earliest layer on the basis that in the biblical texts consumption of meat in villages (separate from a sanctuary) was a new idea in Israel, so the people would need to know how one should do it. However, the debate over

---

153 Following *IBHS* 11.2.9 (p. 203), the function of the preposition *kě* is best understood in terms of suggesting the "agreement in manner or norm" with the condition that follows.

154 Outside of the appearance of this clause (also found in 12:22, 15:22), the terms only appear together in the regulations of clean and unclean foods in 14:3–21. Cf. Reuter, *Kultzentralization*, 106; Meredino, *Das deuteronomische Gesetz*, 32; Seitz, *Redaktions-geschichtliche Studien*, 211–12. Similar views are developed for the concern for blood in v. 16: Veijola, *5. Buch Mose*, 273–74, argues that this notion reflects the respect for life exemplified in P (Gen 9:4), without implying literary dependence upon P. This conclusion seems predetermined by his presupposition of an exilic or postexilic P. Mayes, *Deuteronomy*, 228, sees v. 16 as a later addition, though Deuteronomistic rather than Priestly.

טמא also appears in Deut 24:4 and 26:14 (possible relevant preexilic occurrences are Hos 9:3–4; Isa 6:5; and 2 Kgs 23:4). טהר occurs in Deut 23:10 (where it is negated). It also occurs in 1 Sam 20:26 in a likely preexilic text.

the provision for non-sanctuary or secular consumption of meat continues. Eberhart states, for example:

> Es ist darauf hinzuweisen, dass in 1Sam 14,32–35 nicht זבח oder שלמים sondern eine Profan-schlachtung beschrieben wird. Sauls Soldaten schlachten und verzehren nach einem Sieg über die Philister spontan Beutetiere. Die Tötung der Tiere wird nicht mit זבח, sondern mit שחט bezeichnet (V. 32.34).[155]

However, because the soldiers belong to the sanctified army of Yhwh (cf. Deut 23:14), they are in some sense already "holy." This fact circumscribes the "secular" nature of their slaughter and consumption and in fact coincides to a large degree with the regulations on decentralized slaughter in Deut 12:15. It may be more important here to separate the (narratival) actions and actual practice from the Deuteronomic prescriptions.

My understanding differs from the recent argument of Volkmar Wagner, who asserts an essentially profane or secular (separate from the Temple?) understanding of ancient Israelite society, especially when it comes to meat consumption.[156] For Deut 12:13–17 he argues that profane slaughter was taken for granted and is clarified as not needing to follow the purity ordinances of the sanctuary.[157] However, this creates a syntactical problem in that it separates the *yiqtol* form *yizbaḥ* from the *weqatal* form *wĕ'ākaltā* and makes them verbs for two separate clauses. *Bāśār* is no longer the object for *zbḥ* but only for *'kl*.

A further problem is that he does not deal with the lexical meaning of *zbḥ* in the rest of the OT. He fails to establish non-cultic possibilities (pre-Deuteronomic) for his theory to be plausible. The woman of Endor

---

155 Eberhart, *Studien zur Bedeutung der Opfer im Alten Testament*, 227 [ET: It should be noted that 1 Sam 14:32–35 does not describe a זבח or שלמים, but a profane slaughtering. Saul's soldiers spontaneously slaughter and consume booty animals after a victory over the Philistines. The killing of the animals is not designation with זבח, but with שחט (vv. 32, 34)].

156 Volkmar Wagner, *Profanität und Sakralisierung im Alten Testament* (BZAW 351; Berlin: de Guyter, 2005), 133–34, 152–54. One of his contentions is the non-cultic origination of Deut 14 and Lev 11, but this misses the fact that culture (which includes and is determined in part by religion) determines what is food and what is not. The lists in Lev 11 and Deut 14 are not lists of edible and inedible substances. Rather they are lists further selected out of edible animals in agreement with what is "food" for a particular culture and what is not. Even if Wagner proposes to argue from some sort of materialist theory (i.e., Marvin Harris, "The Abominable Pig," in *Food and Culture: A Reader* [ed. C. Counihan and P. Van Esterik; New York: Routledge, 1997], 67–79). then his analysis fails to show how "what was good to eat" became "what was good to think."

157 Ibid., 154.

(1 Sam 28:24) might be one possibility, but this is clearly both an unacceptable "sacrifice" from the view of the narrative, and she could also be seen as some sort of ritual functionary, given her role as seer. Wagner is right to point to the "keinerlei kultische Elemente" to modern eyes in Gen 18:7; 27:7, 14; and 1 Sam 25:11.[158] However, to think that Nabal's sheep shearing was a profane event seems counterintuitive in light of the central role of sheep and sheep shearing to ancient Israelite culture. To suggest that this was a profane event seems a distinctly modern suggestion, given the agricultural and cultic connections to the various festivals. Genesis 18:7 is certainly more ambiguous, though the divine nature of the visitors complicates matters here. Rebekah preparing a kid for Isaac would be the clearest example of non-cultic slaughter. However, this slaughter takes on the mask of hunted game, which should not count as sacrificial meat! What seems clear from these narratives is that there were situations when an animal could be consumed away from a "normal" sanctuary. Yet caution must be taken because perhaps the regulations in the legal material were not considered hard and fast laws by the authors of the narrative traditions, or alternatively, the view of cultic regulations from a non-priestly perspective was more ambivalent. In any case, I would argue that meat was a rarity for most, and therefore something quite special. This made its consumption exceptional, and easily tied to the cultic context.

Returning to Deut 12, the suggestion that there was no consumption of meat outside a sacrificial context could possibly speak, however, for the inclusion of v.15b in the original layer of the text, but perhaps also for its later addition, when more "practical" details became desirable. A second argument for viewing v. 15b (and possibly v. 16 as well) as part of the earliest layer is the attempt to set off the local consumption of meat from the "cultic-ritual" consumption of 12:14, 17–18. Yet these attempts could also have arisen later to clarify how these festive meals differ from one another. A third argument is the observation that 12:22–25 exegete vv. 15b–16, therefore suggesting their earlier presence in the text. However, it could simply be that both vv. 15b–16 and vv. 22–25 are later, with vv. 15b–16 being marginally earlier than vv. 22–25. There are, therefore, no solid arguments for dating vv. 15b–16 to the earliest stratum.

In v. 17 the focus returns to the single sanctuary with the listing of foods and drinks that one is not able to consume within the local gates. The various tithe elements (here in their raw forms as in 14:23, but in

---

158 Ibid., 146.

14:26 appearing in their fermented or manufactured forms) are supplemented by oath offerings, freewill offerings, and contributions. Deuteronomy uses a further negative, "You are not allowed to eat" in order to return the focus back to the singular sanctuary, in effect performing a double negative, overturning the earlier *raq* of v. 15.

Having set the return to the sanctuary by prohibiting local consumption of various contributions, v. 18 recalls the syntax of v. 14, emphasizing that one shall eat them before the deity, a spatial designation as seen by the following *bammāqôm* formula.

As mentioned earlier, the move towards centralization envisions a profound *de*-centralization of Israelite life and religion. In contrast to Weinfeld's contention that the move towards centralization accomplishes a definitive secularization of the outlying land of "Israel,"[159] I would instead suggest that Deuteronomy proposes a *sanctification of the entire people of Israel*, especially the heads of households.[160] In effect, the heads of households become *de facto* priests on behalf of their communities. Firstly, they are now responsible for distribution of sacrificial meat and any separation of blood from the meat consumed communally (though only implicitly until v. 16 is added to the text). Secondly, they also are responsible for the distribution of the third year tithe (14:28–29). Thirdly, they pierce the ears of Israelite debt slaves choosing to remain with their masters for the rest of their lives rather than going free in the seventh year (15:16–17).[161] Braulik suggests that in this instance "profane" only makes sense when understood literally, that is

---

159 See Jacob Milgrom, "Review of Moshe Weinfeld *Deuteronomy and the Deuteronomic School*" *IEJ* 23 (1973): 156–61; Vogt, *Deuteronomic Theology and the Significance of Torah*, 78–91; and Lohfink, "Opferzentralisation, Säkularisierungsthese und mimetische Theorie," 225–232; and Weinfeld's response, "Reply to J. Milgrom," *IEJ* 23 (1973): 230–33. Also Joachim Schaper, *Priester und Leviten im achämenidischen Juda: Studien zur Kult- und Sozialgeschichte Israels in persischer Zeit* (FAT 31; Tübingen: Mohr Siebeck), 102–104.

160 This analysis contains many similarities with the position suggested by Suee-Yan Yu, "Tithes and Firstlings in Deuteronomy," 134–70.

161 This could also provide help in understanding the *hqdyš* (consecration) of the firstborn, which is forbidden in the rest of the Pentateuch. For this suggestion see Otto, *Das Deuteronomium*, 320, who argues that the reason why one now has to "make holy" a firstborn is because they are no longer offered on the eighth day, so they must be set aside until the pilgrimage takes place. Or perhaps, as Lohfink, "Opferzentralisation, Säkularisierungsthese und mimetische Theorie," 230, argues, this occurrence is instead declarative, and therefore means, "proclaim holy," rather than an actual "consecration." These interpretations are both contra Weinfeld, *Deuteronomy 1–11*, 43.

spatially, "Denn auch die 'Profanschlachtung' ist nicht aus der Beziehung zu Jahwe entlassen."[162]

The ongoing concern for the Levite[163] does fit into the fabric of the Deuteronomic message, and, therefore, further supports the conclusion that it belongs to the earliest layer (cf. 14:27, 29; 16:11, 14).[164] Dahmen argues for the lateness of 12:19b ("all your days upon your ground," *kol yāmêkā 'al 'admātekā*): "Dieser Orts- und Zeitsbestimmung entspricht die Tatsache, daß literarhistorisch mit/nach DtrH der Levit als soziale Größe verschwindet. Gleichzeitig deutet eine solche Bestimmung wie v.19b eher auf deren spät-dtr Abfassungszeit; bereits dtn (,vorbeugend') ist sie kaum denkbar."[165] However, this expression (as Dahmen admits) is idiosyncratic, not appearing anywhere else in Deuteronomy. Furthermore, the notion of losing the land need not be exilic or later if a Judahite considered the fate of the Northern Kingdom.[166]

Finally, there is certainly no logical reason why the ring structure *must* belong to the original layer rather than first appearing through a later redactional insertion, especially since it can be laid out in several

---

162 Braulik, *Die deuteronomischen Gesetze und der Dekalog*, 24, n. 3. [ET: Because also "profane slaughter" is not released from the relationship to Yhwh.]

163 Nelson, *Deuteronomy*, 231, notes that the relationship between the Levite and the Levitical priest remains an important question for Deuteronomy, resulting partly from the integration of the various redactional strata in the book. He does state, however (ibid., 236 n. 4), that 26:3 and 11 clearly distinguish the priests working at the sanctuary from the Levites. Weinfeld, *Deuteronomy 1–11*, 35, argues similarly. Dahmen *Leviten und Priester im Deuteronomium*, 394, summarizes that the only Levites in the early DC texts were *personae miserabiles*, and that their role changes in later, especially postexilic texts. This line of argumentation (also followed by Reinhard Achenbach, "Levi/Leviten," *RGG* 5:293–95) struggles to account for the likely preexilic cultic roles played by Levites in, for example, Judg 17–18.

164 Veijola, *5. Mose*, 278, follows Dahmen, *Leviten und Priester im Deuteronomium*, 374–79 and argues that the Levite verses are contingent on 10:8–9, which he dates to the beginning of the postexilic period when the Levites are not *personae miserae*, but privileged priests. The distinctions between priests and Levites in the postexilic texts make this contention unsustainable.

165 Dahmen, *Leviten und Priester im Deuteronomium*, 379. [ET: The time and location of this ordinance corresponds with a reality according to which the Levites as social group disappeared, historical-critically with or after DtrH. At the same time such an ordinance like v. 19b points more likely to the late Dtr time of composition; already Deuteronomic ("preventative") is hardly conceivable.] In contrast, Leuchter, "'Levite in Your Gates,'" 419–28, argues that Deuteronomy in the seventh century envisions the country Levites shifted roles from cultic personnel to local judicial officials, as reflected in Deut 16:18–20, 17:2–13, and 21:1–9 with the Levites' location "in the gates" as a result of the cultic centralization, though this conclusion is questionable.

166 Hillers, *Treaty Curses and the Old Testament Prophets*, 33–34, concurs and also cites the curses referencing "siege, exile and attendant horrors" in texts predating the rise of the Babylonians; see also Stohlmann, "The Judaean Exile After 701 b.c.e.," 174–75.

ways. However, the text—even in its various forms or versions—does seem to contain some sort of ring structure, supporting the conclusion that v. 19 most likely belongs to the original composition.

My hypothesized text highlights the role of the heads of household. They remain the implied audience of the ordinances, since they had the power to decide when and where to bring their family's offerings. This becomes most explicit in 12:18, where they are addressed directly (as they often are throughout the text) as *'attā(h)*. They also function as the textual addressees around whom "your son, and your daughter, and your male slave and your female slave, and the Levite in your gates" (12:18) congeal as units. The absence of priests from this discussion further heightens the textual role given to these heads of household. Deuteronomy 12 therefore continues the emphasis of the CC on the role of the people as a whole in sacrifice (cf. Exod 20:24–26), which contrasts with the Priestly presentation in Lev 1–17. In general, Deuteronomy picks up on, reinforces, and extends the local societal structures even into the actions taking place at the central sanctuary.[167]

One might also note that the main focus of 12:13–19 is not specifically to underline the singularity of the sanctuary, but it instead highlights Yhwh's choice as primary for the grounding of a sanctuary. This choice in some ways mirrors Yhwh's causing the divine name to be remembered in various places (Exod 20:24b). However, it parallels the choice of David as Yhwh's king more closely.[168] The early versions— which use the same root for Yhwh's choice in v. 14 and the people's desire for meat in v. 15[169]—also serves to de-center the traditional focus of scholars on the centralization of sacrifice in favor of a focus on Yhwh's choice. This allows for a broader understanding of the text, which can then include the centrifugal and centripetal ordinances as well as the desires of the people.

---

167 Dennis T. Olson, Review of Moshe Weinfeld, *Deuteronomy 1-11: A New Translation with Introduction and Commentary* in *JBL* 112 (1993): 328, critiques Weinfeld's contention that Deuteronomy envisions a secularization of Israel as follows: "But can such a clear distinction between the sacral-holy character of P and the secular-social character of D really be sustained? ... The concern for the worship place, festivals and liturgy in Deuteronomy 12, 16, and 26, the consistent concern for Levitical priests and prophets all suggest that Deuteronomy is not so much a more secular document. Rather, it has a different understanding of the sacral."

168 See Lohfink, "Zur deuteronomischen Zentralisationsformel," 171–73, which links the Deuteronomic election formula to Ps 78:67–70 (David) and 132:8, 14 (place for the Ark).

169 The Peshitta uses *gb'* and the Targums use *r''*.

3.6. Conclusion: Significance of Meat From a Socio-Political Background

At this point I will bring forward the discussions from the beginning of the chapter on the wider archaeozoological, iconographic, ancient Near Eastern historical, and biblical views on meat symbolism in order to enrich my analysis of Deut 12:13–19.

The data from the broader Old Testament has shown that meat parades as a commodity of recognized importance and value in ancient Israelite culture. Its use in Proverbs, the sacrificial cult, and 1 Kings—in other words across various epochs and genres—as a signifier of wealth is taken for granted. Since its significance is assumed throughout the OT (Prov 15:17 is the most obvious example), the choice of meat in Deut 12 offers a powerful symbol in the ancient Israelite context. While desire for meat may only occur once in the earliest layer of the text (v. 15), its very appearance carries deep meaning, so much so that later redactions highlight its importance in 12:20, 21, 22–24, 26–27.

The pericope of vv. 13–19 begins specifically with the burnt offerings. While *'lh* ("burnt offering") in v. 14 may stand as a metonym for the entire offering system, the choice of burnt offerings may also be deliberate because it is the only offering received by the deity in full, with nothing left over for the human participants. There is no cultic meal in this sacrifice, making the burnt offering the best choice for highlighting the centripetal movements in Deut 12.

There is also some textual resonance with Deut 6:4 in 12:14's formulation of the election formula, "in the place where Yhwh chooses in *one* of your tribes."[170] This resonance emphasizes Yhwh's unified nature, replicated in the unified nature of the people of Israel coming together at the singular place.[171]

The mention of a more complete family and extra-familial group in 12:18 emphasizes the general distribution of meat throughout the soci-

---

[170] The debate on whether this statement can be read as distributive continues. For recent views from both perspectives, see McConville, *Law and Theology in Deuteronomy*, chapters 2–3, and Bernard M. Levinson, "McConville's *Law and Theology in Deuteronomy*," *JQR* 80 (1990): 396–404. Römer, *The So-called Deuteronomistic History*, 58, sums up my convictions well: "This precision [of Deut. 12:13–14 in relation to Exod 20:20–26] makes it difficult to read the centralization formula in a distributive manner."

[171] Ibid., 59, considers the connection between 6:4 and 12:14 so strong that he suggests that the seventh-century text began with 6:4–5, followed directly by 12:13–18. Similarly, though seen within a somewhat different context, Kratz, *Composition*, 125–26, 130.

ety. The combination of the localized groups eating together in the central place (v. 18, cf. vv. 7, 12) with the local consumption of meat according to one's desire (v. 15, cf. vv. 20, 21) builds upon the depictions in the iconographic and textual records of banquets from surrounding cultures. The ongoing and central importance of celebratory meals throughout the Mesopotamian and Levantine cultures emerges from the discussion of banquet iconography. This iconography highlights the religious and socio-political implications connected to the use of this motif in the centralizing text of Deut 12. The implied promise that Yhwh, as the true high king deserving fealty, would provide enough meat for the Israelites to eat meat according to their desires in these verses creates the potential for hope that Yhwh will give more than the people need, catering even to their wants (cf. Exod 16), beyond even the provisions the Assyrian king gave his subjects as portrayed in the Neo-Assyrian letters and on the White Obelisk and the walls of Sargon's palace in Dur-Sharrukin.

Furthermore, these joyful feasts occur in the central place (12:18, 26–27) and at home (12:15, 20, 21), thereby ridding the whole Israelite land of non-sacred space in which to eat "foreign" meat.[172] This argument works not only for local non-Deuteronomic traditions, but also for those of imperial Assyria, Egypt, or Babylon as well. The implications of the lack of non-Yahwistic space become evident when placed in conversation with the Neo-Assyrian banquet iconography and the Neo-Assyrian description of the dedication banquet of Calah.[173] Both of

---

172 MacDonald, *Not Bread Alone*, 88, states, "Thus, the joyful feasts that the Israelites consume provide not only a positive memory of the gift of the land and YHWH's acts of salvation, but also make the Israelite remember *and* forget the Canaanite cult through the absence of forbidden meat." He mentions "Canaanite" with a view towards the final form of Deuteronomy. The Canaanite opposition is less present in the pre-Dtr Deuteronomic text. In general, the DC presents a community that contrasts with all forms of royally-focused connections with the divine and royal loci of political power and socio-religious identity, whether from the outside (Assyria and Egypt) or inside (Ugarit/Canaan and other "Israelite" notions of community and communal identity). Egypt then appears as a general symbol for this kind of power and identity, but Egypt plays less of a role in the early version of the DC, and becomes more important with Dtr redaction.

173 Pongratz-Leisten, "The Interplay of Military Strategy and Cultic Practice in Assyrian Politics," 252, argues that the intent to extend royal presence to the edges of the empire was part of the Assyrian ideology: "As pointed out by Mario Liverani, in Assyria the king's presence is documented in the periphery of his empire by the visual documentation of statues or rock-reliefs set up in the mountains. Besides, in addition to the very technical meaning of the celebratory stela, delimiting the state border and marking the possession of the universe by the king, 'other metaphorical implications can be pointed out. Concerning space, if we consider the border as an elastic perime-

these separate media place the Neo-Assyrian king at the apex and center of the feast. While the centrality of meat is more difficult to pinpoint in the iconographic banquet celebrations such as the White Obelisk and the Neo-Assyrian palace wall reliefs—though its presence and therefore importance is difficult to deny—, various types of meat parade as the main course in the Calah text. Furthermore, as Marcus notes,[174] the Assyrian rulers take the place of the seated deity, thereby introducing a strong religious flavor to the presentations of these royal banquets.[175] The Deuteronomic formulation takes on a decidedly anti-imperial and anti-royal stance, since in Deut 12 the entire space of Israel becomes satiated with Yahwistic meals centered around meat. Yhwh's provision and method of provision make significant adjustments to those of the Neo-Assyrian ruler who provides the prolific seven–day feast for 70,000 people in Calah or some select guests in the palace reliefs. Yhwh, working through the human hands of the heads of households throughout the localities of Israel, instead provides both for a centralizing and unifying feast at the central sanctuary and for an ongoing and unending meat-focused meal in the local villages. The Deuteronomic meals promote a decidedly *de-centralized* image when contrasted with the Neo-Assyrian banquet. While the centralization of the chosen place remains intact, especially with its connection to the divine authority of Yhwh, the responsibilities for human hosts spread to the various households even to the periphery of Yhwh's land.

Finally, the archaeozoological analysis of the faunal remains from Iron Age II Judah and the Levant show a significant change in the role of meat in Judah as a result of Neo-Assyrian domination. Though the

---

ter that follows the outwards displacement of the king, the stele (with name and image of the king) acts as a substitute of his presence in order to keep the perimeter fixed at the farthest point, even when the king returns to a more central place.'" One particular example is the Nahr Kalb boundary stela in Lebanon. Perhaps the extension of Yhwh's presence to the local villages in 12:15 functions similarly as a marker of Yhwh's presence throughout his kingdom. An intriguing connection might be posited for the presence of Yhwh at the central and local feasts somehow in the way that the deceased KTMW "eats" a thigh portion offered by his surviving heirs in the communal feast in the KTMW inscription. See Dennis Pardee, "A New Aramaic Inscription from Zincirli," *BASOR* 356 (2009): 51–71, esp. 69.

174 See above, 88 n. 37.

175 Gerald A. Klingbeil, "*Momentaufnahmen* of Israelite Religion: The Importance of the Communal Meal in Narrative Texts in I/II Regum and Their Ritual Dimension," *ZAW* 118 (2006): 27–30, and MacDonald, *Not Bread Alone,*167–83, show the political overtones contained in the meals in 1–2 Kings, while C. L. Seow, *Myth, Drama, and the Politics of David's Dance* (HSM 44; Atlanta: Scholars, 1989) explores the same notion in 2 Samuel. These authors conclude that religion and politics most certainly coalesced around banquets in Israel and Judah as well.

evidence from the various Samarian and Judahite Iron II archaeological sites does not provide conclusive answers for the amount of meat available for local consumption, comparison with the historical events and evidence from Philistia suggest intriguing congruity with my conclusions. The Assyrian army's incursions altered the pattern of meat consumption in Ekron. Assyrian domination also led to intensive olive oil production. So, given the changes in agricultural production on the basis of the massive changes in the local economies of the Levant, changes in the production of animal goods are expected. These changes, coinciding with tribute requirements and the loss of animals taken as booty, gave rise to a lack of meat for local consumption. This picture provides background for how an Iron Age II audience may have understood Deut 12:13–19, especially its references to localized desire for and consumption of meat. Deuteronomy 12 envisions the "Israelites" as a unified, yet politically and socially decentralized people under Yhwh's beneficent rule.

The ritual actions theorized in Deut 12:13–19 prescribe a new distinction of the "sacred" in ancient Israel, a new way of ritualizing the envisioned "Israelites" by following the given ordinances related to festive meat consumption, that, following Bell, theorize the creation of a particular "Israelite" society.[176] The moves made in Deut 12:13–19 exemplify Robertson Smith's conclusion that communal feasts create kinship bonds. Geertz' notion that the symbolic and real worlds fusion in ritual informs the power of Deut 12's reformulation of "Israelite" worship: if enacted, the actors rid themselves of connections to Assyrian and other imperial provision. They become recipients of the divinely-provided blessing, celebrating Yhwh's rich feast like the one

---

176 See above, 2.4. The Use of Ritual Theory. Cf. Sanders, *The Invention of Hebrew*, 75: "Unlike Mesopotamian political ritual and discourse, which imposed a king over a mass of subjects, imagined as a territory or a passive, voiceless group, this West Semitic ideal of political ritual and discourse bonded peoples, imagined as agents, to each other. We find here a model of political communication in which power flows from the ability to *recruit* people into relationships of alliance and fictive kinship through ritual and persuasion."

imagined in the significantly later text of Isa 25:6: "On this mountain
the LORD of hosts will make for all peoples a feast of rich food, a feast
of well-aged wines, of rich food filled with marrow, of well-aged wines
strained clear." Yhwh's victory feast in Isaiah, like in Deuteronomy,
consists of the best wine and the richest foods—foods where meat highlighted in the imagery: *mištēh šĕmānîm:* literally "a feast of fat" and
mištēh mĕmuḥîm: a feast of sucked marrow.

4. The Cultic Meals of the Deuteronomic Cultic Calendar (16:1–17) in Light of Comparative Ancient Near Eastern Texts

4.1. Introduction

Outside the biblical canon, one is hard-pressed to find cultic meals in the midst of a legal code, vassal treaty, or wisdom treatise, a void mirrored by the lack of comparisons by interpreters of the DC cultic meals with texts from surrounding cultures. Interpretations generally attempt to identify the inner-biblical developments of the Israelite festival calendar in its various pentateuchal formulations.

There are, however, a number of cultic meals recorded or described in narrative and ritual texts from the cultures surrounding ancient Israel. Because they come from different genres, sociological continuity provides the most fruitful basis for comparison.[1] While ancient Israel produced unique texts in this regard, it nonetheless still incorporates and uses some elements of cultic meals in similar ways to its neighbors.

This sociological continuity has been pointed out by studies that compare the battle–banquet progressions in iconographic portrayals such as the Royal Standard of Ur and the Banquet of Assurbanipal, and the literary portrayals of the Baal Cycle and 2 Sam 5–7,[2] in addition to the temple building–banquet sequence of Gudea and 1 Kgs 8.[3] These textual and graphic representations point to the overlap of symbolic meanings in cultic meals throughout Mesopotamia and the Levant. As

---

1   This is buttressed by the dietary continuity in the Levant during LBA–Persian Period, and also literarily by the similarities seen in Murray Lichtenstein (see next note). Thanks to Simeon Chavel for help on this point.

2   Seow, *Myth, Drama, and the Politics of David's Dance*, notes a similar sequence in the Annals of Ashurbanipal and the Azitawadda inscription. This similarity highlights the overlap between mythic and historical reporting, showing the pervasiveness of the rhetorical pattern. See also Murray Lichtenstein, "The Banquet Motifs in Keret and in Proverbs 9," *JANESCU* 1 (1968):19–31.

3   See "Gudea Cylinder," translated by Richard Averbeck, (*COS* 2.155:418–35), especially Cylinder B xvii.12–xix.21. This text contains an understanding of the festal day similar to that of the DC. Social boundaries are obliterated during the festal celebration, much as they are in Deuteronomy's formulation of Israel during the feasts.

argued in the previous chapter, the historical connotations and implications of these meal depictions often display the politics implied in the cultic meals. One example addressed below is Marduk's invitation to come and celebrate the completion of his Esagila temple in Babylon (*Enuma Elish*), which both signifies Marduk's ascendancy over the divine realm and the ascendancy of Babylon over the earthly realm.

The following chapter will also address the composition-historical analysis important for this chapter of Deuteronomy, especially insofar as it is possible to identify Exod 23 as the source text of Deut 16. Comparison with the other pentateuchal descriptions of the festivals enrich the reading of the DC material because of their differences. However, the main focus will be on the ancient Near Eastern conception of the cultic meal in ritual and literary texts as an important additional perspective for the interpretation of Deuteronomy's cultic festivals, especially their socio-political implications for the divine and human realms.

The comparison of the DC festive meals with ancient Near Eastern analogues draws on texts with intriguing comparisons and relatively secure comparative footing. I have chosen texts that come from contexts that can be compared analogically to late preexilic Judah, or texts that arise from cultures that might have influenced the thinking of those writing and those first receiving the DC. I therefore hope to follow Talmon's assertion that comparison should take place with cultures that are in the same historical and geographic stream as Israel, and the comparisons should take place on a total culture level, rather than atomistically.[4] Furthermore, because the Deuteronomic meals are in a ritual context, with Deut 16:1–17 forming a festival calendar, comparisons are limited to texts related to ritual, either as ritual texts or texts speaking of ritual meals.

My discussion of the texts focuses on two particular questions: 1) What is the nature of the meal? 2) What do the meals set out to accomplish rhetorically? In other words, what seems to be the desired result of the writing and reading of the meal text? This point can be made most clearly from the narratival texts that give some context for exploring the rhetorical potential of the meal. I intend these texts to provide further depth to the interpretation of Deut 16:1–17 by way of what they

---

4   Shemaryahu Talmon "The 'Comparative Method' in Biblical Interpretation—Principles and Problems," VTSup 29 (1977): 320–56; repr. in *Essential Papers on Israel and the Ancient Near East* (Ed. Frederick E. Greenspahn; New York: New York University Press, 1991), 381–419.

share in common, how they differ, and what remains unclear.[5] To give a glimpse of my conclusions, the following analysis will show how the cultic meals of Deuteronomy adapt and reshape cultural conceptualizations of meals available in the Syro-Palestinian and Mesopotamian texts. The ritual texts I explore share the DC's concern for social cohesion, showing how cultic meals were an important vehicle toward this end across the ancient Near East.

The DC meal texts rework the connection between divine and royal hosts found in the Akkadian *akītu–Enuma Elish* complex (and implied in the Ugaritic material). The notion of the meal in these Deuteronomic texts could be viewed as an anti-imperial (and anti-"Canaanite")[6] feast in which Yhwh plays the role of divine host, as especially apparent in the tithe text of Deut 14:22–29, and *each head of household* serves as the human host (rather than the king). This conception parallels the *zukru* festival of Emar in omitting an important role for the king. The DC accomplishes this minimization by reworking the meal conception in accordance with earlier Israelite traditions.[7] As a result, the conception of cultic meals in the DC enhances the view of limited human kingship present in the rest of the code.[8]

---

5   Especially helpful is the comment of Peter Machinist, "The Question of Distinctiveness" in *Ah Assyria...Studies in Assyrian History and Ancient Near Eastern Historiography Presented to Hayim Tadmor* (ed. M. Coogan and I. Eph'al; Scripta Hierosolymitana 33; Jerusalem: Magnes, 1991), 202: "We may find, in fact, that certain facets do look different by comparison with other cultures; but the goal here is not so much to seek out the differences as to understand, whether different or not, what the culture of Israel was."

6   By this term I mean both non-Yahwistic and also non-Deuteronomic Yahwistic formulations of the feast.

7   This anti-imperial polemic also suggests that the DC significantly circumscribes the power of the Israelite monarchy and may attempt to incorporate ancient traditions of the desert mountain (Sinai or Horeb)—which were possibly promoted by tribal leaders (*'am hā'āreṣ*)—into the Neo-Assyrian dominated eighth-seventh century. This argument draws on Gerhard von Rad's emphasis on the importance of this group of leaders; see *Studies in Deuteronomy*, 64–67, and the West Semitic political tradition found in Mari, Emar, and even in Ugarit as found in *CTU* 1.40 below (see Sanders, *Then Invention of Hebrew*, 52–66), which ritually circumscribe royal power.

8   An example of this view of "limited human kingship" can be seen in the fact that the king in the DC is not the promulgator of the law code nor a Mosaic descendent, but rather a reader of and adherent to the given code. See J. Gordon McConville, "King and Messiah in Deuteronomy and the Deuteronomistic History," in *King and Messiah in Israel and the Ancient Near East: Proceedings of the Oxford Old Testament Seminar* (ed. J. Day; JSOTSup 270; Sheffield: Sheffield University Press, 1998): 271–95, also Knoppers, "Rethinking the Relationship between Deuteronomy and the Deuteronomistic History," 405–13; and Levinson, "The Reconceptualization of Kingship."

4.2. Ritual Texts

4.2.1. Emar and the *zukru* Festival Texts

Excavations carried out in the 1970s at Emar revealed a West Semitic culture influenced by its Hittite overlords and by Mesopotamian traditions that was destroyed violently at the beginning of the 12th century.[9] The high point of the tell had two temples, one devoted to the storm god dIM[10] and another to Aštarte. The ritual texts were, however, located in a single room of a third temple complex (M₁) associated with "the diviner," whose role lay in cultic administration for the cults of various deities. Among the various ritual and other texts[11] were two priestess installation rituals and texts related to the central *zukru* festival that occurred on a yearly and seven year cycle.

The respective natures of the Emar *zukru* texts and Deut 16, as well as the political situations of Judah and Emar, suggest similarities that make the comparison intriguing. Both the DC festivals and the *zukru* are concerned with calendrical changes and their respective high deities, while also positing the presence of the entire community at the ritual events. Furthermore, texts of the *zukru* make up the longest tablets and appear more often than any other rituals at Emar, much like the ubiquity of the three festival cycle that appears at least four times just in the legal portions of the Pentateuch. The *zukru* was likely the most expensive celebration, and the main part of each celebration day was spent feasting outside the city.

---

9   Lorenzo d'Alfonso et al, eds., *The City of Emar Among the Late Bronze Age Empires: Proceedings of the Konstanz Emar Conference, 25.–26.04.2006* (AOAT 349; Münster: Ugarit-Verlag, 2008) provides the most recent overview of the scholarly understanding of Emar.

10   Daniel E. Fleming, *The Installation of Baal's High Priestess at Emar: A Window on Ancient Syrian Religion* (HSM 42; Atlanta: Scholars Press, 1992), 71, notes that the convergence of Hittite, Mesopotamian, and West Semitic cultures in Emar could allow for this Akkadian logogram to be read as Teššub, Baal, or Adad. Daniel Schwemer, *Die Wettergottgestalten Mesopotamiens und Nordsyriens im Zeitalter der Keilschriftkulturen: Materialien und Studien nach den schriftlichen Quellen* (Wiesbaden: Harrassowitz, 2001), 552, concludes as part of his thorough study of onomastica and other documents that the weather god was known as both Adad and Baal.

11   Fleming, *Time at Emar*, 6, notes: "A large number of tablets record transactions and events from local religious life, not restricted to one primary deity and temple cult. Many texts mention rites never previously known, and the documents themselves do not copy familiar templates. They are composed in Akkadian but evidently account for the practices of Emar and its environs. Although some rites claim participation by the whole town and all its gods, the texts show only a secondary interest in the king, and this temple was not an arm of palace administration."

Like the DC, the king plays at most a minor background role in the rituals and their meals.[12] Despite the historical and geographical differences, the relative absence of royalty in both the DC and Emar ritual texts may also provide important insights. The Emar king appears in numerous documents such as real estate transactions and also as the provider of many offerings in the later septennial *zukru* found in the diviner's archive, showing royalty's importance in some spheres of the city's life. This makes his absence from the local rituals more noteworthy. This phenomenon parallels the centrality of the king in biblical Zion traditions, rendering the limited kingship in Deuteronomy even more intriguing, perhaps bearing a parallel to the society envisioned by the DC. While constructed in part under the monarchy, the DC laws reflect the relative importance of other institutions.[13]

Yet this does not take away a few pressing differences.[14] The texts from Emar come from the late second millennium and from a Syrian city-state, rather than from Assyrian-dominated Iron Age II Judah. However, both sets of texts emerge from the context of smaller vassal states which project significant independence from the hegemonic em-

---

12 Daniel E. Fleming, "A Limited Kingship: Late Bronze Emar in Ancient Syria," *UF* 24 (1992): 59, notes, "Emar had kings in the 13th century, but their influence in local city life appears to have been limited, restricted, by other, perhaps older traditional leadership: city elders in legal and administrative affairs, temples and deep native traditions in religious affairs." Also Sopie Dömare-Lafont, "The King and the Diviner At Emar," in *The City of Emar Among the late Bronze Age Empires: History, Landscape, and Society: Proceedings of the Konstanz Emar Conference 25.–26.04.2006* (ed. L. d'Alfonso et al; AOAT 349; Münster: Ugarit-Verlag, 2008), 209–213, who notes that the king of Emar became more powerful over time, but without leaving the *primus inter pares* status behind. The elders of the town remained important.

13 Regardless of whether one sees Deuteronomy as generally supportive or resistant to monarchy, only a few verses even mention kingship, and these picture the ideal king as similar to the rest of the Israelites. The judges, priests, elders of towns, and perhaps above all individual family units (however conceived) receive far more attention in the DC. Timothy M. Willis, *The Elders of the City: A Study of the Elders-Laws in Deuteronomy* (SBLMS 55; Atlanta: SBL, 2001), 78, comments, "Based, then, on what one finds at the local level in these contemporary societies [Mesopotamia and Hatti], it is not surprising to find that, even in the highly-centralized polities of the ancient Near East, local judicial and legal matters are generally handled by community leaders ('elders') and one or more local officials." This conclusion stands even if Deut 16:18–18:22 stem from a later (exilic or postexilic period) since the trajectory of Deut 12:13–16:17 moves not only towards the center (Jerusalem), but also toward the periphery ("in your gates").

14 Daniel E. Fleming, "The Israelite Festival Calendar," *RB* 106 (1999): 34, remarks that the temples of both cultures are constructed similarly, both have standing stones, and both anoint the high priest(ess) with oil.

pires in the region (whether Hittite, Hurrian, Assyrian, or Egyptian).[15] The ritual texts of Emar and Israel diverge from the ritual traditions in the imperial cultures' texts, continuing their own indigenous traditions in spite of the local presence of the imperial cultures' traditions (cf. 2 Kgs 23:11–12). The language of the Emar ritual texts also reflects this independence: although written in Akkadian, there are numerous idioms both unattested in Mesopotamia proper or stemming from Hittite origins.[16] Finally, the architectural remains also point to the relative distinctiveness of Emar religion. All of the buildings excavated reflect Hittite influence except for the four temples, which exhibit Syrian characteristics.[17]

Prior to the discovery of the Emar *zukru*[18] texts, the only mention of this ritual came in a Mari letter ordering the king of Mari to give a

---

15   The diviner's house at Emar also included some foreign rituals from Mesopotamian and Hittite localities. Notably, as observed by Daniel E. Fleming, "The Emar Festivals: City Unity and Syrian Identity under Hittite Hegemony," in *Emar: the History, Religion, and Culture of a Syrian Town in the Late Bronze Age* (ed. M. W. Chavalas; Bethesda, Md.: CDL, 1996), 121, texts for deities of *Ḫatti* were kept separate within the diviner's archive.

16   Mark W. Chavales, "Ancient Syria," in *New Horizons in the Study of Ancient Syria* (ed. M. W. Chavalas & J. H. Hayes; Bibliotheca Mesopotamica 25; Malibu: Endena, 1992), 19. See also Fleming, "The Emar Festivals: City Unity and Syrian Identity under Hittite Hegemony," 102. Most decisively, Eugen J. Pentiuc, "West Semitic Terms in Akkadian Texts From Emar," *JNES* 58:2 (1999): 83–84, notes, "As a language written by non-native speakers, the Western Peripheral Akkadian of Emar reflects a native dialect, influenced from one generation to another by foreign contacts and pressures. This means that not all non-Akkadian words in the Emar texts must necessarily be of West Semitic origin. The most immediate non-Semitic influence on the natives is the incorporation of Emar in the Hittite Empire. Thus, some of these non-Akkadian words found in the Emar corpus are of Hittite or Hurrian origin. Others are Akkadian words exhibiting nonnormative spellings. A great number of forms are so far of unknown origin … In the Emar corpus, the religious texts constitute a special category. These texts are unique in describing local rituals and ceremonies, and thus they are commonly considered of Emar origin. They are, in fact, one of the main sources of evidence for West Semitic vocabulary."

17   Fleming, "The Rituals From Emar: Evolution of an Indigenous Tradition in Second-Millennium Syria," 55.

18   Initially the word *zukru* was understood in connection to *zikaru* "male" (*AHw*, 1536), but the connection to *zakāru* "to remember, recall" is more compelling for most scholars. Yoram Cohen, review of Daniel Fleming, *Time at Emar, Orientalia* 72 (2003): 270, notes that while Fleming understands *zukru* as invocation, Eugen J. Pentiuc, *West Semitic Vocabulary in the Akkadian texts from Emar* (HSS 49; Winona Lake, Ind.: Eisenbrauns, 2001), 198, argues instead for 'memorial service.' In the end, I concur with Cohen that it is hard to rule out one or the other.

zukru to Adad of Aleppo.[19] While only an incomplete picture of the diachronic development of the Emar *zukru* exists, like the biblical festivals there appears to have been significant growth over time in the ways the *zukru* was celebrated, especially movement towards more detail. Having grown from the early beginnings in the yearly ritual texts, the later septennial texts reveal an additional and more elaborate festival that occurs every seventh year. The tablets containing the earlier (annual) version of the text are fragmentary, making the underlying structure of the ritual difficult to determine. Therefore, my analysis of these yearly festival texts requires supplementation from the analysis of the more elaborate septennial festival text. Diachronically speaking, the celebration reflected in the septennial festival text is best viewed as growth from the earlier annual *zukru* celebration: in other words, as growth from the modest core of the annual texts.[20]

The difference in genre and focus in the *zukru* texts and Deuteronomy complicates comparative analysis. The Emar *zukru* includes detailed accounts of the offering material (animals, anointing oil, etc.), matters that the DC texts generally omits. Fleming notes that these texts appear to have been actually practiced,[21] while this remains an open question for Deut 16.[22] The *zukru* texts highlight details of ritual practice (like the practicalities of which actions take place at which times), while

---

19 A.1121 + A.2731. See J. J. M. Roberts' translation, pages 172–77 in *The Bible and the Ancient Near East* (Winona Lake, Ind.: Eisenbrauns, 2002). As others have noticed, both the Mari and Emar texts use similar language, specifically that one "gives a *zukru*" (*nadāru*). It is important to note that this ritual is not done in Mari, but rather in Aleppo, thereby increasing its proximity to Israel.

20 Fleming, *Time at Emar*, 49. Lluís Feliu, *The God Dagan in Bronze Age Syria* (trans. W. G. E. Watson; CHANE 19; Leiden: E. J. Brill, 2003), 217, is more cautious about Fleming's reconstruction of the ritual's historical change, but he generally follows Fleming.

21 Fleming, *Time at Emar*, 46.

22 Robert R. Wilson, "Deuteronomy, Ethnicity, and Reform," in *Constituting the Community: Studies on the Polity of Ancient Israel in Honor of S. Dean McBride Jr.* (ed. J. T. Strong and S. S. Tuell; Winona Lake, Ind.: Eisenbrauns, 1995), 107–23; Kenneth Sparks, *Ethnicity and Identity in Ancient Israel: Prolegomena to the Study of Ethnic Sentiments and Their Expression in the Hebrew Bible* (Winona Lake, Ind.: Eisenbrauns, 1998), 225; S. Dean McBride, "Polity of the Covenant People: The Book of Deuteronomy," *Interpretation* 41 (1987): 229–44, all consider Deuteronomy (or at least the DC) as written for actual practice, while it is viewed as more of a utopian projection by von Rad, *Studies in Deuteronomy*, 64 n. 2, and Lohfink, "Recent Discussion on 2 Kings 22–23," 58.

Deuteronomy is more general with regard to the way festivals are carried out.[23]

Fleming constructs a fairly uniform annual *zukru* text can be reconstructed on the basis of four tablets, in contrast to Arnaud who considers the four tablets to represent three different texts (his Emar 375, 448, and 449).[24] Most significantly, Msk 74289b contains portions of the annual *zukru* from both the recto and verso of the other tablets on one side, thereby showing that they belong together, making Fleming's reconstruction preferable. At any rate, these four copies of the annual *zukru* make it the only calendar ritual text at Emar found in multiple copies.

Before offering my interpretation, I provide the following translation to acquaint the reader with the annual festival text:[25]

(1) [...][26] of the *zukru*. When Emar

(2) gives [the *zukr*]*u* to Dagan:

(3) During Zarati [on] the 15th [day], they set aside a lamb[27] for Dagan.

---

23   This is not completely true, especially for Passover, where a month, type of meat and bread, as well as directives on what to do with leftovers are given (this last element also appears in the Emar *zukru*, where they are to be returned after the seventh day of the festival, in contrast to the burning of the leftover Passover meal on the next morning).

24   In the *edition princips* of the annual *zukru* texts Daniel Arnaud, *Recherches au Pays d'Ashtata: Emar VI:3 Textes Sumeriens et Accadiens* (Paris: Editions Recherche sur les Civilisations, 1986), 368–70, concludes that there are three different tablet fragments which attest to an annual *zukru*. He constructs his text Emar 375, which he calls the beginning of the *zukru*, from the texts of Msk 74146l, Msk 74303f, and the recto of Msk 74298b. The third fragment contains significantly more text. Arnaud considers the verso of this tablet (Msk 74298b) another annual liturgical order, calling it Emar 448 (ibid., 426–28). This collation amounts to 25 lines, based on the length of the recto of Msk 74298b. However, Fleming, *Time at Emar*, 258–59, convincingly shows that the recto and verso of Msk 74298b belong together based especially on the collation of Msk 74289b (listed as a variant text of Emar 448 by Arnaud). This tablet does contain some variant readings from the other texts, but the overlap is quite pronounced (Msk 74289b, called "Text D" by Fleming, *Time at Emar*, contains portions of ll. 22–28).

25   My numbering follows Fleming, *Time at Emar*, 258–65 (as does most of my reading).

26   Fleming and Arnaud disagree on whether the yearly *zukru* also received the designation of "festival" (Akkadian logogram EZEN). Arnaud reconstructs the first line of the yearly celebration (Emar 375:1) as *ṭuppi* EZEN *zu*]*kri*, "Tablet of the *zukru* festival" (as does Feliu, *The God Dagan in Bronze Age Syria,* 217), on analogy with the Emar *kissu* ritual texts. Fleming (*Time at Emar*, 258–59; cf. 106) instead suggests *párṣu*(?) *ša zu*]*kri*, "Cultic ordinance(?) of *zukru*. He bases his conviction that EZEN did not appear here in part on its absence in Dagan's titulary "head of the *zukru*" (*rêš zukri*) in 375:17. While it might add to my argument if the determinative EZEN did appear, either way the rite still occurred on a yearly basis and included the cultic meal.

(4) On the 15th day, the Šaggar—that same day—[…][28] goes out,[29] his face uncovered.

(5) [The divine axe] goes behind him. Two sheep [of the cit]y(?)[30] are in their midst.

(6) One with(?) the divine axe […among][31] the stelae.

(7) […] goes out between the stelae.

(8) On the 15th(?) day [… bet]ween the ste[lae…]

(9) […] … on that same day […]

(10) […] oxen, roasted meat, not[32] […] Dagan above, they cover his face.

(11) […d] NIN.KUR,[33] […] they bind (for) the gods.

(12) […]x du[34] fo[r …]and the divine axe

(13) […][35] bet[ween the stelae] they lift up.

(14) […] to d[…] They anoint the stelae with blood and anointing oil.

(15) […the peo]ple (?) [of Emar e]at, they drink.[36]

---

27 This follows Fleming, *Time at Emar,* 258–59, since the logogram SILA[4] ("lamb") is not followed by the plural determinative.

28 Fleming, ibid., 259, inserts Dagan here, which fits well considering the considerable attention this deity receives throughout the ritual text.

29 This expression likely means "to go out in procession," as Marduk's proceeding from the city of Babylon to the *akītu* house is called. See the references in Annette Zgoll, "Königslauf und Götterrat: Struktur und Deutung des babylonischen Neujahrsfests," in *Festtraditionen in Israel und im Alten Orient* (ed. E. Blum and R. Lux; VWGT 28; Gütersloh: Gütersloher Verlagshaus, 2006), 21.

30 I am using the "?," following Fleming's usage, for places in the text where he has been able only partially to make out the signs.

31 Fleming (ibid., 261) reconstructs, "[They go out in procession] [between] the upright stones."

32 Ibid., "They must not." This reconstruction is likely based on analogy with the second half of this line.

33 Fleming (ibid.) has "dNIN.KUR, to […]," but I am unable to see any signs for "to" (*i-na*) in the cuneiform drawings in Arnaud, *Emar VI:2,* 634.

34 Fleming, *Time at Emar,* 260–61, reconstructs "the sacrificial homage (?) (is)…"

35 Ibid., "[follows him.] They lift these up (in procession) between the upright stones."

36 Arnaud, *Emar VI:3,* 368, does not translate this line, likely deeming it too broken, but Fleming's reconstruction is supported by the corresponding sections of the longer septennial *zukru* festival text (Emar 373:34/32, 60/57, 173/178 [the first number is according to Fleming's numbering, the second Arnaud's]). It also appears in l. 30, which Fleming understands to be the second part of the yearly *zukru* text because it appears on the reverse side of the tablet with the yearly *zukru.* As argued above, I see little basis to separate the two sides of the tablet into separate texts.

(16) [...the s]tela of Ninurta.

(17) [...D]agan, head of the *zukru*.

(18) [...] If the lambs

(19) [...] They prepare[37] They gather (them) to the temple of Dagan.

(20) [...] S/he goes and

(21) [...for] the gods and temples they set aside oil.

(22) [...] equipment and the divine axe[38]

(23) [...] one sheep, one calf before the stela.

(24) [...] between the stelae.

(25) [...] in its midst two food offerings.

(26) And the *ḫarṣi* stones [...] they throw down in its midst, and[39]

(27) [...] women[40] eat the ox, the sheep, bread, (and) beer before Dagan.

(28) [to]the stelae,[41] on the seventh day just as on the [15th(?)] day.

(29) Dagan[42] and the gods and the divine axe

(30) [...][43] go out. They eat, they drink. On

(31) that same day, in the evening (is) the return to the sanctuaries.

---

37 Arnaud (ibid., 370) reconstructs "le chariot," arguing that the line begins [...
    GIŠ.mar.gíd.]da. Fleming, 266 n. 19 disputes this on the basis of the same sequence of
    verbs (*ṣamādu + paḫāru*) in l. 32. Fleming also seems unable to concur with Arnaud's
    reading of the *da* sign.

38 Text A (Msk 74298b for this line) reads "equipment and the divine axe of the deity
    KASKAL," but as Fleming, 266 n. 22 notes, "with unclear implication."

39 This is the end of the recto of Msk 74298b, and therefore the end of the text according
    to Arnaud. As mentioned, earlier, he lists the verso as a different ritual, appearing as
    Emar 448.

40 Fleming reconstructs "*sarmātu*-women," keeping with their actions in ll. 46–47 in
    conjunction with the root *sarāmu* "to cut," which is used at Mari and likely related to
    šarāmu according to CAD S:172. This verb, *sarāmu*, could mean pruning and weed-
    ing, fitting the agricultural context of the "ones who plant" in l. 47 (CAD Š III:49
    suggests this possible meaning). Arnaud, followed by Pentiuc, *West Semitic Vocabu-
    lary*, 81 and 192, reads the deity Zarmatu here whom CAD does not mention (see
    448:20–21). Cf. Fleming, *Time at Emar*, 266 n. 27.

41 In his translation of "[*a-nana*]⁴ *sí-ka-na-tí*" (l. 28) Fleming, *Time at Emar*, 263 moves the
    location "[to] the upright stones," to l. 30.

42 Arnaud, *Emar VI:3*, 427, (represented as l. 4') writes "devant Dagan et les dieux et la
    hache divi[ne...], as if the Akkadian were "]*a-na pa-ni* ᵈ*Da-gan*..." However, the cu-
    neiform text he provides, *Emar VI:2*, 635, begins only with "*Da-gan*."

43 Fleming, *Time at Emar*, 263 reconstructs "the ox and sheep."

(32) is clothed,[44] and they prepare everything, gather, and

(33) [...] with their food offerings and the lambs (and) the sheep of the city,[45]

(34) [...] during[46] the return they repeat three times

(35) [...] They make (the people?)[47] eat. The citizens[48] and leaders of the city

(36) on that day go out and destroy their lumps of earth.

(37) [...in order] to cleanse her sheep, she consecrates it.

(38) [...] her sheep, she purifies it.

Line 39 is too fragmentary for sensible translation.

(40) [...] and homage[49]

(41) [...] they sacrifice for great homage before [...][50]

Line 42 is too fragmentary for sensible translation.

(43) [...] They gather to the temple of Dagan.

(44) [...][51] They carry them.

(45) During the same month, the Lord of *Bitaru*[52]

(46) [...] the *sarmātu*-women cut, the land is not [...]

(47) The Lord of Aleppo,[53] on the 16th day the *sarmātu*-women prepare [xxx]

(48) the land shall not ...[54]

---

44 Ibid., Fleming suggests Dagan.
45 Ibid., Fleming interprets—correctly in my opinion—*sa* URU.KI (my "of the city") to mean "provided by the city."
46 Ibid., Fleming translates "in the midst of the return," which I find unnecessarily awkward. *CAD* L:174, notes *ina libbi* is used in the genitive referring to a time span.
47 This insertion of "people" follows Fleming (ibid.), the basis for which is found below, p. 144 n. 55.
48 The underlying Akkadian here is DUMU^meš *u₂* GAL^hi.a *ša* URU.KI, but Fleming, *Time at Emar,* 267 n. 35 states that an alternative reading as TUR^meš (the small) for DUMU^meš (the people), which bolsters the notion that all city inhabitants are to take part in the cultic meal.
49 Ibid., 263, translates *kubāde* as "sacrificial homage," which puts a helpful interpretive slant on the word.
50 Ibid., 267 n. 41, suggests that Dagan is most appropriate since *ana pani* works best with a single deity.
51 Ibid., 265, suggests "[...] (and) they carry them [to the gods(?)]."
52 Ibid., translates, "During the same month (is the celebration of) the Lord of Bitaru. On the [...day...]."
53 Ibid., Fleming suggests that the Lord of Aleppo refers to the celebration for this deity.

The festival represents the yearly high point of Emar religion and is the only ritual text in which all occupants of the city, divine and human, take part.[55] The human inhabitants gather at a particular location outside the city on the first day of the celebration where various animal sacrifices are made before the uncovered face of the high god, Dagan (ll. 10, 14, 23, 33, 41). Afterwards the people of the Emar eat and drink, ritually anoint the stelae, and cover the deity's face. Similar festivities would last for seven days (ll. 28–30, 35).[56] The text does not detail the rations for the people, though it does mention the setting aside (*pâdu*) of lamb, beef, roast meat, bread, and beer.[57] Too few details are given for the determination of how the food was distributed and how to imagine the citizens' feasting. What remains striking for this text is the absence of the king, and the only provider of an offering is the city (l. 33; which is Arnaud 448:8).

While my interpretive focus will remain on the annual text, a brief glance at the diachronic changes proves insightful. The significant developments in the larger and later septennial *zukru* text add to the amount of food and sacrifices, the number of deities involved, and the length of the festival.[58] Another important change is the recording of who provides the foodstuffs and who receives it. The king (and palace), city, and "House of the Gods" are named as providers of the offerings, with the king providing by far the most. Fleming remarks, "Throughout the festival no individual human participant played a role deemed worthy of mention, but the wealth of the palace is evident behind every expansion."[59] The final line of this text notes that the celebration required 700 lambs as well as 50 calves, while the number of bread loaves and jars of wine are absent. The text also records preparatory festivities

---

54   There are approximately another eight fragmentary lines.

55   Fleming, *Time at Emar*, 49, 106, 133–34. All human residents take part in both the annual and seven year festivals, but it is unclear whether the whole divine family participates in the annual festival.

56   Lines 28–30, 35 (Emar 448:3–5, 10 in Arnaud) could plausibly refer to the consumption by the deities, but, when compared with the longer septennial *zukru* text, 373:169–73 (ll. 174–78 in Arnaud), and the various events taking place "before" Dagan and the deities, the actions fit better for the people of Emar. This is Fleming's interpretation as well (cf. Fleming, *Time at Emar*, 266 n. 27, where he argues that the appearance of *akālu* and *šatû* together suggests general festal consumption).

57   The text does suggest some special consumption, likely by the "*sarmātu*-women,"(l. 27, cf. l. 46) which means that all portions were not equal, or at least some were eaten with special symbolic import.

58   This text is known as Emar 373. As with references to the earlier text, I will follow Fleming's line numbers, and when appropriate include those from Arnaud.

59   Fleming, *Time at Emar*, 49.

for the year prior and month prior to the actual *zukru* itself. Now the entire divine pantheon is invoked, represented by the "seventy deities" (373:39/37),[60] and they are listed at length later in the text along with the sacrifices that each receives. The focus nonetheless remains on the Syrian high god Dagan, here called "Lord of Offspring," (373:41/39).[61]

The text enumerates the provisions for the people (22/19), as well as repeatedly mentioning the people's consumption (22/19,[62] 34/32, 60/57, 173/178). The rations include two kinds of bread as well as jugs (of wine). If this was their entire portion, then it would only have been a small tidbit. However, it is likely that the contents dedicated to the entire host of deities were distributed among them, which would make this portion a special ritual amount separated out from the rest of the feast.[63]

The rhetorical goal of the yearly celebration text is difficult to understand given its fragmentary nature. However, its important place among the local constellation of rituals is assured based on its regular repetition, rich assortment of offerings, and inclusion of a wide swath of residents. Yet this does not suggest that all participants were involved in the same manner or allowed to take the same roles. The fact that the high deity appears unveiled and outside the city hints at something of a *mysterium tremendum*. In general, the annual text describes a seven-day celebration of eating and drinking conducted by the whole

---

60 Seventy is also used to signify an entirety in the Baal Cycle, where the "seventy children of Athirat" means all the deities (1.4.VI.46). For a brief discussion, see Mark S. Smith, "The Baal Cycle" *UNP*, 134, n. 135.

61 EN *bu-ka-ri*. Arnaud, *Emar VI*:3,351, and Pentiuc *West Semitic Vocabulary*, 36–37, read EN *bu-qa₂-ri*. Pentiuc argues for this reading based on the parallel in Emar 446:50 to "lord of seeds," which makes the connection to fertility likely. Fleming's translation here ("offspring") is an adjustment from his earlier translation of the same term in *The Installation of Baal's High Priestess*, 269, where he read "firstborn." "Offspring" allows both for the fertility connection and for Fleming's argument (*Time at Emar*, 89) that the sign "KA" at Emar should almost always be read 'ka' rather than *qa₂*." Neither *CAD* nor *AHw* list an entry for "*baqar*," nor do they give any attestation of "*buqru*" (offspring, firstborn) written as it is here. The balance of the evidence supports Fleming's interpretation.

62 Fleming's version contains this addition to Arnaud, which Fleming was able to read based on a different joining of pieces.

63 Fleming, *Time at Emar*, 78–79, states: "It is hard to judge the relationship of these portions to the size of the crowd. This quantity of bread, perhaps baked from roughly one bushel of flour each time, would not feed a cast of thousands or even several hundred … Actual consumption may have included some part of the larger offering as well, so that the specific portions provided for the people may represent a ceremonial allotment for a smaller component of the feast."

city focusing on the high god of the pantheon, all of which suggests a fundamental reaffirmation of the accepted worldview of the city.[64]

Some of the rhetorical aims of the longer septennial *zukru* text are more easily understood. While the king continues to remain dispensable to the ritual acts, the royal coffers provide the extensive offerings. This text also emphasizes the primary role of Dagan even more than the earlier text. Even though more deities are included in the festivities presented in the septennial text, Dagan receives the most offerings and maintains the spotlight in the ritual drama between the stelae,[65] suggesting that the pantheon was rearticulated at the *zukru* festival, when all the divine and human inhabitants gather around and celebrate the fatherhood of Dagan.[66] As a unified group, Emar's particular identity is dramatically reenacted on a yearly and septennial cycle. As a peripheral city belonging to a large empire, this indigenous ritual connected the populous with the ancient and local identity of Emar,[67] distinct from its Hittite overlords.[68]

---

64   Interpreting the festival title *"zukru"* as related to invocation or memorial also suggests the importance of speech, and while the contents cannot be reconstructed based on the available evidence, this nonetheless points to an important similarity to Deuteronomy's presentation of Israelite festivals. Fleming, *Time at Emar*, 124, sees the rite as "… a spoken approach to Dagan, a prayer that renewed the link between the people and the god who was ultimately responsible for its survival as a community." The fact that the spoken portion of the ritual would take place in a local West Semitic language, rather than in Akkadian, may account for its omission from the text, but there are other plausible explanations.

65   Fleming, *Time at Emar*, 91, notes, "Only Dagan is honored at this shrine of sacred stones, with the entire divine and human populace of Emar looking on."

66   This gathering around and glorifying of Dagan parallels the similar actions in the *akītu* and *Enuma Elish* where Marduk is raised up and given the ability to determine destinies.

67   Cf. Fleming, "The Emar Festivals: City Unity and Syrian Identity under Hittite Hegemony," 107.

68   This does not necessarily imply that it was seditious. Cohen, "Review of Daniel Fleming, *Time at Emar*," 268–69, shows that the diviner was able to appeal directly to the Hittite authorities at the regional capital of Carchimesh, bypassing the local Emar king. This gave the diviner a measure of independence from the Emar royalty and also hints at direct Hittite support for the diviner's roles in the *zukru* and other rituals. Fleming, "The Emar Festivals: City Unity and Syrian Identity under Hittite Hegemony," 112–15, argues that Hittite policy toward vanquished vassals included a certain benevolence that allowed for religious continuity in the vassal states. Emar was not only allowed, but encouraged to maintain its own links to the past, as long as tribute was paid. In the Neo-Assyrian context the worship of Sin at Harran was similarly encouraged, supported, and even subverted for the rhetorical goals of the Assyrian Empire.

Stepping back from the image of the rituals projected by the texts, the writing and preservation of these ritual texts themselves has cultural significance. The larger septennial *zukru* text was carefully constructed, including double lines to separate sections, suggesting conscious effort to visually display a particular meaning and reading of the text. Furthermore, this text goes through the ritual twice, focusing on different information each time.[69] Fleming is only able to identify one set of festival texts comparable to the Emar collection in the Syrian area, those from Ḫattuša, the Hittite capital.[70] These ritual festival texts exhibit many similar characteristics to the *zukru*, hinting that the Emar texts—and likely the ritual itself—may have been influenced by and respond to the Hittite ones. However, the king plays a significant role in the Hittite EZEN rituals.[71] In fact, "the very project of recording Emar festivals may consciously both embrace an administrative ambition modeled by scribes of the Hittite capital and by the very effort distinguish their subject from imperial custom and identity."[72]

In summary, these ritual texts from Emar provide several important clues for the DC meals. The historical situation in which Emar found itself, as a small vassal on the edge of the Hittite empire, provides a suggestive parallel to Israel's political situation. In this historical context, both forms of the *zukru* festival text promote a city-wide communal ritual in which the collective inhabitants of the city gather together to focus on one high deity at a particular location, similar to the DC formulation. The *zukru* texts focus on the material food and drink provisions. They also reflect a local non-royal rite—especially in its earlier annual form—separate from the rituals and traditions of the larger Hittite and Mesopotamian cultures.

---

69 Lines 1–167 begins with the sixth year and goes through the actual *zukru* festival in the seventh year. They generally focus on the provisions—what they are, who provides them, and who receives them (both divine and human). Lines 168–211 again start with the sixth year and walk through the entire festival, this time focusing on the movements between the stones and the city. The main subjects of these daily ritual movements are the deities (specifically Dagan, Ninurta, Shaggar, and the *šaššabēyānātu*) and the foodstuffs. Here the divinities and the communally consumed foodstuffs are the focal points.

70 Fleming, "The Emar Festivals: City Unity and Syrian Identity under Hittite Hegemony," 119–20.

71 Oliver R. Gurney, *Some Aspects of Hittite Religion: The Schweich Lectures of the British Academy 1976* (Oxford: Oxford University Press, 1977), 31–43.

72 Fleming, "The Emar Festivals," 121.

4.2.2. Ugaritic *CTU* 1.40 (*RS* 1.002)

When compared with pentateuchal ritual texts, the Ugaritic material generally evades theological interpretation and "reasoned literary presentation"[73] in favor of lists naming the deities and types of offerings. Because little explicit interpretation of the ritual actions is found, any insights garnered come primarily by way of inference. What can generally be ascertained from the Ugaritic material is that the king and his functionaries played a much larger role in ritual texts in Ugarit, and also in some biblical texts such as the Psalms, than in Deuteronomy. The king's role includes leading rituals through ceremonial washing, sacrificing, and even providing an oracle (*CTU* 1.41; 1.87).[74]

Pardee concludes that the majority of the extant texts are prescriptive rituals (based on the imperfective or imperative verbal forms and typically chronological order) meant generally for one specific occurrence.[75] They are drawn from the background of an orally known tradition and are formulated for particular situations, a situation allowing for marginal differences in texts, even when dealing with the same ritual.

The ritual texts incorporate numerous sacrificial terms whose meaning can sometimes be determined by their particular usage.[76] The *dbḥ* sacrifice was the general term for sacrifice. However, placing 1.4.III 17–22 (Baal Cycle),[77] where a shameful feast is described, in conjunction with *CTU* 1.91, an administrative text giving the provisions for a royal

---

73   Dennis Pardee, *Ritual and Cult at Ugarit* (SBLWAW 10; Atlanta: SBL, 2002), 253.

74   David Toshio Tsumura, "Kings and Cults in Ancient Ugarit," in *Priests and Officials in the Ancient Near East: Papers of the Second Colloquium on the Ancient Near East — The City and its Life Held at the Middle Eastern Culture Center in Japan (Mitaka, Tokyo), March 22-24, 1996* (ed. K. Watanabe; Heidelberg: Winter, 1999), 216, notes "There are some forty texts concerned with religious rituals in Ugarit; nearly three quarters of them refer to the king and his involvement." Cf. Pardee, *Ritual and Cult at Ugarit,* 2.

75   Pardee, *Ritual and Cult at Ugarit,* 2, 25. Baruch Levine, "Ugaritic Descriptive Rituals," *JCS* 17 (1963): 105, instead suggests that the *yqtl* forms be read "as the usual narrative tense rather than the jussive or subjunctive," making them descriptive rather than prescriptive. In general, this distinction is not important for my argument. The texts read "prescriptively" but seem most likely to have been carried out as well.

76   David M. Clemens, "A Study of the Sacrificial Terminology at Ugarit: a Collection and Analysis of the Ugaritic and Akkadian Textual Data" (Vol. 1; Ph.D. diss., University of Chicago, 1999), 20–51, gives a fairly exhaustive list and studies the various technical terms.

77   See below, p. 177.

dbḥ, shows that the *dbḥ* sacrifice implies a banquet celebration.[78] This sacrifice is especially important for determining the banquet quality of the particular ritual discussed here.

The Ugaritic ritual text under discussion, *CTU* 1.40 (*RS* 1.002),[79] was rather important in Ugarit, which is striking because the king plays only a minor rule. Multiple copies were found in different parts of the city, including in the house of the high priest, the royal palace, and the House of the Divination Priest. This wide dispersal implies that the text did not belong to one particular group or school, and the large number of texts is "without parallel at Ugarit."[80]

CTU 1.40. 18–43[81]

Section IV:

(18)[and the well-]being of the foreigner [(in) the walls of Ugarit and the well-be]ing

(19)[   ] x and the well-[being] or if you si[n whether by the account of the Qaṭien]

---

78   *CTU* 1.91 includes wine rations. From this, Del Olmo Lete, *Canaanite Religion According to the Liturgical Texts of Ugarit* (trans. W. G. E. Watson; Bethesda, Md.: CDL, 1999), 263, concludes that these imply both ritual slaughter and a sacrifice which was "essentially a 'festival' that includes a sacred 'banquet.'" There are around twenty such texts which give some sense of what was consumed (in this text wine, according to *CTU* 1.106:18–28 cows and ewes, fresh stews, and other provisions). Paolo Merlo and Paolo Xella, "The Ugaritic Cultic Texts," in *Handbook of Ugaritic Studies* (ed. W. G. E. Watson and N. Wyatt; HO 39; Leiden: E. J. Brill, 1999), 292, note, "The so-called polyglot vocabulary of *Ug* 5 (137 iii 6) gives the equivalents EZEN = *i-si-nu* = *e[l]i* = *da-ab-ḫu*, from which can be deduced the clear meaning 'feast', 'soirée.'" Pardee, *Ritual and Cult at Ugarit*, 78, also accepts this conclusion on the nature of the *dbḥ* sacrifice. See also Adonijah's *zbḥ* for a coronation feast in 1 Kgs 1.

79   Further copies of this ritual are found in *CTU* 1.84; 1.121; 1.122; and 1.54. There is some variation in the texts, perhaps pointing to an underlying oral tradition.

80   Pardee, *Ritual and Cult at Ugarit*, 78. Johannes C. de Moor and Paul Sanders, "An Ugaritic Expiation Ritual and its Old Testament Parallels," *UF* 23: 283, boldly claim, "We know for certain that the people of Ugarit regarded it at one of their most important rituals."

81   The translation is my own. I concur with the estimation in *CTU* and all recent articles that this text originally consisted of six sections for a total of 43 lines. Of these 43 lines, the text becomes readable in line 18 (which is in section IV). The structure of the earlier lines can be reconstructed because of the repetitive nature of the text (for example, see ll. 36–43 and ll. 29–34 which repeat ll. 20–25), yet there is some disagreement about just how repetitive the text was, spawning discord over specific reconstructions. My translation and analysis generally follows Dennis Pardee, *Les Textes Rituels I* (vol. 12:1 of *Ras Shamra-Ougarit*; Paris: Editions Recherche sur les civilizations, 2000), 101–42; idem, *Ritual and Cult at Ugarit*, 77–83; and idem, "The Structure of RS 1.002." in *Semitic Studies in Honor of Wolf Leslau* (ed. A. S. Kaye; Wiesbaden: Harrassowitz, 1991), 2:1181–95.

(20) by the account of the DDM-ite, by the account [of the Hurrian, by] the account of the Hittite, by the account of [the Aluṭian, by the account of the] GBR,

(21) by the account of your migrant laborer, by the account of the [your opp]ressed, by the account of the Q[RZBL],

(22) or you sin through your anger, or through [your] impatience, [or through your xxx] (23) which you commit, or you sin in your sacrificial feast, or your ṭʿ offerings. ["Our sac]rificial feast [we cel]berate

(24) it. The ṭʿ offering, we offer it. The *nkt* offering we offer. May (they) be carried [to the father of the gods],

(25) carried to the circle of the sons of El, to the council of the sons of E[l, to ṮKMN W Š]NM: this is the ram."

Section V:

(26) Now, bring near the donkey of integrity—the integrity of the son of Ugarit and [the well-being of the foreigner in the walls of] Ugarit[82]

(27) and the well-being of YMʾAN, and the well being of ʿRMT, and the well-being [ ]

(28) and the well-being of Niqmaddu. Whether your beauty be altered by the account of the Qa[ṭien by the account of the DDM]-ite,

(29) by the account of the Hurrian, by the account of the Hittite, by the account of [the Aluṭian, by the [account of the GBR,] by the account of

(30) your migrant laborer, by the account of your op[pr]essed, by the account of the Q[RZBL], whether your beauty be altered

(31) or you sin through your anger, or through your im[pa]tience, or through your xxx which you committed,

(32) whether your beauty be altered regarding the sa[cr]ificial feast, or your ṭʿ offerings. "Our sacrificial feast [we cel]ebrate it. The ṭʿ offering, we offer it.

(33) The *nkt* offering we offer. May (they) be carried to the father of the gods, El, carried to the circle

(34) of the sons of El, to ṮKMN [W] ŠNM: this is the donkey."

Section VI:

(35) Now returning to the recitation of in[teg]rity: the integrity of the daughter of Ugarit and the well-being of the foreigner

---

82 I am reading ʾugr<ṯ>, given the parallelism with l. 36. The <ṯ> is missing from the tablet.

(36) in the walls of Ugarit and the [well-be]ing of the woman. Whether your beauty be altered by the account of the Qaṭien

(37) by the account of the DDM-ite, by the [account of the Hu]rrian, by the account of the Hittite, by the account of [the Aluṭian,

(38) by the [account of the GBR,] by the account of your mi[grant laborer], by the account of the your op[pr]essed, by the account of the Q[RZBL]

(39) whether your beauty be altered or you sin through yo[ur] anger, [or through] your [im]patience, or through your xxx

(40) which you committed, whether [your] beauty be altered [regarding the sacrificial feasts,] or the ṯ' offerings. "Our sacrificial feast

(41) we celebrate it. The ṯ' offering, we of[fer it. The *nkt* offering we offer. May (they) be c[arr]ied to the father of the gods, El,

(42) carried to the cir[cle of the sons of El, to] the council of the sons of El,

(43) to *ṮKMN* [*W ŠNM*]: this is the donkey."

The ritual text falls in the category of prescriptive sacrificial rituals,[83] and it has often been called an atonement or expiation ritual.[84] Yet while expiation certainly plays a role in the text as evidenced in the terms *ḥṭ'* and *šn yp* ("sin" and "changing of the beauty"), more space in the text is given to the various parties who fall under the category of *gēr*, suggesting that a goal of the text is societal unity.[85] While there are numerous disputed terms, scholars recognize an overarching structure containing six sections, alternating between ritual actions performed by the *bn ugrt* (sons of Ugarit) and *bt ugrt* (daughters of Ugarit).[86] Three separate sacrifices appear, the general feast (*dbḥ*; ll. 23, 32, 41) the uni-

---

83   Del Olmo Lete, *Canaanite Religion*, 144, places it in the category of "Non-sacrificial liturgies;" he then states, however, "This, therefore, is a 'sacrificial' ritual." His reasoning for placing it in this category is that it goes beyond merely a sacrificial ritual because it names the offerer, motives, and recipients of the ritual.

84   Ibid., 144; de Moor and Sanders, "An Ugaritic Expiation Ritual," 295.

85   Similar Pardee, *Ritual and Cult at Ugarit*, 78: "The three principal themes in order of appearance would thus have been communion between human classes as well as between humans and gods, expiation of sin, and 'rectitude' in human and divine relationships."

86   These should be understood as collectives. *CTU* actually suggests a scribal error in the writing of *bt*, which the editors write as *b<n>t* to show that the plural is to be understood. By reading *bt* as collective, this is unnecessary. See Josef Tropper, *Ugaritische Grammatik* (AOAT 273; Münster: Ugarit-Verlag, 2000), 53.121, 122, 13 under "Singular: Form und Funktionen," 288–89, for similar collective or exemplary usages of singular nouns. He does happen to list the use of *gr CTU* 1.40, showing that other singular nouns function this way in this particular text, therefore increasing the likelihood that this could be the case with *bt* as well.

dentified *ṯ'y* (ll. 24, 32, 41), and the *nkt* (ll. 24, 32, 41). Pardee relates the three separate offerings to three distinct movements in the ritual.

The first (*dbḥ*) focuses on unity between various social factions within Ugarit as well as the honored deities.[87] One of the key interpretive points in this text is the meaning of the various gentilics which appear as a group in every section and are introduced by *ulp*. As first suggested by Caquot, the literal meaning is "whether according to the mouth of X."[88] The nuance of this preposition in context arises from the status of the peoples referred to by the gentilics. Two proposals have been that either the people of Ugaritic have sinned by acting according to unacceptable foreign customs,[89] or they have sinned by mistreating these foreigners in their midst. The second answer is preferable as seen through consideration of the various types of people mentioned. While not all are known, the mention of the Hittite (*ḫty*, ll. 20, 29, 37) and especially the Hurrian (*ḫry*, ll. 20, 29, 37) show that these cannot be enemies or even peoples whose customs the "natives" of Ugarit despised.[90] Therefore the long, repeated list of various peoples, both those from surrounding cities and those without standing for other reasons[91] (including those who had little recourse to justice in the political structure

---

87   Pardee, *Ritual and Cult at Ugarit*, 78.

88   *'ū lě pī.* Compare to Hebrew *'ô* + *lěpî*, as in Gen 47:12 (*lě pî haṭṭop:* "According to the (number of) children or 1 Kgs 17:1 (*lěpî děbārî:* "by my word"). See also *KAI 11* (The tomb inscription of BTN 'M) which describes the adornment of the deceased *lpy* "according to" one related to the king. Cf. André Caquot, "Un sacrifice expiatoire à Ras Shamra," *RHPR* 43 (1962): 201–11, here, 208; also Del Olmo Lete, *Canaanite Religion*, 155–56; Pardee, "The Structure of RS 1.002," 1191; and de Moor and Sanders, 291–92.

89   So Del Olmo Lete, *Canaanite Religion*, 147–160, esp. 155, who translates "according to the custom of the X," similarly de Moor and Sanders, 284–87. Contrast with Pardee, *Les Textes Rituels I*, 112–14.

90   The Hittites were overlords of Ugarit, so their customs could be either revered or despised, but the Hurrian culture was in large part accepted in Ugarit. Numerous Hurrian rituals were found among more indigenous Canaanite/Syrian ones at Ugarit. This interpretation finds further support in the mention of the *npy gr ḥmy ugrt* (the well-being of the foreigner [within] the walls of Ugarit) in lines 35–36, also fragmentary in ll. 18, 26, for whom expiation is also mentioned, thereby bringing together the whole community residing in Ugarit, regardless of social standing.

91   These include the *mudāllilu* (Dp participle from "*dll*" meaning "oppressed") and the *ḫabbātu* (either the "robbed" or the "migrant laborer;" see *AHw* 303, *CAD* Ḫ:13–14).

of the city), might instead cry out to the deities,[92] thereby bringing sin upon and marring the "beauty" of the citizens and king of Ugarit.[93]

This analysis lays open intriguing similarities to the DC meals. Like Deut 16:9–15, a primary emphasis here is on the ritual participants, namely, that they include all classes, genders, and ethnicities present in the society.[94] There are of course significant differences between *CTU* 1.40 and the DC cultic meals. Most glaring is the lack of any expiation

---

92 Crying out to the deity for legal recourse suggests two interesting parallels in Deut 15:7–9 and 24:14–15. The correspondence to 15:7–9 is especially intriguing because it combines the ill treatment of the poor with "sin being reckoned to you" (*ḥēṭĕ*').

93 Line 28 mentions *nqmd* and presumably refers to "king Niqmaddu." There are several kings by this name in Ugarit, making it difficult to identify which king this text refers to (cf. Pardee, *Les Textes Rituels I*, 137–38). Ithamar Singer, "A Political History of Ugarit," in *Handbook of Ugaritic Studies* (ed. W. G. E. Watson and N. Wyatt; HO 39; Leiden: E. J. Brill, 1999), 603–733, concludes that there were two possibilities, Niqmaddu II and Niqmaddu III between 1390 and the fall of Ugarit (1190/85).

94 There is also a possible first common plural proclamation: "(As for) our cultic feast, we celebrate it. Our *ṭ'y* offering we *ṭ'y* it," (ll. 23–24 and parallels). This statement provides a further possible parallel, this time to Deut 26:13–15, where the bearer declares his or her innocence of various iniquities with regard to social injustices (giving the tithe to those without legal recourse) and non-Deuteronomistic worship practices. Pardee, *Les Textes Rituels I*, 125, notes that the first common plural only appears in one other instance in the Ugaritic ritual corpus (*CTU* 1.119, which is part of a prayer to Baal in hopes that the deity will protect the city from enemy siege; there is some question as to whether this prayer, which includes obvious ritual sacrificial elements, should be connected with the more straightforward prose ritual text that is on the other side of the tablet; cf. del Olmo Lete, *Canaanite Religion*, 292–306 for the status of this question). Pardee argues that *ndbḥ* is an N-stem; yet *dbḥ* ("sacrifice, celebrate a cultic feast") never occurs in the N-stem in the entire Northwest Semitic or Akkadian corpus, suggesting the likelihood of this form instead being a 1cp prefix conjugation. Both *ndbḥ* and *nty* are best understood as G *yaqtulu* and D *yuqattilu* respectively (*nadbiḥu* and *nuṭa'ʻiyu*), "Our sacrifice, we will sacrifice it," following Tropper, *Ugaritische Grammatik*, 669, also his article, "Ugaritic Grammar," in *Handbook of Ugaritic Studies* (ed. W. G. E. Wyatt and N.Wyatt; HO 39; Leiden: E. J. Brill, 1999), 105–110. This also is in keeping with the imperfective tone of the prescriptive ritual texts which Pardee himself highlights (see above, p. 148 n. 75). This possible 1st person highlights the involvement of the community, much like the 2nd person address in early Deuteronomy, beginning with the imperative *Shema!* Cf. Sanders, *The Invention of Hebrew*, 137: "In Mesopotamia, laws are declared by a king to a non-speaking third-person subject, 'a citizen.' In Exodus and Deuteronomy, precisely this kind of law is addressed by a prophet, speaking on behalf of God, to a collective 'you.' And it was fundamental to the entire enterprise that 'you' 'listen' and respond: at issue is something far beyond mere legal punishment. Only by accepting and enacting (typified in Hebrew as *šm'*, 'hearing/heeding') the biblical laws can the audience become who they are, the 'you' addressed as Israel … biblical law is founded in a dynamic identity that emerges through engagement with the text of the law itself. The deictic shift in person is one way biblical law rejects a foundation in royal sovereignty and founds itself instead through participation in discourse: the words of the law and their reception."

language in the DC (except *kpr* in 21:8, which is generally seen as a late text), which instead leads de Moor and Sanders to compare the Ugaritic text with the Priestly rituals and feasts.[95] In addition, this Ugaritic ritual text not only brings in aspects of "social" grievances, but also anger, impatience, and turpitude—internal sins avoided in the DC meal texts.[96] What the DC meal texts lack in language of expiation they make up for with language of human enjoyment. Implicit in the Ugarit *dbḥ*,[97] enjoyment is a primary emphases for Deut 14:22–29 and 16:9–15. In fact, the ritual meal itself only exists in the background in *CTU* 1.40 through this three-fold (extant) mention of the participants announcing their performance of the *dbḥ*. The emphasis placed on the sacrifice for consumption by all ritual participants in the 1cp utterance "We celebrate it," brings some focus to the meal that these participants would then consume.

The texts also exhibit a similar underlying thrust of the ritual meals. The DC meals aim at unity through the presence of multiple facets of Israelite society, and *CTU* 1.40 speaks not only of the need for good will between various parts of the society, but also (in sections V and VI) focuses on a ritual peace offering of a young donkey bringing about "moral integrity" (*mêšaru*).[98] This non-native ritual—extremely rare at Ugarit and nonexistent in ancient Israel[99]—appears to have come from

---

95   Especially Lev 23:19 and Num 28:22, 30; 29:16, etc. Cf. de Moor and Sanders, 295–96.

96   Though when considered together with Deut 15:7–9, then the DC does entertain the notion of interiority with regard to keeping the society cohesive.

97   This argument could be made on analogy from *CTU* 1.114 (El's Feast).

98   The reading of this word is especially controversial. In the past *mšr* has been understood as 1) a song (from the root *šr*); 2) a D imperative *muššurū* meaning "release!" (see *AHw*, 1485, followed by Johannes C. de Moor, "Ugaritic Lexicographical Notes I," *UF* 18 [1986]: 258–61); and 3) as "justice, justification, rectitude" (on analogy with Hebrew *mêšār*, Akkadian *mīšaru*; see del Olmo Lete, *Canaanite Religion*, 154–55 and Pardee, *Les Textes Rituelles I*, 133–36). The first option does not make contextual sense. The second assumes that the text is poetry because of the repetition in the text, but this does not fit the genre. The final option, "rectitude," or "moral integrity" as I have translated, goes well with the similar donkey sacrifice text from Mari, where the phrase *išariš dabādum* (*CAD* I–J:223 translates, "to come to an agreement") is found.

99   For the Ugaritic material Pardee, *Les Textes Rituelles II*, 1044–45, notes that the only appearances of the practice are here and in *CTU* 1.119, mentioned above, p. 153 n. 94 with regard to the first common plural. In Israel, Exod 13:13 (34:20) prescribes that a sheep or lamb redeem a firstborn donkey. It is possible that the donkey was eaten: while given as a worst case scenario, 2 Kgs 6:25 lists a donkey's head as selling for eighty shekels at a time of dire famine, and donkey bones at Iron IIA Tel Reḥov have been found with cut marks, showing slaughter, and possibly implying human consumption: see Marom et al, "Backbone of Society: Evidence for Social and Economic Status of the Iron Age Population of Tel Rehov, Beth She'an Valley, Israel," 70.

Amorite traditions found in an OB Mari text, whose goal was "to establish peace between two potentially bellicose groups."[100] Given the focus in *CTU* 1.40 on various "ethnic minorities"[101] and legally underprivileged groups at Ugarit, perhaps the donkey ritual functioned as a symbolic pact between these groups and the indigenous and empowered people of Ugarit in an attempt to assuage potentially volatile situations.

In summary, less attention is given to the actual performance of cultic rituals focusing on the meal in *CTU* 1.40 than in the Emar *zukru* and Deut 16. In those texts there is a large quantity of food and drink expressly mentioned (*zukru*) or implied (Deut 16:11, 14). The extant text of *CTU* 1.40 makes mention of one donkey and one sheep, and it has been suggested that one head of cattle would meet the demands of the reconstructed text.[102] These sacrifices would not serve the basis of communal consumption in the same way that the Emar and DC cultic texts imply, which means that the actual consumption itself is only in the background of the Ugaritic text. Nonetheless, the banquet is present in the background through the repeated mention of the shared feast (*dbḥ*; ll. 23, 24, 32, 40, 41).

The importance of *CTU* 1.40 for reading the DC meal texts lies in their shared focus on the goal of social cohesiveness and the unification of the whole divine and human communities in Ugarit in ritual texts concerning festive meals. These texts envision the diverse members of their communities coalescing around cultic meals, much like Robertson Smith and Victor Turner suggest. While there is a distinct possibility, given the many overlaps between the Ugaritic traditions and those in the Old Testament that this ritual text tradition might have somehow been carried down to late preexilic Judah, this is unlikely. Instead, *CTU* 1.40 demonstrates the *kinds of concerns* that could arise in such small patrimonial kingdoms caught between larger powers in the region of the Levant, sharing West Semitic languages.

---

100 Pardee, "The Structure of RS 1.002," 1193. See ARM 2.37:6–14 for the OB Mari text. Cf. discussion by Scurlock, "Animal Sacrifice in Ancient Mesopotamian Religion," 408 and Kuhrt, *The Ancient Near East*, 1:104. Recently, Sanders, *The Invention of Hebrew*, 71.
101 Just because a group was named does not mean that they all were underprivileged. The Hittite residents in Ugarit may even have been "above the law" of the Ugaritic society since they belonged to the culture of the overlords, but they were still outsiders according to this text.
102 Pardee, *Les Textes Rituels I*, 141.

4.3. Narrative Texts

While narratival texts are rarely called upon as prime comparative texts
for the pentateuchal law corpora, the following discussion will argue
that certain narratives and narratival texts provide compelling context
for understanding the DC meal texts. As with the turn to ritual texts
earlier, I presume that the common cultural conception of cultic meals
in the ancient Near East provides a plausible basis for comparing the
Enuma Elish and various Ugaritic narrative descriptions of cultic meals
with Deuteronomy. A further connection underlies my choice of these
texts, namely, their cultural proximity to late eighth–seventh century
Israel. For *Enuma Elish* one can point to the long and growing shadow
of the Neo-Assyrian Empire, which repeatedly darkened the Levantine
sky. Furthermore, the narratives found at Ugarit permeate the worldview of the biblical texts.

4.3.1. Akkadian *Akītu* and *Enuma Elish*

Much has been made in the past century of Old Testament scholarship
about the importance of *Enuma Elish* and its recitation at the Babylonian
akītu festival. I do not wish to return to interpretations that subsume the
various peculiarities of ancient Near Eastern cultures into a myth and
ritual pattern constructed from features of the Enthronement Psalms
and *Enuma Elish* or *akītu* references among other documents. Yet these
Mesopotamian documents (and cultural phenomena) remain important
for the interpretation of the Israelite feasts. However, past scholarship
does make some disclaimers necessary, especially with regard to the
manner in which the entire history of the *akītu* has been assumed for
the ritual at every stage. Pongratz-Leisten argues that the *akītu* festival
was not monolithic throughout Mesopotamia, being celebrated in various months and in various ways throughout its long history and wide
geographic practice.[103] While without a unified meaning or ritual for
the festival, it was often highly politicized.

---

103 Beate Pongratz-Leisten, "Neujahr(sfest). B" *RlA* 9: 294–98 provides brief orientation
   to the various practices of the *akītu* throughout the different eras and regions (her
   longer statement can be found in her *Ina Šulmi Īrub: Die kulttopographische und ideologische Programmatik der* akītu-*Prozession in Babylonien und Assyrien im 1. Jahrtausend v.
   Chrs.* [BF 16; Mainz: von Zabern, 1994]). Her description should be contrasted,
   however, with that of Andrew George, "Studies in Cultic Topography and
   Ideology" (Review of Beate Bongratz-Leisten, *Ina Šulmi Īrub: Die kulttopographische*

The Babylonian *akītu* and its counterpart in the city Assur[104]—
especially during the time of Sennacherib and following—are of primary importance for determining the significance of the festivals for
Deuteronomy.[105] While the *akītu* finds its origins in Sumerian literature,
Lambert, Pongratz-Leisten, and George argue persuasively that the
Babylonian and Assyrian *akītu* texts and artifacts in the seventh century, perhaps even as early as the ninth, do make identifiable allusions
to the story of the *Enuma Elish*.[106] This intertextuality parallels the use of
Israelite narratives as mythemes for the Passover and other yearly festival texts. Both the *Enuma Elish* myth and the *akītu* festival served to
reestablish the divine and human rulers, maintaining continuity with
the accepted social and divine orders.[107]

Similar to the Babylonian festival and myth, Sennacherib's adaptation of *Enuma Elish*, which sets Aššur as *paterfamilias* over the divine
family in place of Marduk as part of Sennacherib's glorification of

---

und ideologische Programmatik der akītu-*Prozession in Babylonien und Assyrien im 1.
Jahrtausend v. Chrs*), BibOr 53:3/4 (1996): 376: "In my view the ideology of P.-L.'s triumphal *akītu* is not so very different from that of Marduk's festival. Though other
business takes place during the course of the Babylonian New Year, notably the assembly of the gods, the principal point of the *akītu* festivals of Marduk (and Aššur) is
the defeat of the enemy and the triumphal return."

104 I use "Assur" to refer to the city and "Aššur" to refer to the deity.
105 My interpretation focuses on texts linked to this era, rather than using *akītu* texts
from vastly different epochs that cannot necessarily be used for reconstructing the
meaning of the ceremony from this period.
106 W. G. Lambert, "The Great Battle of the Mesopotamian Religious Year: The Conflict
in the Akītu House, A Summary," *Iraq* 25 (1963): 189–90; George, "Studies in Cultic
Topography and Ideology," 376; Pongratz-Leisten, *Ina Šulmi Īrub*, 74. She states, "Ein
Kultdrama im Sinne einer dramatischen Aufführung von *Enūma eliš* hat sicherlich
nicht stattgefunden. Andererseits lassen Textgattungen wie die Kultkommentare
erkennen, daß rituelle Handlungen mythische Ereignisse symbolisieren oder eine
mythische Ausdeutung erfahren können." [ET: A cultic drama such as a dramatic
performance of *Enūma eliš* certainly did not take place. However, text genres such as
the cultic commentaries allow for the recognition that ritual actions could either
symbolize or be given mythic meanings.]
107 Karel van der Toorn, "The Babylonian New Year Festival: New Insights From the
Cuneiform Texts and Their Bearing on Old Testament Study," in *Congress Volume
Leuven, 1989* (ed. J. A. Emerton; Leiden: E. J. Brill, 1991), 331–44, esp. 339, has ques-
tioned this connection, but his concerns are answered by Pongratz-Leisten, *Ina Šulmi
Īrub*, 75; and Benjamin R. Foster, *Before the Muses: an Anthology of Akkadian Literature*
(3d ed.; Bethesda, Md.: CDL Press, 2005), 436, who states: "This poem should not be
considered 'the' Mesopotamian creation story; rather, it is the individual work of a
poet who viewed Babylon as the center of the universe, and Marduk, god of Babylon, as head of the pantheon, This message was not lost on contemporary readers,
for, in some Assyrian versions of the poem, Assur was substituted for Marduk.
Therefore this poem can be read as a document of Babylonian nationalism."

Aššur,[108] provides an intriguing comparison to the DC because both respond to the powerful religious (as well as social and political) claims of foreign cults. In the Assyrian adaptation of the ritual and the corresponding text, Sennacherib claims to have refurbished the *akītu* house of the city Assur:

> Sennacherib, king of Assyria, maker of the images of Aššur and the great gods. I restored the *akītu* house of the steppe, whose cult had been forgotten since ancient times, at the command of the oracle of Shamash and Adad...[109]

He also remodeled the Aššur temple in order to accommodate the incorporation of the altered *Enuma Elish* and Babylonian style *akītu* festival. As one of the rituals that took place during this celebration, the deities would gather to determine destinies. Significantly, evidence for the determination of destinies (Akkadian *parak šīmāte*) which required a larger courtyard—directly related to the *Enuma Elish* II:155–62, where Marduk asks to be the ordainer of destinies in place of Anshar if he defeats Tiamat—first appears in the Aššur temple during Sennacherib's reign.[110] Thus the *akītu*, which according to Sennacherib's rhetoric had not been celebrated "since ancient times," seems also to have taken on a significantly different shape in the late eighth to early seventh centuries when Sennacherib remodeled the Aššur temple.[111] Sennacherib used

---

108 W. G. Lambert, "The Assyrian Recension of *Enūma Eliš*," in *Assyrien im Wandel der Zeiten: XXXIX Rencontre Assyriologique Internationale, Heidelberg 6.-10. Juli 1992* (eds. H. Waetzoldt and H. Hauptmann; Heidelberger Studien zum Alten Orient 6; Heidelberg: Heidelberger Orientverlag, 1997), 77, notes that only the Neo-Assyrian text from 700–612 contain this glorification of Aššur. The two texts, KAR 117–118 (of Tablet I) and K 3445+ (of Tablet V), replace "Bēl" and Marduk with Aššur and Babylon with Assur. Cf. Alasdair Livingstone, *Court Poetry and Literary Miscellanea* (SAA III; Helsinki: Helsinki University Press, 1989), 84–85 (texts 34, 35) for the related phenomenon in the ritual explanatory texts.

109 K 1356:1–3. Translated in Daniel David Luckenbill, *The Annals of Sennacherib* (Chicago: University of Chicago Press, 1924), 139–42.

110 Pongratz-Leisten, *Ina Šulmi Īrub*, 63; W. G. Lambert, "Myth and Ritual As Conceived by the Babylonians," *JSS* 13 (1968): 106.

111 This remodeling took place as part of Sennacherib's attempt to embrace and Assyrianize the older, more established Babylonian customs. While *akītu* festivals took place in various geographic locations throughout Mesopotamia and were not uniform, Sennacherib specifically adapts the Aššur temple to accommodate the Babylonian style celebration. Cf. Brigitte Menzel, *Assyrische Tempel* (vol 1; Rome: Biblical Institute Press, 1981), 55. Also, Galo W. Vera Chamaza, *Die Omnipotez Aššurs: Entwicklungen in der Aššur-Theologie unter den Sargoniden Sargon II., Sanherib und Asarhaddon* (AOAT 295; Münster: Ugarit-Verlag, 2002), 114, notes the close connections between and the Babylonian celebration of the *akītu* ritual and the timing of Sennacherib's remodeling of the *akītu* house, which follows the time of the Babylonian celebration: "Es ist sicher kein Zufall, daß Sanherib gerade im *Nisan* den

the *akītu* and its religious implications as a rhetorical means for promoting his kingship over Assyria and Assyria's burgeoning empire, especially Babylon. He did this by incorporating traditional Babylonian elements of the *akītu* celebration, which earlier were not part of the Assyrian *akītu* celebration. "Sennacherib mentions in his inscriptions regarding the building of the *akītu* house that the *akītu* festival had already been celebrated in Assur …; but one can surmise that the *akītu* festival had not earlier been bound with the same ritual actions and mythological implications exhibited in the Babylonian New Year's celebration, but that these were first transferred to Assyria by Sennacherib."[112]

Like the Assyrian rituals, the Israelite festivals—as they are portrayed in the Psalms—endeavor to consolidate the rule of the dynastic deity (Aššur or Yhwh) as well as the human king.[113] However, as they are constructed in the DC, the lack of emphasis on the king is striking. An intriguing question arises: Does the DC put a different human authority in place of the Assyrian king?

Both celebrations intend the re-articulation and reemphasis of an old order. However, in the case of the DC, this old accepted order was something—similar to the situation at Emar—parallel to but also perhaps apart from the monarchy.[114] In the case of Sennacherib's texts, the goal is to infuse an older ritual with a new mythological background to further royal projections of power both in Assyria proper and also to the empire's periphery. When celebrating the *akītu* in other cities, a

---

Grundstein des *akitu*-Tempels legte: dem Monat, in dem das Neujahrsfest stattfindet—ein Fest, das in den jährlichen Aššur-Feiern eine zentrale Rolle spielt, zumindest unter Sanherib." [ET: It is certainly not by chance that Sennacherib laid the cornerstone of the *akītu* temple in Nisan, the month when the New Year's festival took place, a festival that played a central role in the annual Aššur festival, at least under Sennacherib.]

112 Pongratz-Leisten, *Ina Šulmi Īrub*, 63 (translation my own). Vera Chamaza, *Omnipotenz Aššurs*, 115, notes a single reference to *akītu* prior to the time of Sennacherib: "Der einzige Beleg für die Existenz dieses Festes in Aššur—bereits in altassyrischer Zeit—liefert uns Šamši-addu I.: nach ihm feierte man das *akītu*-Fest am 16. Addar in der Stadt Aššur, wofür der König befahl, die Pferde (?) und die Maulesel von Mari nach Aššur zu bringen," (This reference is found in ARM 50.5–20). [ET: The only record of the existence of this festival in Assyria—already in the Old-Assyrian period—comes to us from Šamši-addu I: according to him one celebrated the *akītu* festival on the 16th of Addar in the city Assur, for which the king commanded that the horses (?) and the donkey from Mari be brought to Assur.]

113 Van der Toorn, "The Babylonian New Year Festival," 340.

114 The parallel nature of the Emar *zukru* to the monarchy is apparent in the divergent forms of the text: the earlier and shorter text never mentions a king, while the later and longer text mentions the royal contributions.

local deity accompanied the Assyrian king in order to highlight the king's authority (like Ishtar in Arbela). This points to the primary rhetorical goal of the Assyrian ritual, which was Assyrian political ascendancy rather than the particular religious connection with the god Aššur.[115] What can be gleaned from these observations for the interpretation of the DC cultic meals? The DC uses a similar methodology to the Assyrian royal scribes, who expressly link older rituals with known culture-founding narratives and placed a particular emphasis on ordinances dealing with feasts in these texts.

In the narrative of *Enuma Elish* itself, the celebratory meal sets the stage for the final scene. This placement makes the meal the setting for the denouement in which the details of Marduk's authority receive articulation. In the narrative the gods complete the Esagila temple (Marduk's earthly residence) as a tribute to Marduk's authority over them, and Marduk is enthroned upon the raised dais above them (l. 70). The display of Marduk's ascendancy is then emphasized by his banquet-throwing (VI:69–80):

> (69) The three hundred Igigi-gods of heaven and the six hundred of Apsu all convened.
>
> (70) The Lord, on the exalted Dais, which they built as his dwelling,
>
> (71) Seated the gods his fathers for a banquet,
>
> (72) "This is Babylon, your place of dwelling.
>
> (73) Take your pleasure there, seat yourselves in its delights!"
>
> (74) The great gods sat down,
>
> (75) They set out cups, they sat down at the feast.
>
> (76) After they had taken their enjoyment inside it,
>
> (77) And in awe-inspiring Esagila had conducted the offering,
>
> (78) All the orders and designs had been made permanent,
>
> (79) All the gods had divided the stations of heaven and netherworld,
>
> (80) The fifty gods took their thrones,
>
> The seven gods of destinies were confirmed forever for rendering judgment.[116]

As in Deut 16 and Ugaritic banquet texts, in *Enuma Elish* it is the empowered who throw banquets: Marduk, though a latecomer to the di-

---

115 Pongratz-Leisten, "Neujahr(sfest). B," 296.
116 Translation from Foster, *Before the Muses*, 472–73.

vine council, is in fact their ruler. He is able to call his fathers and seat them at the banquet (l. 71; AD.MEŠ-*šu qeretašu uštešīb*), an action by which Adonijah claims the kingship in 1 Kgs 1. The text then summarizes the feast itself in a matter of a couple of lines (ll. 74–76). The meal gives way to ordering the heavens and the world (ll. 78–80), followed finally by the very detailed and prolonged name-giving (VI:101–VII:135).

The determining of destinies is an important *topos* for divine authority throughout Mesopotamian literature. According to the Sumerian "Anzu Myth" Ninurta recovers the tablets of destinies from the Anzu bird and returns them to his father so that regular determination of the future (the destinies) may take place. Sennacherib, as mentioned above, enlarged the courtyard of the Aššur temple so this ritual event could take place there in accordance with the Babylonian *akītu* manner of celebration. The extensive name-granting ceremony accentuates the rhetorical goal of *Enuma Elish*, which is to proclaim Marduk as supreme deity by granting Marduk the names and thereby also the abilities of other deities. A related goal is to proclaim Babylon the ruling city because Marduk's residence was in Esagila, located in that city. In short, the cultic meal becomes the stage for and part of the act of proclaiming this central message of the text.

Turning from the literary text itself, Annette Zgoll attempts to relate the mythological events of the *Enuma Elish* directly to the proceedings of the *akītu* festival in Babylon.[117] The *akītu* festival in Babylon took place between Markuk's Esagila temple in the city and the *bit-akīti*, also called the house of prayer or festival house, located outside the city. During the festival deities and humans would travel from Esagila to the *akītu* house in procession and then back to the city three days later.

As has been long noted, the myth was read before the statue of Marduk in his temple on the fourth day of the *akītu* celebrations. This was a private ritual, however, leading some interpreters to conclude that it negates the public and political connection between the narrative and ritual.[118] Yet Esagila's iconography, architecture, and temple furni-

---

117 Zgoll, "Königslauf und Götterrat," 11–80. She uses a synchronic approach to the events and texts, which is subject to some difficulties: certainly one cannot assume that the *akītu* festival was always celebrated the same. This problem means that her conclusions, while enlightening as far as they go, must also be viewed with some caution.

118 E.g., Van der Toorn, "The Babylonian New Year Festival," 337.

ture reveal the importance of the chaos battle for the Marduk cult.[119] For example, Marduk's pedestal in Esagila was called "Tiamat." Furthermore, the installation where Marduk sat in the *akītu* house was also referred to as being "in the middle of *timti*" (a genitive form of "Tiamat").

Zgoll notes a number of parallel events between the narrative of *Enuma Elish* and the *akītu* ritual, including a stay in the *akītu* house from the eighth to the eleventh day of the festival to pray, celebrate, and bring Marduk gifts, parallel to the banquet celebrated in tablet VI:69–80. [120] With regard to the banquet, she concludes that the whole festival was shaped concentrically with the celebration in the *akītu* house in the middle.[121] If so, then one may conclude that while the divine banquet does not receive much direct attention in the myth, it is of primary importance for the ritual practice of the *akītu* ritual, at least at certain periods in its history. This seems particularly the case shortly after 700 B.C.E. when Sennacherib's annals refers to the *akītu* celebration as the "celebration of the banquet of the king of the gods, Aššur."[122]

The nature of the feast, as glorification of the high deity, works as a central ritual articulation of the king's claim to power. Zgoll argues (like Foster) that the underlying message of the myth is not really to explain the events of creation, but rather to celebrate the glorification of Marduk, so its modern title as creation myth should be augmented with "Epic of the Kingship of Marduk:" "… was henotheistische Tendenzen erkennen lässt."[123] Marduk's ascendency is explicit in the last line of the narrative: "Let them sound abroad the song of Marduk, How he defeated Tiamat and took kingship" (VII:161). This reading of the epic allows for its carryover into the political realm. The political aspects of the myth are further highlighted when considered together with the fact that the king or his official (wearing the royal garments)

---

119 Zgoll, "Königslauf und Götterrat," 54; George, "Studies in Cultic Topography and Ideology," 376, n. 32.
120 Zgoll, "Königslauf und Götterrat," 38, 57. She also notes (ibid., 38) that Sennacherib's emphasis on the banquet aspect shows the central role that cultic meals play in the very period when Deuteronomy is composed.
121 Ibid., 43.
122 Ibid., 38. For an English translation, see Luckenbill, *Annals of Sennacherib*, 143.
123 Zgoll, "Königslauf und Götterrat," 51 [ET: which allows henotheistic tendencies to be recognized]; Foster, *Before the Muses*, 436. Both elements are certainly present, but if meaning is an event that takes place *between* the text and audience, there is then room for multiple accentuations of meaning throughout the history of its centuries-long performance.

played the role Marduk/Aššur in the ritual celebration, thereby confirming the political authority and election of the king.[124]

The feast, as a central point of the ritual, serves as the rallying point for the religious, political, and social cohesion of the city and empire. For although the city, temple, and people are themes throughout the ritual, on the fifth day the king receives the formal declaration of responsibility for them all. As an action repeated annually, the king receives annual affirmation of his authority and dominion. The king also naturally plays the host to the celebration, emphasizing his role as head of the political household. This position as host echoes one of Marduk's fifty names in the *Enuma Elish* (VI:135): "'MARUTUKKA' shall be the trust of his land, city, and people."[125] In this way the *akītu* and *Enuma Elish* work to form a communal identity through a ritual that places the banquet at its center and the king at its head.[126]

As mentioned above, in the Assyrian version of *Enuma Elish*, the banquet plays a decisive role. Vera Chamaza notes that in Sennacherib's reform, the element received from the Babylonians that the Assyrian evidence seems to emphasize in comparison with the Babylonian material is the banquet.[127] The centrality of the banquet-sacrifice for the short-lived Assyrian version initiated by Sennacherib highlights the cultic meal as a central political and theological *topos* at the beginning of the seventh century. Vera Chamaza notes that Sennacherib provided dedication inscriptions for no other building with the care that he did

---

124 Zgoll, "Königslauf und Götterrat," 52, notes, "Im Fest wird u.a. gerade dieses Credo von Marduk als dem idealen und höchsten Herrscher gefeiert. Daran schließt sich die Bestätigung des irdischen Herrschers an, welcher in bestimmten Teilen des Festes die Rolle Marduks rituell übernimmt ..." [ET: In the festival, among other things it was this creed about Marduk as the ideal and most exalted ruler that was celebrated. The earthly ruler is also affirmed in this because he plays the part of Marduk in the festival.]

125 Translation from Foster, *Before the Muses*, 474.

126 Zgoll, "Königslauf und Götterrat," 67, comments, "Solcherart auf die gemeinsamen Feierns an sich stifteten unter der Bevölkerung Solidarität und das Gefühl einer »social cohesion«." [ET: In this way the nature of the shared feast grounds solidarity and a feeling of 'social cohesion' among the people.]

127 Vera Chamaza, *Omnipotenz Aššurs*, 120: "Die Ritualbeschreibung des babylonischen Neujahrsfestes kümmert sich nicht um die Opfermaterie im *bīt akīti*. Es gibt aber berechtigte Gründe anzunehmen, daß diese Feier dort von Opfergaben begleitet war. Im Gegensatz dazu findet man in Assur festgelegte Vorschriften für die Opfermahlzeit." [ET: The ritual description of the Babylonian New Year's festival is not concerned with the sacrificial material in the *bīt akīti*. There are, however, legitimate reasons for assumed that the celebration there was accompanied by the giving of sacrifices. On the contrary, in Assur fixed prescriptions are found for the sacrificial banquet.] Cf. ibid., 121 and 122 n. 933.

for the *akītu* house (where the celebration meal that took place), which emphasizes its importance for his reform.[128] This evidence provides a specific reason why the composers of the DC might themselves take up the cultic meal as an important cultic ritual in the formation of their text: the cultic meal was highlighted in the central ritual at the heart of the Neo-Assyrian Empire under Sennacherib.

A third avenue for comparison of the *akītu–Enuma Elish* complex and the DC is through the Assyrian mythological explanatory works, texts that use well-known mythic elements to elaborate the meanings of particular ritual acts. According to Livingstone, "It is certain that these mythological explanations do not represent the actual meaning of the ritual acts but put forward an interpretation on the parts of the ancient scholar or scholars responsible for them."[129] His analysis of various mythological explanatory works found in Nineveh and Assur[130] concludes that the rituals and myths that occur in these texts are not coterminous, perhaps like the Israelite festive rituals and their exodus-related motifs.[131] Livingstone explains that mythemes or entire myths were used to explain the meanings of rituals as follows:

> Myths were chosen from a limited range of stories the true meaning of which may have been relevant to the meaning and purpose of the rituals,

---

128 Ibid., 114.

129 Livingstone, *Court Poetry and Literary Miscellanea*, xxix.

130 Because these cities were destroyed when Assyria fell in the late seventh century, the texts have a relatively firm *terminus ad quem* as Alasdair Livingstone notes, *Mystical and Mythological Explanatory Works of Assyrian and Babylonian Scholars* (Oxford: Clarendon, 1986), 130. Yet I think it is important to consider them in connection to the Aššur theology of Sennacherib. For example, his annals omit the mention of Marduk as one of the deities responsible for victory. Furthermore, Vera Chamaza, *Die Omnipotez Aššurs*, 111, argues that no Neo-Assyrian king was as concerned with the Aššur cult as Sennacherib as seen in the temple building and renovations and altered theology of this deity. Vera Chamaza (ibid., 163) comes out in favor of a date from the time of Esarhaddon (681–669) for these mythological explanatory texts. Whatever the actual date, the connections to Sennacherib's glorification of Aššur at the expense of Marduk are striking, especially since Esarhaddon took a much more conciliatory approach to Babylon and the Babylonian Marduk priesthood than his father.

131 The voluminous literature attempting to explain the origins of the feasts in Israel can minimally be said to show that the origins of the feasts are difficult to pin down. Regardless of whether Passover was originally an apotropaic rite of shepherds, or Unleavened Bread began as an agricultural rite, or Booths as a festival related primarily to harvest or the booths of the Ugaritic *CTU* 1.41, Livingstone's work allows for the important insight that rituals and narratives can be wedded together and reinterpreted by one another. This insight refocuses the question to instead focus on which connections the DC is making, rather than attempting to find the meaning of the feasts in their original theoretical purpose (if this was ever unitary).

as understood by the composers. The works therefore have meaning on two distinct levels. On one level individual ritual procedures are explained in detail by myths, and on another level certain types of rituals are explained by a certain type of myth.[132]

There are a few specific elements of the *Enuma Elish* alluded to in these works, for example, the defeat of Tiamat, usually by Marduk, appears at several points in these texts.[133] One text (K 3476) explains the meaning of a (wine?) vat opening ritual as follows: "The king, who opens the vat in the race, is Marduk, who [defeat]ed Tiamat with his penis."[134] Though the actual ritual procedure is both unclear and highly sexualized, one may conclude that the king's action is explained as his assumption of Marduk's role in these ritual acts. In his actions he (the king as Marduk) subdues Tiamat, thereby reaffirming both Marduk's authority and the king's. The connection to *Enuma Elish* is explicit, since it is in the mythic narrative that Marduk defeats Tiamat, though minus the overt sexual connotation.[135]

The destruction of Qingu, commander of Tiamat's army, is also mentioned: "They throw a sheep on the oven and roast it in the fire: It is Qingu when he burns him in the fire."[136] This explanation of a particular ritual act—roasting a sheep—is provided by reference to a narrative event, thereby connecting the ritual with the myth. This appropriation of the myth may also point to the conclusion that the *Enuma Elish* was available to a wider audience for use in explaining reality on various levels.

In addition to mythological explanatory texts employing allusions to *Enuma Elish* there are two versions of the so-called "Marduk Ordeal"[137] that specify Aššur's domination of the family of the gods in contrast to the "accepted" Babylonian version with Marduk at the pin-

---

132 Livingstone, *Mystical and Mythological Explanatory Works*, 115.
133 KAR 0143+; KAR 6333+; K 3476; KAR 307. Translations are from Alasdair Livingstone, *Court Poetry and Literary Miscellanea*, 82–91, 92–95, 99–102 (texts 34, 35, 37, 39).
134 K 3476:18, translated in ibid., 94. Cf. VAT 8917:r.1–3; translated in ibid., 101 as follows: "ʳ.1[The…]… of *muṣu* stone on the horn is Tiamat. Bel defeated [her]. He [sm]ote her, established her destiny and split her into two parts like the fish of the drying place. ³The Tigris is her right eye. The Euphrates is her left eye." Whether this text interprets ritual action or rather geographic features is unclear.
135 The explanation of the king's actions with the *Babylonian* version of the *Enuma Elish* shows that Sennacherib's attempt to replace Marduk with Aššur was unsuccessful—at least in the case of this text—since Marduk, not Aššur, plays the role of hero in the reference to *Enuma Elish*.
136 Ibid., 93, line 11. Cf. ibid., 99: text 39, rev. ll. 17–19.
137 KAR 143+ and KAR 6333+, collated and translated in ibid., 82–91: texts 34 and 35. These are two versions of the ritual, one found in Assur and the other in Nineveh.

nacle. These Assyrian texts identify Aššur as the high god who controls Marduk's destiny. This hierarchy is a specific reversal of the destiny determining position allotted to Marduk in the Babylonian *Enuma Elish*. These two texts do not simply insert Aššur into the narrative, but instead, "… the work interprets Babylonian cult in such a way as to accord with Assyrian ideas."[138]

Marduk (here called Bel) is described as a raving madman who gets thrown into prison. Marduk's alleged crime is not acting like Ninurta did after vanquishing Anzu (according to the "Anzu Myth").[139] Marduk should have brought the Tablets of Destiny to Aššur, but instead Marduk proclaimed that he himself should control the destinies (as is the case in the Babylonian version of *Enuma Elish*).[140] Marduk defends himself saying, "I only did what was good to Aššur! What is my crime?"[141]

The particular references to the myth in these "Ordeal of Marduk" texts display a rhetorical strategy that employs foundational narratives in order to argue for Aššur's ascension to divine kingship.[142] Furthermore, these Assyrian references reveal how certain scribes drew on a stock group of mythological texts in order to explain the specific practices of rituals. This ancient methodology is intriguing for comparison to the DC because of the similar textual practice at work in both. They stem from the same time period, and both texts incorporate known founding narratives to explain ritual practices. Regardless of whether the Akkadian rituals and myths were created with one another in mind,[143] scribes in this period came to associate them with one another, bringing together specific ritual practices with ritual explanations (or theories).

The extant cultic commentaries and other mythological explanatory texts never allude to the temple dedication banquet from *Enuma Elish*. This fact certainly limits its use for understanding the DC cultic meals. However, the incorporation of other scenes from *Enuma Elish* provides

---

138 Livingstone, *Mystical and Mythological Explanatory Works*, 232.
139 See Foster, *Before the Muses*, 555–78 for an English translation. In this myth Ninurta returns the Tablets of Destiny to his father.
140 Livingstone, *Court Poetry and Literary Miscellanea*, 85 (text 34:54–58).
141 Ibid., 84 (line 35).
142 In a similar way, one can argue that (especially Deuteronomistic) Deuteronomy employs references to Egypt and the exodus to affirm Yhwh's supreme power and authority.
143 Most scholars do not see them as initially related, but instead argue that this connection is made later. For this point, see Pongratz-Leisten, *Ina Šulmi Īrub*, 74; Livingstone, *Mystical and Mythological Explanatory Works*, 166.

suggestive ways that the banquet scene could have been called upon. Therefore, what this section does give is an ancient Near Eastern analogue to the way in which narratives were productive for explaining the meanings of ritual practices—precisely what is at work in Deut 16:1b, 3b, 12. [144]

The connections between foundational myths explaining the dominion of a certain deity in relation to a particular human ruler in the early seventh century shows the socio-political and religious climate into which the DC was received. Such mythic and ritual bonds between divine and human monarchs suggest similar categories to which the DC responds, also through cultic meals. While Sennacherib's description of the *akītu* house as a banquet house combines divine and royal banqueting and their attending claims for authority, the DC conspicuously omits the royal link.

4.3.2. Ugaritic Narratives

In this section I will draw comparisons with various meal texts from the Ugaritic narratival corpus. Analysis of the texts will show how the Ugaritic formulations of divine and human banquets characterized in these narratival texts provide a potent background for understanding the DC cultic meals. The importance of the Ugaritic narrative material for the interpretation of OT texts is generally well established, so I will commence by providing analysis of the particular texts and by highlighting the specific points of comparison with the DC meal texts.[145]

---

144 This analogue establishes an important point, namely, that it is not of necessary importance to trace the origins of the festivals in order to determine their meaning in Deuteronomy. Rituals and ritual practice (or rituals in texts, in this case) do not maintain the same meaning as though the meaning of the ritual were somehow indelibly inscribed into its practice or its textual description. Different practitioners or observers can attribute variable meanings, just as happens in the various pentateuchal accounts of the festivals. I highlight this point in order to note the difference in my approach to Deut 16:1–17 from attempts to explain the festivals in terms of their origin and long-term development (i.e., Rolf Rendtorff, "Die Entwicklung des altisraelitischen Festkalenders," in *Das Fest und das Heilige: religiöse Kontrapunkte zur Alltagswelt* [ed. J. Assman and T. Sundermeier; Gütersloh: Gütersloher Verlaghaus, 1991], 185–204).
145 Though the general acceptance of the importance of Ugaritic texts does not answer the question of the temporal distance between the two, nor the question of the Ugaritic texts' relationship with the "Canaanites" of the biblical texts and of reality. Keel, *Die Geschichte Jerusalems und die Entstehung des Monotheismus*, 1:112, argues, for example that the cult of the sun god from Egypt was far more important in Jerusalem than in Ugarit, pointing to one of the many differences between the two situations.

While the ritual texts discussed above[146] give some details about similar cultic festive formulations across Syro-Palestine, they do not provide detailed information about how an ancient audience may have conceptualized such a ritual feast. The narratival texts presented in this section reveal more explicit hints.

David Wright offers a useful framework for the use of narrative texts for interpreting rituals. One the one hand, he critiques the approach found in de Moor and Loretz that explicitly links the Ugaritic narratives to calendar-based ritual practices.[147] Rather than assuming a direct link between myth and ritual, Wright notes that the narratives use the language and motifs of ritual for their own purposes.[148] Yet, in Wright's opinion, the ritual motifs in the narratives of Aqhat, the Baal Cycle, and Kirta can still be helpful: "the fact that rituals appear in contexts that elucidate them and that describe them clearly enough to contribute to the sense of the story means that these narrative examples can aid in assessing the nature and significance of ritual in Ugarit and the larger ancient Near East.[149] Wright focuses on the nature of the rituals within the narrative texts, rather than speculating on their relationship to rituals external to the texts.[150] However, further insight into ritual practice can be garnered because these texts do have a relationship with real human experience.[151] Wright's hesitation is a necessary

---

He does note later (ibid., 189–90) that a link between the northern Syro-Hittite culture may be seen in name of Jerusalem's Amarna period ruler, Abdi-Cheba, and such remnants as 'Uriah the Hittite.'"

146 See above, 4.2. Ritual Texts.

147 David P. Wright, *Ritual in Narrative: the Dynamics of Feasting, Mourning, and Retaliation Rites in the Ugaritic Tale of Aqhat* (Winona Lake, Ind.: Eisenbrauns, 2001), 4. Cf. Johannes de Moor, *Seasonal Pattern of the Ugaritic Myth of Ba'lu According to the Version of Ilimilku* (AOAT 16; Kevelaer: Butzon & Bercker, 1971), 56; and Oswald Loretz, "Das Neujahrsfest im syrisch-palaestinischen Regengebiet: Der Beitrag der Ugarit- und Emar-Texte zum Verständnis biblischer Neujahrstradition," in *Festtraditionen in Israel und im Alten Orient* (ed. E. Blum and R. Lux; VWGT 28; Gütersloh: Gütersloher Verlagshaus, 2006), 81–110.

148 Wright, *Ritual in Narrative*, 4.

149 Ibid. He notes (ibid., 5) that since ritual motifs occur in Aqhat, the Baal Cycle, and Kirta, as well as *Enuma Elish* that this does "justify explorations in these direction. But these interpretations [such as those offered by de Moor and Loretz] may also be disputed because of the questionable supposition that myth is necessarily connected with ritual and, more particularly, because of the hypothetical and even arbitrary character of many of the observations and conclusions."

150 Ibid., 6.

151 Ibid., 228: "Interpretation of the rituals embedded in narrative allows us to estimate the way a particular society viewed the effect and purpose of their ritual practices. Narrative thus provides indirect access to the manifest native interpretation of ritual." Belnap, Fillets of Fatling and Goblets of Gold, 66–67, echoes Wright: "The ritual

caution, but exploration of the connection between ritual action (and texts) and narrative texts can produce more results.

4.3.2.1. The Rephaim texts (*CTU* 1.20–22)

The Rephaim texts provide some hints about an Ugaritic conception of ritual banquets.[152] Wright notes that some Ugaritic narratives (such as Aqhat and Kirta) contain so many references to ritual because they deal with interaction of the divine and human realms, which, at least in Ugarit, happened primarily in ritual.[153]

The portrayals of ritual in the Rephaim texts repeat certain features that are also echoed in the Kirta and Aqhat narratives.[154] The first of these elements is the occurrence of a seven-day sequence:[155]

One day passed, and a second. The Rephaim eat, they drink.

A third, a fourth day, a fifth, a sixth day the Rephaim eat, they drink (in) the eating house on the summit in the heart of Lebanon.

Then, on the seventh [day] Mighty Baal [...] (*CTU* 1.22.I.22–26) [156]

---

actions performed by the deities do not emerge from a vacuum, even if they are literary creations. Therefore the ritual acts, as described in the texts, even if they are imaginary ritual acts, provide the hearer with insight into the creation and use of myths within the larger Ugaritic society."

152 For a succinct summary of the argument against the Rephaim texts being the fourth tablet of the Aqhat narrative see Wayne T. Pitard, "The *RPUM* Texts," in *Handbook of Ugaritic Studies* (ed. W. G. E. Watson and N. Wyatt; HO 39; Leiden: E. J. Brill, 1999), 263.

153 Wright, *Ritual in Narrative*, 229.

154 Wayne T. Pitard, "A New Edition of the 'Rāpi'uma' Texts," *BASOR* 285 (1992): 73, notes: "It is important to remember that the texts are fragments of two or three different tablets written by two scribes, and that the relationship among the three fragments remains unclear. Also, on these three fragments are parts of 95 lines, of which only 22 are completely preserved, some 24 others a bit more than half preserved, and the rest less than half preserved." This conclusion suggests that the tablets should not be read as a consecutive narrative (especially across the tablet transition from 1.20 to 1.21–22, according to ibid., 41).

155 The period of seven days parallels the frequent sevens in Deut 16—the seven days of Unleavened Bread, counting of seven weeks until Shabu'ot, and finally the seven days of Sukkot. While this framework certainly extends beyond ritual meals (even within the DC itself where the seven year cycle appears in Deut 15), the seven-day period *does* remain significant for cultic meals. Note that both the seven-day and septennial periods are important in the Emar *zukru* as well.

156 The text breaks off at this point. As is often the case, the divine banquet takes place on the mountaintop (cf. Sinai and Zion in the OT as well as the Baal Cycle 1.4.VI.38–

A second repeated element in these texts is the notion that the deities come from afar (the Rephaim travel for three days on horses and chariots in 1.22.II.20–26 to get to the banquet or sacrifices). Furthermore the Rephaim text also sets the general term for sacrificial feast (*dbḥ*) parallel to *mrzḥ*. This parallel explicitly connects the general sacrifices provided by the humans with the notion of divine and human banqueting. A further crucial note is that Dan'el (from Aqhat) , as the human person in a position of power, plays the role of host and is responsible for providing adequate meals for the guests.

Lewis notes that there is no certainty about the genre of the Rephaim text.[157] Regardless of this difficulty, the combination of *dbḥ*, *hkl* ("temple," "palace"), and *aṯr* ("sanctuary") does imply some type of narratively-couched description of a cultic feast. The mention of the threshing places and plantations (1.20.II.6–7) certainly suggests an earthly locus of action distant from urban sanctuaries; however, the combination of these agrarian locations with the "palace/temple" and "sanctuary" language points to a cultic background for the banquet.[158] Regardless of whether this is a small village shrine or some sort of makeshift harvest sanctuary, there is a stable connection in this text to the cultic meal setting, providing a basis for comparison with the DC meals.

Given the above similarities in banquet location (a sanctuary), a journey or pilgrimage to the feast, and the seven-day duration in the cultic banquets of the Rephaim text and the DC cultic meals, what insights from *CTU* 1.20–22 meals might be garnered for the DC meals? First, the Rephaim texts bear many similarities to Lichtenstein's observations of the general ancient Near Eastern banquet motif: beginning with preparation of the meal (first meat and then wine), followed by the invitation, and finally the consumption (again first meat and then wine).[159] Second, the meal in the Rephaim text offers a rich array of

---

59 treated below). This meal bears similarities with those in Aqhat: *CTU* 1.17.I.5–16, 1.17.II.32–39.

157 Theodore J. Lewis, "The Rapiuma," in *UNP*, 197.

158 The agrarian location provides an intriguing connection with 2 Sam 6:10–13, where the Ark resides at Obed-Edom's threshing floor. Cf. the agricultural connection in Isa 9:2 as well.

159 In this text, however, the invitation and travel take place before the hunt and preparation of food. Lichtenstein, "The Banquet Motifs in Keret and in Proverbs 9," 19–31, notes that the preparation of the meal usually precedes the invitation. Cf. J. B. Lloyd, "The Banquet Theme in Ugaritic Narrative," *UF* 22 (1990): 170. Lloyd (ibid., 173), notes the differences between a meal (1.3.IV.40–46 where Baal provides a meal for Anat and 1.16.VI.17–21, where Ḥurray feeds Kirta) and a full-fledged banquet. The

food and drink. The divine feast emphasizes the various types of meat and wine available (*CTU* 1.22.I.12–20):

(12) They slaughtered cattle, also sheep.

They brought low bulls (13) and fatling rams

Yearling calves, (14) lambs and a handful[160] of kids.

Like silver (15) for travelers is the olive (oil),

Like gold for travelers is KŠ.[161]

(16) DPR[162] a table with fruit, with royal fruit.

(17) Look! Daylong they pour wine ṬMK,[163]

(18) the must of rulers. Wine BLD.(19) ĠLL.[164]

Gladdening[165] wine (from) a necklace of vines[166] of (20) Lebanon,

pleasant must that El has tilled."

The multiple types of meat—cattle and sheep, young and old—highlight the luxurious nature of the feast. The various wines, while

---

complete banquet is also seen in Aqhat with Dan'el's feast for the Kotharāt (*CTU* 1.17.II.32–38), Dan'el's feast for Kothar-wa-Hasis (*CTU* 1.17.V.15–25) , and in the Baal Cycle (*CTU* 1.3.I.2–22 and 1.4.VI.38–59).

160 I read *qmṣ* ("a handful") as a cognate of BH *qōmeṣ*, "closed hand, fist" (BDB, 888; *HALOT*, 1109; *DUL*, 704 reads "heap, pile") like Lev 2:2; 5:12; especially important is *liqmāṣîm* in Gen 41:47 referring to the abundance produced during the seven years of plenty under Joseph. Lewis, "The Rapiuma," 204, translates "They butchered lambs and even kids," either omitting a translation of *qmṣ* or viewing it as a verb form (his "butchered") perhaps from *DUL*, 703: / *q-m-ṣ*/ "to curl up, to bend."

161 Possibly "cooking fat," with BH *kśh* (BDB, 505). In Deut 32:15 ("you became fat, you grew thick") *kāśîhā* appears parallel to *šāmantā 'ābîtā*. Arabic *kśy* means "grow fat."

162 Marvin H. Pope, "Notes on the Rephaim Texts from Ugarit," in *Probative Pontificating in Ugaritic and Biblical Literature: Collected Essays* (ed. M. S. Smith; UBL 10; Münster: Ugarit-Verlag, 1994; repr. from *JCS* 20 [1966] 95–118), 209, suggests "redolent" from an Arabic cognate *dafira* as a possible construal (cf. *DUL*, 277).

163 Wilfred G. E. Watson, "Wonderful Wine (KTU 1.22 I 17–20)," *UF* 31 (1999): 779, argues that *ṭmk* should be construed as a "vessel" based on Akk. *šumkalaṯu*, rather than a place name. Watson's article also provides a survey of various renditions of the difficult lines 17–20.

164 Lewis' ("The Rapiuma," 204) translation of BLD and ĠLL as "sweet and abundant," appears quite tenuous.

165 I am understanding Ugaritic *'išryt* here as cognate to the Hebrew *'ašēr* (happy), which makes sense in this context. See Watson, "Wonderful Wine," 781; *DUL*, 118.

166 This translation follows that found in Watson, "Wonderful Wine," 780–81, taking *'nq* as a necklace (cf. Song 4:9, Judg 8:26, and Prov 1:9), and *smd* as "vines," derived from Akk. *asmidu* "eine Gartenpflanze" (*AHw*, 75). While tenuous, this reading allows for a parallel with the following line set in the vineyards tilled by El.

difficult to interpret, emphasize this opulence. Expensive oil (perhaps used as perfumes), cooking oils, and some fruit also appear. Since fruit is not always included in banquets, it is possible that it is present here because the occasion is a harvest festival. In any case, the food and drink is supplied to the deities in order to provide for ample enjoyment and satisfaction for a full seven-day party. The fact that it was sufficient might be extrapolated from the final intelligible lines in which Baal, on the seventh day, is about to take action in response to the felicity of the feast.[167]

4.3.2.2. El's Feast (*CTU* 1.114)

While some of the details of this text remain unclear,[168] this text's basic plot consists of El throwing a banquet in which he and other deities eat and drink to satisfaction and drunkenness (ll. 1–4, 14–16). The deities Yariḫu (the cook?), Anat, and Attart have some sort of interaction about a particular cut of meat, for which the gatekeeper rebukes El (ll. 4–14).[169] When El later attempts to return home, supported by a certain ṬKMN-W-ŠMN, he is confronted by ḤBY, another divine being (ll. 17–20). El then passes out in his own excrement (ll. 20–22). Finally, Anat and Attart cure El of his drunken state with a special concoction (ll. 26–28). So the narration of the feast displays the hangover remedy's power: it even helps the father of the gods recover!

This short text enhances the conception of cultic meals in the above discussion by showing the general pattern of preparation, invitation, and consumption (ll. 1–4):

> El sacrifices game in his house,
> wild meat in the midst of his palace.

---

167 This hypothesis finds support in Baal's response to Dan'el's hospitality in *CTU* 1.17.I.6–16: at the end of a seven-day banquet Baal comes in a show of compassion towards Dan'el and answers his request for an heir.

168 See Theodore J. Lewis, "El's Divine Feast," in *UNP*, 193–96; Marvin H. Pope, "A Divine Banquet at Ugarit," in *Probative Pontificating in Ugaritic and Biblical Literature: Collected Essays* (ed. M. S. Smith; UBL 10; Münster: Ugarit-Verlag, 1994), 153–80; repr. from *The Use of the Old Testament in the New and Other Essays: Studies in Honor of William F. Stinespring* (ed. J. M. Efird; Durham, N.C.: Duke, 1972), 170–203; and Dennis Pardee, "El on a Toot," *COS* 1.97:302–305 for detailed analysis.

169 Pardee's theory of two separate banquets in different places seems unnecessary. He seeing a progression from El's house to a banquet hall *(marziḫu)* in l. 15 (*COS* 1.97:304), but the movement implied in his translation in ll. 14–16 is not present in the text. It seems easier to instead place all the feasting in one place with El returning to his own quarters in ll. 17–18.

He invites the gods to the cutlets,
Then the gods will eat and drink—

Wine until satisfied,
new wine until drunk.

Philologically speaking, the verb *dbḥ* is used to describe El's preparation of game in his palace/temple (ll. 1–2) , which accords with the conception of sacrifices as cultic meals. The notion of eating and drinking
to satisfaction also finds a reflex in Deut 14:26 and the mention of "all
your desires" in Deut 12:15, 20, 21 (cf. 1 Kgs 11:37). The extravagant
consumption in the Ugaritic texts adds emphasis to the similar understanding in the biblical material, though the genres and themes of the
texts are vastly different.[170]

Also important is that the high deity hosts the party. His authority
is certainly contested and mocked in various ways in this text, but El is
nevertheless the primary mover who invites and prepares the meal,
who receives help to get home, and for whom the remedy is prepared.
Similarly, the DC meal texts are addressed to the heads of household.
They are responsible for providing an adequate spread for their households and for "special insiders" (the Levite, widow, and others) when
at the pilgrim festivals.

4.3.2.4. Baal Cycle

I have held discussion of the Baal Cycle banquets until last in order to
show that there is a broad notion of cultic meals in place even without
this particular text. This move should prevent the Baal Cycle (like the
Enuma Elish in the previous section) from becoming too dominant as a
contextual background for understanding the ancient Israelite feasts as
presented in the DC. This step counteracts an over-identification of the
DC cultic meal with the "fertility rite" interpretation of the Baal Cycle
or the "Enthronement Ritual" interpretation of the fall feast.[171] Given
the joyous nature of the DC presentation of Weeks, Booths, and Tithes,

---

170 *CTU* 1.114 is labeled a "burlesque" by Theodor H. Gaster, *Thespis: Ritual Myth, and
Drama in the Ancient Near East* (rev. ed.; Garden City: Doubleday, 1961). Given the
recipe for a headache cure at the end, perhaps an etiological explanation might be
more appropriate.

171 As seen in Johannes C. de Moor, *New Year With Canaanites and Israelites* (Vol. 1–2;
Kampen: Kok, 1972), 1:29; idem, *Seasonal Pattern of the Ugaritic Myth of Ba'lu*, 59, 155.

some checks are necessary to prevent a return to such readings.[172] The Baal Cycle, following Smith's understanding, cannot be reduced thematically to a ritual myth related to fertility rites at the autumnal New Year.[173] The narrative also does not present itself as a cosmogonic myth since there is little focus on the cosmos or its creation, but rather on relationships between the deities themselves. While fertility is certainly a key theme in the various laments over Baal's death in tablets V–VI, citing this as the main theme misses wide swaths of the text. Finally, the assumption that the narrative was part of an annual ritual festival is based on an argument from silence.[174]

Two banquet scenes from the Baal Cycle are of particular importance for my analysis—1.3.I.2–27, which may be the celebration of Baal's defeat of Yamm and the celebration of the completion of Baal's palace (1.4.VI.38–59).[175] The context of the former is quite uncertain in

---

172 The main pitfall I have in mind here is the conflation of various rituals and myths into one overarching cultic drama, whether it be an underlying pattern across the Levant, or pressing them all into an enthronement New Year's festival. For a short synopsis of the critique, see Hans-Joachim Kraus, *Worship in Israel: a Cultic History of the Old Testament* (trans. G. Buswell; Richmond: John Knox, 1966), 9–19.

173 Mark S. Smith, "Interpreting the Baal Cycle," *UF* 18 (1986): 313–39. Belnap, "Filets of Fatling and Goblets of Gold," 110, argues, "It appears that one of the overall purposes of the Baal Myth was to explain the order that existed within the pantheon and thus of Ugaritic society." He continues (ibid., 113), "… it is possible that it was used to present a Ugaritic national view, the fashion in which Ugaritians viewed themselves, maintainers of the political order, not through might, but by emphasizing the unique nature of the political neighbors." Sanders, *The Invention of Hebrew*, 51 (cf. 50–53), comments that in line with West Semitic tribal governing, "Sovereignty in the first alphabetic epic is negotiated in speech as much as it is won in battle."

174 I am not opposed to some connection here, but basing conclusions on the necessary connection between the myth of the Baal Cycle and a particular ritual seems questionable. The difficulty with this identification is that it is based on the arrangement of the tablets—1.3–1.1–1.2–1.4–1.5–1.6 to follow the Syrian climate and its agricultural year (see de Moor, *Seasonal Pattern of the Ugaritic Myth of Ba'lu*, 42). This makes the whole myth into one cycle rather than a double cycle. The main problem with this sequence is that it does not adequately account for the two primary battles (with Yamm and Mot). I find it more convincing to follow the traditional order, which also happens to parallel the two-battle structure of *Enuma Elish*.

175 There are other banquets, such as the victory banquet thrown by Anat (1.3.II.36–37), but the details are not as pertinent to discussion of the DC since Anat washes in blood, arranges tables and chairs, and draws water. Baal and Anat's feast for Athirat in 1.4.III.33–44 is rather broken, but does seem to display the general formulation of banquets: eating, then drinking. In 1.3.III–IV Baal invites Anat, who then travels to him for a feast. This text contains the progression of invitation–travel–feasting on meat (discussed above, p. 170). In 1.4.IV.33–38 El offers Athirat a meal after her journey, but the individual nature of this meal and different structure (lack of invitation and preparations) put it in a different category of meal than the dedication and victory banquets.

that it occurs at the beginning of a new tablet and much text is missing at the end because of the broken nature of the tablet.[176] The text of the first celebration includes the following description of a feast:

> He served Might[iest] Baal,
>
> Waited on the Prince, Lord of the Earth
>
> He stood, arranged and offered him food,
>
> Sliced a breast before him,
>
> With a salted knife, a cut of fatling.
>
> He stood, served and offered him drink,
>
> Put a cup in his hand,
>
> A goblet in both his hands:
>
> A large, imposing vessel,
>
> A rhyton for mighty men …
>
> A thousand jars he drew of the wine,
>
> A myriad he mixed in his mixture. (ll. 2–13; 15–17)[177]

Smith and Pitard assume that this banquet is the victory celebration of Baal's defeat of Yamm, and that it is different from the typical banquet scene because of its solitary nature.[178] The absence of the divine council emphasizes Baal's outsider role and the fact that he has yet to be accepted as ruler of the gods. In spite of its atypical nature and broken context, the text of 1.3.I.2–27 still highlights the centrality of meat and wine for a banquet. Furthermore, even though Baal does not do the serving, he is clearly the host of the banquet, implying that he is the one in power in the situation.[179]

The meal celebrating the dedication of Baal's palace stands on more secure ground. Its context is more readily understood since the text is more complete and it occurs in the middle of a tablet, so that the events

---

176 About 25 lines are missing at the beginning of the tablet as well. For an overview see Mark S. Smith and Wayne T. Pitard, *The Ugaritic Baal Cycle, Vol II: Introduction with Text, Translation and Commentary of KTU/CAT 1.3-1.4* (Leiden: E. J. Brill, 2009), 69.

177 This translation is from Smith and Pitard, *The Ugaritic Baal Cycle II*, 69.

178 Ibid., 102. There are some solitary banquets portrayed in seal iconography, however.

179 Cf. Belnap, "Fillets of Fatling and Goblets of Gold," 71, who argues for Baal's hosting abilities based on his mixing of the wine in l. 16. In the iconographic depictions servants are portrayed bringing the food.

prior and following are known.[180] This second text provides ample helpings of description for the meal itself:

(38) The preparations in his house [Ba]al (39) prepared;

Haddu prepared the [prepara]tion in (40) his palace.[181]

He slaughtered cattle, [also] (41) a sheep.

He brought low bulls, (42) a fatted ram,

Yearling calves, (43) Lambs, a handful of kids.[182]

(44) He called his siblings into his house;

His kin (45) into the midst of his palace;

He called the seventy, the children of Athirat.

(47) He provided rams for the gods;[183]

(48) He provided ewes for the goddesses.

(49) He provided male cows for the gods;

(50) He provided heifers for the goddesses.

(51) He provided thrones for the gods;

(52) He provided chairs for the goddesses.[184]

---

180 Ibid., 84. Between two and five lines are missing from the end, however.

181 Dennis Pardee, "Baal Cycle," *COS* 1.86:261, connects these first two lines with the previous section which narrates the building of Baal's palace rather than the feast. He argues (1.86:261, n. 176) this on the basis that *'dbt* ("preparations" here, or "furniture") is a general term. There are numerous occasions, however, where *'db* is used as a verb (as it also is in these lines) for the preparation of food (cf. *CTU* 1.41.10; 1.14.II.27; and 1.17.V.16). I think it makes the most sense to see these lines as providing a transition from the completion of the palace to the preparation of the feast. See the similar analysis in Smith and Pitard, *The Ugaritic Baal Cycle II*, 626–28.

182 Lines 41b–43 are very similar to the beginning of the description of the Rephaim feast in 1.20.I.12–14 (see above, p. 171).

183 With Pardee, Baal Cycle," 262 and Smith and Pitard, *The Ugaritic Baal Cycle II*, 630–34, I do not think that the animals are deities, though animals are used to symbolize deities elsewhere in the Ugaritic corpus (see Patrick D. Miller, Jr., "Animal Names as Designations in Ugaritic and Hebrew," *UF* 2 [1970]: 177–86). My reading is supported by the difficulty with reading the thrones and chairs (ll. 51–52) as "throne deities" and "chair deities." Furthermore, my reading allows for the consumption to loosely mirror the preparation of the meal in the preceding lines.

184 Lines 47–52 in *CTU* include an addition of [*yn*], but since Baal provides the deities with numerous other items *followed* by provision of wine in ll. 53 [and 54], these additions are superfluous. See discussion in Smith and Pitard, *The Ugaritic Baal Cycle II*, 631–34 and Belnap, "Fillets of Fatling and Goblets of Gold," 96–97.

(53) He provided wide (vessels) of wine for the gods;

(54) He provided bowls [of wine] for the goddesses.

(55) While they ate, the gods drank,

(56) And they took animals which suck the breast,

(57) with a salted knife, pieces of [fat]ling.

(58) They drank [wi]ne from gob[lets]

(59) [from cu]ps of gold the blo[od of trees].

In this feast Baal gives a lush housewarming party for the other deities, over whom he claims sovereignty. The first set of parallel lines depicts Baal as the giver of the feast: he prepares the palace, slaughters the animals, and invites the guests. This establishes the host, similar to *CTU* 1.114 (and *Enuma Elish*), as the recognized person in power, also an important dynamic in Deut 16:9, 13. After naming the rich fare that shows this to be a lavish banquet, ll. 44–47 provide the guest list. The mention of seventy deities implies a great number of gods, likely the totality of the divine pantheon.[185] Belnap concludes that this feast's intent is consolidation of Baal's kingship and solidification of past rivalries.[186]

An often-overlooked feasting text in the Baal Cycle is found in the proverbial sayings or cultic ordinances about proper conduct at banquets.[187] These lines counter the mockery that Baal experienced in the previous section where he recounts his disgraceful treatment including being spat on at a banquet (1.4.III.10–16). Baal then declares various stipulations for a pleasing banquet (1.4.III.17–22):

(17) There are two feasts Baal hates;

Three (18) the Cloud rider:

A feast (19) of shame, a feast of strife

And a feast (20) of lewdness of (21) maidservants.

For in it shame surely appears;

(22) Because in it is the lewdness of maidservants.

---

185 Cf. Mark S. Smith, "The Baal Cycle," 134, n. 135 and above, p. 145 n. 60.

186 Belnap, "Fillets of Fatling and Goblets of Gold," 101.

187 Smith and Pitard, *The Ugaritic Baal Cycle II*, 475, compare ll. 17–22 to numerical proverbs.

The exact nature of these regulations has not been settled. Pardee understands them as relating to the quality of the food, low class participants, and banquets where female servants misbehave.[188] His reading minimizes the sexual connotations of the first and third terms (which might be rendered as follows *bṯt* – "shame" and *tdmmt* – "lewdness" or "infamy").[189] The middle term, *dnt*, has often been taken as cognate to BH *znh* "fornication, degradation." However, Smith and Pitard reconstruct the meaning of *dnt* through comparison with the hollow root *dyn* ("strife, contention") in Hebrew.[190] As they note, the connection to Prov 17:1 "feasts of strife" is quite suggestive, making the emphasis on sexuality in the line seem out of place. Instead they propose that a general connection to disregard and dishonor is more appropriate and understand *tdmm* as "whisper."[191] However, it seems difficult to negate the role of gender at such a feast to simply "whispering." More likely is some sort of sexual boundary crossing. This statement could describe orgiastic celebration by focusing its spotlight on the women, rather than more directly on the act or on all the participants. Or, instead of laying the blame at the feet of the women, the text may exhibit concern for those who would be prone to be taken advantage of when the banquet participants become inebriated. Perhaps the events in Sodom, Judg 19, and Esth 1 are appropriate comparisons in which meals events are disturbed by strife, general inhospitality, and inappropriate sexuality.

In contrast to early interpretations like those of Humbert who imagines Canaanite feasts as drunken orgies,[192] the Ugaritic festivals which form an important cultural background for the DC cultic meals do not necessarily imply orgiastic fertility bacchanals or raucous events.

---

188 Pardee, "Baal Cycle," *COS* 1.86:258, n. 144. Also Smith and Pitard, *The Ugaritic Baal Cycle II*, 475–80.

189 The first term is related to BH *bwš*, Akk. *būštu* and cognate terms. In neither language does it necessarily imply sexual shame, though this can be the case. See Horst Seabass, "בוש" *TDOT*, 2:56–60. The rare Ugaritic term *tdmm(t)*, found only in these lines, could either be related to BH *zimmâ* which could lead to the meaning "infamy, fornication," and to the Arabic *ḏamma* which suggests "blame."

190 Smith and Pitard, *The Ugaritic Baal Cycle II*, 477, state, "The Arabic cognate of BH *znh* is *zana*, which indicates that the first root consonant is *z*." Ugaritic /d/ can only be related to BH /z/ with significant difficulty (cf. ibid., 476–78).

191 In this case, *tdmm* might be understood in relation to Arabic *damdama* "murmur" or Middle Hebrew *dmm* "to speak under one's breath." Cf. *HALOT*, 226. These options seem better than their citations (Smith and Pitard, *The Ugaritic Baal Cycle II*, 477) of Job 4:15 and 1 Kgs 19:12, which instead seem to imply "silence."

192 Paul Humbert, "»Laetari et exultare« dans le vocabulaire religieux de l'Ancien Testament (Essai d'analyse des termes *Sāmaḥ* et *Gîl*)" *RHPR* 22 (1942): 200–201.

Events such as El's drunken stupor are portrayed, but they are not the whole picture. In the (broken) context, Baal here responds to his treatment at a previous divine council when he was treated shamefully.[193] There is a general lack of hospitality, which reflects poorly on the host.[194] Baal addresses this lack of hospitality, which correlates to the necessary preparations and invitations that an addressee of the DC meal texts (the heads of household) should make to provide a meal that meets the hospitality protocol for the family and other "special insiders" such as slaves, Levites, and sojourners. Baal's declaration on the nature of an acceptable feast draws an important connection with the DC conception of cultic worship: their nature should be characterized by hospitality and peace (or unity), while remaining free of general debauchery.

4.3.2.5. Conclusions from the Ugaritic Narrative Material

These banquet texts provide significant background for the interpretation of the DC cultic meals. In order to show this, I will contrast my conclusions with the views of de Moor and Loretz, whose views I highlight because they form the underpinning for Braulik's interpretation of Deut 16:1–17, which is the most exhaustive to date.

De Moor conflates the various Ugaritic narratives into a grand New Year celebration, which in Israel was largely mirrored in the Feast of Booths. With regard to the difference between the celebrations of the two cultures he states, "Of course only JHWH could be the deity upon whom the ritual focused. It must have been claimed that He was the One who in the year to come would give new life to all creatures by renovating the vegetation by his rains."[195] He further suggests that Israelite priests attempted to make the celebration a more sober affair.[196] So for de Moor, the main issues are the provision of fertility and a curbing of orgiastic worship.

Oswald Loretz continues de Moor's emphasis on fertility in his recent essay on the New Year festival.[197] Loretz's primary concern is to connect the fall festival to an agrarian background in Syria and Pales-

---

193 Cf. Smith and Pitard, *The Ugaritic Baal Cycle II*, 473–75.
194 Belnap, "Fillets of Fatling and Goblets of Gold," 87–88.
195 De Moor, *New Year With Canaanites and Israelites*, 1:14.
196 Ibid., 15.
197 Oswald Loretz, "Das Neujahrsfest im syrisch-palaestinischen Regengebiet," 81–110.

tine, rather than to the Mesopotamian celebration.[198] This prime objective of his argument is persuasive, but Loretz unfortunately follows de Moor in using "The Birth of the Goodly Gods" (*CTU* 1.23), the Rephaim texts (*CTU* 1.20–1.22), and Aqhat (*CTU* 1.017–1.19) as primary texts for reconstructing the Ugaritic New Year celebration.

Loretz bases his OT analysis on various Psalms texts, which can be tied to the Ugaritic narrative material through their common use of royal language, connecting them both to the mythic realm. Yet his focus on royal language keeps his discussion largely separate from the pentateuchal festive formulations. This omission is provocative: the Psalms provide more compelling comparative material with regard to the ancient Near Eastern fall festival traditions because the Psalms contain more pro-king Zion theology, but the Psalms do not articulate festival calendars like the Pentateuch.[199] In this manner the Psalms provide a distinct contrast to the non-royal festivals of the Pentateuch. Deuteronomy, for example, contains significantly more "limited kingship" Sinai theology,[200] which can therefore be interpreted as a rebuttal to this pro-royal tradition.

Braulik bases his understanding of the Canaanite religious roots on the conceptions found in Loretz and de Moor for his approach to the Deuteronomic festivals. Since his position has occupied center stage in interpretation of Deuteronomy's cultic meal texts, I will trace his position in more depth. He states that, on the one hand, this comparison of Canaanite and Deuteronomic festivals

> confronts the question of adaptation to some very attractive features of the Canaanite fertility cult. In the cult of YHWH, too, one may—indeed one should—rejoice. Those features of the Canaanite cult which are accepted because of their human value and which are, for the first time, introduced into the Israelite cult with a theological explanation must first be freed from all traits which are incompatible with the authentic traditions of faith in YHWH. And so there is, on the other hand, a rejection of rites.[201]

---

198 Ibid., 82.

199 Belnap, "Fillets of Fatling and Goblets of Gold," 15, also notes the absence of pentateuchal ritual texts in comparisons between the Ugaritic narratives and biblical material.

200 Levenson, *Sinai to Zion*, 21, agrees: "'the mountain of God,' … is out of the domain of Egypt and out of the domain of the Midianites, an area associated, by contrast, with the impenetrable regions of the arid wilderness, where the authority of the state cannot reach."

201 Braulik, "The Joy of the Feast," 40. It is unclear from Braulik's formulation whether he understands Israelite religion to have become syncretistic with Canaanite religion or if it emerged out of Canaanite religion similar to Mark S. Smith, *The Early History*

Braulik's formulation of the background for the DC cultic meals insightfully identifies the Canaanite formulation of cultic meals (as seen in the Ugaritic texts) as the primary cultural background for the DC's explication of meals. Furthermore, Braulik notes that various features are accepted, which highlights the question of which elements of Canaanite worship the Deuteronomic authors rejected.[202] Braulik understands the rejection of Canaanite rites directly in relation to fertility rituals, an interpretation heavily reliant on the interpretation of the Baal Cycle as a fertility ritual.[203] For Braulik then, the key difference between Yahwistic and "Canaanite" joy is the source of fertility: "It is YHWH, not Baal, who grants fertility and the success of human endeavor. The

---

of God: Yahweh and the Other Deities in Ancient Israel (San Francisco: Harper & Row, 1990), xxii: "The [archaeological] record would suggest that the Israelite culture largely overlapped with, and derived from, Canaanite culture. In short, Israelite culture was largely Canaanite in nature."

202 Braulik relies on Humbert, "Laetari et exultare," 200–01, 213, who suggests that the main element rejected was either worship at manifold sanctuaries or the rejection of orgiastic worship characterized in the verb *gyl*, never used in the Deuteronomic material. The former seems much more plausible than the latter.

203 Like de Moor, whom Braulik cites later in "The Joy of the Feast," 39 n. 70. One of the difficulties with Braulik's argument here is that he does not provide sufficient detail for his understanding of the Canaanite ritual. He relies on the work of Dorothea Ward Harvey, "Rejoice Not, O Israel!," in *Israel's Prophetic Heritage: Essays in Honor of James Muilenburg* (ed. B. W. Anderson and W. Harrelson; New York: Harper and Brothers, 1962), 116–27. She argues, (ibid., 122), "There seems to be no doubt that the Canaanite fertility ritual was for the purpose of causing the gods to bring about fertility of the land and of the flocks. And it is precisely those terms which seem to have been associated with a specific Canaanite ritual (*ṣāḥaq* and *gîl*) that are omitted from the official language of the Israelite cult." She goes on to comment that in the prophets the problem is not only the magical use of rites but also certain techniques meant to insure the deity's favor, such as human rejoicing which leads to divine rejoicing. With regard to Deuteronomy she argues for the insistence on joy as a response to the past history (citing Deut 16:12), which circumvents the possibility of coercing God into action. Braulik follows Harvey considerably, (Braulik, "The Joy of the Feast," 40): "This rejection [of Canaanite rites] can be concluded from a comparison between the ancient Israelite and the Canaanite (that is, alien) practice with what is stipulated by Deuteronomy—and not only with what is positively determined, but also with those elements of joy which are deliberately not mentioned in Deuteronomy." He proposes (ibid., 45) that "Canaanite" cultic joy was supposed to magically bring about the joy of the deity, again relying on Harvey, "Rejoice Not, O Israel!," 122 ("There seems to be no doubt that the Canaanite fertility ritual was for the purpose of causing the gods to bring about fertility of the land and of the flocks"). Braulik differs from Harvey in that he sees the connection to the past history as a later redactional insertion (idem, "The Joy of the Feast," 43): "The relation of the yahwistic faith to history does not constitute an essential element in the Deuteronomic festival theory." In contrast I see history as an essential element in the Deuteronomic approach to cultic meals. Removing the exodus background, especially from the Deuteronomic formulation of the Passover, seems very difficult.

commandment to rejoice—the very core of the Israelite cult—is also oriented towards the 'first commandment,' the 'principal commandment.'"[204] One may ask, "Is Baal worship really the foe here?" Braulik assumes that the DC is arguing for an anti-Baalistic "Israel," but there is little presence of Baalism in the pre-Deuteronomistic DC.

He also argues, "The 'joy before YHWH' is neither a particular action within the sanctuary nor indeed an act at all in the literal sense of the word. Rather, this joy characterizes human behavior as the expression of an inner religious attitude."[205] He thereby denies that this joy needs to be connected to any particular religious celebration, but rather emerges from the paradigmatic type of celebration that one would experience at harvest time (and therefore every celebration?) "… when the ever-present danger of famine has disappeared, and the rejoicing when the spoils of war are shared out and one passes from war with all its dangers to a peaceful and more prosperous life."[206]

While these feelings undoubtedly characterized the model harvest celebration, they should also, contra Braulik, be understood in light of the mythological and ritual analogues in Ugaritic literature. In the Ugaritic texts discussed above the notion of "joy" is not merely some ephemeral feeling. The celebration of harvest and the enjoyment of a meal belong in the center of religious rites. The Baal Cycle (and *Enuma Elish*) speaks directly to the victory celebration, while the Rephaim text (*CTU* 1.20) and the rites for the vintage (*CTU* 1.41//1.87)[207] are set as religious harvest celebrations. These connections suggest the impor-

---

204 Ibid., 42. Later, (ibid., 44) Braulik makes the connection between Canaanite fertility religion and Deut 26:14a, interpreting the negative confession "I have not given a portion of it to the dead" as referring to sacrifices for the dying and rising Baal. I find it more compelling to interpret this confession in relation to some sort of cult of the dead ancestors (*kispu*) celebration, or mourning rites (See Theodore J. Lewis, *Cults of the Dead in Ancient Israel and Ugarit* [HSM 39; Atlanta: Scholars, 1989], 103–104). Braulik ("The Joy of the Feast," 46) further highlights the distinction from his point of view, saying "As far as the external rites went, there was probably little difference between the sacrifices of Israel and those of the Canaanite religion." I concur with this statement, and the following discussion of various Ugaritic narrative texts explores such correspondences.

205 Braulik, "The Joy of the Feast," 38. See further discussion below, p. 205. For another recent critique, see Houston, "Rejoicing Before the Lord: the Function of the Festal Gathering in Deuteronomy," and my review, "Review of Christopher Tuckett, ed. *Feasts and Festivals. Journal of Hebrew Scriptures* 9 (2011)." Cited 28 March, 2011. Online: http://www.arts.ualberta.ca/JHS/reviews/reviews_new/review526.htm

206 Ibid. Deut 12:8–12 also highlights security as a prerequisite for celebration.

207 For an analysis see Baruch A. Levine and Jean-Michel de Tarragon, "The King Proclaims the Day: Ugaritic Rites for the Vintage (*KTU* 1.41//1.87)," *RB* 100 (1993): 76–115; and Levine, "Ugaritic Rites for the Vintage (*KTU* 1.41//1.87)," *COS* 1.95:299.

tance of relating the DC cultic meals to the Ugaritic conception of meals because of the specific festive links.

Specific human and divine celebrations are further linked in other biblical uses of *śmḥ* and *śimḥāh*. Braulik does in fact mention key texts— 1 Sam 11:15, 2 Sam 6:12–19, Isa 9:2, 22:13, and Hos 9:1—as exemplifications of the general feeling of joy.[208] Yet these very texts display cultic overtones: Saul's coronation in 1 Sam 11:15 takes place at the holy site of Gilgal and includes sacrifices. Offerings, David as priest, and the Ark show the cultic nature of 2 Sam 6. These two texts even draw upon the literary motifs which appear in the Ugaritic corpus, following the description of a victory celebration in the Baal Cycle and *Enuma Elish*.[209] The latter three (Isa 9:2, 22:13; and Hos 9:1) refer to harvest festivals.[210] Isaiah 9:2 states, "They rejoice before you like the rejoicing of harvest, just as they exalt when dividing war spoils." This text shows that the two streams of Ugaritic imaginative thought about festive celebrations (which are not necessarily separate!) were received in an Israelite, specifically Jerusalemite, context. Both a harvest celebration and a victory banquet are portrayed in the various texts as cultic events, which is exactly what I argue lies in the background for the DC. Biblical "joy" is both tangible and cultic, not merely a general feeling.

My reading differs from Braulik's on a second point as well. In general, he accepts de Moor's interpretation of the Baal Cycle and "Canaanite" religion, which I contend makes too much of the fertility and seasonal trajectory.[211] It is more profitable to consider various dimen-

---

208 Braulik, "The Joy of the Feast," 3.

209 Seow, *Myth, Drama, and the Politics of David's Dance,* 104–105, 132. Note that Seow also highlights the agricultural hues of David's victory celebration, which takes place at a threshing floor and employs agricultural terminology, much like Anat's defeat of Mot in *CTU* 1.6.II.30–35. Also Humbert, "Laetari et exultare," 192. Humbert, (ibid., 198) states, "Dans l'ancien Israël la *Śimḥâ* religieuse avait donc une allure franchement dionysiaque et c'est peut-être le motif pout lequel le Yahviste et l'Elohiste ne lui font jamais place." [ET: In ancient Israel religious *śimḥa* was quite Dionysian and so had no place at all in the Yahwist or the Elohist.] The Philistine victory banquet in Judg 16:23 employs similar terms to the DC formulation, bringing together *zbḥ, śimḥāh,* and rowdy religious celebration.

210 Like the Rephaim text of *CTU* 1.20.

211 As Frank M. Cross, *Canaanite Myth and Hebrew Epic: Essays in the History of Israelite Religion* (Cambridge, Mass.: Harvard, 1973), 116–20; and Mark S. Smith, "Interpreting the Baal Cycle," 314–15, have shown, an interpretation of the Baal Cycle focused solely on the theme of fertility cannot take large swathes of material into consideration. It focuses too myopically on the death of Baal, subsequent mourning rites, and Baal's return to life. The six tablets together show an ongoing focus on the struggle for kingship and palace building as a symbol of sovereignty. This broader reading of

sions of existence—physical, political, and religious—all conjoined in Ugaritic religion and coalescing in the Baal Cycle under the rubric of "kingship."[212] Smith states:

> The central unifying thematic of the cycle is Baal's kingship, which affects the natural, human and divine levels of reality. The text plays out the action on the divine level, yet behind this stage are the concerns for humanity and nature ... Hence Baal's rule lies at the heart of the great chain of relations between nature, humanity and divinity.[213]

This inclusive approach takes the whole gamut of human concerns into consideration, but especially reflects the socio-political situation that confronted second millennium Ugarit, a small state caught between powerful antagonistic empires. This situation also parallels that of seventh-century Judah. There is therefore not only significant overlap in the linguistic and thematic concerns in the texts of Ugarit and the Israelites, but there is also an overlap in the socio-political situations that gave rise to similarly focused texts. Like the Baal Cycle, Deuteronomy emphasizes the question of kingship: Yhwh—and no other deity or empire—is Israel's sovereign lord according to the covenant motif of the DC. In agreement with Braulik's analysis, the emphasis of the DC is on the worship of Yhwh and no other, yet more directly political than fertility related and, therefore, perhaps anti-imperial because of the political situation confronting Judah in the late preexilic period.

This overlap between the Ugaritic and Israelite conceptions of banquets suggests that it is important to flesh out the rhetorical use of banquets in the Ugaritic texts for religious, social, and political purposes in order to broaden interpretation beyond the issue of fertility. Furthermore, it is necessary to expand (or perhaps explicitly lay out) the notion of the banquet Braulik identifies, showing the overlap between cultures. Lloyd provides a helpful summary of the Ugaritic narrative material that carries over into the biblical understanding:

> Such lavishness, apparent in the divine banquet, may have been a reflection of the high social status that the gods enjoyed in Ugaritic society. The wide range of meats and wine depicted in the formulae were available for these mythological banquents at every meal, precisely because of the use of formulae. However, whether these formulae were restricted solely to the

---

the cycle is able to take the fight with Yamm and the section on Athtar into consideration.

212 This terminology follows Smith's formulation, "Interpreting the Baal Cycle," 332. His reading builds on insights from many earlier scholars, including Ginsberg, Gordon, Kapelrud, and Kaiser.

213 Mark S. Smith, "The Death of 'Dying and Rising Gods' in the Biblical World," *SJOT* 12/2 (1998): 308–309.

description of divine banquets, or whether they could be used by the poets for any mythological banquet, divine or otherwise, we cannot be sure; we simply do not have enough material.[214]

What is important to recognize from his conclusion is how the literary construction of the banquet meal for the deities is restricted to the highest echelons of Ugarit.[215] Yet, there is no need for Lloyd's scepticism about whether these lavish descriptions could be imagined for human meals as well. According to *CTU* 1.91, which details wine provisions for a certain royal festival (*dbḥ mlk*), the Ugaritic royalty did partake in such extravagant celebrations.

Going a step further, when comparing with the Gudea cylinder, the Azitawadda inscription, the Calah banquet, as well as 2 Sam 6:18–19, one may conclude that not only royalty, but all factions of society supposedly join in some celebrations.[216] Certainly the DC cultic meals take part in this broadening of the invitation to the feast to all the people.

The key move that the Deuteronomic conception makes in comparison to these texts is the change in the human host for the feast. In the DC cultic meal, it is the addressees, the heads of households, who are responsible for providing the banquet for their families, servants, Levites, and the various legally marginalized groups. Not only are various social levels of society present—they have been present in some form in the Emar and Ugaritic rituals—but the emphasis in Deut 14:22–27, 16:9–15, and other texts is that all should eat and drink until satisfied on a banquet provided by Yhwh through the multiplicity of households instead of the royal house. This particular emphasis conceives of a corporate identity re-articulated and created afresh with a focus on individual households (likely something of the *bêt 'ab*), rather than a politically centralized focus on the human monarch found in the banqueting of the Ugaritic narratival corpus.

---

214 Lloyd, "The Banquet Theme in Ugaritic Narrative," 190.

215 This can also be said for the feeding of the deities in Assur, as apparent in each of the four daily meals (*naptanu*) which the god Aššur was served; cf. G. Van Driel, *The Cult of Ashur* (SSN 13; Assen: Van Gorcum, 1969), 159. However, as van Driel notices (idem, 161; cf. *CAD* Q:240–41), both the meal served in the *akītu* house according to Sennacherib and Marduk's feast in *Enuma Elish* VI:71 are called *qerītu*, "banquet, festival," a term used almost exclusively for special celebrations.

216 Seow, *Myth, Drama, and the Politics of David's Dance*, 132–33, notes that David gives everyone a ring-bread, date-cake, and raison cake as a symbolic banquet parallel to Baal giving a banquet for in *CTU* 1.4.VI.40–59 as demonstration of beneficence as victor.

4.4. Inner-biblical Comparison

At this point I would like to take a detour from discussion of the DC and ancient Near Eastern texts in order to highlight a few important connections and distinctions discernable when comparing the DC meals with the various formulations of the same festivals in other pentateuchal material. This foray will display the richness that the ancient Near Eastern material can then bring to the DC in contrast to the different flavors found in Exod 12–13 and the CC. These texts also show some of the concerns of the DC as well as providing some hints about the relationships between the texts.[217]

4.4.1. Exodus 12:1–13:16

The extended narrative and ritual instructions in this (canonically) first telling of Passover/Unleavened Bread give an extensive narratival grounding for the practice of these cultic celebrations. Fretheim sums up one theme of modern analysis: "liturgy has shaped literature ... Many different layers of tradition from centuries of religious practice have been integrated into the final form of the narrative."[218] Typically these layers are identified as Priestly or post-Priestly (12:1–20, 28; 12:40–13:2), Yahwistic (or non-Priestly) (12:21–23, 27b, 29–39), and Deuteronomistic (12:24–27a; 13:3–16) or post-Priestly for 13:1–16.[219] There is

---

217   I am omitted detailed discussion of the Priestly texts (Num 28–29 and Lev 23) because of their significantly difference foci and formulations. In brief, while both Num 28–29 and the DC attempt to set a community apart for Yhwh, the DC's emphasis on communal meals contrasts with the rhythm and order reminiscent of Gen 1 that is found in Num 28–29. Deuteronomy provides a broad listing of food and drink elements that can be part of the celebrations, also giving general dates for the celebrations. Numbers commands specific amounts of grain, oil, and meat offerings for specific days. The concept of rest is central in Lev 23, which deviates from the DC's focus on meals and participants. Another significant contrast from the DC festival calendar is Lev 23's repeated occurrence of exact calendrical dates for the festivals.

218   Terrence Fretheim, *Exodus* (Interpretation; Louisville: John Knox, 1991), 133.

219   Except for his suggested identification of E in 12:35–36 Fretheim's analysis generally follows that of Childs, *Exodus*, 184; cf. Martin Noth, *Exodus* (trans. J. S. Bowden; OTL; Philadelphia: Westminster, 1962), 95–109, for a similar analysis. While the existence of J is now disputed, broad consensus on the identification of P material continues. Molly Zahn, "Reexamining Empirical Models: The Case of Exodus 13," in *Das Deuteronomium zwischen Pentateuch und Deuteronomistischem Geschichtswerk* (ed. E. Otto and R. Achenbach; FRLANT 206; Göttingen. Vandenhoeck & Ruprecht, 2004), 42–43, provides a brief overview of the history of scholarship in the dating of the

significant Deuteronomistic terminology,[220] including emphasis on action taken once one is in the land (Exod 12:25). In general, the "ritualistic" concerns in Exod 12:1–20 diverge from Deut 16:1–8, though both mention the hurried nature of the celebration (*běḥippāzôn* in Deut 16:3 and Exod 12:11).[221] Exodus 12:1–20 gives the date, type of animal, blood ritual (omitted in Deut 16), and cooking process with significantly more detail. It differs from the DC in the way it forbids that meat be left to the next day (Exod 12:10) and calls the celebration to take place on the seventh day a "feast" (*ḥag* in Exod 12:14), unlike the "assembly" (*ʿăṣeret*) in Deut 16:8.[222] The DC, in contrast, assumes much more common knowledge about the Passover, what it celebrated, and how it is celebrated. There is minimal interest in a precise date—only a particular month in mentioned (Deut 16:1). The nature of the sacrificial animal is significantly more flexible. It is rather the particular place (vv. 2, 5–6, 7) , the repetition of Egypt (vv. 1, 3 [twice], 6), and the incorporation of Unleavened Bread to make it one united ritual that are important for the DC.

Exodus 12:1–13:16 also specifically connects Passover and Unleavened Bread with the consecration of the firstborn, a connection absent from the DC formulation. While the law of the firstborn does appear *next to* the Passover/Unleavened Bread prescriptions (Deut 15:19–23) in the DC, no explicit connection is made between the festival meal texts and the firstborn of Egypt like in Exod 13:11–15.

The possible Deuteronomistic redaction of Exod 12:24–27a; 13:3–16 (or post-Priestly or KD[223] for this text) includes language very similar to formulations in Deuteronomy,[224] though often with the Deuteronomis-

---

passage. Zahn (ibid., 43) argues for a post-Priestly date for Exod 13:1–16, , which seems to be dependent on the direction of dependence between this text and Exod 34 (see ibid., 51–53).

220 See below, next page.

221 This mention in Deut 16:3 makes the most sense in light of the tradition mentioned in Exod 12:33–34, 39.

222 The SamP (*ḥag*) and OG (ἑορτή) of Deut 16:8 disagree with MT. MT preserves the better reading because of its independence here, whereas the other versions appear to be flattening out the differences in favor of Exod 12:14 and what was likely a more common word. The same word "festival"(*ḥag*) also appears in Exod 13:6, which can be affiliated with a Deuteronomistic source.

223 Blum, *Studien Zur Komposition Des Pentateuch*, 18–19, 202–203, includes these texts in his KD, which he places in a later literary layer than the DC and the DtrH (cf. ibid., 164).

224 There are various problems with the attribution of Exod 12:24–27a; 13:3–16 to D, especially the use of *ʿăbōdâ* for a type of liturgical work (Exod 12:25, 26; 13:5), which is generally considered P terminology. While it does appear in Josh 22:27 (though

tic passages outside Deut 16 and the DC. A number of commonalities can be found with Deut 6, such as the idiom "a land flowing with milk and honey,"[225] the mention of wearing signs upon one's hand and *ṭôṭāpōt* on one's head,[226] and the catechesis of children.[227] The oath to the ancestors also appears in both.[228] Yet the fact that these similarities are *not* found with the DC version of Passover and Unleavened Bread (in Deut 16:1–8) is significant, suggesting that the composer(s) of Exod 12:24–27a; 13:3–16 is influenced by or shares a tradition similar to that preserved by Deuteronomy, especially chapters 6–11.[229] I therefore conclude that Exod 12–13 were formed with little regard for Deut 16, since each deals with some rather different concerns—Deut 16:1–8 with the centralized place for celebration (which one might expect in Exod 13:3–16 if it knew of Deut 16), and the teaching of children in 12:24–27a; 13:3–16, which is absent from Deut 16.

The ritual requirements of Exod 12:43–51 contain some intriguing traditions for my understanding of the DC Passover. Past scholarship has generally assigned these verses to a secondary Priestly source[230] or a conglomeration of redactional editions.[231] Within the context of Exod 12, they make the most sense when read in conjunction with the fact that a "mixed crowd" (12:38: *'ēreb rab*) went up with the Israelites. This narrative fact provides the impetus for why the Passover is designated as a particularly "Israelite" celebration—both in Exod 12–13 and in the DC. The presence of an "other" in the Israelites' midst leads to the prescription of a further action which will reveal the identification of the

---

this may not be Dtr) with this meaning, the overwhelming appearance of this usage appears in Priestly passages, i.e., Exod 30:16; 35:21, Num 4, 7, 8, 16, 18. This data supports Zahn's contention, "Reexamining Empirical Models: The Case of Exodus 13," 47–48, that Exod 13 incorporates Deut 16, but with many other texts as well.

225 Exod 13:5; Deut 6:3; 11:9; 26:9, 15.
226 Exod 13:16; Deut 6:8; 11:18. In Exod 13:9 a different expression (*zikkārôn*) appears.
227 Exod 12:24–26; 13:8, 14; Deut 6:7, 20–21; 11:19; Josh 4:6, 21–22.
228 Exod 13:5,11; Deut 6:10; 7:12–13, etc.
229 Contra Jan Wagenaar, "Passover and the First Day of the Festival of Unleavened Bread," 253–54, who sees Deut 16:1–8 as dependent on the Exodus material. Marc Vervenne, "Current Tendencies and Developments in the Study of the Book of Exodus," in *Studies in the Book of Exodus: Redaction—Reception—Interpretation* (ed. M. Vervenne; Leuven: Leuven University Press and Peeters, 1996), 47–54 and Norbert Lohfink, *Das Hauptgebot: Eine Untersuchung literarischer Einleitungsfragen zu Dtn 5–11* (AnBib 20: Rome: Pontifical Bible Institute, 1963), 121–24, argue instead that they are "proto-deuteronomic." Vervenne gives a summary of recent positions.
230 Noth, *Exodus*, 95.
231 Fretheim, *Exodus*, 142–43.

community of the Israelites as "Israelites."[232] The overarching principle
articulated in Exod 12:43 is that no foreigner (*nēkār*) may eat the Passover. The following verses (vv. 44–49, except for the prohibition on
breaking the animal's bones) explicate the meaning of "foreigner." A
foreigner is defined as someone not attached to the "house" of Israel (or
an Israelite) so integrally that if male, they have been circumcised.[233]
The notion of "house" receives further emphasis in v. 46, which locates
the celebration in the house and forbids celebrants from going outside.
So "house" becomes the place of celebration as well as the marker of
who may take part.

The identification between bodily mark and the group meal is most
explicit in 12:48: "for a sojourner sojourning with you to do Passover
for Yhwh, let all of his males be circumcised … but no one who is un-
circumcised may eat of it." This connection between the irremovable
bodily mark and communal consumption reflects the extreme importance that communal consumption of the Passover plays in this text for
one's identification as an Israelite. An important consequence follows
from circumcision and communal Passover: these actions—rather than
one's genetic kinship identity—determine one's belonging to the community and standing under the Yhwh's ordinances (cf. 12:49).

The formulation of the Passover celebration in Exod 12:42–49 may
provide an important insight into the meaning of Deut 16:1–8. While I
see little chance of genetic connection between the two traditions, Exod
12:42–49 reveals a parallel tradition which is, like Deut 16, concerned
with fostering in-group identity through the practice of a communal
meal. For both texts, the *nēkār* is an outsider to be shunned (Exod 12:43;
cf. Deut 15:3), while the *gēr* is a "special insider" to be incorporated into
the group.[234] The important similarity is that communal consumption in

232 Childs, *Exodus,* 202, reaches a similar conclusion: "The present position following the
exodus narrative may have arisen from the redactor's concern to specify at this point
the qualifications for participation in the future feast, mentioned in v. 42. Moreover,
the exodus of a large mixed multitude with Israel (v. 38), who had presumably not
participated in the first passover, but now joined Israel would have made the issue
of the non-Israelite role an acute one."
233 Cornelis Houtman, *Exodus* (vol. 2; trans S. Woudstra; Kampen: KOK, 1996), 207,
concurs that there must be a permanent tie to the Israelites like that symbolized in
circumcision.
234 I see it as an open question as to whether *gēr* in Deuteronomy refers to those of a
"foreign ethnicity" or rather to Israelites who have traveled outside their clan (with
Otto, *Gottes Recht als Menschenrecht,* 242, and Christoph Bultmann, *Der Fremde im antiken Juda: eine Untersuchung zum sozialen Typenbegriff »ger« und seinem Bedeutungswandel in der alttestamentlichen Gesetzgebung* [FRLANT 153; Göttingen: Vandenhoeck und Ruprecht, 1992], 30). Bultmann, *Der Fremde im antiken Juda,* 55, defines the

both texts can only be done by the Israelite—whether by birth or by incorporation through circumcision. In Deut 16 the Passover-Unleavened Bread ritual is the only one of the three festivals that does not specifically mention the inclusion of the *gēr*. This omission is a response to the basic premise of the Deuteronomic celebrations—they are based on Yhwh's actions on behalf of the Israelites. Following Braulik, no mention of *gēr* or Levite occurs in the celebration of Passover because the celebration of that festival concerns the cultic representation of Israel and its origins.[235] The *gēr* must become attached to an Israelite house. Furthermore there is no mention of the Levite because the ritual takes place within the context of the "whole people," a conceptualization that already includes the Levite.

4.4.2. Exodus 23 and Source-Critical Analysis of Deuteronomy 16

When comparing the Deuteronomic feasts with other biblical formulations, the DC's emphasis on cultic centralization must be taken into consideration.[236] It is this change, which, as with Deut 12, highlights the importance of the relationship between the DC and the CC. As argued with regard to Deut 12, in the following I will contend that the festival calendar of Deut 16 builds upon the festival calendar of the CC, Exod 23. One of the main developments is the centralization of the feasts, though this move can be seen as building on Exod:23:17, (cf. with its tri-

---

gēr as a foreigner only in the sense that he lives in an area within Judah where he does not own land. This definition paves the way for understanding the *gēr* as a fellow "Israelite" rather than a person of foreign ethnicity. In general I see *gēr* as signifying a non-Israelite for Exod 12:42–49 because the *gēr* here must be circumcised in order to join the Israelite ritual community, a ritual action that one would expect of every Israelite even if they sojourned to another part of the land. A different conclusion can be made for Deuteronomy as a whole based on the differentiation between the of *'aḥ* and *nokrî* in Deut 15:3 and the similar (but subtly different) treatment of the *gēr* and *nokrî* in Deut 14:21. These two conceptions allow for a hierarchical system from "related kinsperson" (*'aḥ*) to "special insider" (*gēr*) to clear outsider (*nokrî*). While Deut 14:21 is likely a later text, given its attachment to the dietary laws in Deut 14:3–20, the fact that it prescribes Israelites to give the *gēr* meat that has died on its own suggests either that the *gēr* is either somewhat "outside" or else so in need that the purity laws no longer matter, a situation that likely occurred with some regularity.

235 Braulik, "Commemoration of Passion and Feast of Joy," 75.
236 Taking the theme of centralization is most certainly an over-generalization with regards to the whole DC, yet I think it is justified for the purposes of this argument. This emphasis is most pronounced in texts related to meals (12:2–28; 14:22–29; 15:19–23; 16:1–17; 26:1–15) , while its importance is less pronounced in other sections.

annual visit to a (then regional) sanctuary. One further development in Deut 16 is the amalgamation of the Passover and the Feast of Unleavened Bread. A final change is the emphasis on enjoyment (*smḥ*).

With regard to centralization, as Knoppers has noted, one would expect such a move to have "entailed the ascent of royal authority," given the fact that feasts were a prime *topos* for the demonstration of royal prerogatives, but in fact the DC legislation envisions the opposite.[237] Centralization of worship in Deuteronomy serves as the primary festive distinction—both from the named Canaanite practices and from other Yahwistic formulations, whether biblical (Exod 20:24, though not P) or archaeological (Arad, Khirbet el Qom, and Kuntillit 'Ajrud). And, as has also been noticed by many, this centralization follows the general impulse of Deut 12 (see esp. vv. 17–18) to proclaim the sovereign reign of the Great King Yhwh. Veijola states

> Wie der Festkalender am Ende des vor-dtn Bundesbuches dem Altargesetz an dessen Anfang (Ex 20,24–26) kompositionell entspricht, so stellt der dtn Festkalender (16,1–17) das Gegenstück zu dem dtn Kultzentralisationsgesetz (Dtn 12) dar, und beide zusammen bilden den Rahmen für das sog. Privilegrecht Jahwes (Dtn 12,2–16,17). ... dessen Fundament und Dach in den Hoheitsrechten Jahwes bestehen.[238]

The fact that a human royal figure is missing from Deut 16, notably a feature that undergoes change in Josiah's Passover in 2 Kgs 23:21–23, so that Josiah then becomes the focal point of the festival.[239] The framework of Yhwh as single sovereign demanding his portion (*"Privilegrecht"*) brings certain features of Deut 16:1–17 to the fore. As is commonly stated, the main emphasis of the first section (vv. 1–8) is on the centralization of what likely had been a local Passover. This is only half of the story: Deut 16:1–8 also works the material received from the CC formulation of the Festival of Unleavened Bread into its vision of Passover.[240]

---

237 Knoppers, "Rethinking the Relationship between Deuteronomy and the Deuteronomistic History," 405; cf. Levinson, "The Reconceptualization of Kingship."

238 Veijola, *5. Mose*, 329. [ET: Just as the festival calender at the end of the pre-Deuteronomic Covenant Code corresponds to the altar law at its beginning (Exod 20:24–26), the Deuteronomic festival calendar (16:1–17) stands in juxtaposition to the Deuteronomic centralization law (Deut 12). And together they form the frame for the so-called *Privilegrecht* of Yhwh (Deut 12:2–16:17). ...whose foundation and roof exist in Yhwh's sovereign rights.]

239 Knoppers, "Rethinking the Relationship between Deuteronomy and the Deuteronomistic History," 413 (and n. 81).

240 Following Levinson, *Deuteronomy and the Hermeneutics of Legal Innovation*, 65–66, even if Exod 23:14–19 (the festive calendar of the CC) was not an original part of the CC, Deut 16:1–17 displays close dependence on it. For this reason and because there

¹Keep the month of Abib. Now you shall do Passover for Yhwh your God because in the month of Abib Yhwh your God brought you out of Egypt[241] by night. ²You shall sacrifice of the flock or herd [for] Passover to Yhwh your God in the place that Yhwh will choose to make his name dwell there. ³You may not eat [anything] leavened along with it; seven days you shall eat unleavened (bread)—the bread of suffering—along with it because in a hurry you went out from the land of Egypt. Therefore you shall memorialize the day of your going out of the land of Egypt all the days of your life. ⁴Yeast shall not be seen in all your borders for seven days, and you shall not leave any part of the meat that you sacrifice in the evening on the first day until the [next] morning. ⁵You are not permitted to sacrifice Passover in any of your villages that Yhwh your God gives to you. ⁶Rather in the place that Yhwh your God will choose to make his name dwell you shall sacrifice Passover in the evening when the sun sets—the time of going out of Egypt. ⁷You shall cook[242] and eat in the place that Yhwh your God will choose, then you shall turn on the [next] morning and go to your tents. ⁸Six days you shall eat unleavened (bread), and on the seventh day will be an assembly for Yhwh your God. You shall not do work. (Deut 16:1–8)

The scholarly community has long disagreed about the original text of Deut 16 because separation of layers in vv. 1–8 has proved difficult. There is no *numeruswechsel*, so this criterion does not help. The earlier text of the CC includes the Feast of Unleavened Bread and thereby points to ordinances concerning this festival as early; however, cen-

is no sign of Dtr (or other later) editing or conflation of Passover and Unleavened Bread in Exod 23:14–19, it is best to conclude that this section were part of the CC prior to the earliest writing of the DC.

241 Most *OG* texts read "you came out" (ἐξῆλθες), which agrees with Deut 16:3, 6, Exod 23:15, and 34:18. It is difficult to determine which variant represents the older formulation: against *OG* is its similarity with the above mentioned texts; against MT is its general conformity to the biblical notion of Yhwh leading the Israelites out of Egypt.

242 I have translated Heb *biššaltā* with the non-descript "cook" instead of "boil" because "cook" is a more general term, reflecting the general nature of *bšl*. I expect that an ancient Israelite audience would understand that cooking here would, however, mean "in water," matching the connotations found in other sacrificial uses of the root (cf. 1 Sam 2:13–14, Lev 8:31, and esp. 2 Chr 35:13, which attempts to bring together the traditions of roasting and boiling) and contrasting with "roasted" (*ṣĕlî*) meat of the Passover found in Exod 12:8–9. The early translations (*OG*, which adds "and fry," καὶ ὀπτήσεις) and *Sipre* mirror 2 Chr 35:13 in reflecting the tension between Deut 16:7 and the corresponding command to "roast" in Exod 12:8. The notion of cooking as boiling is a development by the DC to bring Passover in line with other cultic feasts; this conclusion is supported by the opening up the choice of meat to include beef, the removal of the celebration from the villages and placement of it at the central sanctuary, and the use of the verb *zbḥ*. For an overview, see McConville, *Law and Theology in Deuteronomy*, 116–17; idem, "Deuteronomy's unification of Passover and Massôt: a response to Bernard M. Levinson," *JBL* 119 (2000): 47–58; and Bernard M. Levinson, "The Hermeneutics of Tradition in Deuteronomy: a Reply to J. G. McConville," *JBL* 119 (2000): 269–86.

tralization is only found in relation to the Passover material, thus placing these two criteria in opposition to one another. Veijola represents
one group of scholars that generally see the Passover ordinances (i.e.
vv. 1–2, 5–7) as the original layer.[243] A number of earlier scholars have
also argued that the Mazzot material was primary.[244] Kratz rejects these
attempts, concluding instead that only vv. 16–17 were the original DC
festive calendar:

> I cannot find an old, pre-Deuteronomic calendar of festivals in vv. 1-15.
> These verses do not arise for the basic Deuteronomic version simply be-
> cause of the combination of Passover and exodus, which has its closest
> parallel in the Priestly Writing and the post-Priestly expansions in Exod.
> 12-13, is no part of Ur-Deuteronomy, and if it is taken by itself, the feast of
> unleavened bread in Deut. 16.1a*a*, 3a lacks the clause about centraliza-
> tion.[245]

Such a skeptical position seems overdone in my mind. I agree that the
Unleavened Bread section does not appear to have existed alone. But if
one takes Exod 23:14–17 (18) as the underlying text, which Kratz himself generally does for CC texts, then it makes plenty of sense for Deut
16 to be reworking this text. Furthermore, the connection between Deut
16 and Exod 12–13 is really not that significant. The connections are
much stronger with Deuteronomistic sections (i.e. Deut 6) and Exod 12–
13, not the language found in Deut 16. This problem is also alleviated
by recognizing the centralization formula with *lškn šmo šm* as one of the
original options available for the original construction of the DC. Dependence on Exod 23 does not mean that the DC could not introduce
concerns of its own, such as Passover.

Several points seem decisive to me: 1) the reliance of the DC on the
CC is a prevalent factor throughout, and these connections are also
present here beyond v. 16. 2) Passover and Unleavened Bread took
place during the same season, so reformulation of one in light of centralization could logically expand to include the other.

Gesundheit notes that the passage begins with the observance during a particular month, in order that both festivals occurring in Abib
may be subsumed under one term.[246] He views this verse, however, as a

---

243 Veijola, *5. Mose*, 330–33. Similarly, though for vv. 2, 5–7 are Gesundheit, "Intertextu-
     alität und literarhistorische Analyse," 207; and Wagenaar, "Passover and the First
     Day of the Festival of Unleavened Bread in the Priestly Festival Calendar," 251.
244 I.e., Rose, *5. Mose*, 42–46; Merendino, *Das deuteronomische Gesetz*, 125–49, argues for a
     pre-Deuteronomic version of the Unleavened Bread festival.
245 Kratz, *Composition*, 122.
246 Gesundheit, "Intertextualität und literarhistorische Analyse," 199, argues that *ḥōdeš*
     does not mean "new moon" here (also *Sipre* 127, which addresses the problem of ad-

later addition because of its use of *šmr*, similarly to the Sabbath Commandment (Deut 5:12). Beginning with an imperatival use of an infinitive absolute is found elsewhere in the early DC (12:13, and *šmr* itself is also at home in the pre-Dtr DC. Furthermore, as Veijola points out, without v. 1*, the section lacks a beginning.[247] The use of *ḥodeš hā'ābîb* comes from Exod 23:15, though with perhaps a decisive change: in Exod 23:15 the phrase is *lĕmô'ēd ḥodeš hā'ābîb*, implying a specific time. Omitting this *lĕmô'ēd* allows for the time determination to be broadened to include both festivals. The DC thus amalgamates the previously separate rituals of Passover and Unleavened Bread (Exod 23, cf. Exod 34).[248] This observation leads to the recognition that Deut 16:(1) 2, 5–6 (7) (material dealing only with Passover) do not rely on a prior (known) source, but are Deuteronomic innovations.[249]

In addition, the basic outline of 16:1, 3–4 should also be included in this original layer, thereby foregoing the complex redactional history proposed by Gesundheit.[250] Rather, the DC is attempting to rearticulate the material provided by the CC in vv. 1, 3–4 so that it fits with the

---

justing the lunar calendar to the seasons, arguing that Abib means a spring month). He sees the observation of the month of Abib as implying the observation of all relevant festival events in the month, both Passover and Unleavened Bread. He notes the use for the term "Passover" in Ezekiel, the NT, and rabbinic writings for the seven-day Mazzot celebration as well. I do not see Deut 16:1 as attempting to pinpoint a specific day or calendar month for these celebrations, but rather, it is keeping with the seasonal changes which vary as to their specific dates from year to year. This is in contrast to Lev 23:4–6, which attempts to identify a particular date.

247 Veijola, *5. Mose*, 331, n. 1198.

248 Even if the mention of *ḥag happāsaḥ* in Exod 34:25 is a pre-Deuteronomic identification of the specific festival meant by *ḥaggî* in Exod 23:18, the discussion of this sacrifice is presented *separately* from the spring festival of Unleavened Bread.

249 This observation is largely in agreement with those of Veijola, *5. Mose*, 330–33, and Gesundheit, "Intertextualität und literarhistorische Analyse," 207. However, I agree with Gesundheit, against Veijola, that v. 7 belongs with this original stratum because it contains original material which fits with the overall Deuteronomic program (centralization), as well as its attempt to bring together the two spring rituals.

250 See also Gertz, "Die Passa-Massot-Ordnung im deuteronomischen Festkalender," 69, who states "Ist die Verbindung von Passa und Massotfest demzufolge eine unmittelbare Konsequenz der Zentralisationsidee, so geht auch die Festsetzung des Passa auf den Termin des Massotfestes durch die Nennung des Passa in V. 1aγ auf den dt Gesetzgeber zurück." [ET: If the combination of Passover and the Mazzot Festival is, therefore, a direct consequence of the centralization idea, then the setting of the date of Passover to the time of the Mazzot Festival through the mention of Passover in v. 1aγ also goes back to the Deuteronomic lawgiver.] Gesundheit argues, "Intertextualität und literarhistorische Analyse," 205, that the Unleavened Bread material was added later, and that the relative order of redaction goes from Exod 23:14–19 > Deuteronomic redaction of CC > Exod 34 as redaction of CC in relationship with Deut 16 and P > secondary redaction of Deut 16 with Exod 34 as direct *Vorlage*.

main thrust of the Deuteronomic program. The reference in v. 1b to leaving Egypt in the month of Abib parallels Exod 23:15b, though it changes the focus from the Israelites' action of leaving to Yhwh's work to make this happen (in Exod: *yāṣā'*, but in Deut *hôṣî'ăkā*).

Along these lines the injunctions concerning the Passover meat— that it should neither be left until morning (Deut 16:4b, like the sacrifice in Exod 23:18) nor slaughtered along with leaven (Deut 16:4b; Exod 23:18 has *lō' tizbaḥ*)—are set into the framework of 1a, 2, 5–7. This attempt to incorporate the material from the CC gives rise to the choppiness found especially in 16:3a with regard to the twice mentioned *'ālāyw*. The first half of the verse—"You shall not eat (anything) leavened along with it"—fits well with the sacrifice of the flock or herd mentioned in 16:2, while at the same time it is a reworked quotation from Exod 23:18 (*lō' tizbaḥ 'al ḥāmēṣ dam zibḥî*). The reformulation of the CC material is also apparent in the avoidance of *zibḥî*, which only appears in later layers of the DC, since the early DC redefines the implications of the verbal form of *zbḥ* and avoids the noun.

The following clause—"seven days you shall eat unleavened (bread) along with it"—is a quotation as well, this time from Exod 23:14 (cf. Exod 34:18). This quotation has been supplemented with an insertion of the prepositional phrase *'ālāyw* ("along with it") in order to fit it into the context of Deut 16:2–3aα.[251] The date of v. 3b is more difficult: the term *ḥippāzôn* is rare, though it also appears in this context in Exod 12:11. Without it the meaning of the following clause ("you went out from the land of Egypt") does not fit seamlessly. It might be possible to imagine this entire clause as late, which would then leave v. 3 as "You may not eat (anything) leavened along with it; seven days you shall eat unleavened (bread) along with it in order that you shall memorialize the day of your going out of the land of Egypt." However, *tizkōr* often appears in later, generally Dtr texts of Deuteronomy, (5:15; 8:2, 18; 9:7; though perhaps 15:15 is earlier?), which may pose some problems for this reconstruction, since there is no firm anchor for this clause in Exod 23.

---

251 The final verse of the spring festival material, 16:8, need not be understood as a contradictory insertion, even though it is likely a later addition. Mayes, *Deuteronomy*, 254, views the seventh day in v. 8 as contradicting the seven days mentioned in v. 3. I do find his reasoning compelling that v. 8 is an addition though, because if v. 3 had been more clear, then the mention of the seventh day (which might be understood as the eighth day!) in v. 8 would not be so disjunctive. However, this presumably later update works out the intentions of the DC to extend the concept of holiness to the whole land. This intention is exemplified in the "tents" of v. 7 and the removal of leaven from the borders of the land in v. 3 (cf. local meat consumption in 12:15a).

As has perhaps become apparent to the reader, my analysis thus far has focused solely on 16:1–8. In this focus my discussion follows most scholarly work on the chapter.[252] The point of the discussion thus far has been to demonstrate the close connections between the DC formulation of the festivals of Abib with the text of Exod 23:14–19, mirroring the similarities found in Deut 12:13–19's reception of Exod 20:24–26. Deut 16:9–15 also imply that Deut 16:1–17 is a reworking of the Exod 23.

> [9]You shall count seven weeks: from [the] beginning of setting a sickle in the standing [grain] you shall begin to count seven weeks. [10]Then you shall do the Festival of Weeks for Yhwh your God. From the sufficiency of the freewill offering of your work you shall give, in accordance with how Yhwh your God has blessed[253] you. [11]And enjoy before Yhwh your God—you and your son and your daughter, your male slave[254] and your female slave, and the Levite who [resides] in your gates, and the sojourner and the orphan and the widow who [reside] in your midst—in the place where Yhwh your God will choose to make his name dwell. [12]And you shall remember that you were a slave in Egypt. Now be careful to do all these ordinances.
>
> [13]The Festival of Booths you shall do [for] seven days when you have gathered from your threshing floor and from your wine vat. [14]And enjoy your festival—you and your son and your daughter, your servant and your maidservant, and the Levite and the foreigner and the orphan and the widow who [reside] in your gates. [15]Seven days you shall celebrate for Yhwh your God in the place that Yhwh will choose, for[255] Yhwh will bless you. (Deut 16:9–15)

---

252 Contrast, however, MacDonald, *Not Bread Alone,* and Houston, "The Function of the Festal Gathering in Deuteronomy."

253 The Peshitta, *OG* (– *Vaticanus*), 4QDeut[c] read *brkk* (3ms pf.) instead of MT *ybrkk* (3ms impf.). The two readings may connect the blessing to different events: if the majority reading (pf.) is read as past tense, then it could refer to the exodus-conquest narrative. However, it could also simple denote general blessing, therefore also agricultural fecundity, similar to the implications of the MT variant. A perfective form is used in 15:13 clearly referring to past agricultural blessing. One might also propose some kind of indefinite or persistent perfective (cf. *IBHS,* 487–88, §30.5.1c) in keeping with ongoing agricultural blessing. The variant in MT could more easily be explained as a scribal change made to bring it in line with the appearance of the 3ms imperfective forms in Deut 15:10; 24:19, which could have been given perfective forms and still fit their context (The states [tenses] of the forms in 15:4, 6, 14 are determined by their context). The imperfective MT form would then be understood as an "habitual non-perfective" (cf. *IBHS,* 506, §31.3e).

254 Following Peshitta and *OG* I see the *waw* as a later smoothing out the participants list.

255 NRSV, NJPS, and NIV translate the BH *kî* with "for," while NAS has "because." NAS implies that the Israelites give *in response to* Yhwh's prior action, while the other

The festivals of Weeks and Booths emphasize ties to agricultural pro-duction, with language different from that in Exod 23. The Exodus treatment of the harvest festival (*qāṣîr*) specifies bringing the firstfruits, while in Deut 16:10 the audience is left to decide what the vaguer (*mis-sat nidbat yādĕkā:* literally, "the fullness of the freewill offering of your hand") refers to for the Festival of Weeks.[256] Both are related to one's work, but Deuteronomy lays the emphasis on responding to the bless-ing provided by Yhwh (16:10b). Sukkot in Deut 16:13 occurs *bĕ 'ospĕkā* ("when you have gathered") maintaining the connection to gathering, while Exod 23:16 simply calls the festival *ḥag hā'āsip* (the gathering festival).

The summarizing vv. 16–17 again show that they are reworking the earlier version of the festival calendar:

> [16]Three times a year each of your males shall appear before Yhwh your God in the place which He will choose: in the Festival of Unleavened Bread and in the Festival of Weeks and in the Festival of Booths, and (they) shall not appear before Yhwh empty-handed. [17]Each according to the gifts of his hand, according to the blessing of Yhwh your God, (the blessing) which He has given you. (Deut 16:16–17)

Most of v. 16 is lifted straight out of Exod 23:15b, 17 (cf. Exod 34:23), which partially explains the repeated emphasis on "each of your males" *(kol-zĕkûrĕkā* in Exod 23:17 and Deut 16:16). The emphasis on the men does not directly fit the DC festival logic, which mandates the presence of a much wider swath of the Israelite population (cf. Deut 12:18; 16:11, 14), yet it maintains the focus on the heads of households as addressees of the DC.

The differences between the Exod 23:14–18 and Deut 16:9–17 sec-tions are also revealing. There is no mention of "enjoyment" (*śmḥ*) in Exod 23, while this is central for the DC text. Secondly, the location for the feasts is specifically articulated within the DC's discussion of each feast (vv. 11, 15) and in the summarizing statement of 16:16 (cf. Exod 23:14,17; also Exod 34:23). Thirdly, the DC articulation extends the

---

three leave the direction open-ended. Does one give to Yhwh *so that* Yhwh will bless, or the opposite? The Hebrew is open to both readings, especially within the context of the Deuteronomic covenant, which sets Yhwh's action in advance of Israel's, but also demands that Israel respond in kind for Yhwh's blessing to continue uninter-rupted. It is, therefore, appropriate to leave the directionality open so that both im-plications can combined.

256 I see no reason to follow the emendation proposed by J. Hempel in BHS of *missat* to *kĕmattĕnat*. While 4QDeut^c reads *mtt*, MT is to be preferred as a more difficult (but comprehensible) reading. 4QDeut^c also smoothes out the MT singular *nidbat* into the plural *ndbwt*.

mandate from only males[257] to entire households and to the special "outsiders" merely tied to one's village who are designated insiders for the festivals (16:11, 14). Finally, Deut 16:12 (while possibly a later addition) works to connect the Feast of Weeks to Egypt, not only to the fruitfulness of the land.

In short, both the Exod 23 source text and Deut 16 provide a narrative continuum for the reader that stretches from the exodus event (Exod 23:15; Deut 16:1, 3, 12?) to fruitful enjoyment and offerings from one's own land.[258] The DC formulation works with this inherited narrative conception and adds extra details for its own particular purposes.

4.5. Interpretation of Deuteronomy 16:1–17

Historical-critical analysis suggests the plausibility of Exod 23 as the source text of Deut 16. However, consideration of the ancient Near Eastern conception of the cultic meal adds an important piece of the conceptual background for the cultic festivals. This final section brings together the analyses of the previous sections in order to show how they provide for a richer reading of the section as a "textual complex."[259]

---

257 This could possibly refer only to heads of households. See David Volgger, *Israel wird feiern: Untersuchung zu den Gesetztexten in Exodus bis Deuteronomium* (Arbeiten zu Text und Sprache im alten Testament 73; St. Ottilien, Germany: EOS, 2002), 63: "Gegenüber den weiblichen Personen in Israel ist der Befehl indifferent ... Die Weisung, die die Männer Israels betrifft, wendet sich somit an Israel, das durch die Hausväter repräsentiert wird." [ET: With regard to female persons in Israel, the command is indifferent ... The directive that concerns the men of Israel is therefore directed to Israel as represented by the household patriarchs.] It seems most likely to me that this is how the ordinance could be read in light of the surrounding DC material, but this does require a certain move from the general Deuteronomic terminology.

258 Volgger, *Israel wird feiern*, 77, makes this argument poignantly: "Ex 23,14–17 blickt also nicht nur auf die Befreiung aus Ägypten und die bereits ergangene Gebotsoffenbarung YHWHs zurück, sondern wendet sich zugleich auch auf die Inbesitznahme des gelobten Landes voraus."[ET: Exod 23:14–17 not only looks back on the liberation from Egypt and the earlier experienced revelation of the law of YHWH, but at the same time also assumes the possession of the promised land.]

259 I use this terminology to mean that I am reading Deut 16:1–17 as a whole, rather than separating vv. 1–7(8) from vv. 9–17, as has often been done in articles which focus specifically on the question of Passover and Unleavened Bread in vv. 1–8. Reading the section as a whole is important insofar as it inspires the interpreter to remember that these are texts (not rituals), yet they are texts about specific ritual actions. I do not mean by this that there were no later additions to the Deut 16 text

The rhetorical potential of the textual complex as a whole—that is, as a text, rather than as the ritual actions behind the text[260]—means that reading (hearing) begins with the narrativized Passover, which lays the framework for the less overtly narrativized Festivals of Weeks and Booths. Egypt and the memory of leaving Egypt are the explicit narrative undergirding Passover: the temporal setting is highlighted by the inclusion of "in the month of Abib Yhwh your God brought you out of Egypt," (v. 1b).[261] This memorial time appears again in the verses 5–7, which deal directly with Passover. The narrative connection to this Israelite founding narrative is also incorporated into the ordinances on the Festival of Unleavened Bread in v. 3, where the DC version picks up on the similar reference in Exod 23:15 (cf. Exod 34:18). Though the Festival of Unleavened Bread contained references to the exodus narrative prior to Deuteronomy's composition, Deut 16:1–8 nonetheless highlights the narrative as the mythic foundation for *both* rituals. The provision of a common narrative interlinks the two more closely.

In the first eight verses of Deut 16 the text progresses spatially from Egypt (vv. 1, 3, 6) to the singular sanctuary (v. 2), and then again from the land in general ("all your borders" in v. 4 and "any of your gates" in v. 5) to the sanctuary (vv. 6, 7). I would call this movement the "exodus pilgrimage" because it combines a move up out of Egypt with a move up out of one's local setting to the central sanctuary.[262] Subsequently a reverse movement takes place, this time from the central

---

(vv. 3b, 8, and 12), but that the major structure of the text was present at the earliest stage. Braulik, "The Joy of the Feast," 43, argues, "Characteristically, the Passover is never called a 'feast' … Its rites do not allow us to assimilate it to the feasts in the strict sense of the word (the Feast of Weeks and the Feast of Booths)." Yet, in spite of his noteworthy objections, this argument misses how the Passover has been joined with Unleavened Bread to form a unified ritual conjoined with the second and third feasts of the yearly cycle. Furthermore, as I noted above, several points in the text remake Passover-Unleavened Bread into something more of a feast—the use of *zebaḥ* ("sacrifice," vv. 2, 5, 6), the addition of *bāqār* ("cattle," v. 2), the use of *biššāl* ("cook, boil"), and the location of the ritual at the central sanctuary. Levinson, *Deuteronomy and the Hermeneutics of Legal Innovation*, 73, notes that the idea of Passover as a boiled sacrifice (*zebaḥ*) indicates an assimilation of Passover to the public cult.

260 See above, 2.1. Methodological Note.

261 The final adverb, *lāylâ* "by night," is often seen as a later addition. It further determines the moment when the exodus occurred, thereby providing a specific reason for celebrating Passover in the evening and coinciding with the prohibition on leaving the meat sacrificed in the evening until the next morning (v. 4b) and the narratival element of v. 6: "in the evening as the sun is setting, the time of your going out from Egypt."

262 Cf. Braulik, "The Joy of the Feast," 51 and above, p. 39.

place (v. 7a) to one's home ("your tents" in v. 7b; also the local "assembly" in the perhaps later addition of v. 8).

The DC Passover-Unleavened Bread regulations therefore take the whole land of Israel into consideration. While there is a focusing of the Passover sacrifice itself at the chosen place to which the community should travel, the people should rid the entire land of leaven. The fact that the land as a whole is in view is also the case if "return to one's tents" (16:7b) means to return home, thereby indicating an extension of the celebration into the entire land.[263] This clause extends the logic found in the ordinances of Deut 12:13–19 that not only fix a special place, but also consider the entire land as Yhwh's domain. As a result Deut 16:1–8 envisions a noteworthy progression, "Der *mqwm* wird in Dtn vom Zielort, zu dem Israel aus Ägypten aufbricht, um sich dort niederzulassen, zum Zielort, zu dem des seßhaft gewordene Israel dreimal im Jahr wandert, ohne jemals dort seßhaft zu werden."[264] The sanctuary is a fixed destination, but one does not remain there. Instead the people extend the sacrality of the place throughout the land through their return journeys.

---

263 See the similar usage in 2 Kgs 14:12. This follows Braulik, *Deuteronomium 1–16,17*, 118–19 (and *OG* which translates "your tents" with "houses": ὃικους and *Tg. Onq.* which translates "your villages": *lqrwk*); Michael Homan, *To Your Tents, O Israel!: The Terminology, Function, Form and Symbolism of Tents in the Hebrew Bible and the Ancient Near East* (Leiden: E. J. Brill, 2002), 16–19, notes that the usage of the term "tents" often occurs as the place to which the Israelites are to return *after battle*, and is then terminology signifying the return home, and perhaps in Deut 16:7 meaning the breaking off of a holy engagement (either as sacred army or temple worship). Thanks to Dan Pioske for this reference. This reading opposes Mayes, *Deuteronomy*, 259, who interprets "go to your tents" in 16:7 "as a reference to the tent encampments of the pilgrims to the central sanctuary for the celebration of the seven-day festival." MacDonald, *Not Bread Alone*, 81, weighs the two opinions and suggests (with Mayes and Braulik), "The problem may be resolved if the author of Deuteronomy was deliberately seeking to relate the conclusion of the Passover feast with Israel's experience of the wilderness. In common with their ancestors the celebrating Israelites leave the Passover and move immediately into an existence of living in tents." If this is the case, then the timeframe for people to return to their local villages for the solemn assembly in v. 8 is omitted. Thus I find the possible symmetry between vv. 2–4 (centralized and dispersed) and v. 7 as more compelling. In either case, MacDonald (ibid.) is correct in seeing the use of "tents" for homes as unusal. In my mind this implies a known tradition behind the usage that is no longer self-explanatory for modern readers.

264 Volgger, *Israel wird feiern*, 114, [ET: The *mqwm* in Deuteronomy changes from the destination towards which Israel sets out from Egypt in order to settle into the destination to which the now-settled Israel travels three times a year without settling there.]

Wagenaar, following Gertz, argues for a six day-seven day schema wherein the first day of the Feast of Unleavened Bread (v. 3a) coincides with Passover, so the seventh day of v. 8 coincides with the seventh day of v. 3.[265] Therefore, v. 8 reinforces the entirety of the celebratory events of the month of Abib, beginning in Egypt, moving into the land, then to the central sanctuary as a unified nation, and ending in local assemblies scattered throughout the land. This progression and interpenetration of feasts builds on the pattern of meat consumption from 12:15 , highlighting the notion elucidated by Sutton.[266]

The Passover-Unleavened Bread spring celebration text conceptually transforms and orients the entirety of Israelite territory, as exemplified in the phrase "all your borders" (*gĕbulĕkā* in v. 4), toward the specific place of worship to which the entire people travel, just as they "went out" (or were "brought out") from Egypt. In this ritual celebration the many people of various villages (v. 5b: "in any of your gates") are subsumed under a singular "you shall sacrifice" at a single place. Like the *zukru* of Emar, the entire population converges at a particular site in order to reaffirm its communal commitment to an ancient narrative. With regard to Deuteronomy, Braulik states:

> … this unification cannot be attributed either to the sacredness of this particular locality or to an absolute centralization. Rather, it arises as a consequence of Israel's relationship to YHWH, their God. This relationship constitutes the heart of deuteronomic theology … More importantly, it gathered the individual families and social classes together into a united people.[267]

This singularity of place, time, deity, and narrative may also explain why there is no mention of household members and social outliers in the celebration of Passover-Unleavened Bread: the community celebrates as one at Passover.[268] Like the *zukru*, in the Passover-Unleavened Bread legislation the people return to a previous era represented by the hurriedness of leaving Egypt or perhaps the oppression that occurred there, before having settled into the "blessed present."[269] This previous

---

265 Wagenaar, "Passover and the First Day of the Festival of Unleavened Bread in the Priestly Festival Calendar," 255; Gertz, "Die Passa-Massot-Ordnung im deuteronomischen Festkalender," 66. Gertz (ibid., 60) argues that because the seven days were originally only for Mazzot that the seven sevens in the section are not by chance and should therefore be viewed as early.

266 See above, 2.2.1.2. Sutton, on the interpenetration of ritual and mundane meals.

267 Braulik, "Commemoration of Passion and Feast of Joy," 80.

268 See also below, p. 236.

269 The DC presents this "blessed present" as a promised future if the people accept the Yhwh's yoke.

difficult era could also be translated in the Iron Age II situation to mean life under the imperial Assyrian yoke, from which the DC offers a reprieve.

Continuing with the spatial category, the discussion of the Feast of Weeks begins in the field where the grain stalks stand in view (v. 9) and around one's locale where the blessings received from Yhwh can be observed (v. 10). The text then moves to the central sanctuary, present both as the place where one enjoys (v. 11a: *wĕśāmaḥtā lipnê yhwh 'ĕlōkêkā*, "And enjoy before Yhwh your God") and the direct mention of the place Yhwh will choose (v. 11b). The progression is, however, made complex by command to include the Levites "in your gates" in v. 11a. Similarly, the regulations for Booths begin locally with the collection from one's vat and threshing floor (v. 13: *bĕ'ospĕkā miggornĕkā ûmiyyiqbekā*). The next verse begins "enjoy your festival" (*wĕśāmaḥtā bĕḥaggekā*) denoting a change in location, but the verse ends with a reminder of the foreigners, orphans, and widows in your gates (v. 14b). The summation of the Festival of Booths (v. 15) repeats the election formula of the central sanctuary, and the concluding section (v. 16) emphasizes the central sanctuary again. However, just like 16:7–8, the final movement (v. 17) returns the spotlight to the land as a whole, where Yhwh blesses each person or head of household.

In the text complex as a whole, the location moves from Egypt (vv. 1, 3, 6, 12) to the land (i.e., "proportional freewill offerings of your own production" in v. 10; cf. v. 13). Yet within these progressions the celebrants travel to the same central location, "the place which Yhwh your God chose." This element frames the festivals within the context of, or better, as worship. The travel also approximates the journeys in the *akītu* festival, in El's Feast, in the travel of the Kothirāt of the Aqhat narrative, and the Emar *zukru*.

In addition to the spatial progression, the second and third celebrations change their formulation of the participants to go along with the temporal sequence. It moves from a solely "Israelite" festival in Passover to the wider, more inclusive listing of the whole community that should participate in the Festivals of Weeks and Booths.

> And enjoy before Yhwh your God—you and your son and your daughter, your servant and your maidservant, and the Levite in your gates, and the sojourner and the orphan and the widow who are in your midst. (Deut 16:11, cf. v. 14)

The broad list of participants intends to include all residents of the land affiliated with Israel. Both commands (or invitations) to enjoy, like all the verbs in this section, are 2ms forms, therefore directed first and foremost towards the heads of households able to take responsibility for the subsequently named groups both inside and outside the larger family structure. This broader inclusion mirrors the societal and social concerns found in *CTU* 1.40, with its inclusion of individuals from different economic and social groups.

Studies comparing the Ugaritic and Akkadian festivals with those of Israel have tended to maintain a focus on the Psalms and other texts that include an easy correspondence to the role of the king, whether that correspondence is found in Yhwh or in a human king. This narrow focus has left relationships between the meals of Deuteronomy and various ancient Near Eastern parallels unexamined. When the meals are viewed along the lines of the subversive reception of the Neo-Assyrian use of the covenant or loyalty oath genre in Deuteronomy, and perhaps of its Judahite analogue ("Zion theology"), it becomes possible to consider these meal texts in relation to the ancient Near Eastern analogues. Yhwh is the analogue to the divine giver of the feasts, whether El or Baal at Ugarit, Marduk or Aššur in Mesopotamia, or Dagan in Emar. However, instead of royalty playing the role of human host as found in 2 Sam 6, 1 Kgs 8:65, or 2 Kgs 23:21–23, Deuteronomy—in keeping with its rejection of foreign suzerains—makes the individual heads of household responsible for throwing the feast for all members of the society.[270] This "leveling" of the feast suggests a radical revision (re-envisioning) of the feasts over against both local celebrations and the imperial (Neo-Assyrian and Babylonian) feasts.[271] Eckard Otto notes, "So durch die gemeinsame Gottesverehrung und nicht durch Hierarchie staatlicher Macht zu einer Einheit zusammengefügt, ergibt sich auch die Abgrenzung nach außen: Religionsgrenzen sind Gemeinschaftsgrenzen."[272] Such is the function of the kind of patronage feasts envisioned in Deut 16: Yhwh offers hospitality in return for homage.[273]

---

270 Cook, *The Social Roots of Biblical Yahwism*, 40–41, notes the ancient stream of tradition in biblical texts (Judg 8:23, 1 Sam 8:7) that conceives of Israel without a human sovereign. This tradition also emerges in the DC's emphasis on the "brother" language for the king (17:15, 20). Cf. Sanders, *The Invention of Hebrew*, 70–72, for ancient *'am* traditions.

271 Canaanite here could imply non-Deuteronomic Yahwistic worship as well.

272 Otto, *Gottes Recht als Menschenrecht*, 242. [ET: A unity is achieved through communal worship rather than the hierarchy of national power, resulting also in the borders against the outside: religious boundaries are community boundaries.]

273 Houston, "The Function of the Festal Gathering in Deuteronomy," 12, argues similarly in reliance on Michael Dietler's typology of meals (see above, 2.3.2 for further discussion of Dietler).

In the textual progression from 16:1–8 to the festivals of Weeks and Booths (16:9–17), the unified and singular narratival foundation of the spring festivals is then textually what precedes the joyful and worshipful recognition of Yhwh's provisions of land and produce in celebration within the unified but variegated society.[274] This connection between the Egypt memory of the spring festivals and the more agricultural focus of Weeks and Booths contradicts Braulik's suggestion that "the relation of the yahwistic faith to history does not constitute an essential element in the deuteronomic festival theory."[275] The textual connection of Passover-Unleavened Bread with Weeks and Booths underscores the importance of "remembered narrative" for Deuteronomy's approach to faith. Braulik can make this claim only by relegating 16:12 to a later redactor (which may be correct, however),[276] and furthermore by neglecting the deliberate and immediate juxtaposition by Deuteronomy itself of Passover with the traditional festivals of Unleavened Bread, along with Weeks and Booths.[277]

The origin of Weeks and Booths may certainly be agrarian as Mayes argues.[278] However, as Mayes recognized, this does not explain the festivals' function within the DC formulation of the festival calendar. Instead of understanding these festivals only within the context of the agricultural connections brought forth by the mention of "threshing

---

274 This textual progression is also mirrored the seriousness of the *'āšeret* (v. 8) and "bread of suffering" (v. 3) , both of which may be later additions, to enjoyment in the latter two festivals. The move from Egypt to enjoyment of the land can also easily be viewed as a move from exodus to promised land; see MacDonald, *Not Bread Alone*, 82. This is the action prescribed in Deut 27:1–7.

275 Braulik, "The Joy of the Feast," 43.

276 However, Mayes, *Deuteronomy*, 206, comments, "The reference to Israel's slavery in Egypt does not appear any earlier than Deuteronomy in connection with the feast of Weeks; moreover, it does not even here explain the observance of the festival, but rather why the Levite and the poor should be invited to join in it—in itself a deuteronomic recommendation."

277 In "Commemoration of Passion and Feast of Joy," 84, Braulik argues, "According to the Deuteronomic calendar, the Passover-Feast of Unleavened Bread as a commemorative passion celebration and the Feast of Weeks and the Feast of Booths as feasts of joy constitute *two* basic forms of liturgy," [italics mine].

278 Mayes, *Deuteronomy*, 257, claims, "[Weeks was a] purely agricultural festival, with no original connection with Israel's saving history … it was derived from the Canaanites." Likewise (ibid.), "as a harvest festival it [Booths/Ingathering] was also of Canaanite origin (cf. Jg. 9:27) but since it is only in Deuteronomy and later legislation (cf. Lev. 23:39, 41f.) that it is a seven-day festival known as the feast of Booths, it is likely that at least in these characteristics it received a distinctive stamp in the Israelite context." See also Houston, "The Function of the Festal Gathering in Deuteronomy," 4.

floor" and "vat" (v. 15) or the "setting of the sickle to the standing grain" (v. 9), the mythological connections of the Ugaritic banquets— with their earthy enjoyment of food and drink—provide enrichment to the interpretation. Consideration of the commands to "enjoy" (śmḥ) recalls the free-flowing wine and generous meat portions in the Ugaritic banquets of the Rephaim, El's Feast, and the Baal Cycle with all their political implications intact.

In his fullest statement on the purpose of the DC meal legislation, Braulik argues:

> In remaining so consistently silent about any cultic meal during the harvest festivals, Deuteronomy is setting a theological accent which cannot be overlooked. Since the Feast of Weeks and the Feast of Booths have their liturgical center in YHWH's blessing, that is, in the fertility he has granted (16:10, 15), Deuteronomy, by not mentioning any meal, intends to put up a barrier against the festive meals of the Canaanite fertility religions. The banquet which is sure to have taken place during the harvest festivals at the central sanctuary is not thereby forbidden. It is simply stripped of its syncretistic-sacral character.[279]

In contrast, Deut 16 does not remain silent at all about the meal or put up a barrier against the festive meals of "Canaanite" religion. Instead, the emphasis and even command in Deuteronomy (vv. 11, 14) to "rejoice" is a direct injunction to enjoy a festive meal in the physical sanctuary of the deity. So, against Braulik's interpretation, Deuteronomy not only accepts, but goes so far as to highlight the meal element of the festival. This command to rejoice implies something that could be materially expressed, reflected in the actual practice of eating and drinking (rather than an imperative to "feel joyful" or something of that sort). The description in Deut 14:26 gives a representative sampling of the food and drink options from which one might choose—according to one's own desires—and caters to the notion of physical fulfillment for the meaning of the verb śmḥ:

> Then spend the money on whatever you desire, whether from the herd, or the flock, or wine, or beer, or whatever you might ask for yourself—then eat there before Yhwh your God, you and your house shall enjoy!

Therefore, I cannot follow Braulik's subsequent statement: "The appeasement of human appetites ought to enter into the cultic joy, but must not be interpreted in accordance with the religion of Baal. In the Canaanite cults drinking wine together was part of the ritual."[280] Braulik admits that wine is part of the Israelite ritual, based on 14:26.

---

279 Braulik, "Commemoration of Passion and Feast of Joy," 81.
280 Ibid., 81–82.

However, he argues that the drinking of wine should be downplayed in Israel because the drunkenness must have been considered wrong since "the intoxication made people experience themselves as one with God and with nature."[281] While intoxication may have a role in certain religious experiences of ecstatic union with the divine, there is no clear evidence from the Ugaritic texts that intoxication in Canaanite worship played a radically different role from Deuteronomic worship. Sometimes alcoholic consumption simply marks religious occasions of joy and celebration. The limitations on certain inappropriate behavior in the Ugaritic formulations of worship, especially as formulated in the Baal Cycle 1.4.III.17–22, suggest that DC (and other "Israelite") and "Canaanite" styles of worship and celebration may not be distinguished on this basis.

Finally Braulik concludes, "Compared to [the portrayals of festivals in Ugaritic literature], Israel's harvest festivals retained a matter-of-fact distance between YHWH and his people. The purpose of this radical de-mystification, however, was the most intimate communion in 'rejoicing before YHWH, your God' (verse 11) ."[282] Here Braulik leans on the interpretation of *lipnê yhwh* offered by Reindl, that "before Yhwh" does not designate a place or particular action but rather a religious attitude.[283] However, simply because not all Israelites can be imagined to be in the sanctuary does not mean that the prepositional phrase *lipnê yhwh* does not designate a particular place, but as Reindl argues, the phrase may be "… ein Ausdruck für den kultischen Charakter der Zeremonie."[284] Because the determination of place is given in conjunction with *lipnê yhwh*, it makes more sense to understand the prepositional phrase spatially as a *terminus technicus* for a cultic place.[285] When turning to the DC, "before Yhwh" makes the most sense when understood spatially. In numerous places the phrase "before Yhwh" occurs specifically in conjunction with the phrase "in the place which Yhwh

---

281 Ibid.

282 Ibid.

283 Joseph Reindl, *Das Angesicht Gottes im Sprachgebrauch des Alten Testaments* (ETS 25; Leipzig: St. Benno-Verlag, 1970), 28–29.

284 Ibid., 29. [ET: an expression for the cultic character of the ceremony.]

285 As is often the case in the Priestly writings. A category Reindl himself includes, see ibid., 33, and also ibid., 27: "Als Ortsangabe ist 'לפני' mehrdeutig; aber die Beschränkung auf kultische Funktionen oder Gegenstände macht seine eigentliche Bedeutung aus." [ET: As spatial designation 'לפני' is multivalient; but the limitation to cultic functions or situations is what determines its unique meaning.]

has chosen" in its various forms.[286] So the very nature of the DC feast is exemplified by communal feasting in the central sanctuary.

As stated above, the Deuteronomic celebration calls each head of household to provide the scrumptious feast, broadening the representative identity of Israel from the singular royal representative of the Ugaritic and Mesopotamian myths. Otto formulates his understanding similarly:

> Ist der literarische Kern des Deuteronomiums ein subversive rezipierter Loyalitätseid des assyrischem Königs Asarhaddon ... dann geht damit auch eine neue Idee davon, was eine Volksgemeinschaft konstituiert, einher. Ist es im gesamten Alten Orient sebstverständlich, daß ein Volk durch die im König repräsentierte und durch die Götter legitimierte Hierarchie staatlicher Macht integriert wird, so setzt das Deuteronomium dem das Model einer durch die gemainsame Feier der Wallfahrtsfeste integrierten Gesellschaft entgegen, die auch den Fremden einschließt.[287]

While I am skeptical of Otto's identification of Deuteronomy as a renunciation of a specific loyalty oath to Esarhaddon,[288] he does point out the kind of communal identity that Deuteronomy fosters. He also highlights the dominant ideology against which Deuteronomy reacts. The DC cultic meals are the specific actions (eating, drinking, and rejoicing) at the special place ("before Yhwh" and "at the place Yhwh chooses") where the congregated group articulates their particular identity as "Israel." Braulik recognizes:

> Certainly the Passover-Feast of Unleavened Bread is above all oriented towards worship ... In the deuteronomic liturgy of the Passover and the

---

286 For example, the two phrases appear together in 12:18 to name where sacrifices should be consumed as a contrast to other meals that may occur in one's village. Similar formulations occur in 14:23 (though "before Yhwh your God is omitted from LXX[B]), 14:26, 15:20, 16:11, 16:16 (2x). Cf. the analysis of Ian Wilson, *Out of the Midst of the Fire: Divine Presence in Deuteronomy* (SBLDS 151; Atlanta: Scholar's Press, 1995), 161–67.

287 Otto, *Gottes Recht als Menschenrecht*, 243 [ET: If the literary core of Deuteronomy is a subversive reception of the loyalty oath of the Assyrian king Esarhaddon ... then a new idea also results that constitutes a national community. If it is self-explanatory in the whole ancient Near East that a people would be represented by their king and the divinely legitimated hierarchy would be integrated into the state's power, then Deuteronomy sets up a model that stands in contradiction through its community celebration of pilgrimage feasts that integrate the society and also includes the foreigners].

288 See the arguments provided by Koch, *Vertrag, Treueid und Bund*, especially the shared use of curse terminology found in both Esarhaddon's loyalty oath and Deut 28:20–44 that is also found in Neo-Assyrian letters. This shared terminology suggests that there need not be direct dependence on this one Neo-Assyrian loyalty oath, but rather wider usage.

Feast of Unleavened Bread, the people first of all render present its proto-
type, its departure and its wanderings and thereby reenacts an event in the
history.[289]

By connecting with this foundational narrative, the audience of the DC
texts is called to reconnect with its deity and with each other.

Braulik rightly notes that the festival law "... decidedly expands the
circle of participants compared with the older festival calendar. Reform
of worship and reform of the community are very closely related in
Deuteronomy."[290] The reform of worship describes the unity of the
community based on a common narrative and grows into satisfying
enjoyment by the whole community.[291] The DC reformulation of worship as community-defining cultic meals, mandating provision for all
individuals of the Israelite community, lays out an Iron Age II Israelite
response to the Neo-Assyrian hegemony that was perpetrated militar-
ily, economically, and also ideologically through foundational myths
and rituals such as the *akītu* and *Enuma Elish*, which connected the divine and political monarchs as a way to augment imperial power.

Nelson claims, "Deuteronomy's liturgical reformulation is driven
by a theology that sees traditional local and private celebrations as
dangerous subversions of Israel's relationship to Yahweh. ... From a
polemic standpoint, these three festivals with agricultural connections
counter the fertility claims of rival cults."[292] I would suggest that this
interpretation fails to note the thrust of the DC's argument in light of
the Assyrian threat and its political theology. The prohibition of local
sanctuaries (or, more specifically, local sanctuary sacrifices) does not
forbid local celebrations; however, it does change their location and
orientation within the local community to the "gates" rather than a
sanctuary. Furthermore, as I have suggested above, one might wonder
how intact the local agnatic groups were after the various Assyrian
invasions.[293] According to Deut 12:15–16, special meals of meat certainly may take place locally. Yet in their very difference from centralized celebrations, these local meals recall the festival meals consumed

---

289 Braulik, "Commemoration of Passion and Feast of Joy," 76.
290 Ibid., 81.
291 Yet this reformulation of worship goes beyond an answer to any seductive Baal
     fertility rites as seen in Hosea and an attempt to circumscribe joy to a context within
     Yhwh worship s Braulik contends (ibid., 76, 83).
292 Nelson, *Deuteronomy*, 203; also Houston, "The Function of the Fesal Gathering in
     Deuteronomy," 9. Mayes, *Deuteronomy*, 255, questions whether Unleavened Bread
     could ever have been an agricultural festival since it takes place at the wrong time of
     year, and unleavened bread does not work well as the basis of a pilgrim festival.
293 See above, p. 33, esp. n. 95.

at the chosen place. These systematic differences therefore serve to remind the receivers of the text that their identity moves beyond their local community to participation in Israel as a whole. The texts are therefore not primarily a response to rival fertility cults, although that may be a subsidiary consideration (in 12:15 the local community eats meat "according to the blessing of Yhwh your God"). The DC texts are better explained as a response to the mythologically enshrined claims found in the Baal Cycle and *Enuma Elish,* which designate the high deity and the human king as giver of the banquet instead of the heads of households addressed in 12:13–19 as well as 16:1–17.[294] Houston rightly highlights the patron role of the heads of household in these feasts as the human hosts, which increases their prestige in the community, though all receive patronage from Yhwh, the ultimate donor.[295] Nonetheless, it is important to go a step further and note the contrast between the Deuteronomically envisioned system and the general ancient Near Eastern pattern on display in the close relationships between royal and divine kings in Ugarit and Mesopotamia (and Egypt). As Levinson observes, "There is no provision for the monarch to participate in the cultus, still less to supervise it or serve as royal patron of the Temple. … Deuteronomy's cultic laws envision no role whatsoever for the monarch."[296] Therefore, much in the manner of Victor Turner's analysis, Deut 16:1–17 reformulates the CC festival calendar in response to the experience of Assyrian domination: the DC festival texts seek to transform Judahite society through a particular experience of liminality (the centralized festivals), the experience of which each "Israelite" carries back with them to their homes, thus affecting the meaning of the identifier "Israelite" so that the festive meal becomes the location for societal change (*a la* Turner). The DC ritual meal texts postulate the meals as "fundamentally a response to the divisiveness, alienation, and exploitation that are associated with everyday social structure,"[297] in this case, that experienced under Assyrian domination.

---

294 Otto, *Gottes Recht als Menschenrecht,* 244, points out that in contrast to the usual ancient Near Eastern pattern of state protection for the weak, in Deuteronomy it is the responsibility of each Judahite. I would modify this to say that it was the task of every Judahite *head of household.*

295 Houston, "The Function of the Fesal Gathering in Deuteronomy," 11–13.

296 Levinson, "The Reconceptualization of Kingship," 523.

297 Turner, *Dramas, Fields, and Metaphors,* 250. Turner defines "liminality" as a boundary situation in which people are freed from their normal social obligations, thereby allowing for different formulations of individual and group identity into a simplified idea of "communitas," which is more egalitarian social relations. Independently, Houston, "The Function of the Festal Gathering in Deuteronomy," 9–13, has simi-

From the perspective of de Certeau's "tactics," Deut 16 takes up the widely used literary *topos* (a "strategy") of the divine and royal feast, a symbol generally used to solidify royal authority by use of a divine imprint, and reorganizes the feast according to its own values, focused on Yhwh, the central sanctuary, and the Israelites as broader family units.

---

larly highlighted Turner's insights especially with regard to *communitas* and solidarity in Deut 16.

5. Deuteronomy 14:22–29 in Light of Ancient Near Eastern Tribute and Modern Anthropology

5.1. Introduction

Deuteronomy 14:22–29 provides the most detailed description of the possible menu for the festive meal in Deuteronomy. The choices for consumption can be established based on both the description of elements to be tithed in v. 23 (grain, oil, wine, and the firstborn of the herd and flock),[1] and especially from the suggestive list of what one could buy for celebration in v. 26 — wine, *šēkār* (alternately understood as "beer" or some sort of grappa), beef, mutton, or "whatever you might ask for." This lavish list marks a special meal in its contrast to the mundane meal.[2] Houston describes the festive meal as follows

> A feast in these circumstances is no mere enhancement of the everyday diet, it is radically different from it, in the type of food and drink, being based on flesh meat and including alcohol, in the quantities, and in the company, being a large gathering as distinct from the private household or smaller group.[3]

This fits well into the notion of festival developed by Pieper: "Absence of calculation, in fact lavishness, is one of its elements. … The way is open to senseless and excessive waste of the yield of work, to an extravagance that violates all rationality. The product of a whole year's labor can be thrown away on a single day."[4]

This chapter turns to the DC tithe within the larger pentateuchal and ancient Near Eastern context. The section finishes with an analysis

---

1   On the possibility that the firstborn animals are a later addition, see below, p. 216.
2   MacDonald, *What Did the Ancient Israelites Eat?*, 68 concludes, "In terms of generalities we can at least say that textual and archaeological evidence agree in the centrality of the so-called Mediterranean triad: bread, wine and olive oil. Fruit, vegetables, legumes, milk-products and meat made a much smaller contribution to calorific intake."
3   Houston, "The Function of the Festal Gathering in Deuteronomy," 4.
4   Josef Pieper, *In Tune With the World: A Theory of Festivity* (trans. R. and C. Winston; South Bend: St. Augustine's Press, 1999), 19–20.

of Deut 14:22–29 itself from text-critical, historical-critical, and other interdisciplinary perspectives. Two particular aspects that arise from my discussion are the DC's lack of a royal recipient for the tithe and the rich festive menu in this text.

5.2. Deuteronomy 14:22–29: A History of Scholarship

Having surveyed several interdisciplinary perspectives from Goody, Sutton, and Montanari in an earlier chapter that offer valuable insights for the meals in Deuteronomy, the next section will introduce the particular concerns raised within biblical scholarship itself with regard to Deut 14:22–29. The tithe regulations of Deut 14:22–29 have generally been interpreted in connection to three sets of questions: 1) What is the development of the tithe in ancient Israelite religion as it relates to the various texts in which the tithe occurs? 2) How does the Israelite tithe compare with other state and temple taxes throughout the ancient Near East? And 3) How does the tithe in Deuteronomy fit in with and support the move to centralization?

5.2.1. Comparison with Pentateuchal Texts
(Num 18:21–32; Lev 27:30–33)

Unlike Deut 12 and 16, the tithe does not receive and interpret an earlier *biblical* text, since a law on tithes does not appear in the Covenant Code.[5] This has led some interpreters to propose a different, non-

---

5   There may, however, be some relation to the command in Exod 22:28a [ET 22:29], *mĕlē'ātĕkā wĕdim'ăkā lō' tĕ'aḥēr* ("You shall not be slow [with] your fullness [harvest] or your tears [wine]"), which bears no verbal resemblance. The same may be said for Exod 23:19a, *rē'šît bikkûrê 'admātĕkā tābî' bêt yhwh 'ĕlōhêkā* ("You shall bring the best of the first fruits of your ground to the house of Yhwh your God"), since there is no corresponding command concerning firstfruits except for Deut 18:4 (the priestly portion) or Deut 26:2. The verbal resemblances between Exod 23:19a and Deut 26:2 suggest that this Deuteronom(ist)ic text is likely an expansion and explanation of the earlier CC ordinance. Kratz, *Composition*, 121, formulates the contrast with the CC as follows: "In connection with 12.17f., 14.22-27, 28-29 deal with the tithe, which replaces the vegetable offering of Exod. 22.28 and 23.19; it is not the surpluses or the best, but the tithe of the produce of the field which is to be given year by year and either consumed as such at the place which Yhwh will choose or, if the journey is too long and the burden too heavy, sold beforehand."

biblical source (either oral or written) underlying the DC tithe.[6] Regardless, the lack of a specific mention of the tithe in the CC may point to the significance of this idea in the DC. Given that it is historically speaking the first tithe law in the Pentateuch, there might have been a particular exigency that gave rise to its construction. Comparison with the later, Priestly versions of the tithe will provide an important backdrop for understanding the specific thrust of the Deuteronomic version.

The (post-)Priestly text Num 18:21–32 views the tithes as an exchange (*ḥēlep* in Num 18:21, 31) for the service rendered by the Levites at the sanctuary: "Now to the Levites I give the whole tithe in Israel as an inheritance in exchange for services they perform, the service of the Tent of Meeting" (Num 18:21). This formulation of the tithe contrasts starkly with the DC version. In both Numbers and Deuteronomy the Levites should receive their portion (cf. Deut 14:27 and 28–29), but the manner in which landowners distribute this portion takes on a remarkably different feel. Numbers 18:21 designates the whole tithe (*kol ma'ăśēr*) as property of the Levites, while in the DC the Levites should be cared for, but more out of a feeling of *communitas* rather than exchange for service. Both actions are prescriptive legal ordinances, yet the two presentations differ significantly. Deuteronomy 14:27 commands the DC audience to "not abandon" (*lō' ta'zennû*)[7] and therefore to include the Levite in the feast with the tithe produce, while Num 18:21 describes the tithe as a payment for Levites' work. Inheritance (*naḥălāh*) also plays a role in both descriptions, yet again with different tones. Deuteronomy 14:27—in the received form—reminds the audience that the Levites have no portion of the land as Num 18:23 also suggests, but Num 18:24 (also v. 25) then adds that therefore the tithe is their inheritance (cf. Deut 18:1–5). The Numbers version also prescribes a tenth of the tenth as the Levites' offering to the deity received by Aaron and the priests, an idea absent, at least explicitly, from the DC version.

Numbers 18:27, 31 elaborate on the produce included in the tithe, naming grain and wine, while leaving out the third member of Deut 14:23's agricultural triad (oil). Numbers 18 also omits any mention of

---

6   Seitz, *Redaktionsgeschichtliche Studien,*193, argues that v. 22 is pre-Deuteronomic since it does not prescribe centralization. Cf. Morrow, *Scribing the Center,* 13.

7   While I view this clause as a possible secondary addition, it still serves to accentuate a possible reading of the earliest text, and even if an addition, it explains the Levites' inclusion. More analysis of the composition history of the text appears below (5.2.2. Compositional History of Deuteronomy 14:22–29).

meat, either conceived of as the firstlings like Deut 14:23 or the tenth animal passing under the keeper's staff in Lev 27:32.[8]

Numbers allows the Levites to eat their portion of the tithe anywhere (18:31), thereby setting it off from the holy portion (v. 32: *qodĕšē bĕnê yiśrā'ēl*). This allowance contrasts with the tithe eaten at the sanctuary in Deut 14:22–27 and corresponding instead to the third year tithe consumed by the Levites, widows, orphans, and sojourners in 14:28–29. This mention of the sojourners, orphans, and widows in Deut 14:28 marks a significantly different social impulse in the DC from the perspectives in Numbers and Leviticus. There seems little room in the Num18 formulation for reconciliation with Deut 14.

Leviticus 27:30–33 presents the tithe in the Holiness Code, where it appears as the final ordinance of the HC. This formulation of the law presents more similarities to the Deuteronomic formulation than the Numbers version. In the HC the tithe first addresses agricultural produce generally (*wĕkol ma'śar hā'āreṣ*, then elaborating with "the seed of the land" and "the fruit of the tree" as distinct categories. Deuteronomy 14:22–23 likewise begins with a general category but is followed by the tripartite *dĕgānĕkā tîrōšĕkā wĕyiṣhārekā* ("your grain, your new wine, and your oil"). Leviticus 23:32 bears a further similarity to Deut 14:23 in its inclusion of an animal tithe. The similarity stops at the mutual inclusion however, since the HC imagines a situation where a flock or herd walks under its keeper's staff and every tenth animal is set apart for the sanctuary.[9] Deuteronomy 14:23 instead subsumes firstlings under the tithe category. The general inclusion of animals in the tithe does find similarities to other tithe practices in Mesopotamia.[10]

Key to the HC's understanding is that these products belong to Yhwh (vv. 30, 32, 33). The farmer does not own them and then give them away, but rather they always begin as and remain the property of the deity. The prices for redemption of the agricultural tithe in v. 31 and the impossibility of redeeming tithed animals in v. 33 underscore this emphasis on ownership.

---

8   Neh 10:37 [ET 10:36–39] follows the understanding of Deut 14, including tithes of plant produce as well as firstlings.

9   The HC conceives of the animal tithe similarly to 1 Sam 8:17, where the king takes a tenth of the flock. The tithe of 2 Chr 31:5–6 also includes a tithe of animals without explaining how the animals were selected.

10   Milgrom, *Leviticus*, 3:2422, comments, "In Mesopotamia, there is evidence of tithes from agricultural produce, cattle and sheep, slaves, donkeys, wool, cloth, wood, metal production, silver, gold, and so on."

In contrast to both Numbers and Deuteronomy, the HC shows no interest in the location of consumption or specification of the persons consuming the tithe. The human receivers are completely avoided, while the divine recipient and owner comes to the fore.

This brief overview brings several aspects of the DC tithe law in Deut 14 into focus. As expected, the Deuteronomic formulation highlights the consumption of the tithe by the whole people of Israel, imagined as a multiplicity of households coming together. The corresponding centripetal and centrifugal movements (first towards the sanctuary and then to the villages for the third year tithe) match the meals of Deut 12:13–19. Finally, Deuteronomy also highlights concern for the marginal elements of society.

5.2.2. Compositional History of Deuteronomy 14:22–29

Kratz, as a representative of recent (Germanic) scholarship, envisions that the earliest layer of the text included v. 22, followed then by vv. 25–26aα, 26b.[11] His view may be set against that of Morrow, who views only 14:23b, 14:27aβ as additions, and everything else as belonging to the original layer.[12] Given these fairly diverse opinions, I will consider each verse in detail in order to build my argument about the earliest layer of the DC text.

The pericope sets itself apart from what precedes with the strong opening in 14:22 of an infinitive absolute followed by the imperfect of 'śr.[13] Since the rest of the section depends on this verse, the prevailing

---

11 Kratz, *Composition*, 121: "The additional regulation in 14.28–9, which was probably added later, is a consequence of the centralization of the offerings. … The text is expanded not only in v. 27 but also in vv. 23f., 29b." See also n. 27. Ibid., 150–51: on additions: "Verse 23 'to make his name dwell there', 'and the firstborn of your cattle and your sheep', v. 24aα²βγ (from 'for the place is too far…'), perhaps also the list of kindnesses in v. 26a (from the oxen) and vv. 23b, 24b, 29b. Thus most scholars. But perhaps all of vv. 23f. were also added later, so that originally v. 25 was directly attached to v. 22." Two mediating positions, from quite different perspectives generally, are Veijola, *5. Mose*, 305, who views vv. 22–23a, 24a, 25–26, 28–29a* as original and Nelson, *Deuteronomy*, 185–86, who calls only vv. 23aβ (possibly all of 23a), the third *kî* clause of v. 24, and the list of v. 26 as additions.

12 Morrow, *Scribing the Center*, 13.

13 Similar constructions are also found in 15:10, 14. Morrow, *Scribing the Center*, 81, 211–15, notes that this construction is rare at the beginning of a section (cf. the late 12:2), and (following the earlier works of Horst, Nebeling, Seitz, and Merendino) concludes that 14:22 comes from a pre-Dtn source. See also Nielsen, *Deuteronomium*, 156.

consensus argues that v. 22 represents traditional (either oral or written) material. Generally speaking interpreters conclude, correctly in my mind, that all of v. 22 belongs to the original text.

The following verse contains several debated phrases and clauses. Seitz suggests that the election formula was not original on syntactical grounds, since it separates the verb ("eat") inordinately far from its object ("the tithe"),[14] yet, as Morrow notes, in Deut 26:5, 13 the object is similarly separated from the verb by a phrase noting the spatial location of the action.[15] This similarity suggests that such a construction is not outside the bounds of typical Deuteronomic style. Of course the question of whether Deut 26 was part of the earliest version of Deuteronomy might complicate this argument. Nonetheless, the question of where the meal is eaten is of decisive importance in the Deuteronomic program, suggesting that its possibly surprising syntactical placement of this clause could be deliberate.

Morrow, among others, also notes that the original tithe ordinance in v. 22 focuses on grain, which v. 23 expands to the triad of grain, wine, and oil in addition to the firstlings.[16] The inclusion of the firstlings in this list of products is often viewed as secondary because tithes often only include plant products[17] and because Deuteronomy addresses firstlings in their own section (15:19–23).

---

14   Seitz, *Redaktionsgeschichtliche Studien,* 193–95. Seitz's position does have textual support in the *OG* of Codex Vaticanus. Nielsen, *Deuteronomium,* 156, also argues that *lĕšakkēn šĕmô šām* in v. 23a should be viewed as a Dtr redaction, likely because it makes the syntax of the sentence more difficult in that it separates the verb even farther from its object, but the present text does not seem outside of Deuteronomic style. Kratz's proposal to eliminate the phrase from the verse seems unduly connected to his contention that this phrase is not part of the original layer, which I have argued is problematic above. Once this presupposition is removed, there is no compelling reason to view the phrase as later.

15   Morrow, *Scribing the Center,* 85.

16   Ibid., 83, "A tension exists between the sense of v. 22 and v. 23, since the former enjoins only the tithing of grain rather than the triad of grain, new wine, and oil. It is clear from other contexts that the harvest which comes out of the field is grain by definition." He offers Gen 47:24 and Exod 23:10–11, 16 as example texts. This has also been noticed earlier by Samuel R. Driver, *A Critical and Exegetical Commentary on Deuteronomy* (3d ed. ICC; Edinburgh: Clark, 1902), 166 and by Nelson, *Deuteronomy,* 184, who comments, "Deuteronomy's law of the tithe grows out of an older 'seed tithe' law, visible behind v. 22, which is converted into an opportunity for joyful familial and social fellowship at the central sanctuary." Nelson's notion of conversion coincides well with the comments of Yu below.

17   This is the opinion of Nelson, *Deuteronomy,* 185. Cf. Num 18:21–32, which is the one clear example of a tithe without animals. Gen 14:20; 28:22; and Amos 4:4 are unclear, while 1 Sam 8:17; 2 Chr 31:5–6; and Lev 27:30–33 include animals.

However, as mentioned above, Lev 27:30–33, while likely a later text, also includes an animal tithe, though conceived quite differently. Furthermore, Yu notes that the Masoretic reading does not include firstlings as part of the tithe, strictly speaking, as the *zaqeph qaton* separating them shows. He suggests, "They are mentioned here presumably because they are to be eaten at the same place."[18] Similarly, Robertson Smith argues that no cultic meal could have taken place without meat.[19] Though much of his analysis is outdated, this point does seem to get to the point of the nature of a particularly festive meal, along with the consumption of alcohol. The decidedly different approach to tithes in Deuteronomy, as part of the cultic meal for the whole household—especially when 14:26 is in view—necessitates that some sort of meat be available when tithes are brought. Furthermore, the inclusion of the firstlings is a direct link to Deut 12:13–19, where tithes are first mentioned and the text upon which 14.22–27 is elaborating. The list appearing in 14:23 is actually a *shortened* version of the one found in 12:17.[20] Finally, as Morrow notes, while firstlings may seem out of place because of the surrounding context which focuses on plant products, perhaps 14:22–29, with the inclusion of the firstlings, means to supply a mode of compensation for the blemished animals of 15:19–23.[21] These considerations speak for the inclusion of 23aβ in the earliest form of the text.

Most interpreters (i.e., Kratz, Braulik, Morrow, Mayes, Nelson) consider 14:23b ("in order that you may learn to fear Yhwh your God for all time") a later insertion. They note that the conception of Israel as a learning community in Deuteronomy primarily occurs in texts generally accepted as late, such as 4:10; 5:29–31; and 31:12–13.[22] Mayes argues

---

18 Yu, "Tithes and Firstlings in Deuteronomy," 66.

19 Robertson Smith, *Religion of the Semites*, 242, 255.

20 Deut 12:17 includes "and everything that you vow and your free-will offerings and the gifts of your hand" (*wĕkol nĕdārêkā 'ăšer tiddōr wĕnidbōtêkā ûtĕrûmat yadekā*).

21 Morrow, *Scribing the Center*, 85 (cf. 205) notes that the repetition of the firstlings in 14:23 "… would be acceptable, however, if it were necessary to incorporate traditional [pre-Deuteronomic] material in 15:19 into a Dtn composition."

22 Morrow, *Scribing the Center*, 206. Cf. Georg Braulik, "Das Deuteronomium und die Gedächtniskulture Israels: Redaktionsgeschichtliche Beobachtungen zur Verwendung von *lmd*," in *Studien zum Buch Deuteronomium* (SBAB 24; Verlag Katholisches Bibelwerk, 1997; repr. from *Biblische Theologie und gesellschaftlicher Wandel* [ed. G. Braulik et al.; Freiburg: Herder, 1993]), 137–38, who dates this clause to an exilic Dtr redaction because its notion of learning is compatible with that found in the law of the king, Deut 17:19. Reuter, *Kultzentralisation*, 159, claims that learning fear is secondary because it contradicts the joyfulness of the feasts. Yu's analysis (below, p. 228–29) provides a different alternative, though the clause is likely still later.

that this clause links offerings with the reading of the law, and thus with the Festival of Booths (cf. 31:10), when men needed to travel to the sanctuary, making it a convenient occasion for the delivery of tithes as well.[23] This argument is plausible, but based on an unnecessary inference because the DC never explicitly connects the tithe with Booths. A second reason for seeing this text as an addition is the phrase *kol hayyāmîm*, which appears chiefly in likely later insertions—5:29; 12:1; 18:5; 19:9. I therefore conclude that vv. 22–23a comprise the original layer of this first section.

The second section, vv. 24–27, displays even more significant overlap with Deut 12, making redaction-critical questions for each text contingent on the other. If one uses the election formula as a criterion for dating, then at least parts of these verses can be seen as later since they contain the long form with *lāśûm šēmô šām* in v. 24aγ.[24] This portion of v. 24 also relates to the broadening of territory using the exact terminology of 12:21a, providing some interpreters further incentive to judge it as a later addition.[25]

The syntax of v. 24 is somewhat ambivalent. There are various ways that the first three *kî* clauses may be put together:[26] "Now if the road becomes too great *so that* you are not able to carry it [the tithe]" or "Now if the road becomes too great *because* you are not able to carry it." The main issue here is whether or not the second *kî* is the reason explaining why the road is too great, or if it is instead a result clause.[27] The notion of a result clause is supported by, possibly superior, text-critical evidence that the second *kî* was originally a *waw*.[28]

---

23   Mayes, *Deuteronomy*, 245.

24   SamP, which like MT and in contrast to the Targums distinguishes between the two different long forms of the election formula (between the use of *śym* and *škn*), uses the infinitive of *škn* rather than *śym*. This variation calls into question the basis of source-critical analyses that separate layers on the basis of which form of the election formula is used. See the more detailed discussion of this phenomenon in 3.5.1. The Election Formula as a Proposed Key to Relative Dating.

25   Rose, *5. Mose*, 1:35, argues that vv. 24–27a in their entirety come from his second layer—dated to Josiah and including 12:20–27—on the assumption that the distance to Jerusalem was passable during Hezekiah's time, but Josiah expanded the boundaries of the kingdom so that it became unreasonably far. Note that Veijola, *5. Mose*, 266, and Otto, *Deuteronomium*, 346–47, among recent interpreters consider 12:21 part of the earliest Deuteronomic layer, however.

26   Reuter, *Cultzentralisation*, 159.

27   Compare *IBHS*, §38.3, 638–39 and §38.4, 640–41.

28   The Peshitta and OG simply have the copulative *waw* in place of *kî*. MT and the other versions seem to be levelling out the use of *kî*, suggesting *waw* was more original, which would read "Now if the way becomes too far for you and you are not able to

Several points complicate the view that the section does not, at least in its entirety, come from a later version. There are significant textual difficulties with using the versions of the election formula as a primary basis for establishing the layers in the text. Furthermore, while the syntax of v. 24 seems overloaded, the theme of divine blessing also appears in 12:15 and 16:10, both of which arguably belong with the earliest Deuteronomic layer.[29] A similar point can be made for the similarity between the first clause of v. 24aα, *wĕkî yirbeh mimmĕkā hadderek*, and the very similar wording in Deut 19:6, which describes the way for the asylum seeker (*kî yirbeh hadderek*).[30] The change in the places of asylum is directly related to centralization, and therefore could easily be original. Furthermore, neither v. 25 or v. 26 make sense without v. 24aα. For these reasons I propose that the earliest layer included 24aα and 24bβ, reading: "And if the way becomes too much and you are not able to carry it when Yhwh your God blesses you, (v. 25) then you shall exchange [it] with silver ..."

Nelson suggests that the list in v. 26 is also secondary, though the DC shows a proclivity for such lists.[31] The repetition of the same idea of personal desire, first *bĕkōl 'ăšer tĕ'awweh napšĕkā* and then *ûkōl 'ăšer tiš'ālĕkā*, underscores the Yhwh's lavish provision in light of the socioeconomic and political-religious situation in Judah during the late pre-exilic period.[32]

---

carry it." There is also some ambiguity about the third *kî* clause. Does it explain how the road could become too great (i.e., because the central sanctuary is too distant), or simply underscore the situation given in the first two clauses? Given the already loaded syntax, it seems best to take the clause as a later insertion that adds emphasis through renaming.

29 Morrow, *Scribing the Center*, 87, also makes the suggestion that v. 24aγ could represent a repetition "with structural value" instead of a literary doublet. The clause mentioning the sanctuary does make explicit *which* way has become too long for transporting the tithe. Without this clause the audience must return back to the beginning of v. 23. However, it does seem most likely that v. 24aγ, "when the place which Yhwh your God has chosen to set his name becomes too distant for you," does come from a later layer. Morrow's notion of the "structural value" of the repetition seems overblown.

30 Included by, i.e., Kratz, *Composition*, 123, in the original layer.

31 Nelson, *Deuteronomy*, 185; also Kratz, *Composition*, 121. Compare the lists of types of offerings: 12:6, 11, 17; household members: 12:12, 18; 16:11, 14; those without normal means of provision: 14:29; and items to tithe: 14:23. Many of these come from the earliest layer of Deuteronomy, though their ubiquity throughout does leave the possibility open that it is added later to describe the elements of such a meal.

32 Note the conclusions of Oded Lipschitz, *The Fall and Rise of Jerusalem Judah Under Babylonian Rule* (Winona Lake, Ind.: Eisenbrauns, 2005), 220–21: "Data from the *archaeological survey* that has been conducted in the Shephelah since 1979 supplement

On the basis of the appearance of the same clause in Deut 12:12b, Rose assigns 14:27b—*kî 'ên lō' ḥēleq wěnaḥălāh*—to his third layer, judged by most as Deuteronomistic or part of some later layer.[33] All of v. 27b ("You shall not abandon him," which may be a later text-critical plus in MT) is found in Deut 12:12b, and the statement about the Levites' lack of inheritance also occurs in Deut 10:9; 14:29; and 18:1. The appearance of the lack of inheritance also occurs in 12:12 and 10:9, which are likely Deuteronomistic. Further support is garnered from the statement's omission from 12:18–19. On the basis of the Levites inclusion in 12:19, and because the Levite is separated from its usual triad of the sojourner, widow and orphan, there seems little textual reason to view v. 27a as an addition.

For the final section, vv. 28–29, there seems little need to question the seamlessness of the text, except for the Levites' lack of inheritance. Mayes summarizes, "The law of vv. 28f. is found in no older source and should be seen as a deuteronomic innovation."[34] However, the mention of the Levites' lack of inheritance also appears here in v. 29, so there is some question about the date of the clause in this verse as well. The lack of this conception's appearance in an earlier source may or may support its inclusion in the earliest layer. The DC tithe demonstrates the texts ability to go beyond the CC source text to address other areas of interest, and the provisions for the Levite, sojourner, and others also fits the DC program.

---

the picture obtained from archaeological excavations. The survey results show that, during the ninth and eighth centuries b.c.e., the Shephelah experienced a flowering of settlement activity: opulation density increased; many new settlements were established (particularly small, agricultural sites); and the settled area extended to new regions, primarily in the western part of the Shephelah … Sennacherib's campaign (701 b.c.e.) dealt the Shephelah a severe blow from which it did not recover. It is also likely that the problematic economic, political, and security conditions in the region, which grew more serious as the seventh century b.c.e. advanced (the rending of territory from Judah, the presence of the Assyrian army, the destruction of forts on Judah's border, and the growth of the kingdom of Ekron) caused the population to continue to dwindle. The decline in settlement is most evident at the smaller sites, and it appears that, as the seventh century b.c.e. progressed, settlement was greatest in the eastern parts of the Shephelah, with the population concentrated mainly in major cities."

33   Rose, *5. Mose*, 1:35. He likewise assigns the same clause in v. 29a to this Dtr layer. Reuter, *Kultzentralisation*, 160–61, also argues that the original text of v. 27 stopped with "and the Levite who is in your gates."

34   Mayes, *Deuteronomy*, 246.

5.3. Ancient Near Eastern and Israelite Background

Deuteronomy 14:22–29 as a whole explains the mention of the tithe in Deut 12:17. But before exploring the connections to chapter 12, this section will explore the meaning of the terms *'śr* and *m'śr* and the ancient Near Eastern background of the tithe. Given the fact that the DC tithe is not following its primary source text, the CC, with the inclusion of a tithe, the search for other possible juxtapositions becomes increasingly important.[35]

Braulik mentions the possibility that *'śr* may not have meant "tenth" before the exile, but rather "serving a meal" (here, for the poor).[36] This meaning is apparent for various Ugaritic texts, such as the Baal Cycle (*CTU* 1.3.I.9) in the context of Baal's victory feast after vanquishing Yamm, when he prepares the meat and then the cup.[37] The problem with Braulik's proposal is that instead of a banquet for the benefit of the poor, the Ugaritic texts refer more to a royal or divine celebration. This is also the case for Deut 14:22–26, which do not seem to have the poor particularly in view. There is also some question about whether the two homonyms are related. Pardee, however, argues, "Un rapport avec 'ŚR « dix, dîme » n'est pas impossible: en guèze les deux mots s'expriment par la même racine. Il se sera agi à l'origine du festin sacré alimenté par la dîme, et le verbe sera donc dénominatif."[38] Fur-

---

35   I find it surprising that this divergence from the CC and acknowledgement of the long-standing existence of the tithe did not lead commentators such as Veijola, *5. Mose*, 306, to reflect on the purpose for the tithe's inclusion in the DC.

36   Braulik, *Deuteronomium 1–16,17*, 96. Mayes, *Deuteronomy*, 245, similarly notes that *'śr* might have the broader meaning, "to offer." He references Cyrus Gordon, *Ugaritic Textbook: Grammar, Texts in Transliteration, Cuneiform Selections, Glossary, Indices* (3 vols.; AO 35; Rome: Pontifical Biblical Institute, 1965), 462.

37   Smith, "The Baal Cycle," 106, and Pardee, "Baal Cycle," *COS* 1:250 translate "serves." In the Aqhat narrative, Anat offers Aqhat to make him like Baal, who revives, and "invites" to drink (*CTU* 1.17.VI.30) . It is translated by Simon B. Parker, "Aqhat" in *UNP*, 61, as "invites." Here again the context is clearly festal. The situation is similar in the Kirta narrative, 1.16.I.39–41, where Kirta gives a feast *(krtn dbḥ dbḥ / mlk 'šr 'šrt*: Kirta is hosting a feast/ The king gives a banquet"). In the ritual text 1.119:32–33 one finds *'šrt b 'l n 'šr*: "the banquet for Baal we will (or "let us") give." There might be a similar banquet for Astarte when she enters the sacred pit in the palace and temple in *CTU* 1.43:2. *DUL*, 188, glosses, "1) 'to invite'; 2) 'to give a banquet.'"

38   Pardee, *Les Textes Rituels*, 1:228–29 n. 61, He also notes (ibid.) that the root meaning "invite" appears in Arabic and Akkadian. [ET: A relationship with 'ŚR "ten, tenth" is not impossible: in Ge'ez the two words are expressed through the same root. It was originally a holy banquet that was financed by the tithe, so the verb is a denominative.]

thermore, Baumgarten argues that both *m'šr* and δεκατη in the Second Temple were used both literally and non-literally, perhaps even within a single document.[39] Baumgarten's references do not necessarily support Braulik's suggestion, but they do imply that there was some elasticity to the term, at least in the Late Bronze Age and in the Second Temple period. Whether this has any bearing on the DC is therefore an open question. If the authors and audience of the DC were well acquainted with the myths and linguistic variations found at Ugarit such as the Baal Cycle, then perhaps '*šr* in Deut 14:22–29 leaves the door open to secondary connotations of "to prepare, to invite to a banquet" in addition to "give a tenth."[40] Within the context of Deut 14:22, there is a relatively clear implication that the text is referring to something of a "tax" or similar type institution, which means that the banquet notions would be secondary, though evocative connotations.[41] These hints of a banquet in relation to the tax or tribute are supported by the wide-reaching connection between tribute paid to a ruler and royal/divine hospitality. This connection should not be forgotten in light of the absence of a royal presence in the DC, especially as host for the cultic banquets in general and here as recipient of the tithe, tribute, or tax.

Because the palace and temple were closely connected throughout the ancient Near East, tithes cannot easily be separated into either a sacred or secular purpose, but they instead bundle both religious and political purposes together. However, the various regimes supported their religious institutions using different methods. In general, as Crüsemann remarks, "Hervorzuheben ist, daß der enge Zusammenhang von Palast und Tempel sich auch auf diesem Gebiet voll bestätigt.

---

39   Joseph M. Baumgarten, "On the Non-Literal Use of *ma'ăśer* / δεκατη," *JBL* 103 (1984): 245–46, states, "It is, in our opinion, possible to demonstrate that the use of *ma'ăśer*, not only in its literal sense of a 10-percent impost but also as a general term for any tax payable to the Temple or the clergy, was characteristic of both Hebrew and Greek sources stemming from the period of the Second Temple." He notes 2 Chr 31:5, 6, 12; Philo, *De virtutibus,* 95; and the *Temple Scroll* (11QTᵃ) 60:4–10 as places where this phenomenon of literal and non-literal usage occurs.

40   As found in *HALOT*, 894. Note that *HALOT*, 898 lists a possible second עשר, (with "š") glossed as "to give drink to" (Ps 65:10) and linked to the above named Ugaritic texts.

41   Yohanan Aharoni, *Arad Inscriptions* (Jerusalem: Israel Exploration Society, 1981), 20, restores the late seventh or early sixth century letter from Arad (5:10–12) , as "who will send (?) you the ti[the](*m'šr*) baths before the month passes," but the broken context precludes any firm reconstruction and subsequent conclusions about the tithe in the Judahite kingdom at the time.

Das Steuersystem ist überall auch ein Ausdruck der religiösen Bedeutung altorientalischen Königtums."[42]

In Akkadian texts from Ugarit entire cities were responsible for delivering tithes of grain, beer, wine, and oxen via royal officials to the king.[43] Yet while the deliveries went to the king, temple personnel in Ugarit were royal officials.[44]

Egypt during the New Kingdom funneled all taxes through the pharaoh. Pharaoh in turn took on the personal support of the temples and deities.[45] Pharaoh alone was to perform temple rituals according to the iconography, thereby making the temple priests and servants his representatives.[46] In the Egyptian conception the pharaoh was the focus point of the meeting between the human, the divine, and the political. Taxes and temple support were no exception, but instead were important methods toward the focus of power in the person or institution of the pharaoh. O'Connor concludes, "As testaments to royal bounty and to pharaoh's unique links to the gods, temples reinforced pharaonic power while systemically serving as state agencies."[47]

In Babylon and Assyria it also seems that temple tithe collection was never completely separate from (or out of the oversight of) the ruling regime.[48] However, the typical connection between temple and

---

42 Crüsemann, "Der Zehnte in der israelitischen Königszeit," 28 [ET: Highlighted is the fact that the close connection beween palace and temple is also completely confirmed in this area. The tax system was an expression of religious significance for the ancient Near Eastern kingdoms everywhere.]

43 Michael Heltzer, "On Tithe Paid in Grain in Ugarit," *IEJ* 25 (1975): 124–25, mentions *PRU* III.16.153 l. 10 and *PRU* III.10.044.

44 Gary A. Anderson, *Sacrifices and Offerings in Ancient Israel: Studies in Their Social and Political Importance* (HSM 41; Atlanta: Scholars, 1987), 79, notes that the priests at Ugarit also receive payments from the tithes, and are treated just like other specialists (traders, administrators, etc.) of the king (*bnš mlk*, see *PRU* V.11). Cf. Frank Crüsemann, "Der Zehnte in der israelitischen Königszeit," *WD* 18 (1985): 24–25.

45 Donald B. Redford, "Studies in the Relations between Palestine and Egypt during the First Millennium B.C.: The Taxation System of Solomon," in *Studies in the Ancient Palestinian World* (ed. J. W. Wevers and D. B. Redford; Toronto: University of Toronto Press, 1972), 145.

46 David O'Connor, "The Social and Economic Organization of Ancient Egyptian Temples," *CANE* 1:320.

47 Ibid., 322.

48 Crüsemann, "Der Zehnte in der israelitischen Königszeit," 26–28. In the Neo-Babylonian period the tithe went to the temples (even the king paid), but there is a striking confluence between the cities receiving tax exemptions and those with major temples. M. A. Dandameyev, "State and Temple in Babylonia in the First Millennium B.C.," in *State and Temple Economy in the Ancient Near East* (vol. 2; ed. E. Lipiński; OLA 6; Leuven: Departement Oriëntalistiek, 1979), 2:590–94, comments that at least by the reign of Nabonidus, royal authority over the previously powerful tem-

monarch was quite different than in Egypt or Ugarit. It has been suggested that the regular contributions from temple communities, while absent from the archival records, provided the major source of sustenance for the Mesopotamian temples.[49] In the Neo-Babylonian period all residents were required to pay a tithe to the closest temple from their livelihood, be it grain, wool, or other goods.[50] Also, until the reign of the Achamaenids, even the kings paid some sort of tithe.[51]

The situation in Assur during the Neo-Assyrian empire has been discussed in some detail above.[52] With regard to regular provision of the Aššur Temple Postgate argues that the provinces of Assyria were responsible for provisions for a fixed period of time, much like the provision of Solomon's table in 1 Kgs 4:7–19.[53] Postgate goes on to suggest

> So when Esarhaddon marched into Egypt in 671, the (albeit brief) incorporation of this new territory within 'Assyria' is marked by the offering in vegetable and other commodities imposed on the defeated land. This is not tribute from a client state, but offerings from one part of the land to its central shrine. The expansion of Assyria did not entail creating new Assur temples across the empire, or interfering with local religious practices, but adding to the constituency from which these symbolic offerings were dispatched.[54]

While the cult of Sin at Harran does appear to have been supported by the Assyrian rulers,[55] if Postgate's position is generally correct, this Assyrian practice and its incumbent ideology might easily have elicited a subversive response from those forced to pay such allegiance to Aššur

---

ples was growing. Royal officials determined the rations of temple personnel. This was also the case for the temples under the Assyrians. In Assyria, the king took on considerably more of a priestly role than in Babylon, as shown by Masetti-Rouault, "Le roi, la fête et le sacrifice," 71–73.

49 John F. Robertson, "The Social and Economic Organization of Ancient Mesopotamian Temples," *CANE* 1:445.
50 M. A. Dandamayev, "State and Temple in Babylonia in the First Millennium B.C.," 2: 593.
51 Stevens, *Temples, Tithes, and Taxes*, 98.
52 See section 1.2.3. Deuteronomy's Relationship to Assyrian Imperialism?, and further comments, in 3.3. Iconography and Records of Meat and Banquets in the Ancient Near East, and 4.3.2. Ugaritic Narratives.
53 J. N. Postgate, "Royal Ideology and State Administration in Sumer and Akkad," *CANE* 1:406 for the time of Tiglath-pileser I, 1:409–10 for Tiglath Pileser III; reference in Yu, "Tithes and Firstlings in Deuteronomy," 39.
54 Postgate, "Royal Ideology and State Administration in Sumer and Akkad," 1:410. See the detailed treatment in Menzel, *Assyrische Tempel*, 293 (also the short summary in Crüsemann, "Der Zehnte in der israelitischen Königszeit," 25–26).
55 See above, p. 34.

the king and his vice-regent, the human king of Assyria.[56] Instead of sending their produce to the central—and only—temple for Aššur in this period in Assyria, the DC suggests communal consumption of the tithe at Yhwh's temple.

Kratz has recently attempted to relativize the importance of this singular temple for Aššur for Deuteronomy, insisting instead on the need to look for Israelite/Judahite internal reasons for centralization.[57] While he may be correct that the singularity of the Aššur temple does not in and of itself lead directly to the DC's cult centralization, the fact that the DC includes a tithe law at all is suggestive.

In general, the evidence from surrounding cultures bears considerable similarity to the threat in 1 Sam 8:11–18, where the king takes the tithe.[58]

> Then he said, "This will be the practice of the king that rules over you: He will take your sons and appoint them his charioteers and his riders, and they will run before his chariot. And to set them as leaders of thousands and leaders of fifties, and to plow his fields and reap his harvest, and to make his weapons and chariot equipment. Your daughters he will also take for his perfumers, his butchers, and his bakers. Your fields, your vineyards, and your best olive groves he will also appropriate and he will make [you] his servants. He will take a tithe of your seed and your vintage and give them to his eunuchs and his servants. Your male and female servants, your good young men and your donkeys he will appropriate and he will use them for his work. He will take a tithe of your flock, and you will become servants to him. But on the day when you cry out because of the king that you have chosen for yourselves, Yhwh will not answer you on that day. (1 Sam 8:11–18)

Such a system, perhaps not always as oppressive as the polemic Samuel text, seems likely throughout the period of the monarchy in both Israel and Judah. It explicitly contains not only general appropriation of re-

---

56 Stefan M. Maul, "Der assyrische König—Hüter der Weltordnung," in *Priests and Officials in the Ancient Near East: Papers of the Second Colloquium on the Ancient Near East—The City and its Life Held at the Middle Eastern Culture Center in Japan (Mitaka, Tokyo), March 22-24, 1996* (ed. K. Watanabe; Heidelberg: Winter, 1999), 207, notes that the king, even in the Neo-Assyrian period, is not seen primarily as a king, but as the regent of the deity, first Enlil and later Aššur). Yet this also worked in reverse so that the human ruler would take on mythic and divine attributes in the royal inscriptions (ibid., 210).

57 Kratz, "The Idea of Cultic Centralization and Its Supposed Ancient Near Eastern Analogies," 125–26.

58 Cf. Anson F. Rainey, "Institutions: Family, Civil, and Military," in *Ras Shamra Parallels: The Texts from Ugarit and the Hebrew Bible* (ed. L. R. Fisher; AO 50; Rome: Pontifical Bible Institute, 1975), 2:93–98.

sources by the crown, but also explicitly mentions a royal tithe both of plant harvests and of animals.

As is well known, Amos 7:10–17 (cf. 1 Kgs 12:26–33, which explicitly connects the monarchy, the temple at Bethel, *and* the centrality of the king during the newly established festival to counter the celebration of Booths in the seventh month, i.e., Lev 23:34) highlights the intimate connection between the sanctuary and priests in Bethel with the monarch of the northern kingdom. It is noteworthy that Amos 4:4 specifically condemns the practice of bringing a tithe to Bethel.

The preexilic (Solomonic) temple had rather close ties to the Judahite king, as shown in the fact that the king repeatedly appropriated its valuables to pay tribute, beginning with the report of Rehoboam's payment to Sheshonq/Shishak (1 Kgs 14:25–28).[59] Asa's payment to Tabrimmon of Damascus for protection from Baasha of Israel included both valuables from the palace as well as from the treasuries of the house of the Lord (1 Kgs 15:18). Ahaz makes a similar gift of allegiance to Tiglath-pileser III of the temple's bronze furniture (2 Kgs 16:17–18), similar to Joash before him (2 Kgs 12:18–19). Finally, Hezekiah too was forced to pay tribute from the palace treasure and temple silver and gold overlaid doorposts, according to 2 Kgs 18:13–16.

Perhaps even more striking are the proportions and location of the First Temple. Keel notes that the amount of time devoted to building the royal palace (13 years) and its size (ca. 50 meters x 25m x 15m) reveal its importance in comparison to the temple (7 years; 30m x 10m x 15m;). More telling is the conclusion, "Setzt man die Maßangaben von 1Kön 6,1–9,9 in eine Rekonstruktion bzw. einen Plan um, schrumpft der Tempel zu einer 'Palastkirche.'"[60]

It is these very connections between temple and palace that have led many interpreters to conclude that the DC was a royal document either under Hezekiah or Josiah that attempted to collect the economic resources of the Judahite kingdom that were usually dispersed among the various sanctuaries all into the central Jerusalem temple.[61] Yet surprisingly, as I have noted in the previous chapters and will argue again below, the king is absent from the tithe, and the proceeds of the tithe are consumed by their bearers. The Israelites are to eat their taxes.

---

59   For an overview of the historical issues surrounding the events this passage see Keel, *Die Geschichte Jerusalems und die Entstehung des Monotheismus*, 1:339–44.

60   Ibid., 248. [ET: If one uses the figures from 1 Kgs 6:1–9:9 as the basis for a reconstruction, the temple shrinks to a "palace church."]

61   I.e., Schaper, *Priester und Leviten im achämenidischen Juda*, 94–95 (below, 230 n. 74).

5.4. Reading of Deuteronomy 14:22–29

Returning to the tithe within the DC, there are significant links back to the first appearance of the centralization law in 12:13–19. Morrow concludes, "The sequence of 14:22–27 and 15:19–23 is a reflection of the requirement of … 12:17. These two clause rows take the general instruction of 12:17 and explore its particulars."[62] In addition to repeating the items belonging to the tithe in 12:17, 14:22–27 also parrots, in abbreviated form, the list of meal participants of 12:18 in 14:26–27aα (also 12:7, 12). Human desire for succulent food and drink from 12:15 (where meat stands as the premium object of desire, just as it is in 12:20, 21) is expanded in 14:26 to include the full range of a banquet. Only here is the spread of food and drink made explicit for what can also be understood as implicit for the cultic meals found throughout the DC, whether in chs. 12, 14 and 16 (or the later texts of chs. 26 and 27).

As mentioned above, this section also overlaps with 12:20–21 about distance to the sanctuary, though the conclusions drawn from this distance are divergent. In 12:20–21 the distance to the sanctuary becomes the reason why one can eat meat in one's village. In 14:24–26 the distance provides the basis upon which one can sell the produce at home and then take the proceeds to the sanctuary, rather than the produce itself.[63] If one lives close, then arguably 14:22–23 remain the operative guidelines.

Perhaps one of the most insightful additions to the section is v. 23b, which suggests that the reason for consuming the tithe at the central sanctuary is "in order that you might learn to fear the Lord." As mentioned above (p. 217), the appearance of the verb *lmd* in this setting has led commentators to make connections with the Booths celebration of Deut 31 and later redactions of the DC. Braulik states,

> Das festliche Lernritual holt also die Gesellschaft Jahwes wieder in ihre Ursituation zurück. … Das aus dem Gotteswort wachsende Gottesvolk findet seine reinste Selbstdarstellung als Festgemeinde. … Die Liturgie ist,

---

62 Morrow, *Scribing the Center*, 14. Similarly, Nelson, *Deuteronomy*, 184.

63 Much has been made of the "desacralization" of the tithe in Deut 14:24–26 because it can be sold. While there is certainly some kind of uncoupling of the particular produce from the gift brought to the sanctuary, conversion into money is also attested in Mesopotamia. Cf. Moshe Weinfeld, "Tithe," in *EncJud*, 19:737. Therefore, it need not signal a move away from the connection between land and deity suggested by Julius Wellhausen, *Prolegomena to the History of Ancient Israel: with a reprint of the article, Israel, from the Encyclopedia Britannica.* (Cleveland: Meridian Books, 1965), 76–78.

im Vergleich zum archaischen Sacrum und Ritual, in rationales und humanisierendes Licht getaucht.[64]

Braulik is correct in his recognition of the reestablishment of group identity through ritual practice. His comment shows how the ritual portrayed in the cultic feasts, such as Deut 14, provides a temporal and spatial mnemonic for the cultic participants to remember their societal connections through the portrayed ritual practice. However, contrary to what Braulik suggests, "learning," at least in 14:23, does not necessarily imply reading and hearing, as it does in 31:12–13. There are multiple ways of learning, also learning that has less to do with cognition and more with action.[65]

For example, Yu counters,

> … in 14:22–29, this fear of Yahweh is meant to be inculcated through the experience of eating the tithe and the firstlings at the sanctuary in the presence of Yahweh. The consumption of the sacred dues—elsewhere in the Pentateuch is [sic] restricted to the priests and Levites—must have been an awesome experience, sufficient to instill a proper sense of reverence toward Yahweh, especially when this took place before Yahweh in the sacred atmosphere of the temple.[66]

This heuristic interpretation of the laity eating the tithe explores an alternative, in this case, a bodily type of learning (akin to MacDonald's use of Connerton's incorporated memory). While Yu's projection needs to be tempered with the reminder that Deut 14:22–29 is a *text* that may or may not have been carried out in the concrete life of the Israelite (Judahite) cult, it is still a text that provides for fruitful imaginative interpretation for cultic life. The notion here of ritual, bodily acquisition of connection to the divine also appears in the unrelated text of Exod 24:9–11, where Moses, Aaron, two of Aaron's sons, and the seventy elders ascend Mount Sinai to encounter God, to eat, and to drink. While "fear" is not explicitly mentioned in these verses, the idea underlies v. 11a: *wě'el 'ăṣîlê běnê yiśrā'ēl lō' šālaḥ yādô* ("but to the Israelite nobles, he [Yhwh] did not stretch out his hand [to strike them]").

---

64 Braulik, *Deuteronomium 1–16,17*, 15. [ET: The festive learning ritual brings the community of Yhwh back to its originary situation. … The people of God growing out of the word of God finds its purest self-portrayal as a festive community. … The liturgy, when compared with archaic sacrality and ritual, is immersed in a rational and humanized light.]

65 See also Otto, *Das Deuternomium*, 318, n. 495. Reuter, *Cultzentralisation*, 158, notes the difference, and though she ultimately dates this clause as later, she suggests that the different method of "learning fear" may mean that this text is older than the other appearances of "learning fear" in Deuteronomy.

66 Yu, "Tithes and Firstlings in Deuteronomy," 69.

As Morrow has argued, the rhythm of Deut 14:22–29 is structured temporally by *hašānāh šānāh* ("annually") in v. 22 and *miqṣēh šālōš šānîm* ("At the end of three years") in v. 28.[67] This temporal structure also accounts for the movement from addressing the situation of the land-owners and their families (*'attāh wĕbêtekā*) to the discussion of the third parties—the Levites, foreigners, orphans, and widows in "your" villages.

In the first section, after introducing the tithe and its annual occurrence, the DC then elaborates. The striking manner of the DC conception is immediately apparent from v. 23 when compared to its biblical and ancient Near Eastern counterparts.[68] As in the citation from Yu above, the notion that one take the normal payment to the temple or crown[69] and consume it with one's family is a striking and new meaning to what was likely an old and respected institution.[70] One may, like Milgrom, explain the change practically with reference to the DC conception of the sacrificial system which abolishes local sanctuaries and its relation to internal politics,[71] yet this suggestion does not account for the change in the use of the tithe: now it belongs to the bringer. It is more helpful to consider this move in light of the international politics where the strong imperial rulers such as the Assyrian king reigned. From this perspective, what the DC seems to underhandedly suggest is

67 Morrow, *Scribing the Center*, 77; cf. Nelson, *Deuteronomy*, 184.
68 Gen 14:18–20; 28:20–22; 2 Chr 31:4–21; Neh 10:38; 1 Sam 8:11–18; Mal 3:8; as well as the Ugaritic, Neo-Assyrian, and Neo-Babylonian appearances of the tithe.
69 It is debated whether the farmer delivered the produce or it was seized by temple and/or royal officials as Milgrom, *Leviticus*, 3:2423, suggests: "Furthermore, the evidence in Neh 10:38 about Levites as tithe collectors in the provincial cities, which some have regarded as a gloss, is now corroborated by Mesopotamian data, according to which tithe collectors were recruited from the temple administration." Also Weinfeld, "Tithe," 19:739.
70 Wellhausen, *Prolegomena*, 155–57, argued the opposite direction, seeing Deut 14:22–27 as the preservation of an ancient tithe tradition, but this view is not corroborated by the ancient Near Eastern corollaries.
71 Milgrom, *Leviticus*, 3: 2424, "This novelty of eating the tithe instead of giving it away to the sanctuary and its ministrants (as was the case before) is to be explained against the background of the cultic reform that stands at the basis of the deuteronomic law code, especially Deut 12:19. After the abolition of the provincial sanctuaries and the provincial cultic officials, the Levites, there was no further need for the tithe, which had been destined for the maintenance of these institutions. The tithe was reduced primarily to a sacred gift." Similarly, Weinfeld, "Tithe," 738–39. The connection between the Levites and local sanctuaries prior to Deuteronomy, 2 Kgs 22–23, and Josiah has been problematized by Dahmen, *Leviten und Priester im Deuteronomium*, 369. Many recent interpreters dispute the connection between early Deuteronomy and an historical book-based Josianic reform in which the Levites *might* be idenitified with the priests of the high places in 2 Kgs 23.

that any resources that might somehow be siphoned off by the Judahite palace to be sent on to the Assyrian Empire should rather remain "at home" (for "you and your house") under the control of the local households.[72] As Crüsemann remarks, "Daß eine von JHWH befreite Bauernschaft im Grunde keinen Zehnten zu zahlen hat, dieser Tenor von 1Sam8 kommt hier auf neue Weise zu seinem Recht."[73]

Schaper disputes Crüsemann's conclusions, and instead follows the theory that cult centralization was proposed to strengthen Josiah's control over the periphery and give him a treasury for war.[74] Schaper also goes one step further, concluding that the Jerusalemite priests were likely the essential carriers of the Deuteronomic reform and its law because they stood to benefit the most from the centralization of goods designated for the deity.[75]

However, Schaper's argument does not account for the third-year tithes, which never come to the central sanctuary (also the seventh year as set out in Deut 15). Nor does he adequately deal with the fact that

---

72   Crüsemann, "Der Zehnte in der israelitischen Königzeit," 44–45, argues that Judah irrefutably developed its own tax system no later than the point in time when it needed to provide regular tribute to Assyria. The eighth-century Samarian Ostraca support this claim by way of analogy with these records of the northern kingdom.

73   Ibid., 46. [ET: That the farmers, freed by Yhwh, basically no longer had to pay a tithe, this tenor can be seen in a new light when viewed from the perspective of 1 Samuel 8.]

74   Schaper, *Priester und Leviten im achämenidischen Juda*, 94–95: "Der deuteronomische 'Verfassungsentwurf' ist eine Antwort auf die Strukturkrise des judäischen Königtums in einer Zeit der äußeren Bedrohung und der inneren Umwälzung. Um das Königtum zu einem effektiveren Herrschaftsinstrument umzuschmieden, war es nötig, das Steuereinkommen im Zentrum, d.h. in Jerusalem, zusammenzuführen." [ET: The Deuteronomic "Constitution" is an answer to the structural crisis of the Judahite monarchy in a time of external threat and internal cataclysm. In order to forge a more effective instrument of authority, it was necessary to bring together the tax income in the center, that is in Jerusalem.] The decentralized procedure of the festivals along with the scattered consumption of meat (Deut 12:15) and distribution of the third year tithes effectively circumvent the king and priest.

75   Schaper, *Priester und Leviten im achämenidischen Juda*, 111–12, states, "In den Kreisen dieses Kultpersonals, d.h. unter den 'levitischen Priestern' — d.h. in Wahrheit: unter den zadokidischen Priestern — im Jerusalem des 7. Jahrhunderts, sind daher mit hoher Wahrscheinlichkeit einige der wesentlichen Träger des dtn Reformgesetzes zu finden. Von diesen Kreisen sind auch von den Schreibern am Hof und/oder am Tempel dürften die dtn Reform und das dtn Reformgesetz initiiert und formuliert worden sein." [ET: In the circles of these cult personnel, that is, among the "Levitical priests" — meaning in reality among the Zadokite priests — of seventh-century Jerusalem with high probability is where some of the essential bearers of the Deuteronomic reform law would be found. From these circles as well as from the scribes of the palace and/or the temple are those who may have initiated and formulated the Deuteronomic reform and Deuteronomic reform law.].

the priests of the central sanctuary must now share with the rural Levites according to Deut 18 (if vv. 6–8 are part of this layer), meaning there are more cultic mouths to feed.[76]

The de Certeauian "tactic" employed by the DC is especially remarkable when viewed from an anthropological perspective. Hayden explains the typical nature of a tribute feast in the non-modern world as follows:

> They may be far larger than any other type of feast. They are held at regular, calendrical intervals and should be as inclusive as possible within a given polity. It seems unlikely that wealth distribution would be common since the goal of these feasts is to amass as much surplus as possible, and to sequester as large a proportion of it as possible for elite use. … Tribute feasts are likely to be intimately tied to rituals honoring polity deities and in many cases are associated with monumental structures and spaces associated with those deities.[77]

The DC formulation of the tithe overthrows the typical nature of the tithe and the tithe feast. Since, as seems to have been the case in Israel and Judah as much as elsewhere in the ancient Near East,[78] the tithe in Israel generally benefited the palace and temple, then the DC meal that benefits those bringing the tribute goes against the fundamental idea of these feasts since tribute functioned as a sign of a submissive bond towards the monarch. Therefore, missing payment amounted to breaking the contract.[79] In a number of ways the DC follows the general "form" of the tribute feast: the tithe is yearly, it includes everyone possible, and it is tied to rituals for the polity deity and his sanctuary. In fact, the tithe is still brought to the reigning king; however, the king is Yhwh. The earthly counterpart—found in Deut 17, which may or may

---

76 See my comments in "What Do the 'Levites in Your Gates' Have to Do with the 'Levitical Priests'? Towards a European-North American Dialogue on the Levites in the Deuteronomic Law Corpus," in *"The LORD Is Their Inheritance": Priests and Levites in History and Tradition* (ed. M. Leuchter and J. Hutton; Ancient Israel and Its Literature Series; Atlanta: SBL, forthcoming).

77 Brian Hayden, "Fabulous Feasts: A Prolegomenon to the Importance of Feasting," in *Feasts: Archaeological and Ethnographic Perspectives on Food, Politics, and Power* (ed. M. Dietler and B. Hayden; Washington: Smithsonian Institution Press, 2001), 58; cf. 1 Kgs 4–5 and above, p. 97 on Neo-Assyrian administrative records of distribution.

78 See Denise Schmandt-Besserat, "Feasting in the Ancient Near East," in *Feasts: Archaeological and Ethnographic Perspectives on Food, Politics, and Power* (ed. M. Dietler and B. Hayden; Washington: Smithsonian Institution Press, 2001), 391–403.

79 Otto, *Gottes Recht als Menschenrecht*, 116, argues that the goal of the tribute system was perhaps even more for the vassal's symbolic show of fealty than filling the imperial coffers.

not have been part of this early form of the DC[80]—is absent from the Deuteronomic tithe. So the surplus is distributed liberally to all present rather than setting it aside for elite consumption or royal distribution for the purpose of increasing royal power (cf. the Assyrian letters, the system of the Persian kings, and also the distribution of meat by Adonijah at his banquet in 1 Kgs 1, which constitutes his claim to power). The fact that the basic "form" of the tithe remains intact suggests that Deuteronomy does not abolish the tithe strategy, nor its compulsory nature. One cannot "opt" out, and it still must be disposed of correctly.[81] Furthermore, in this DC tithe, the two semantic fields of the root *'śr* merge: the percentage of produce is brought in order to form a rich banquet.

Not only does the household consume the tithe, but they also do so in the presence of the deity.[82] Milgrom explains, "Thus D ordained that the tithes should revert to their owners. But by insisting that the tithes be brought to Jerusalem, D endeavoured to maintain their sacred character."[83] Furthermore, this concept binds the laity with the sanctuary through the people's physical presence and religious experience.[84]

There are two lists of suggestive products (vv. 23, 26) that one would bring as part of the tithe for consumption, and they take on a different tone when they are no longer lists of items that one gives away, but instead lists of items that one may consume as part of sacred festive meals. The list of tithe goods in v. 23 may be envisioned for those who live close enough to the central sanctuary to transport their goods there. The second list, in v. 26, on the contrary, could be imagined for those living further away. The repetition between the lists—the primary difference between the two lies in the mention of unquestionably fermented drinks in the latter versus the raw products in the former—highlights the importance for the DC festal vision that all "Israel"

---

80   Against: , i.e., Braulik, *Deuteronomium II*, 122–23, Ernest Nicholson, "Traditum and traditio: the Case of Deuteronomy 17: 14-20," in *Scriptural Exegesis: The Shapes of Culture and the Religious Imagination: Essays in Honour of Michael Fishbane* (ed. D. A. Green and L. S. Lieber. Oxford: Oxford University Press, 2009), 46–62; Kratz, *Composition*, 133. For: Crüsemann, *Die Tora*, 274–77, Richard D. Nelson, "A Response to Thomas Römer, *The So-called Deuteronomistic History*" in "In Conversation with Thomas Römer, *The So-Called Deuteronomistic History: a Sociological, Historical and Literary Introduction* (London: T. & T. Clark, 2005), ed. R. F. Person, Jr.)," in *JHebS* 9/17 (2009): 9. Cited 7 December, 2009. Online: http://www.arts. ualberta. ca /JHS/ Articles/-article_119.pdf; and Levinson, "The Reconceptualization of Kingship," 524 n. 37.

81   Yu, "Tithes and Firstlings in Deuteronomy," 82–83.

82   See above, p. 228–29.

83   Milgrom, *Leviticus*, 3:2427.

84   Cf. Tigay, *Deuteronomy*, 142, and Crüsemann, "Der Zehnte in der israelitischen Königzeit," 46.

should enjoy (cf. *śmḥ* in v. 26) the tithe together. Their length and re-peated nature suggests their central role in the passage. These lists pro-vide an overlap between center and periphery through their shared items. The mention of being able to eat what one desires also provides contact with memory of past special meals, allowing for meals to con-tinue and recreate the memories of the past.[85] The fact that one could turn one's tithe into silver also allows for purchase of the specific items for consumption that the individual desires, rather than only being stuck with what each group brought along. Not having to carry one's goods also makes the physical journey easier, which is of course the explicit meaning of v. 24.

The portrayed experience highlights the goodness of the deity, from whom one receives the gifts, as noted in v. 24. Secondly, the tone is set to one of human desire—both as an individual and a group. Since fami-lies are envisioned as consuming the tithes together, there is an element of group unification. This aspect is displayed prominently throughout the literature on commensality.[86] However, an aspect of individuality also emerges through the mention of *bĕkōl 'ăšer tiš'ālēkā* ("whatever you ask for yourself"). This individuality, though, seems somewhat limited to the heads of household, who are addressed as *'attāh* (you).

The section of vv. 24–26 as a whole highlights the celebration that emerges as a consequence of divine blessing (v. 24). The blessing is twofold: in the first case it is divine blessing that allows the territory to become so large that the distance to the central sanctuary might become a hardship (v. 24); secondly, divine blessing nourishes the fields so richly that a tithe becomes too much to carry. The picture, as mentioned above, overflows into celebration.[87] Reuter notices that perhaps the real—if not explicit—intent of the section is less about the question of delivering goods to the central sanctuary, and more about the connec-tion between good harvests and divine blessing,[88] and I would add, consumption of the goods harvested. The bond between divine blessing

---

85   See discussion above, pp. 46ff. and 51ff.
86   Sutton, *Remembrance of Repasts*, 5, summarizes, "Anthropological work has reached a consensus that food is about commensality—eating to make friends—and competi-tion—eating to make enemies."
87   Nelson, *Deuteronomy*, 185, argues that the third *kî* clause of v. 24 (because the place … is too far) "confuses the notion of distance by presenting the reason for one's in-ability to bring the tithe as due to the rich extent of Yahweh's blessing." I do agree that this phrase is later; however, both the distance and fertility of the land could function as signs of blessing and reasons one could not transport the tithe to the sanctuary.
88   Reuter, *Cultzentralisation*, 160.

and the produce of the land appears throughout the DC meal texts, and plays a foundational role in their logic. Just as Yhwh blesses those who accept the DC formulation of society in 12:15 with meat to eat when-ever one desires, so also enjoyment in 16:11, 14–15 grow out of Yhwh's concrete blessing of the people so that they have the necessary elements for the feast.

An important insight may be gleaned from the Ugaritic rituals at this point: "The strict association of meat and wine does not seem to be typical … of just any kind of ceremonial meal, but belongs exclusively to the banquet."[89] While such a stark dichotomy cannot be made for the DC banquets, nonetheless the inclusion of portions of the entire yield (meat, grains, grapes, and oil) implies that the foodstuffs take on the character of and should be understood as an exquisite feast, thereby portraying the people of the DC banquets as Yhwh's chosen guests at a sumptuous banquet, akin to the those portrayed in the Neo-Assyrian palace reliefs.

There are also some conceptual difficulties with the picture in these verses. Tigay notes that it seems improbable for the people to consume such a great percentage of their yearly produce in such a short period of time.[90] This question has received various answers. Some interpret this over-consumption as a sign of Deuteronomy's utopian tint.[91] Oth-

---

89   Lucio Milano, "Food and Diet in Pre-Classical Syria," in *Production and Consumption in the Ancient Near East* (ed. C. Zaccagnini; Budapest: University of Budapest, 1989), 242.

90   Tigay, *Deuteronomy*, 143: "It is not clear how the farmer and his household could consume the entire tithe during pilgrimages to the sanctuary. In the course of a 354-day lunar year, a household producing at subsistence level would theoretically re-quire 35.4 days to consume ten percent of its produce. The three pilgrimage festivals require farmers and their households to be present in the chosen city for only nine days each year (16:1–17). In so short a time they could not consume thirty-five days worth of produce plus firstlings, festival offerings, and other sacrifices that would have to be consumed at the same time. … Assuming that the farmers invited the Le-vites and poor to the meals, as required, even if they doubled their normal consump-tion at the festivals, they could not dispose of all the food involved unless there were as many Levites and poor as there were members of the farmers' households, which is unlikely. Conceivably the law aimed to encourage farmers to travel to the sanctu-ary more often, but it would have been extremely difficult for those living far away to do so…" Cf. Nelson, *Deuteronomy*, 186. The number of days spent feasting could perhaps be increased to 15, since Passover-Unleavened Bread is spread out over a week total (though not all at the sanctuary), and no particular number of days is given for the Feast of Weeks. Deut 16:13 calls for Booths to be seven days. Whether the tithe need be exactly ten percent is also questionable, see above p. 222.

91   Tigay, *Deuteronomy*, 143; Nelson, *Deuteronomy*, 186, Weinfeld, "Tithe," 1161; and most recently Pakkala, "The Date of the Oldest Edition of Deuteronomy," 399. Pak-kala's reasoning seems remarkably modern. In response to the idea that the DC leg-

ers, such as Mayes, see here the unspoken requirement to leave the unconsumed produce with the temple personnel.[92] Yu suggests that portions of the tithe could have been brought during *each* of the three festivals, which spreads out consumption, but this hypothesis seems forced.[93] Yet, when compared to various ethnographic studies of feasting, the problem dissipates. Dietler shows that a remarkable percentage of resources in many "subsistence level" and non-modern societies goes to festal consumption, especially in the form of alcoholic beverages.[94] This is, of course, *exactly* what appears in Deut 14:26–27. He further notes that this situation can be so extreme that it leads to serious impoverishment for the rest of the year.[95]

A further difficulty involves the ordinances pertaining to the Levites. It is often assumed that they are the social group that stands to lose the most in any movement towards implementation of the DC social vision. If there is a movement towards cultic centralization, the Levites' livelihood would be at stake if they were the cult personnel at the local shrines. If, as Nelson argues, their inclusion in the list of cultic meal participants means to "cushion the negative economic effect of centralization …,"[96] then the DC conception places maintenance of the Levites squarely on the shoulders of the local households. This conclusion finds support in the mention that it is the "Levites within your gates" (14:27) for whom the addressees of the DC should care. The conception of the Israelites cast here is radically *decentralized* in this aspect. Perhaps one may go so far as to say that the local households had previously been responsible for maintaining the local shrines and their

---

islation was only utopian, Yu, "Tithes and Firstlings in Deuteronomy," 80, notes, "It is true that as part of the Deuteronomic reform, the tithe law may not directly reflect the prevailing practice, but this does not mean that it was not meant to be implemented."

92   Mayes, *Deuteronomy*, 244–45. Cf. Otto Eissfeldt, *Erstlinge und Zehnten in Alten Testament* (BWANT 22; Leipzig: Hinrich, 1917), 152–63, and McConville, *Law and Theology*, 73–74. Nelson's analysis, *Deuteronomy*, 186, leaves this open as a possibility as well.

93   Yu, "Tithes and Firstlings in Deuteronomy," 81.

94   Dietler, "Theorizing the Feast: Rituals of Consumption, Commensal Politics, and Power in African Contexts," 80–82. He surveys results from various African and East Asian societies and finds percentages between fifteen and fifty percent of total grain consumption (and this is often just for the alcoholic portion of the feasts!).

95   Ibid., 82: "Hence, it is clear that recognizing the importance of feasting for both social reproduction and political action in agrarian societies should provoke a corollary recognition of the scale of productive labor and resources necessarily devoted to these crucial features of social life." Dietler's study serves to show just how fitting Deut 14:22–27 is for its agrarian society.

96   Nelson, *Deuteronomy*, 186.

personnel (cf. the situation reflected in Num 18), so the DC provision for "the Levite within your gates" does not change their support, but the channels through which support for the Levites travels is what changes.[97]

Milgrom, however, contends that Levites would not really accept the offer to go to the Temple for a free meal, and this is included in Deuteronomy because of guilt about depriving them of rights to the tithe.[98] Whether this would practically be the case does not really matter for the DC. Firstly, the implied audience of the DC is primarily the heads of households, not the Levites, and the DC seems more concerned with winning the household heads' approval of the DC formulation of Israelite society. One may further suggest that the "brotherly ethic" espoused by the DC is conceived of in such a way as to make the treatment of the Levites the outward sign of the community's obedience to Yhwh.[99]

One might question whether the various persons described in vv. 28–29 are somehow implicitly included in the happenings of vv. 22–27. Are they connected to the households of v. 26? While not explicitly mentioned (the same is true for the Passover rules of 16:1–8, and the foundational cultic feast laws of 12:13–19), these "others," treated as special insiders, likely take part in the celebrations. As argued above for the Passover-Unleavened Bread celebrations,[100] it is more likely that the DC, at certain points, attempts to highlight the unity of the people instead of naming all parties entitled to take part in the feast, though the reason behind this choice is less clear in this section.

The final section of the pericope begins with a new temporal marking, "At the end of three years." This section marks a change in its concern from the general cultic meals at the central sanctuary towards the effects of the DC program in the mundane life of the community. While an event that only happens every third year can hardly be called "mundane," vv. 28–29 return the focus to issues that touch the everyday ethos of the people. The connection between these verses and what preceded are the Levites. Since the Levites fall into the category of limi-

---

97   Ibid., 187, notes the similar idea in vv. 28–29, "Keeping this tithe under local control seems to preserve an element of the earlier practice of tithing to the neighborhood sanctuary."

98   Milgrom, *Leviticus*, 3:2433. Earlier Eissfeldt, *Erstlinge und Zehnten*, 50–51.

99   McConville, *Law and Theology*, 149–51, sees the Levites as idealized people of God, and should be prosperous, thereby showing the entire community's realization of their dependence on Yhwh. He also links remembering the Levites to remembering Yhwh through 8:11; 12:19; and 14:27 (ibid., 74).

100 See above, 191, 202.

nal figures themselves, the text then moves to other similar societal categories.[101] What sets these groups of people apart is not their *economic* status, but rather their *social* status, which Yu describes as "precarious," in light of "their inability to defend their rights, hence making them vulnerable to oppression by others."[102] Given the close connection in Deuteronomy between "your land" and the people (i.e., 12:19), anyone falling outside of this category is viewed as liminal, and therefore requires special treatment. This is supported by the—perhaps later—reassertion in 14:29 that the Levites have no "portion or inheritance with you." The Levites "in your gates" only appear in conjunction with cultic ordinances in the DC.[103]

This ordinance only focuses on the care of liminal groups on the land, omitting any consideration of an urban setting. Perhaps such an urban context might only have been found around the central sanctuary, and therefore provided for by the temple personnel.[104] This is not altogether too surprising, given the fact that most of Judah—especially the cities—had been devastated by Sennacherib, so the world into which the DC was written was (outside of Jerusalem) quite rural.

---

101 As Lohfink, "Opferzentralisation, Säkularisierungsthese und mimeische Theorie," 241, explains, these people do not necessarily need to be viewed as "the poor," but rather as those without their own fields, though this is often quite related. If 18:8 can be brought into the discussion for this time period, then it does seem that the Levites could own land as well.

102 Yu, "Tithes and Firstlings in Deuteronomy," 8, who cites Donald Gowan, "Wealth and Poverty in the Old Testament: The Case of the Widow, the Orphan, and the Sojourner," *Interpretation* 41 (1987): 344–45. Cf. Zech 7:9–10, and the tenuous situation encountered by Naomi and Ruth. As these biblical citations show, there absolutely may be some overlap between the economic and social situations, but this is not necessarily the case. Gowan (ibid., 344) suggests the following relationship, "… it would be easier for them to become poor than any other group, because it was so easy to cheat them and their options were so few."

103 Reuter, *Kultzentralisation*, 141, cf. 142–45. She, like Dahmen, argues that it is not clear that the Levites functioned as priests at country shrines before the centralization law (as Nelson, *Deuteronomy*, 186, among others, suggests). She agrees, (*Kultzentralisation*, 145), however, that they did undergo a significant change in status with cult centralization.

104 Reuter, *Kultzentralisation*, 161. However, Mayes, *Deuteronomy*, 246, "It is unlikely that it [the law of vv. 28–29] arose out of the new situation created by the abolition of the local sanctuaries (so supposedly depriving the poor of their former annual share of the tithe), for there is no evidence that before Deuteronomy the tithe was devoted to the welfare of the needy." Nonetheless, care for the weak was a typically the responsibility of the king in the ancient Near East.

5.5. Synthesis of Exegesis, Social Scientific, and Biological Evidence

Let me begin putting these sections together with the following two quotations from the sociologist Anderson:

> Experience appears more important than genetics. Foods we were raised with are typically our favorites ... children learn to love the foods their parents and older peers prefer. [105]

> One main message of food, everywhere, is *solidarity*. ... The other main message is *separation*. Food transactions define families, networks, friendship groups, religions, and virtually every other socially institutionalized group.[106]

These two statements bring together the basis for understanding the rhetorical potential for individuals to take on the specific "Israelite" identity imagined for the community in the cultic meal described in Deut 14:22–27 and assumed in Deut 12:13–19 and 16:1–17. These texts exhibit and make use of the realities affirmed in the conclusions of current social scientific studies. By setting apart a variety of culturally desirable foods in 14:23, 26 (cf. meat in 12:15), Deuteronomy creates a system that entices and encourages people to throw their allegiance to the Israelite group imagined in the DC,[107] especially because their taxes and gifts are returned to them.

The process at work here can be compared with the narrative of Adonijah's attempt to take on the mantle of kingship in 1 Kgs 1.[108] His claims are demonstrated through a number of reported actions—his preparation of a chariot and accompanying guard (1 Kgs 1:5), his gathering of key supporters such as the army commander Joab and the priest Abiathar (1:7), and finally his hosting of a sacrificial banquet for his brothers and the powerful in Judah (1:9, 19, 25). The feast—and its focus on the sacrifice and consumption of sumptuous and liberally apportioned meat—is the central location for the determination and declaration of allegiance to Adonijah: "For he descended today and sacrificed many oxen, fattened [calves], and sheep. And he invited all the king's sons and the commanders of the army,[109] and Abiathar the

---

105 Anderson, *Everyone Eats*, 97.
106 Ibid., 125.
107 See above, 49–50.
108 See Klingbeil, "'Momentaufnahmen' of Israelite Religion," 38–39, 43–44, on the ritual nature and implications of Adonijah's banquet.
109 This follows MT; OG reads "and Joab, the commander of the army."

priest. Now they are eating and drinking before him, and they have said, "Long live King Adonijah!" (1:25).

Deuteronomy plays on the same theme: just as Adonijah served rich meals to those he attempted to draw to his side, in Deut 14:22–27 and elsewhere, Yhwh plays liberal host to tasty banquets through his regular blessings for those who are willing to come in order to consume food and drink at his banquets and to become part of the Deuteronomic "Israelite" community.

The festive meals also create a mechanism for the incorporation of newcomers and children to grow into and reaffirm their belonging to the "Israelite" group. "Children are most prone to love foods that are used as treats, rewards, and markers of special events,"[110] and the foods in Deut 14:23, 26; 12:15 fall into these categories. They are the markers of special events, which establish their ongoing desirability. In addition, the lists of tasty foods and beverages in Deut 14:23, 26, all of which are well-known, indigenous items rather than foreign imports, appeal to the regional tastes of home.[111] These lists are constructed in such a way as to allow the audience to assume that they would be able to pick the items that appeal most strongly to their tastes, since the lists especially contain the items that would be "local favorites."

Furthermore, they are designated as treats for the people in the way that Deuteronomy uses them rhetorically. They are given as gifts from the deity when the people take on Yhwh's yoke in place of the Assyrian or other possible "foreign" options. The rhetorical function here is similar to biblical texts from various periods, such as Isa 25:6–8, where Yhwh prepares a rich banquet on Zion, an image meant to provide hope and to bring embolden the audience to remain faithful to Yhwh (cf. Deut 32:10–14, Psalm 128).

Though oft repeated, communal consumption of the sacred meal works anthropologically to foster inner-group identity—the intended result of David's inclusion of Mephibosheth at his table (1 Sam 9:7, 10) —as suggested by the quote at the beginning of this conclusion. Eating together in the DC equates to defining oneself as "Israelites" by acting in the manner that Israelites should act. This eating before Yhwh also works to distance the Israelites from those absent, namely, from those

---

110 Anderson, *Everyone Eats*, 97.

111 This contrast can be seen in the difference between the foods on offer in Deuteronomy and those on Solomon's table in 1 Kgs 5:2–3 [ET 4:22–23]. Cf. Anderson, *Everyone Eats*, 130, who notes, "As we all know, nothing brings back a place, time, or occasion more powerfully than a scent or taste. To eat the familiar home food is to be at home, at least in the heart—as well as the stomach."

who might eat in the shade of an alternative deity, political structure, or formulation of Yahwism. A poignant narrative example may be found in Saul's violent response to David's absence from the royal feast in 1 Sam 20, when David should have been present to show his allegiance to King Saul's house by eating the banquet Saul hosts.

Finally, Sutton's category of "prospective memory" illuminates the imaginative power of the DC formulations. The DC, which is generally building on the CC, takes for granted that the people understand the basic contours of the festival celebrations, including the general seasons in which they take place. Therefore, writing of the festivals and highlighting their meal qualities marks time "prospectively" by naming the elements of the meal that will take place at future festive celebrations and meals.[112] The special nature of Deut 14:23–26 marks a powerful link between agriculture and ritual consumption, rather than a break made between agriculture and sacrifice. However, even though Deut 14:25 makes provisions for a household to exchange its tithe goods for silver and then buy their foodstuffs for the sacred meal at the central sanctuary, the subsequent mention of the desirable foods in 14:26 returns the focus to agriculture. In reference to modern Greece, Sutton comments that people in Greece mark time prospectively by when they will again eat the red dyed eggs of Easter.[113] Similarly, even while distant from the singular sanctuary, Deuteronomy projects the image of Israelites counting the days until they may again consume their choice foods together at that sacred place (cf. Deut 16:9).

---

112 See above, 46–47.
113 Sutton, *Remembrance of Repasts,* 30.

6. Conclusion

This study brings together diverse strands of evidence in order to explore the meaning of early DC cultic meal texts (Deut 12:13–19; 14:22–29; 16:1–17) for a preexilic audience familiar with the experience of the political and ideological domination by the Neo-Assyrian Empire in Judah. My argument suggests that the original construction of the Deuteronomic text took place as a Yahwistic answer to the material and ideological hegemony experienced in Judah at the hands of the their Neo-Assyrian overlords.[1] To state the thesis positively, these texts highlight Yhwh's beneficence and strength through his willingness and ability to provide the community of Israelites who accept his claim to covenantal kingship with rich concrete blessings in the form of plentiful feasts, especially at the central sanctuary, but also in their local villages.

Generally speaking, the discussion seeks to broaden the interpretive categories for these particular texts of Deut 12, 14, and 16, arguing that the typical bounds of interpretation—the Covenant Code of Exod 20–23 as a *Vorlage*, or comparison with the other biblical law corpora—are too restrictive. Building within Old Testament studies on the works of Braulik and MacDonald, there are further bodies of data than can be incorporated into the interpretation of these texts, and I attempt to take steps in this direction.

I begin by presenting various lines of evidence that illuminate the focus on meat in Deut 12. The archaeological data of faunal remains provides an important piece for furthering the understanding of the dynamics of Judahite meat consumption during the Assyrian period and the related emphasis on the desire for meat reflected in the biblical text (Deut 12:13–19). The negative effects of Neo-Assyrian imperialism made inroads into the amounts of meat available for consumption in the seventh-century Levant.

Other significant data comes from the iconographic and administrative records of the broader ancient Near East. The iconography of ban-

---

1   The response can be compared to de Certeau's "strategies" of the central power taken up and used in the "tactics" of those on the periphery. See above, pp. 64–65, for an overview.

quets reveals a long and highly-developed tradition that began no later than the third millennium Ur III period and spread throughout Mesopotamia and the Levant. This tradition contained highly political and symbolic portrayals of rulers (human and divine) at table, often celebrating their military victories. This data supports the assertion that the portrayal of cultic meals in the DC receives and incorporates a widely-known political and religious symbol: banquets in the ancient Near East were not only about food. They also carried implications concerning power relations and theological devotion.

Select letters from the Neo-Assyrian period show the importance of meat distribution for status in the inner workings of the empire as well. Albeit spotty, the administrative record points to the long distances that consumable animals were transported for enjoyment at centralized royal and temple banquets.

I then place these threads in dialogue with composition-critical analysis of Deut 12. After identifying the plausible earliest text of Deut 12, namely, vv. 13–15a, 17–19, I explore the implications of this text in light of the broader material and political context of the Neo-Assyrian period previously outlined. I conclude that Deut 12:13–19* incorporates and responds to the particular concerns of a Judahite audience that experienced scarcity as a result of the Neo-Assyrian appropriation of Judahite resources with a vision of abundant Yahwistic provision at both the central sanctuary and in the local villages.

Further insight into understanding the DC cultic meals arises from comparison with ritual and narrative texts from Emar, Ugarit, and Mesopotamia. The ritual texts concerning the *zukru* festival celebrations in Emar note the persistence of local, non-royal cultic celebrations involving the entire community in West Semitic cultures even when they were under the hegemony of the great empires. The Ugaritic *CTU* 1.40 ritual text envisions reconciliation and unification of various in-power and marginalized groups within the city of Ugarit in part through the act of a cultic feast. Here again communal identity is imagined as emerging from a shared ritual that brings together all parts of the society.

Discussion of the *akītu-Enuma Elish* ritual and myth noted its importance as a *topos* for community identification and political power throughout the history of ancient Mesopotamia. Sennacherib's reformulation of the Aššur cult at the beginning of the seventh century adapted the *Enuma Elish* and the Babylonian practice of the *akītu* festival to his purposes. By asserting the dominance of Aššur over Marduk and by emphasizing the banquet, Sennacherib and his officials raised the profile of cultic banquets as a *topos* for the projection of political might and imperial identification. Other Assyrian ritual texts, the so-called cultic commentaries, employed mythemes from *Enuma Elish* in an effort to explain ritual actions, thereby showing the use of foundational myths in the theoretical interpretations of a wide variety of rituals. So in the same period as the construction of the DC, Assyrian scribes used a similar methodological approach to give meaning to ritual action, comparable especially to the Passover-Unleavened Bread text of Deut 16:1–7.

Likewise, the Ugaritic narratives of *CTU* 1.20–22 (the "Rephaim"), 1.119 ("El's Banquet"), and 1.1–1.6 (the Baal Cycle) employ the banquet as a prominent theme. Its joyful and lively nature provides an important background for the interpretation of the Deuteronomic cultic meals, which also fixate on enjoyment. They agree with *Enuma Elish* in placing the high deity as host, often with royal overtones, setting the absence of a royal human host for the Deuteronomic banquets into sharp relief.

In essence, the DC receives and redeploys the Neo-Assyrian and general ancient Near Eastern royal strategy of projecting the state's identity and power through the *topos* of the cultic banquet by tactically reorganizing the banquet into a still-centralized banquet, now with one divine host and many human hosts—more in line with the Emar *zukru*. This tactic is on display in Deut 16:1–17, which connects the exodus story of origins with both centralized pilgrimage feasts and Yhwh's presence extending to the periphery. The hosts at the three annual feasts are the numerous heads of households, and Deut 16:1–17 highlights the shared eating experience by all "Israel," which vv. 9–15 enumerates as "you, your son, your daughter, your male and female slaves, the Levite, the widow, the orphan, and the foreigner."

Turning to Deut 14:22–29, the particular conception of the DC tithe comes to light through comparison with other ancient Near Eastern and OT/HB formulations of the tithe and tribute taxes. The DC envisions the striking return of taxes to those who paid them to use for their own enjoyment as ingredients for the shared festivities. The "Israelites" celebrate their good fortune from Yhwh as one body in Yhwh's presence. The special nature of this meal is that all "Israel" takes part in the bounty, a bounty that defines and deepens the connections with this DC conception of Israel through the anthropological link between taste, memory, and identity. This feast also leads to specific ethical action with food in the local villages (14:28–29).

In conjunction with exploration of the ancient background of the Deuteronomic feasts, modern anthropological studies of food and medical studies of human taste and smell offer insight for the Deuteronomic cultic meals. Anthropologists since Goody have identified the cross-cultural (though always culturally-defined) importance of food and meals as a sign system, perhaps second only to verbal language. This conclusion grows out of the observation that meals serve as important group and individual identifiers because of their links both with memory and with dynamics of inclusion and exclusion. In this regard, Sutton's analysis highlights the maintenance of connection to a shared and individual past through the mnemonics of food.

Studies of eating in the OT/HB further confirm the importance of social factors for the determination of the meaning of meals. These textual meanings begin from the extra-textual reality of writers and readers, and rely on the audience's experiences for understanding the literary and social symbolism implied in the textual projections of communal consumption.

In line with Otto's helpful summary of the rhetorical thrust of the early DC material that the specific contribution of DC Yahwism is not covenant theology in itself, but rather the revolt against the Assyrian rule and royal ideology of the covenant theology,[2] I argue that the DC receives and reuses the ritual banquet as a second widely used form of religious and political relations. Again, the DC's unique contribution is not the creation of this form of divine-human (or royal-subject) relationship. Rather, the DC's contribution is the application of the king-subject metaphor to an exclusive Yhwh-Israel context as an important *topos* for the formation and concretization of "Israel" as Yhwh's people, celebrating the one God in one place, in the form of a multiplicity of households.

Briefly restated, this project uses an eclectic, interdisciplinary approach to emphasize the centrality of meals for identity formation as well as for political and religious rhetoric in the texts of Deut 12:13–19; 14:22–29; and 16:1–17.

---

2   Otto, *Gottes Recht als Menschenrecht*, 166; see also Levinson, "The Reconceptualization of Kingship," 527–28, and Knoppers, "Rethinking the Relationship between Deuteronomy and the Deuteronomistic History," 405.

Bibliography

Abusch, Tzvi. "Sacrifice in Mesopotamia." Pages 39–48 in *Sacrifice in Religious Experience*. Edited by A. I. Baumgarten. Leiden: E. J. Brill, 2002.

Achenbach, Reinhard. "Levitische Priester und Leviten im Deuteronomium: Überlegungen zur sog. "Levitisierung" des Priestertums." *Zeitschrift für altorientalische und biblische Rechtsgeschichte* 5 (1999) 285-309.

Aejmelaeus, Anneli. "Die Setuaginta des Deuteronomiums." Pages 1–22 in *Deuteronomium und seine Querbeziehungen*. Edited by T. Veijola. Schriften der Finnischen Exegetischen Gesellschaft 62. Helsinki: Finnische Exegetische Gesellschaft & Göttingen: Vandenhoeck & Ruprecht, 1996.

Aharoni, Yohanan. "Arad: Its Inscriptions and Temple," *Biblical Archaeology* 31 (1968): 2–32.

___. *Arad Inscriptions*. Jerusalem: Israel Exploration Society, 1981.

___. "The Horned Altar of Beer-sheba," *Biblical Archaeology* 37 (1974): 2–6.

Albenda, Pauline. *The Palace of Sargon, King of Assyria: Monumental Wall Reliefs at Dur-Sharrukin, from Original Drawings Made at the Time of Their Discovery in 1843–1844 by Botta and Flandin*. Synthèse 22. Paris: Editions Recherche sur les Civilisations, 1986.

Alexander, Bobby C. *Victor Turner Revisited: Ritual as Social Change*. American Academy of Religion Academy Series 74. Atlanta: Scholars Press, 1991.

d'Alfonso, Lorenzo. "Die hethitische Vertragstradition in Syrien (14.–12. Jh. v. Chr.)." Pages 303–29 in *Die deuteronomistischen Geschichtswerke: Redaktions- und religionsgeschichtliche Perspektiven zur "Deuteronomismus"-Diskussion in Tora und Vorderen Propheten*. Edited by M. Witte et al. Beihefte zur Zeitschrift für die alttestamentliche Wissenschaft 365. Berlin: de Gruyter, 2006.

___. Yoram Cohen, and Dietrich Sürenhagen. *The City of Emar Among the Late Bronze Age Empires: Proceedings of the Konstanz Emar Conference, 25.–26.04.2006*. Alter Orient und Altes Testament 349. Munster: Ugarit-Verlag, 2008.

Alt, Albrecht. "Die Heimat des Deuteronomiums." Pages 250–75 in *Kleine Schriften zur Geschichte des Volkes Israel*. Volume 2. Munich: Beck, 1953.

Alter, Robert. "A New Theory of Kashrut." *Commentary* 68 (1979): 46–52.

Altmann, Peter. "Review of Christopher Tuckett, ed. *Feasts and Festivals. Journal of Hebrew Scriptures* 9 (2011)." Cited 28 March, 2011. Online: http://www.arts.ualberta.ca /JHS/ reviews/reviews_new/review526.htm.

___. "What do the 'Levites in Your Gates' Have to Do with the 'Levitical Priests'? Towards a European-North American Dialogue on the Levites in the Deuteronomic Law Corpus." I*"The LORD Is Their Inheritance": Priests and Levites in History and Tradition* Edited by M. Leuchter and J. Hutton. Ancient Israel and Its Literature Series. Atlanta: SBL, forthcoming.

Anderson, Eugene N. *Everyone Eats: Understanding Food and Culture.* New York: New York Press, 2005.

Anderson, Gary A. *Sacrifices and Offerings in Ancient Israel: Studies in Their Social and Political Importance.* Harvard Semitic Monographs 41. Atlanta: Scholars Press, 1987.

Appadurai, Arjun. "Gastro-politics in Hindu South Asia." *American Ethnologist* 8 (1981): 494–511.

Arnaud, Daniel. *Recherches au Pays d'Ashtata: Emar VI: Textes Sumeriens et Accadiens.* 4 Volumes. Paris: Editions Recherche sur les Civilisations, 1985–87.

Assman, Jan. *Das kulturelle Gedächtnis: Schrift, Erinnerung und politische Identität in frühen Hochkulturen.* Munich: Beck, 1992.

Ballentine, Samuel. *Leviticus.* Interpretation. Louisville: John Knox, 2003.

Bär, Jürgen. *Der assyrische Tribut und seine Darstellung: Eine Untersuchung zur imperialen Ideologie im neuassyrischen Reich.* Alter Orient und Altes Testament 243. Kevelaer: Butzon & Bercker and Neukirchen-Vluyn: Neukirchener, 1996.

Barnett, Richard D. "Assurbanipal's Feast." *Eretz Israel* 18 (1985): 1–6.

___. *Sculptures From the North Palace of Ashurbanipal at Nineveh (668-627 B.C.).* London: The Trustees of the British Museum, 1976.

___. *Sculptures From the Southwest Palace of Sennacherib at Nineveh.* London: British Museum, 1998.

___ and M. Falkner. *The Sculptures of Aššur-Nasir-Apli II (883-859 B.C.), Tiglath-Pileser III (745-727 B.C.), Esarhaddon (681-669 B.C.) From the Central and South-West Palaces at Nimrud.* London :British Museum, 1962.

Barthes, Roland. "A Psychosociology of Contemporary Food Consumption." Pages 166–73 in *European Diet from Pre-Industrial to Modern Times.* Volume 5 of *Food and Drink in History. Selections from the Annales: Economies, Sociétés, Civilisations.* Edited by R. Forster and O. Ranum. Translated by E. Forster and P. M. Ranum. Baltimore: Johns Hopkins University Press, 1979.

Batto, Bernard. "The Sleeping God: an Ancient Near Eastern Motif of Divine Sovereignty." *Biblica* 68 (1987): 153–77.

___. *Slaying the Dragon: Mythmaking in the Biblical Tradition.* Louisville: Westminster John Knox, 1992.

Baumgarten, Joseph M. "On the Non-Literal Use of *ma'ăśer / dekatē.*" *Journal of Biblical Literature* 103 (1984): 245–51.

Beckwith, Roger T. and Martin J. Selman, eds. *Sacrifice in the Bible.* Grand Rapids: Baker, 1995.

Beardsworth, Alan and Teresa Keil. *Sociology on the Menu: An Invitation to the Study of Food and Society*. London: Routledge, 1997.

Bell, Catherine. *Ritual: Perspectives and Dimensions*. Oxford: Oxford University Press, 1997.

___. *Ritual Theory, Ritual Practice*. Oxford: Oxford University Press, 1992.

Bell, David and Gill Valentine, *Consuming Geographies: We Are Where We Eat*. London: Routledge, 1997.

Belnap, Daniel. "Fillets of Fatling and Goblets of Gold: The Use of Meat Events in the Ritual Imagery of the Ugaritic Mythological and Epic Texts." Ph.D. diss., The University of Chicago, 2007.

Ben-Dov, Jonathan. "Writing As Oracle and As Law: New Contexts for the Book-Find of King Josiah." *Journal of Biblical Literature* 127 (2008): 223–39.

Bennett, Harold V. "Triennial Tithes and the Underdog: A Revisionist Reading of Deuteronomy 14:22–29 and 26:12–15." Pages 7–18 in *Yet with a Steady Beat: Contemporary U.S. Afrocentric Biblical Interpretation* Edited by R. Bailey. Semeia Studies 42, Society of Biblical Literature: Atlanta, 2003.

Berman, Joshua. "Who Was the Vassal King of the Sinai Covenant?" Paper presented at the annual meeting of SBL, Boston, 25 November, 2008.

Berquist, Birgitta. "Bronze Age Sacrificial Koine in the Eastern Mediterranean? A Study of Animal Sacrifice in the Ancient Near East." Pages 11–43 in *Ritual and Sacrifice in the Ancient Near East: Proceedings of the International Conference Organized by the Katholieke Universiteit Leuven from the 17th to the 20th of April 1991*. Edited by J. Quaegebeur. Orientalia Lovaniensia analecta 55. Leuven: Peeters, 1993.

Biddle, Mark E., *Deuteronomy*. Macon, Ga.: Smyth and Helwys, 2003.

Bietenhard, Hans and Hernik Ljungman. *Der Tannaitische Midrasche Sifre Deuteronomium*. Judaica et Christiana 8. Bern: Peter Lang, 1984.

Birch, Leann L. and Jennifer A. Fisher, "The Role of Experience in the Development of Children's Eating Behavior." Pages 113-41 in *Why We Eat What We Eat: The Psychology of Eating*. Edited by E. Capaldi. Washington D.C.: American Psychological Association, 1996.

Black, Jeremy, Andrew George, and Nicholas Postgate, eds. *A Concise Dictionary of Akkadian*. SANTAG: Arbeiten und Untersuchungen zur Keilschriftkunde. Wiesbaden: Harrassowitz, 2000.

Blenkinsopp, Joseph. *Isaiah 1–39*. Anchor Bible 19. New York: Doubleday, 2000.

___. "Memory, Tradition, and the Construction of the Past in Ancient Israel." *Biblical Theology Bulletin* 27 (1997): 76–82.

Bloch-Smith, Elizabeth. "Assyrians Abet Israelite Cultic Reforms: Sennacherib and the Centralization of the Israelite Cult." Pages 35–44 in *Exploring the* Longue Durée: *Essays in Honor of Lawrence E. Stager*. Edited by J. D. Schloen. Winona Lake, Ind.: Eisenbrauns, 2009.

Blum, Erhard. "The Decalogue and the Composition History of the Pentateuch." Paper presented at "The Pentateuch: International Perspectives on Current Research," Zurich, 12 January, 2010.

___. "Solomon and the United Monarchy: Some Textual Evidence." Pages 59–78 in *One God - One Cult - One Nation: Archaeological and Biblical Perspectives.* Edited by R. G. Kratz and H. Spieckermann. Beihefte zur Zeitschrift für die alttestamentliche Wissenschaft 405. Berlin: de Gruyter, 2010.

___. *Studien zur Komposition des Pentateuchs.* Beihefte zur Zeitschrift für die alttesta-mentliche Wissenschaft 189; Berlin: de Gruyter, 1990.

___. and Rüdiger Lux, eds. *Festtraditionen in Israel und im Alten Orient.* Veröffent-lichungen der Wissenschaftlichen Gesellschaft für Theologie 28. Gütersloh: Güter-sloher Verlagshaus, 2006.

Borowski, Oded. *Agriculture in Ancient Israel.* Winona Lake, Ind.: Eisenbrauns, 1987.

___. *Daily Life in Ancient Israel.* Archaeology and biblical studies 5. Atlanta: Society of Biblical Literature, 2003.

___. *Every Living Thing: Daily Use of Animals in Ancient Israel.* Walnut Creek, Calif.: Al-tamira, 1998.

Bottéro, Jean. "The Cuisine of Ancient Mesopotamia." *Biblical Archaeology* 48: 36–47.

___. *Everyday Life in Ancient Mesopotamia.* Translated by A. Nevill. Edinburgh: Edinburgh University Press, 2001.

___. *The Oldest Cuisine in the World: Cooking in Mesopotamia.* Translated by T. L. Fagan. Chicago: University of Chicago Press, 2004.

Botterweck, G. Johannes and Helmer Ringgren, eds. *Theological Dictionary of the Old Tes-tament.* Rev. ed. Translated by J. T. Willis. 15 vols. Grand Rapids, Eerdmans: 1977–2006.

Bourdieu, Pierre. *Distinction: A Social Critique of the Judgement of Taste.* Translated by R. Nice. Cambridge, Mass.: Harvard University Press, 1984.

___. *Outline of a Theory of Practice.* Cambridge Studies in Social Anthropology 16. Trans-lated by R. Nice. Cambridge: Cambridge University Press, 1977.

Braulik, Georg. "Das Buch Deuteronomium." Pages 76–88 in *Einleitung in das Alte Testament* . Edited by E. Zenger. Stuttgart: Kohlhammer, 1995. Reprinted as pages 11–38 in *Studien zum Deuteronomium und seiner Nachgeschichte.* Stuttgarter biblische Aufsatzbände 33. Stuttgart: Verlag Katholisches Bibelwerk, 2001.

___, ed. *Bundesdokument und Gesetz: Studien zum Deuteronomium.* Herders biblische Studien 4. Freiburg: Herder, 1995.

___. "Commemoration of Passion and Feast of Joy: Popular Liturgy According to the Festival Calendar of the Book of Deuteronomy (Deut 16:1–17)." Pages 67–85 in *The Theology of Deuteronomy: Collected Essays of Georg Braulik. O.S.B.* Translated by U. Lindblad. N. Richland Hills, Tex.: BIBAL Press, 1994. Translation of "Leidens-gedächtnisfeier und Freudenfest: 'Volksliturgie' nach dem deuteronomischen Fest-kalender (Dtn 16, 1-17)." Pages 95–122 in *Studien zur Theologie des Deuteronomiums.* Stuttgarter biblische Aufsatzbände 2. Stuttgart: Verlag Katholisches Bibelwerk, 1988.

___. "Conservative Reform": Deuteronomy from the Perspective of the Sociology of Knowledge." *Old Testament Essays* 12 (1999) 13–32. Translation of "'Konservative Reform': das Deuteronomium in wissenssoziologischer Sicht." Pages 39–58 in *Studien zum Deuteronomium und seiner Nachgeschichte.* Stuttgarter biblische Aufsatzbände 33. Stuttgart: Verlag Katholisches Bibelwerk, 2001.

___. "Die dekalogische Redaktion der deuteronomischen Gesetze: Ihre Abhängigkeit von Levitikus 19 am Beispiel von Deuteronomium 22,1–12; 24,10–22; 25,13–16." Pages 1–25 in *Bundesdokument und Gesetz: Studien zum Deuteronomium.* Edited by G. Braulik. Freiburg: Herder, 1995.

___. *Die deuteronomischen Gesetze und der Dekalog: Studien zum Aufbau von Deuteronomium 12–26.* Stuttgarter Bibelstudien 145. Stuttgart: Verlag Katholisches Bibelwerk, 1991.

___. *Deuteronomium I: 1–16,17.* Neue Echter Bibel 15. Würzburg: Echter Verlag, 1986.

___. *Deuteronomium II: 16,18–34,12.* Neue Echter Bibel 28. Würzburg: Echter Verlag, 1992.

___. "Das Deuteronomium und die Gedächtniskultur Israels: Redaktionsgeschichtliche Beobachtungen zur Verwendung von *lmd.*" Pages 119–46 in *Studien zm Buch Deuteronomium.* Edited by N. Lohfink. Stuttgarter biblische Aufsatzbände 24. Verlag Katholisches Biblewerk, 1997. Reprinted from Pages 9–31 in *Biblische Theologie und gesellschaftlicher Wandel.* Edited by G. Braulik et al. Freiburg: Herder, 1993.

___. "Deuteronomy and the Commemorative Culture of Israel," Pages 183–98 in *The Theology of Deuteronomy: Collected Essays of Georg Braulik, O.S.B.* Translated by U. Lindblad. N. Richland Hills, Tex.: BIBAL Press, 1994.

___. "Durften auch Frauen in Israel opfern?: Beobachtungen zur Sinn- und Festgestalt des Opfers im Deuteronomium." Pages 59–89 in *Studien zum Deuteronomium und seiner Nachgeschichte.* Stuttgarter biblische Aufsatzbände 33. Stuttgart: Verlag Katholisches Bibelwerk, 2001.

___. "Geschichtserinnerung und Gotteserkenntnis: Zu zwei Kleinformen im Buch Deuteronomium." Pages 165–83 in *Studien zu den Methoden der Deuteronomiumsexegese.* Stuttgarter biblische Aufsatzbände 42. Stuttgart: Verlag Katholisches Bibelwerk, 2006.

___. "The Joy of the Feast: The Conception of the Cult in Deuteronomy." Pages 27–65 in *The Theology of Deuteronomy: Collected Essays of Georg Braulik. O.S.B.* Translated by U. Lindblad. N. Richland Hills, Tex.: BIBAL Press, 1994. Translation of "Die Freude des Festes: Das Kultverständnis des Deuteronomium—die älteste biblische Festtheorie." Pages 161–218 in *Studien zur Theologie des Deuteronomiums.* Stuttgarter biblische Aufsatzbände 2. Stuttgart: Verlag Katholisches Bibelwerk, 1988.

___. "Die Politische Kraft Des Festes: Biblische Aussagen." Pages 65–79 in *Liturgie Zwischen Mystik und Politik: Österreichische Pastoraltagung 27. bis 29. Dezember 1990.* Edited by H. Erharder. Vienna: Herder, 1991.

___. "The Rejection of the Goddess Asherah." Pages 165–82 in *The Theology of Deuteronomy: Collected Essays of Georg Braulik. O.S.B.* Translated by U. Lindblad. N. Richland Hills, Tex.: BIBAL Press, 1994. Translation of "Die Ablehnung der Göttin Aschera in Israel: War sie erst deuteronomistisch, diente sie der Unterdrückung der Frauen?" Pages 81–118 in *Studien zum Buch Deuteronomium* Edited by N. Lohfink et al. Stuttgarter biblische Aufsatzbände 24. Stuttgart: Verlag Katholisches Bibelwerk, 1997.

___. "The Sequence of the Laws in Deuteronomy 12-26 and in the Decalogue. Pages 313–35 in *A Song of Power and the Power of Song: Essays on the Book of Deuteronomy.* Edited by D. L. Christensen. Translated by L. M. Maloney. Winona Lake, Ind.: Eisenbrauns, 1993 Translation of "Die Abfolge der Gesetze in Deuteronomium 12–26 und der Dekalog." Pages 252–72 in *Das Deuteronomium: Entstehung, Gestalt und Botschaft.* Edited by N. Lohfink. Bibliotheca ephemeridum theologicarum lovaniensium 68. Leuven: Leuven University Press, 1985.

___. *The Theology of Deuteronomy: Collected Essays of Georg Braulik. O.S.B.* Translated by U. Lindblad. N. Richland Hills, Tex.: BIBAL Press, 1994.

___. "Von der Lust Israels vor seinem Gott: Warum Kirche aus dem Fest lebt." Pages 91–112 in *Studien zum Deuteronomium und seine Nachgeschichte.* Stuttgarter biblische Aufsatzbände 33. Stuttgart: Verlag Katholisches Bibelwerk, 2001. Reprinted from pages 113–122 in *Den Himmel offen halten: ein Plädoyer für Kirchenentwicklung in Europe.* Edited by I. Baugartner, C. Riesl and A Mate-Toth. Innsbruck: Tyrolia, 2000.

Brenner, Athalya and J. W. van Henten. "Our Menu and What Is Not On It: Editor's Introduction." Pages ix–xvi in *Food and Drink in the Biblical Worlds.* Semeia 86. Atlanta: Society of Biblical Literature, 1999.

Briant, Pierre. *From Cyrus to Alexander: a History of the Persian Empire.* Winona Lake, Ind.: Eisenbrauns, 2002.

Brichto, Herbert C. "On Slaughter and Sacrifice, Blood and Atonement." *Hebrew Union College Annual* 58 (1976): 1–17.

Brown, Francis, Samuel R. Driver, and Charles A. Briggs, eds. *A Hebrew and English Lexicon of the Old Testament, with an Appendix Containing the Biblical Aramaic. Based on the Lexicon of William Gesenius as Translated by Edward Robinson.* Oxford: Clarendon, 1907.

Brown, James W. "On the Semiogenesis of Fictional Meals." *Romanic Review* 69:4 (1978): 322–35.

Bultmann, *Der Fremde im antiken Juda: eine Untersuchung zum sozialen Typenbegriff »ger« und seinem Bedeutungswandel in der alttestamentlichen Gesetzgebung.* Forschungen zur Religion und Literatur des Alten und Neuen Testaments 153. Göttingen: Vandenhoeck und Ruprecht, 1992.

Burkert, Walter. "Oriental Symposia: Contrasts and Parallels." Pages 7–26 in *Dining in a Classical Context.* Edited by W. J. Slater. Ann Arbor, Mich.: University of Michigan Press, 1991.

Buttrick. George A., ed. *The Interpreter's Dictionary of the Bible.* 5 Volumes. Nashville: Abingdon, 1962.

Çambel, Halet and Aslı Özyar. *Karatepe-Aslantaş: Azatiwataya: die Bildwerke.* Mainz: Philippe von Zabern, 2003.

Capaldi, Elizabeth D. "Conditioned Food Preferences." Pages 53–80 in *Why We Eat What We Eat: The Psychology of Eating.* Edited by idem. Washington D.C.: American Psychological Association, 1996.

___. "Introduction." Pages 3–9 in *Why We Eat What We Eat: The Psychology of Eating.* Edited by idem. Washington D.C.: American Psychological Association, 1996.

Caquot, André. "Un sacrifice expiatoire à Ras Shamra." *Revue d'Histoire et de Philosophie Religieuses* 43 (1962): 201–11.

Carmichael, Calum M. *The Laws of Deuteronomy.* Ithaca, N.Y.: Cornell University Press, 1974.

Carr, David M. "Method in Determination of Direction of Dependence: An Empirical Test of Criteria Applied to Exodus 34,11–26 and its Parallels." Pages 107–40 in *Gottes Volk am Sinai: Untersuchungen zu Ex 32–34 und Dtn 9–10.* Edited by M. Köckert and E. Blum. Veröffentlichungen der Wissenschaftlichen Gesellschaft für Theologie 18; Gütersloh: Gütersloher Verlaghaus, 2001.

___. *Writing on the Tablet of the Heart: Origins of Scripture and Literature.* Oxford: Oxford University Press, 2005.

Carroll, Robert P. "Prophecy and Society." Pages 203–25 in *The World of Ancient Israel.* Edited by R. E. Clements. Cambridge: Cambridge University Press, 1989.

Certeau, Michel de. *The Practice of Everyday Life.* Translated by S. Rendall. Berkeley: University of California Press, 1984.

___, Luce Giard, and Pierre Mayol. *The Practice of Everyday Life, Volume 2: Living and Cooking.* New Revised and Augmented Edition. Edited by L. Giard. Translated by T.J. Tomasik. Minneapolis: University of Minnesota Press, 1998.

Chapman, Stephen B. *The Law and the Prophets: A Study in Old Testament Canon Formation.* Forschungen zum Alten Testament 27. Tübingen: Mohr Siebeck, 2000.

Chavalas, Mark W. "Ancient Syria: A Historical Sketch." Pages 1–22 in *New Horizons in the Study of Ancient Syria.* Edited by M. W. Chavalas and J. H. Hayes. Bibliotheca Mesopotamica 25. Malibu, Calif.: Endena, 1992.

Chavel, Simeon. "Religious Law and Society in the Layers of Deuteronomy 12." Paper presented at "The Pentateuch: International Perspectives on Current Research," Zurich, 12 January, 2010.

Childs, Brevard S. *Biblical Theology of the Old and New Testaments: Theological Reflection on the Christian Bible.* Minneapolis: Fortress, 1992.

___. *The Book of Exodus.* Old Testament Library. Philadelphia: Westminster, 1974.

___. *Memory, and Tradition in Ancient Israel.* Studies in Biblical Theology 37. London: SCM Press, 1962.

Chilton, Bruce. "The Hungry Knife: Towards a Sense of Sacrifice." Pages 122–38 in *The Bible in Human Society : Essays in Honour of John Rogerson.* Edited by M. D. Carroll R., D. J. A. Clines and P. R. Davies. Sheffield: Sheffield Academic Press, 1995.

Cholewinski, Alfred. *Heiligkeitsgesetz und Deuteronomium: Eine vergleichende Studie.* Analecta biblica 66. Rome: Biblical Institute Press, 1976.

Christian, Mark A. "Priestly Power That Empowers: Michel Foucault, Middle-Tier Levites, and the Sociology of 'Popular Religious Groups' in Israel." *Journal of Hebrew Scriptures* 9/1 (2009): 1–81. Cited 27 March, 2010. Online: http://www.arts. ualberta.ca/JHS/Articles/article_103.pdf.

___. "Revisiting Levitical Authorship: What Would Moses Think?" *Zeitschrift für Altorientalische und Biblische Rechtsgeschichte* 13 (2007): 194–236.

Christensen, Duane L., ed. *A Song of Power and the Power of Song: Essays on the Book of Deuteronomy.* Winona Lake, Ind.: Eisenbrauns, 1993.

___. *Deuteronomy 21:10-34:12.* Word Biblical Commentary 6B. Nashville: Word, 2001.

___. "Deuteronomy in Modern Research: Approaches and Issues." Pages 3–17 in *A Song of Power and the Power of Song: Essays on the Book of Deuteronomy.* Edited by D. L. Christensen. Winona Lake, Ind.: Eisenbrauns, 1993.

Civil, Miguel. "Enlil and Ninlil: The Marriage of Sud." *Journal of the American Oriental Society* 103.11 (1983): 43–66.

Claassens, L. Julia M. *The God Who Provides: Biblical Images of Divine Nourishment.* Nashville: Abingdon, 2004.

Clarke, Ernest G., with the collaboration of Sue Magder. *Targum Pseudo-Jonathan: Deuteronomy with Notes.* Aramaic Bible 5B. Edinburgh: Clark, 1998.

___, with collaboration by W. E. Aufrecht, J. C. Hurd, and F. Spitzer. *Targum Pseudo-Jonathan of the Pentateuch: Text and Concordance.* Hoboken, N.J.: KTAV, 1984.

Clemens, David M. "A Study of the Sacrificial Terminology at Ugarit: a Collection and Analysis of the Ugaritic and Akkadian Textual Data." Vol. 1. Ph.D. diss., University of Chicago, 1999.

Clements, Ronald E. *Deuteronomy.* Old Testament Guides. Sheffield: JSOT Press, 1989.

Cody, Aelred. "'Little Historical Creed' or 'Little Historical Anamnesis'?" *Catholic Biblical Quarterly* 68 (2006): 1–10.

Cogan, Mordechai. "Judah Under Assyrian Hegemony: a Reexamination of *Imperialism and Religion.*" *Journal of Biblical Literature* 112 (1993): 403–14.

Cohen, Mark E. *The Cultic Calendars of the Ancient Near East.* Bethesda, Md.: CDL 1993.

Cohen, Yoram. Review of Daniel Fleming, *Time at Emar. Orientalia* 74 (2003): 267–74.

Collins, Billie Jean. *The Hittites and Their World.* Society of Biblical Literature Archaeology and Biblical Studies 7. Atlanta: SBL, 2007.

Collon, Dominique. "Banquets in the Art of the Ancient Near East." Pages 23-30 in *Banquets D'Orient.* Edited by R. Gyselen. Res Orientales IV. Bures S/Y: Groupe pour L'Étude de la Civilisation du Moyen-Orient, 1992.

___. *First Impressions: Cylinder Seals in the Ancient Near East.* Chicago: University of Chicago, 1987.

Connerton, Paul. *How Societies Remember*. Cambridge: Cambridge University Press, 1989.

Cook, Stephen L. *The Social Roots of Biblical Yahwism*. Studies in Biblical Literature 8. Atlanta: Society of Biblical Literature, 2004.

Counihan, Carole and Penny Van Esterik. *Food and Culture: A Reader*. New York: Routledge, 1997.

Craigie, Peter C. *The Book of Deuteronomy*. New International Commentary on the Old Testament. Grand Rapids, Mich.: Eerdmans, 1976.

Croft, Paula. "Archaeozoological Studies, Section A: The Osteological Remains (Mammalian and Avian)." Pages 2254–2348 in *The Renewed Archaeological Excavations at Lachish (1973-1994)*. Vol 5. Edited by D. Ussishkin. Tel Aviv: Tel Aviv University, 2004.

Cross, Frank M. *Canaanite Myth and Hebrew Epic*. Cambridge, Mass.: Harvard, 1973.

Crüsemann, Frank." Der Zehnte in der israelitischen Königzeit." *Wort und Dienst* 18 (1985): 21–47.

___. *The Torah: Theology and Social History of Old Testament Law*. Translated by Allan W. Mahnke. Minneapolis: Fortress Press, 1996. Translation of *Die Tora: Theologie und Sozialgeschichte des alttestamentlichen Gesetzes*. Munich: Kaiser, 1992.

Dahm, Ulrike. *Opferkult und Priestertum in Alt-Israel: Ein kultur- und religionswissenschaftlicher Beitrag*. Beihefte zur Zeitschrift für die alttestamentliche Wissenschaft 327. Berlin: de Gruyter, 2003.

Dahmen, Ulrich. *Leviten und Priester im Deuteronomium: Literarkritische und redaktionsgeschichtliche Studien*. Bonner Biblische Beiträge 110. Bodenheim: Philo, 1996.

Dandamayev, M. A. "State and Temple in Babylonia in the First Millennium B.C." Pages 590–94 in *State and Temple Economy in the Ancient Near East* II. Edited by E. Lipiński. Orientalia Lovaniensia Analecta 6. Leuven: Departement Oriëntalistiek, 1979.

Daniels, Dwight R. "The Creed of Deuteronomy XXVI Revisited." Pages 231–42 in *Studies in the Pentateuch*. Edited by J. A. Emerton. Vetus Testamentum Supplement 41. Leiden: E. J. Brill, 1990.

Davies, Philip R., "Food, Drink, and Sects: The Question of Ingestion in the Qumran Texts." *Semeia 86* (1999): 151–63.

Davis, Simon. "The Faunal Remains." Pages 249–50 in *Tell Qiri: A Village in the Jezreel Valley*. Edited by A. Ben Tor and Y. Portugali; Jerusalem: Hebrew University, 1987.

Detienne, Marcel. "Culinary Practices and the Spirit of Sacrifice." Pages 1–20 in *Cuisine of Sacrifice Among the Greeks*. Edited by M. Detienne and J.-P. Vernant. Translated by P. Wissing. Chicago: University of Chicago Press, 1989.

Dietler, Michael. "Feasts and the Commensal Politics in the Political Economy: Food, Power, and Status in Prehistoric Europe." Pages 87–125 in *Food and the Status Quest*. Edited by P. Wiessner and W. Schiefenhövel. Providence: Berghahn Books, 1996.

___. "Theorizing the Feast: Rituals of Consumption, Commensal Politics, and Power in African Contexts." Pages 65–114 in *Feasts: Archaeological and Ethnographic Perspectives on Food, Politics, and Power*. Edited by M. Dietler and B. Hayden; Washington D.C.: Smithsonian Institution Press, 2001.

___ and Brian Hayden, eds. *Feasts: Archaeological and Ethnographic Perspectives on Food, Politics, and Power.* Washington D.C.: Smithsonian Institution Press, 2001.

Dietrich, Manfred and Oswald Loretz. "Baals Ablehnung niedriger Gäste." *Ugarit-Forschugen* 18 (1986): 447–48.

Dietrich, Manfred, Oswald Loretz, and Joaquín Sanmartín. *The Cuneiform Alphabetic Texts from Ugarit, Ras Ibn Hani and Other Places.* Abhandlungen zur Literatur Alt-Syrien-Palästinas und Mesopotamiens 8. Münster: Ugarit-Verlag, 1995.

Díez Macho, Alejandro, et al, editors. *Neophyti 1, Targum Palestinense ms. de la Biblioteca Vaticana.* Volume 5. Seminario Filológico Cardenal Cisneros del Instituto Arias Montano. Textos y estudios 11. Madrid: Consejo Superior de Investigaciones Científicas, 1968–1979.

Dion, Paul E. "Deuteronomy 13: The Suppression of Alien Religious Propaganda in Israel during the Late Monarchical Era." Pages 147–216 in *Law and Ideology in Monarchic Israel.* Edited by B. Halpern and D.W. Hobson. Journal for the Study of the Old Testament Supplement Series 124. Sheffield: Sheffield Academic Press, 1991.

Dobbs-Allsopp, F. W., J. J. M. Roberts, C. L. Seow, and R. E. Whitaker. *Hebrew Inscriptions: Texts From the Biblical Beriod of the Monarchy with Concordance.* New Haven: Yale University Press, 2005.

Donner, Herbert and Wolfgang Röllig. *Kanaanäische und aramäische Inschriften.* 5t ed. Wiesbaden: Harrassowitz, 2002.

Douglas, Mary. "Deciphering a Meal." Pages 61–80 in *Myth, Symbol, and Culture.* Edited by C. Geertz. New York: Nortand and Co, 1971. Reprinted from *Daedalus* 101 (1972): 61–81.

___. *Purity and Danger: An Analysis of the Concepts of Pollution and Taboo.* London: Routledge, 1966.

Drazin, Israel. *Targum Onkelos to Deuteronomy: an English Translation of the Text With Analysis and Commentary.* Based on A. Sperber's edition. New York: Ktav, 1982.

Driel, G. van. *The Cult of Ashur.* Studia Semitica Neerlandica 13. Assen: Van Gorcum, 1969.

Driver, Samuel R. *A Critical and Exegetical Commentary on Deuteronomy.* 3d ed. International Critical Commentary. Edinburgh: Clark, 1902.

Durkheim, Emile. *The Elementory Forms of the Religious Life.* Translated by R. Needham. New York: Free Press, 1965.

Dutcher-Walls, Patricia. "The Circumscription of the King: Deuteronomy 17:16–17 in its Ancient Social Context." *Journal of Biblical Literature* 121 (2002): 601–616.

___. "The Social Location of the Deuteronomists: a Sociological Study of Factional Politics in Late Pre-Exilic Judah." *Journal for the Study of the Old Testament* 52 (1991): 77–94.

Eberhart, Christian. *Studien zur Bedeutung der Opfer im Alten Testament: Die Signifikanz von Blut- und Verbrennungsriten im kultischen Raum.* Wissenschaftliche Monographien zum Alten und Neuen Testament 94. Neukirchen-Vluyn: Neukircherner, 2002.

Eidelman, Jay M. "Be Holy for I am Holy: food, Politics, and the Teaching of Judaism." *Journal of Ritual Studies* 14/1 (2000): 45–50.

Eissfeldt, Otto. *Erstlinge und Zehnten in Alten Testament*. Beiträge zur Wissenschaft vom Alten und Neuen Testament 22; Leipzig: Hinrich, 1917.

Eitam, David. "The Olive Oil Industry at Tel Miqne-Ekron in the Late Iron Age." Pages 16–35 in *Olive Oil in Antiquity: Israel and Neighbouring Countries from the Neolithic to the Early Arab Period*. Edited by D. Eitam and M. Heltzer . History of the Ancient Near East Studies 7. Padua: Sargon, 1996.

Eliade, Mircea. "Toward a Definition of Myth." Pages 3–5 in *Mythologies*. Vol 1. Edited by Yves Bonnefoy. Translated by G. Honigsblum et al. Chicago: University of Chicago, 1991.

Elliger, K. and W. Rudolph, eds. *Biblio Hebraica Stuttgartensia*. 5t., corrected edition. Stuttgart: Deutsche Bibelgesellschaft, 1997.

Ellison, R. "Diet in Mesopotamia: The Evidence of the Barley Ration Texts (c. 3000–1400 B.C.)." *Iraq* 43 (1981): 35–45.

Engen, Trygg. "The Acquisition of Odour Hedonics." Pages 79–90 in *Perfumery: the Psychology and Biology of Fragrance*. Edited by S. Van Toller and G. H. Dodd. London: Chapman & Hall, 1988.

___. *Odor Sensation and Memory*. New York: Praeger, 1991.

Fales Frederico M. and J. N. Postgate, eds. *Imperial Administrative Records, Part 1: Palace and Temple Administration*. State Archives of Assyria VII. Helsinki: Helsinki Univ. Press, 1992.

___, eds. *Imperial Administrative Records, Part 2: Provincial and Military Administration*. State Archives of Assyria VII. Helsinki: Helsinki Univ. Press, 1995.

Fazzini, Richard A. *Egypt, Dynasty XXII–XXV*. Iconography of Religions XVI:10. Leiden: E. J. Brill, 1988.

Faust, Avraham and Ehud Weiss. "Judah, Philistia, and the Mediterranean World: Reconstructing the Economic System of the Seventh Century B.C.E." *Bulletin of the American Schools of Oriental Research* 338 (2005): 71–92.

Feely-Harnik, Gillian. *The Lord's Table: The Meaning of Food in Early Judaism and Christianity*. Washington D.C.: Smithsonian Institution Press, 1981.

Feliu, Lluís *The God Dagan in Bronze Age Syria*. Translated by W. G. E. Watson. Culture and history of the ancient Near East 19. Leiden: E. J. Brill, 2003.

Fensham, F. Charles. "Malediction and Benediction in Ancient Near Eastern Vassal-Treaties and the Old Testament." Pages 247–55 in *A Song of Power and the Power of Song: Essays on the Book of Deuteronomy*. Edited by D. L. Christensen. Winona Lake, Ind.: Eisenbrauns, 1993. Reprinted from *Zeitschrift für altestamentliche Wissenschaft* 74 (1962): 1–9.

___. "Widow, Orphan, and the Poor in Ancient Near Eastern Legal and Wisdom Literature." Pages 176–92 in *Essential Papers on Israel and the Ancient Near East*. Edited by F. E. Greenspahn. New York: New York University Press, 1991.

Fernandez, James. *Persuasions and Performances: The Play of Tropes in Culture.* Bloomington, Ind.: Indiana University Press, 1986.

Ferrera, A. J. and Simon B. Parker. "Seating Arrangements at Divine Banquets." *Ugarit-Forschungen* 4 (1972): 37–39.

Fiddes, Nick. *Meat: A Natural Symbol.* London: Routledge, 1992.

Finet, Andre. "Le Banquet de Kalah offert par le Roi d'Assyrie Ašurnasirpal II (883–859)." Pages 31–44 in *Banquets d'Orient.* Edited by R. Gyselen. Res Orientales IV. Bures S/Y: Groupe pour L'Étude de la Civilisation du Moyen-Orient, 1992.

Finkelstein, Israel. *The Quest for the Historical Israel: Debating Archaeology and the History of Early Israel: Lectures Delivered at the Annual Colloquium of the Institute for Secular Humanistic Judaism, Detroit, October 2005.* Edited by B. B. Schmitt. Society of Biblical Literature Archaeology and Biblical Studies 17. Atlanta: SBL, 2007.

___ and Neil Asher Silbermann, "Temple and Dynasty: Hezekiah, the Remaking of Judah and the Rise of the Pan-Israelite Ideology." *Journal for the Study of the Old Testament* 30 (2006): 259–85.

Fishbane, Michael, *Biblical Interpretation in Ancient Israel.* New York: Oxford University Press, 1985.

Fischler, Claude. "Food, Self, and Identity." *Social Scientific Information* 27 (1988): 275–92.

Fleming, Daniel E. "A Break in the Line." *Revue biblique* 106 (1999): 161–74.

___. "The Emar Festivals: City Unity and Syrian Identity under Hittite Hegemony." Pages 81–121 in *Emar: The History, Religion, and Culture of a Syrian Town in the Late Bronze Age.* Edited by M. W. Chavalas; Bethsaida, Md.: CDL, 1996.

___. *The Installation of Baal's High Priestess at Emar: A Window on Ancient Syrian Religion.* Harvard Semitic Monographs 42. Atlanta: Scholars Press, 1992.

___. "The Israelite Festival Calendar." *Revue biblique* 106 (1999): 8–34.

___. "A Limited Kingship: Late Bronze Emar in Ancient Syria." *Ugarit-Forschungen* 24 (1992): 59–71.

___. *Time at Emar: the Cultic Calendar and the Rituals from the Diviner's Archive.* Mesopotamian Civilizations 11. Winona Lake, Ind.: Eisenbrauns, 2000.

Foster, Benjamin R. *Before the Muses: an Anthology of Akkadian Literature.* 3d ed. Bethesda, Md.: CDL Press, 2005.

Fox, Nili Sacher. Review of Stephen Cook, *The Social Roots of Biblical Yahwism. Journal of the American Oriental Society* 127 (2007): 86–88.

Freedman, David Noel., ed. *Anchor Bible Dictionary.* 6 Volumes. New York: Doubleday, 1992.

Fretheim, Terrence *Exodus.* Interpretation. Louisville: John Knox, 1991.

Frow, John. *Genre.* London: Routledge, 2005.

Gadamer, Hans-Georg. *Truth and Method.* Rev. ed. Translated by J. Weinsheimer and D. Marshall. New York: Continuum, 2004.

Gardella, Peter. "Food." Pages 3167–74 in vol. 5 of *Encyclopedia of Religion.* 2nd Ed. Edited by Lindsay Jones. 15 Volumes. Detroit: Thomson Gale, 2005.

Garnsey, Peter. *Food and Society in Classical Antiquity*. Key Themes in Ancient History. Cambridge: Cambridge University Press, 1999.

Gaster, Theodore H. *Thespis: Ritual, Myth and Drama in the Ancient Near East*. Rev. ed. New York: Harper & Row, 1961.

Geertz, Clifford. *The Interpretation of Cultures: Selected Essays*. New York: Basic Books, 1973.

Gelb, I. J., ed. *The Assyrian Dictionary of the Oriental Institute of the University of Chicago*. Chicago: Oriental Institute, 1956–2007.

George, Andrew. "Studies in Cultic Topography and Ideology" (Review of Beate Bongratz-Leisten, *Ina Šulmi Īrub: Die kulttopographische und ideologische Programmatik der akītu-Prozession in Babylonien und Assyrien im 1. Jahrtausend v. Chrs.*). *Biblica Orientala* 53:3/4 (1996): 363–95.

Gerstenberger, Erhard S. *Das dritte Buch Mose: Leviticus*. Das Alte Testament Deutsch 6. Göttingen: Vandenhoeck & Ruprecht: 1993.

Gertz, Jan C. *Die Gerichtsorganisation Israels im deuteronomischen Gesetz*. Forschungen zur Religion und Literatur des Alten und Neuen Testaments 165. Göttingen: Vandenhoeck und Ruprecht, 1994.

___. "Die Passa-Massot-Ordnung im deuteronomischen Festkalender." Pages 56–80 in *Das Deuteronomium und seine Querbeziehungen*. Edited by T. Veijola; Helsinki: Finnische Exegetische Gesellschaft, 1996.

___. "Die Stellung des kleinen geschichtlichen Credos in der Redaktionsgeschichte von Deuteronomium und Pentateuch." Pages 30–45 in *Liebe und Gebot: Studien zum Deuteronomium*. Edited by R. G. Kratz and H. Spieckermann. Forschungen zur Religion und Literatur des Alten und Neuen Testaments 190. Göttingen: Vandenhoeck & Ruprecht, 2000.

___. "Tora und Vordere Propheten." Pages 193–311 in *Grundinformation Altes Testament*. 3d ed. Edited idem. Göttingen: Vandenhoeck & Ruprecht, 2008.

Gesenius, Wilhelm and Andrew E. Cowley. *Gesenius' Hebrew Grammar as Edited and Enlarged by the Late E. Kautzsch*. 2d. English ed. Translated by A.E. Cowley. Oxford: Clarendon Press, 1983.

Gesundheit (Bar-On), Shimon. "Intertextualität und literarhistorische Analyse der Festkalender in Exodus und im Deuteronomium." Pages 190–220 in *Festtraditionen in Israel und im Alten Orient*. Edited by E. Blum and R. Lux. Veröffentlichungen der Wissenschaftlichen Gesellschaft für Theologie 28. Gütersloh: Gütersloher Verlaghaus, 2006.

___. "The Festival Calendars in Exodus XXIII 14–19 und XXXIV 18–26." *Vetus Testamentum* 48 (1998): 161–95.

___. "The Riddle of Exodus 13, 1–16." Paper presented at "The Pentateuch: International Perspectives on Current Research," Zurich, 12 January, 2010.

Gieselmann, Bernd. "Die sogenannte josianische Reform in der gegenwärtigen Forschung." *Zeitschrift für die alttestamentliche Wissenschaft* 106 (1994): 223–42.

Ginsburger, Moses. *Das Fragmententhargum: Targum Yerushalmi la-Torah*. Berlin: S. Calvary & Co., 1899.

Gitin, Seymour. "Tel Miqne-Ekron in the 7th Century B.C.: City Plan Development and the Oil Industry." Pages 219–42 in *Olive Oil in Antiquity: Israel and Neighbouring Countries from the Neolithic to the Early Arab Period*. Edited by D. Eitam and M. Heltzer . History of the Ancient Near East Studies 7. Padua: Sargon, 1996.

Glaser, Gabrielle *The Nose: A Profile of Sex, Beauty, and Survival*. New York: Atria, 2002.

Goldstein, Bernard R. and Alan Cooper. "The Festivals of Israel and Judah and the Literary History of the Pentateuch." *Journal of the American Oriental Society* 110 (1990) 19–31.

Goody, Jack. *Cooking, Cuisine and Class: A Study in Comparative Sociology*. Cambridge: Cambridge University Press, 1982.

Gordon, Cyrus. *Ugaritic Textbook: Grammar, Texts in Transliteration, Cuneiform Selections, Glossary, Indices*. 3 Volumes. Analecta Orientalia 35. Rome: Pontifical Biblical Institute, 1965.

Gottwald, Norman K. Review of Stephen Cook, *The Social Roots of Biblical Yahwism*. *Interpretation* 60 (2006): 210–212.

Gowan, Donald. "Wealth and Poverty in the Old Testament: The Case of the Widow, the Orphan, and the Sojourner." *Interpretation* 41 (1987): 341–53.

Grayson, A. K. "Chronicles and the Akitu Festival." Pages 160–70 in *Actes de la XVIIe Rencontre assyriologique internationale. Université libre de Bruxelles, 30 juin-4 juillet 1969*. Edited by A. Finet. Publications du Comité belge de recherches historiques, épigraphiques et archéologiques en Mésopotamie 1. Ham-sur-Heure, Belgium: Comité belge de recherches en Mésopotamie, 1970.

Greenberg, Moshe. "Some Postulates of Biblical Criminal Law." Pages 5–28 in *Yehezkel Kaufmann Jubilee Volume*. Edited by M. Haran. Jerusalem: Magnes, 1960. Reprinted as pages 283–300 in *A Song of Power and the Power of Song: Essays on the Book of Deuteronomy*. Edited by D. L. Christensen. Sources for Biblical and Theological Study 3. Winona Lake, Ind.: Eisenbrauns, 1993.

Greer, Jonathan S. "A Marzeah and a Mizraq: A Prophet's Mêlée with Religious Diversity in Amos 6.4–7." *Journal for the Study of the Old Testament* 32 (2007): 243–62.

Gurney, Oliver R. *Some Aspects of Hittite Religion: The Schweich Lectures of the British Academy 1976*. Oxford: Oxford University Press, 1977.

Hallo, William W., ed. *Canonical Compositions from the Biblical World*. Vol. 1 of *The Context of Scripture*. Leiden: E. J. Brill, 1997.

___, ed. *Monumental Inscriptions from the Biblical World*. Vol. 2 of *The Context of Scripture*. Leiden: E. J. Brill, 1997.

___, ed. *Archival Documents from the Biblical World*. Vol. 3 of *The Context of Scripture*. Leiden: E. J. Brill, 1997.

___. "The Origins of the Sacrificial Cult: New Evidence from Mesopotamia and Israel." Pages 3–14 in *Ancient Israelite Religion: Essays in Honor of Frank Moore Cross*. Edited by P. D. Miller, Jr. et al. Philadelphia: Fortress, 1987.

Halpern, Baruch. "The Centralization Formula in Deuteronomy." *Vetus Testamentum 31* (1981): 20–28.

___. "Jerusalem and the Lineages in the seventh Century BCE: Kinship and the Rise of Individual Moral Liability." Pages 11–107 in *Law and Ideology in Monarchic Israel*. Edited by B. Halpern and D. W. Hobson. Journal for the Study of the Old Testament Supplement Series 124. Sheffield: JSOT Press, 1991.

Hamilton, Mark. W. "At Whose Table? Stories of Elites and Social Climbers in 1–2 Samuel. *Vetus Testamentum* 59 (2009): 513–32.

Haran, Menahem. *Temples and Temple Service in Ancient Israel: An Inquiry Into the Character of Cult Phenomena and the Historical Setting of the Priestly School*. Oxford: Oxford University Press, 1978.

Harris, Marvin. "The Abominable Pig." Pages 67–79 in *Food and Culture: A Reader*. Edited by C. Counihan and P. Van Esterik. New York: Routledge, 1997. Reprinted from pages 67–81 in *Good To Eat: Riddles of Food and Culture*. New York: Simon & Schuster, 1985.

Harvey, Dorothea Ward. "Rejoice Not, O Israel!" Pages 116–27 in *Israel's Prophetic Heritage: Essays in Honor of James* Muilenburg. Edited by B. W. Anderson and W. Harrelson; New York: Harper and Brothers, 1962.

Hayden, Brian. "Fabulous Feasts: A Prolegomenon to the Importance of Feasting." Pages 23–64 in *Feasts: Archaeological and Ethnographic Perspectives on Food, Politics, and Power*. Edited by M. Dietler and B. Hayden. Washington D.C.: Smithsonian Institution Press, 2001.

Hellwing, S., M. Sadeh, and V. Kison. "Faunal Remains." Pages 309–50 in *Shiloh: The Archaeology of a Biblical Site*. Edited by I. Finkelstein. Tel Aviv: Tel Aviv University, 1993.

Heltzer, Michael. "On Tithe Paid in Grain in Ugarit," *Israel Exploratory Journal* 25 (1975): 124–28.

___ and David Eitam, eds. *Olive Oil in Antiquity: Israel and Neighboring Countries from Neolithic to Early Arab Period*. Haifa: University of Haifa, 1987.

Hendel, Ronald S. " The Exodus in Biblical Memory." *Journal of Biblical Literature* 120 (2001): 601–22.

___. *Remembering Abraham: Culture, Memory, and History in the Hebrew Bible*. Oxford: Oxford University Press, 2005.

Henkelman, Wouter F. M. "'Consumed Before the King': The Table of Darius, that of Irdabama and Irtaštuna, and that of his satrap, Karkis." Pages 667–776 in *Der Achämenidenhof / The Achaemenid Court: Akten des 2. Internationalen Kolloquiums zum Thema »Vorderasien im Spannungsfeld klassischer und altorientalischer Überlieferungen« Landgut Castelen bei Basel, 23.–25. Mai 2007*. Edited by B. Jacobs and R. Rollinger. Classica et Orientalia 2. Wiesbaden: Harrassowitz, 2010.

Herzog, Ze'ev. "Perspectives on Southern Israel's Cult Centralization: Arad and Beersheba." Pages 169–99 in *One God - One Cult - One Nation: Archaeological and Biblical Perspectives*. Edited by R. G. Kratz and H. Spieckermann. Beihefte zur Zeitschrift für die alttestamentliche Wissenschaft 405. Berlin: de Gruyter, 2010.

Hesse, Brian. "Animal Use at Tel Miqne-Ekron in the Bronze Age and Iron Age." *Bulletin of the American Schools of Oriental Research* 264 (1986): 17–28.

___. Review of Melinda A. Zeder, *Feeding Cities: Specialized Animal Economy in the Ancient Near East. American Antiquity* 59:2 (1994): 171–72.

Hillers, Delbert R. *Covenant: The History of a Biblical Idea*. Baltimore: Johns Hopkins University Press, 1969.

___. *Treaty Curses and the Old Testament Prophets*. Biblica et Orientalia 16. Rome: Pontifical Biblical Institute, 1964.

Hoftizjer, Jean and K. Joengling. *Dictionary of the North-West Semitic Inscriptions*. Handbook of Oriental Studies 21. 2 Volumes. Leiden: E. J. Brill, 1995.

Holloway, Steven W., *Aššur Is King! Aššur Is King! Religion in the Exercise of Power in the Neo-Assyrian Empire*. Culture and History of the Ancient Near East 10. Leiden: E. J. Brill, 2002.

___. Review of Eckart Otto, *Das Deuteronomium: politische Theologie und Rechtsreform in Juda und Assyrien. Journal of Near Eastern Studies* 66:3 (2007): 205–208.

Hölscher, Gustav. "Komposition und Ursprung des Deuteronomiums." *Zeitschrift für die alttestamentliche Wissenschaft* 40 (1922): 161–255.

Holtzman, Jon D. "Food and Memory." *Annual Review of Anthropology* 35 (2006): 361–78.

Homan, Michael. *To Your Tents, O Israel!: The Terminology, Function, Form and Symbolism of Tents in the Hebrew Bible and the Ancient Near East*. Leiden: E. J. Brill, 2002.

Hopkins, David C. *The Highlands of Canaan: Agricultural Life in the Early Iron Age*. Sheffield: Sheffield University Press, 1985.

Horwitz, Loira Kolska. "Faunal Remains from Mount Ebal." *Tel Aviv* 13–14 (1986–87): 173–87.

Houston, Walter J. "Rejoicing Before the Lord: the Function of the Festal Gathering in Deuteronomy." Pages 1–14 in *Feasts and Festivals*. Edited by C. Tuckett. Contributions to Biblical Exegesis and Theology. Leuven: Peeters, 2009.

Houtman, Cees. *Der Pentateuch: Die Geschichte seiner Erforschung neben einer Auswertung*. Contributions to Biblical Theology 9; Kampen: Kok Pharos, 1994.

Houtman, Cornelis. *Exodus*. Volume 2. Translated by S. Woudstra. Kampen: KOK, 1996.

Humbert, Paul. "»Laetari et exultare« dans le vocabulaire religieux de l'Ancien Testament (Essai d'analyse des termes Śāmaḥ et Gîl)." *Revue d'histoire et de philosophie religieuses* 22 (1942): 185–214.

Hundley, Michael. "To Be or Not to Be: A Reexamination of Name Language in Deuteronomy and the Deuteronomistic History." *Vetus Testamentum* 59 (2009): 533–55.

Hutzli, Jürg. *Die Erzählung von Hanna und Samuel: Textkritische und literarische Analyse von 1. Samuel 1–2 unter Berücksichtigung des Kontextes.* Abhandlungen zur Theologie des Alten und Neuen Testaments 89. Zurich: Theologischer Verlag Zürich: 2007.

Ikram, Salima. *Choice Cuts: Meat Production in Ancient Egypt.* Orientalia Lovaniensia Analecta 69. Leuven: Peeters Press, 1995.

Jagt, Krijn van der. "What Did Saul Eat When He Visited Samuel?" *The Bible Translator* 47 (1996): 226–30.

Janzen, David. *The Social Meanings of Sacrifice in the Hebrew Bible: A Study of Four Writings.* Beihefte zur Zeitschrift für die alttestamentliche Wissenschaft 344. Berlin: de Gruyter, 2004.

Janzen, J. Gerald. "The 'Wandering Aramean' Reconsidered." *Vetus Testamentum* 44 (1994): 359–75.

Jastrow, Marcus. *Dictionary of the Targumim, Talmud Bavli, Talmud Yerushalmi and Midrashic Literature.* Peabody, Mass.: Hendrickson, 2004.

Jenks, Alan W. "Eating and Drinking in the Old Testament." Pages 250–54 in vol. 2 of *Anchor Bible Dictonary.* Edited D. N. Freedman. New York: Doubleday, 1992.

Johnstone, William. "The Use of the Reminiscences in Deuteronomy in Recovering the Two Main Literary Phases in the Production of the Pentateuch." Pages 247–73 in *Abschied vom Jahwisten: Die Komposition des Hexateuch in der jüngsten Diskussion.* Edited by J. C. Gertz, K. Schmid, and M. Witte. Beihefte zur Zeitschrift für die alttestamentliche Wissenschaft 315. Berlin: de Gruyter, 2002.

Joüon, Paul. *A Grammar of Biblical Hebrew.* Translated and revised by Takamitsu Muraoka. 2 volumes. Subsidia biblica 14/1–2. Rome: Pontifical Bible Institute, 2006.

Juengst, Sara Covin. *Breaking Bread: the Spiritual Significance of Food.* Louisville: Westminster John Knox, 1992.

Kaufman, Cathy K. *Cooking in Ancient Civilizations.* Westport, Conn.: Greenwood Press, 2006.

Kaufman, Stephen A. "The Structure of Deuteronomic Law." *Maarav* 1 (1978/79): 105–58.

Keel, Othmar. *Die Geschichte Jerusalems und die Entstehung des Monotheismus.* Orte und Landschaften der Bibel IV. 2 Volumes Göttingen: Vandenhoeck & Ruprecht, 2007.

Kelle, Brad E. *Metaphor and Rhetoric in Historical Perspective.* Academia Biblica 20. Atlanta: SBL, 2005.

Keller, Martin. *Untersuchungen zur deuteronomisch–deuteronomostichen Namenstheologie* Bonner biblische Beiträge 105. Weinheim, Germany: Beltz Athenäum Verlag, 1996.

Kelm, Georg and Amichai Mazar, "7th Century B.C. Oil Presses at Tel Batash, Biblical Timnah." Pages 121–25 in *Olive Oil in Antiquity: Israel and Neighbouring Countries from the Neolithic to the Early Arab Period.* Edited by D. Eitam and M. Heltzer. History of the Ancient Near East Studies 7. Padova: Sargon, 1996.

King, Philip J. and Lawrence E. Stager, *Life in Ancient Israel*. Louisville: Westminster John Knox Press, 2001.

Kislev, M. E. "Food Remains." Pages 354–61 in *Shiloh: The Archaeology of a Biblical Site*. Edited by I. Finkelstein. Tel Aviv: Tel Aviv University, 1993.

Kittel, Rudolf, ed. *Biblia Hebraica*. 3d ed. Stuttgart: Württembergische Bibelanstalt, 1937.

Kline, Meredith G. *Treaty of the Great King: the Covenant Structure of Deuteronomy, Studies and Commentary*. Grand Rapids, Mich.: Eerdmans, 1963.

Klingbeil, Gerald A. "'Momentaufnahmen' of Israelite Religion: The Importance of the Communal Meal in Narrative Texts in I/II Regum and Their Ritual Dimension." *Zeitschrift für die alttestamentliche Wissenschaft* 118 (2006): 22–45.

Knierim, Rolf. "The Concept of the Text, not of the Performance." Pages 17–22 in *Text and Concept in Leviticus 1:1-9: a Case in Exegetical Method*. Forschungen zum Alten Testament 2. Tübingen: J. C. B. Mohr, 1992.

Knohl, Isaac. *The Sanctuary of Silence: the Priestly Torah and the Holiness School*. Minneapolis: Fortress, 1995.

Knoppers, Gary N. "Rethinking the Relationship between Deuteronomy and the Deuteronomistic History: The Case of Kings." *Catholic Biblical Quarterly* 63 (2001) 393–415.

Koch, Christoph. *Vertrag, Treueid und Bund: Studien zur Rezeption des altorientalischen Vertragsreachts im Deuteronomium und zur Ausbildung der Bundestheologie im Alten Testament*. Beihefte zur Zeitschrift für die alttestamentliche Wissenschaft 383. Berlin: de Gruyter, 2008.

Koehler, Ludwig, Walter Baumgartner, and J. Jacob Stamm. *The Hebrew and Aramaic Lexicon of the Old Testament, Study Edition*. 2 Volumes. Translated by M. E. J. Richardson. Leiden: E. J. Brill, 2001.

Köckert, Matthias. Review of Galo W. Vera Chamaza, *Die Omnipotez Aššurs: Entwicklungen in der Aššur-Theologie unter der Sargoniden Sargon II., Sanherib und Asarhaddon*. *Zeitschrift für alttestamentliche Wissenschaft* 116/2 (2004): 317–18.

Kratz, Reinhart G. *The Composition of the Narrative Books of the Old Testament*. Translated by J. Bowden. London: T & T Clark, 2005. Translation of *Komposition der erzählenden Bücher des Alten Testaments: Grundwissen der Bibelkritik*. Göttingen: Vandenhoeck & Ruprecht, 2000.

___. "The Idea of Cultic Centralization and Its Supposed Ancient Near Eastern Analogies." Pages 121–44 in *One God - One Cult - One Nation: Archaeological and Biblical Perspectives*. Edited by R. G. Kratz and H. Spieckermann. Beihefte zur Zeitschrift für die alttestamentliche Wissenschaft 405. Berlin: de Gruyter, 2010.

___. "Der literarische Ort des Deuteronomiums." Pages 101–20 in *Liebe und Gebot: Studien zum Deuteronomium*. Edited by R. G. Kratz and Hermann Spieckermann. Forschungen zur Religion und Literatur des Alten und Neuen Testaments 190. Göttingen: Vandenhoeck & Ruprecht, 2000.

___ and Hermann Spieckermann, eds. *Liebe und Gebot: Studien zum Deuteronomium.* Forschungen zur Religion und Literatur des Alten und Neuen Testaments 190. Göttingen: Vandenhoeck & Ruprecht, 2000.

___ and Hermann Spieckermann, eds. *One God - One Cult - One Nation: Archaeological and Biblical Perspectives.* Beihefte zur Zeitschrift für die alttestamentliche Wissenschaft 405. Berlin: de Gruyter, 2010.

Kraus, Hans-Joachim. *Worship in Israel: a Cultic History of the Old Testament.* Translated by G. Buswell. Richmond: John Knox, 1966.

Kreuzer, Siegfried. "Die Exodustradition im Deuteronomium." Pages 81–106 in *Das Deuteronomium und seine Querbeziehungen.* Edited by T. Veijola. Schriften der Finnischen Exegetischen Gesellschaft 62. Helsinki: Finnische Exegetische Gesellschaft and Göttingen: Vandenhoeck & Ruprecht, 1996.

Kuhrt, Amélie. *The Ancient Near East c. 3000-330 BC.* 2 Volumes. London: Routledge, 1995.

___. *The Persian Empire.* London: Routledge, 2007.

Lambert, Wilfred G. "The Assyrian Recension of *Enūma Eliš.*" Pages 77–79 in *Assyrien im Wandel der Zeiten: XXXIX Rencontre Assyriologique Internationale, Heidelberg 6.-10- Juli 1992.* Edited by H. Waetzoldt and H. Hauptmann. Heidelberger Studien zum Alten Orient 6. Heidelberg: Heidelberger Orientverlag, 1997.

___. "Donations of Food and Drink to the Gods in Ancient Mesopotamia." Pages 191-201 in *Ritual and Sacrifice in the Ancient Near East*: *Proceedings of the International Conference Organized by the Katholieke Universiteit Leuven from the 17th to the 20th of April 1991.* Orientalia Lovaniensia analecta 55. Edited by J. Quaegebeur. Leuven: Peeters, 1993.

___. "The Great Battle of the Mesopotamian Religious Year: The Conflict in the Akītu House, A Summary." *Iraq* 25 (1963): 189–90.

___. "Myth and Ritual As Conceived by the Babylonians." *Journal of Semitic Studies* 13 (1968): 104–112.

Leuchter, Mark. "'The Levite in Your Gates': The Deuteronomic Redefinition of Levitical Authority." *The Journal of Biblical Literature* 126 (2007): 419–28.

Lev-Tov, Justin. "The Social Implications of Subsistence Analysis of Faunal Remains from Tel Miqne-Ekron." *ASOR Newsletter* 49 (1999): 15.

Levenson, Jon D. *Sinai to Zion: An Entry into the Jewish Bible, New Voices in Biblical Studies.* San Francisco: Harper and Row, 1985.

Levin, Christoph. "Das Deuteronomium und der Jahwist." Pages 121–36 in *Liebe und Gebot: Studien zum Deuteronomium.* Edited by R. G. Kratz and Hermann Spieckermann. Forschungen zur Religion und Literatur des Alten und Neuen Testaments 190. Göttingen: Vandenhoeck & Ruprecht, 2000.

___. "Über den 'Color Hieremianus' des Deuteronomiums. Pages 107–26 in *Das Deuteronomium und seine Querbeziehungen.* Edited by T. Veijola. Schriften der Finnischen Exegetischen Gesellschaft 62. Helsinki: Finnische Exegetische Gessellschaft and Göttingen: Vandenhoeck & Ruprecht, 1996.

Levine, Baruch. *Numbers 1–20: A New Translation With Introduction and Commentary.* Anchor Bible 4. New York: Doubleday, 1993.

___. *In The Presence of the Lord: A Study of Cult and Some Cultic Terms in Ancient Israel.* Leiden: E. J. Brill, 1974.

___. "Ugaritic Descriptive Rituals." *Journal of Cuneiform Studies* 17 (1963): 105–111.

___ and Jean-Michel de Tarragon, "The King Proclaims the Day: Ugaritic Rites for the Vintage (*KTU* 1.41//1.87)." *Revue biblique* 100 (1993): 76–115.

Levinson, Bernard. "But You Shall Surely Kill Him! The Text-critical and Neo-Assyrian Evidence for MT Deuteronomy 13:10*." Pages 37–63 in *Bundesdokument und Gesetz: Studien zum Deuteronomium.* Edited by G. Braulik. Freiburg: Herder, 1995.

___. *Deuteronomy and the Hermeneutics of Legal Innovation.* Oxford: Oxford University Press, 2002.

___. "The Hermeneutics of Tradition in Deuteronomy: a Reply to J. G. McConville." *Journal of Biblical Literature* 119 (2000): 269–86.

___. "Is the Covenant Code an Exilic Composition? A Response to John Van Seters." Pages 272–325 in *In Search of Pre-exilic Israel: Proceedings of the Oxford Old Testament Seminar.* Edited by J. Day. Journal for the Study of the Old Testament Supplement Series 406. London: T & T Clark, 2004.

___. "McConville's *Law and Theology in Deuteronomy.*" *Jewish Quarterly Review* 80 (1990): 396–404.

___. "The Neo-Assyrian Origins of the Canon Formula in Deuteronomy 13:1." Pages 25–45 in *Scriptural Exegesis: The Shapes of Culture and the Religious Imagination: Essays in Honour of Michael Fishbane.* Edited by D. A. Green and L. S. Lieber. Oxford: Oxford University Press, 2009.

___. "The Reconceptualization of Kingship in Deuteronomy and the Deuteronomistic History's Transformation of Torah." *Vetus Testamentum* 51 (2001): 511–34.

___. "The Revelation of Redaction: Exodus 34:10–26 as a Challenge to the Standard Documentary Hypothesis." Paper presented at "The Pentateuch: International Perspectives on Current Research," Zurich, 12 January, 2010.

Lévi-Strauss, Claude. *The Savage Mind.* Chicago: University of Chicago, 1966.

Levy, B. Barry. *Targum Neophyti 1 : a Textual Study; Leviticus, Numbers, Deuteronomy.* Volume 2. Studies in Judaism, Lanham, Md.: University Press of America, 1987.

Lewis, Theodore J. *Cults of the Dead in Ancient Israel and Ugarit.* Harvard Semitic Monographs 39. Atlanta: Scholars, 1989.

___. "El's Divine Feast." Pages 193–196 in *Ugaritic Narrative Poetry.* Edited by S. B. Parker. Writings from the Ancient World 9. Atlanta: Scholars Press, 1997.

___. "The Rapiuma." Pages 196–205 in *Ugaritic Narrative Poetry.* Edited by S. B. Parker. Writings from the Ancient World 9. Atlanta: Scholars Press, 1997.

Lichtenstein, Murray. "The Banquet Motifs in Keret and in Proverbs 9." *Journal of the Ancient Near Eastern Society of Columbia University* 1 (1968):19–31.

Lichtheim, Mariam. *Ancient Egyptian Literature: a Book of Readings.* Vol 1. Berkeley, Calif.: University of California Press, 2006.

Livingstone, Alasdair. *Court Poetry and Literary Miscellanea*. State Archives of Assyria III. Helsinki: Helsinki University Press, 1989.

___. *Mystical and Mythological Explanatory Works of Assyrian and Babylonian Scholars*. Oxford: Clarendon, 1986.

___. "New Dimensions in the Study of Assyrian Religion." Pages 165–77 in *Assyria 1995: Proceedings of the 10th Anniversary Symposium of the Neo-Assyrian Text Corpus Project, Helsinki, September 7-11, 1995*. Edited by S. Parpola and R. M. Whiting. Helsinki: The Project, 1997.

Lloyd, J. B. "The Banquet Theme in Ugaritic Narrative." *Ugarit-Forschungen* 22 (1990): 169–93.

Lohfink, Norbert. "The Cult Reform of Josiah of Judah: 2 Kings 22–23 as a Source for the History of Israelite Religion." Pages 459–75 in *Ancient Israelite Religion: Essays in Honor of Frank Moore Cross*. Edited by P. D. Miller, Jr., P. D. Hanson, and S. D. McBride. Philadelphia: Fortress, 1987.

___. "Das deuteronomische Gesetz in der Endgestalt – Entwurf einer Gesellschaft ohne marginale Gruppen." Pages 205–18 in *Studien zum Deuteronomium und zur deuteronomistischen Literatur III*. Stuttgarter biblische Aufsatzbände 20. Stuttgart: Katholisches Bibelwerk, 1995. Reprinted from *Biblische Notizen* 51 (1990): 25–40.

___. "Das Deuteronomium: Jahwegesetz oder Mosegesetz? Die Subjektzuordnung bei Wörter für »Gesetz« im Dtn und in der dtr Literatur." Pages 157–65 in *Studien zum Deuteronomium und zur deuteronomistischen Literatur III*. Stuttgarter biblische Aufsatzbände 20. Stuttgart: Katholisches Bibelwerk, 1995. Reprinted from *Theologie und Philosophie* 65 (1990): 387–91.

___. "Deuteronomium und Pentateuch. Zum Stand der Forschung." Pages 13–38 in *Studien zum Deuteronomium und zur deuteronomistischen Literatur I*. Stuttgarter biblische Aufsatzbände 20. Stuttgart: Katholisches Bibelwerk, 1995.

___. "*'d(w)t* im Deuteornomium und in den Königsbüchern."Pages 167–77 in *Studien zum Deuteronomium und zur deuteronomistischen Literatur III*. Stuttgarter biblische Aufsatzbände 20. Stuttgart: Verlag Katholisches Bibelwerk, 1995. Repr. from *Biblische Zeitschrift* 35 (1991): 86–93.

___. "Dtn 26, 6–9: Ein Beispiel altisraelitischer Geschichtstheologie." Pages 291–303 in *Studien zum Deuteronomium und zur deuteronomistischen Literatur I*. Stuttgarter biblische Aufsatzbände 8. Stuttgart: Verlag Katholisches Bibelwerk, 1990. First published as "Un exemple de théologie de l'histoire dans l'ancien Israël. Deut 26, 5–9." *Archivio di filosofia* 39 (1971): 189–199. Reprinted from pages 100–107 in *Geschichte, Zeugnis und Theologie*. Edited by F. Theunis. Kerygma und Mythos VI/7 and Theologische Forschung 58. Hamburg-Bergstedt: Herbert Reich—Evangelischer Verlag, 1976.

___. "Fortschreibung?: Zur Technik von Rechtsrevisionen im deuteronomischen Bereich, erörtert an Deuteronomium 12, Ex 21,2–11 und Dtn 15,12–18." Pages 163–204 in *Studien zum Deuteronomium und zur deuteronomistischen Literatur IV*. Stuttgarter biblische Aufsatzbände 31. Stuttgart: Verlag Katholisches Bibelwerk, 2000. Reprinted from pages 127–71 in *Das Deuteronomium und seine Querbeziehungen*. Edited by T. Veijola. Schriften der Finnischen Exegetischen Gesellschaft 62. Helsinki: Finnische Exegetische Gesellschaft & Göttingen: Vandenhoeck & Ruprecht, 1996.

___. "Gab es eine deuteronomistische Bewegung?" Pages 65–142 in *Studien zum Deuteronomium und zur deuteronomistischen Literatur III*. Stuttgarter biblische Aufsatzbände 20. Stuttgart: Verlag Katholisches Bibelwerk, 1995. Reprinted from pages 91–113 in *Jeremia und die »deuteronomistische Bewegung«*. Edited by W. Groß. Bonner biblische Beiträge 98. Winheim: Beltz Athenäum, 1995.

___. "Gibt es eine deuteronomistische Bearbeitung im Bundesbuch." Pages 39-64 in *Studien zum Deuteronomium und zur deuteronomistischen Literatur III*. Stuttgarter biblische Aufsatzbände 20. Stuttgart: Verlag Katholisches Bibelwerk, 1995. Reprinted from pages 91–113 in *Pentateuchal and Deuteronomistic Studies: Papers Read at the XIIIth IOSOT Congress Leuven 1989*. Edited by C. Brekelmans and J. Lust. Bibliotheca ephemeridum theologicarum lovaniensium 94. Leuven: Peeters, 1990.

___. *Das Haupgebot: eine Untersuchung literarischer Einleitungsfragen zu Dtn 5–11*. Analecta Biblica 20. Rome: Pontifical Bible Institute, 1963.

___. "Kultzentralisation und Deuteronomium" (Review of Eleanore Reuter, *Kultzentralisation: Entstehung und Theologie von Dtn 12*). Pages 131–61 in *Studien zum Deuteronomium und zur deuteronomistischen Literatur IV*. Stuttgarter biblische Aufsatzbände 31; Stuttgart: Katholisches Bibelwerk, 2000. Reprinted from *Zeitschrift für altorientalische und biblische Rechtgeschichte* 1 (1995): 117–48.

___. "Opferzentralisation, Säkularisierungsthese und mimeische Theorie." Pages 219–60 in *Studien zum Deuteronomium und zur deuteronomistischen Literatur III*. Stuttgarter biblische Aufsatzbände 20. Stuttgart: Katholisches Bibelwerk, 1995.

___. "Recent Discussion on 2 Kings 22–23: The State of the Question." Pages 36–61 in *A Song of Power and the Power of Song: Essays on the Book of Deuteronomy*. Edited by D.L. Christensen; Winona Lake, Ind.: Eisenbrauns, 1993. Translated from "Zur neueren Diskussion über 2 Kön 22–23." Pages 24–48 in *Das Deuteronomium: Entstehung, Gestalt und Botschaft*. Edited by N. Lohfink. Bibliotheca ephemeridum theologicarum lovaniensium 68. Leuven: Leuven University Press, 1985. Reprinted as pages 179–207 in *Studien zum Deuteronomium und zur deuteronomistischen Literatur I*. Stuttgarter biblische Aufsatzbände 20. Stuttgart: Verlag Katholisches Bibelwerk, 1995.

___. "Zum 'kleinen geschichtlichen Credo' Dtn 26, 5–9." Pages 263–90 in *Studien zum Deuteronomium und zur deuteronomistischen Literatur I*. Stuttgarter Biblische Aufsatzbände 8. Stuttgart: Stuttgart: Katholisches Bibelwerk, 1995. Kaltholisches Bibelwerk, 1990. Reprinted from *Theologie und Philosophie* 46 (1971): 19–39.

___. "Zur deuteronomischen Zentralisationsformel." Pages 147–77 in *Studien zum Deuteronomium und zur deuteronomistischen Literatur II*. Stuttgarter biblische Aufsatzbände 20. Stuttgart: Verlag Katholisches Bibelwerk, 1991. Reprinted from *Biblica* 65 (1984): 297–329.

Loretz, Oswald. "Das Neujahrsfest im syrisch-palaestinischen Regengebiet: Der Beitrag der Ugarit- und Emar- Texte zum Verständnis biblischer Neujahrstradition." Pages 81–110 in *Festtraditionen in Israel und im Alten Orient*. Edited by E. Blum and R. Lux. Veröffentlichungen der Wissenschaftlichen Gesellschaft für Theologie 28. Gütersloh: Gütersloher Verlagshaus, 2006.

Luckenbill, Daniel David. *Ancient Records of Assyria and Babylon: Volume II: Historical Records of Assyria From Sargon to the End*. Chicago: University of Chicago Press, 1927.

___. *The Annals of Sennacherib*. Chicago: University of Chicago Press, 1924.

Lust, Johan, Erik Eynikel and Karin Hauspie. *Greek-English Lexicon of the Septuagint*. Rev ed. Stuttgart: Deutsche Bibelgesellschaft, 2003.

MacDonald, Nathan. "Ancient Israelite Diet: Problems and Prospects." Paper presented at the annual meeting of SBL, Philadelphia, 21 November, 2005.

___. *Deuteronomy and the Meaning of 'Monotheism.'* Forschungen zum Alten Testament, II/1. Tübingen: Mohr Siebeck, 2003.

___. "Issues in the Dating of Deuteronomy: A Response to Juha Pakkala." *Zeitschrift für die alttestamentliche Wissenschaft* 122 (2019): 431–35.

___. *Not Bread Alone: The Uses of Food in the Old Testament*. Oxford: Oxford University Press, 2008.

___. Review of Sven Petry, *Die Entgrenzung JHWHs: Monolatrie, Bilderverbot und Monotheismus im Deuteronomium, in Deuterojesaja und im Ezechielbuch. Journal of Hebrew Scriptures* 9 (2009). Cited 10 January, 2010. Online: http://www.arts.ualberta .ca/JHS/reviews/reviews_new/review385.htm.

___. *What Did the Israelites Eat? Diet in Biblical Times*. Grand Rapids, Mich.: Eerdmans, 2008.

Machinist, Peter. "The Question of Distinctiveness." Pages 196–212 in *Ah Assyria…Studies in Assyrian History and Ancient Near Eastern Historiography Presented to Hayim Tadmor*. Edited by M. Coogan and I. Eph'al. Scripta Hierosolymitana 33. Jerusalem: Magnes, 1991. Reprinted as pages 420–42 in *Essential Papers on Israel and the Ancient Near East*. Edited by F. E. Greenspahn. New York: New York University Press, 1991.

Magen, Ursula. *Assyrische Königsdarstellungen—Aspekte der Herrschaft: eine Typologie*. Baghdader Forschungen 9. Mainz: von Zabern, 1986.

Markoe, Glenn. *Phoenician Bronze and Silver Bowls from Cyprus and the Mediterranean*. University of California Classical Studies 26. Berkeley: University of California, 1985.

Marom, Nimrod, Noa Raban-Gerstel, Amihai Mazar, Guy Bar-Oz, "Backbone of Society: Evidence for Social and Economic Status of the Iron Age Population of Tel Rehov, Beth She'an Valley, Israel," *Bulletin of the American Schools of Oriental Research* 354 (2009), 55-75.

Martin, Geoffrey T. *The Memphite Tomb of Horemheb Commander-in-Chief of Tut'ankhamūn*. London: Egypt Exploration Society, 1989.

Marx, Alfred. "Familiarité et transcendance. La fonction du sacrifice d'aprés l'Ancien Testament." Pages 1–14 in *Studien zu Opfer und Kult im Alten Testament*. Edited by A. Schenker. Forschungen zum Alten Testament 3. Tübingen: Mohr Siebeck, 1992.

___. "The Theology of Sacrifice According to Leviticus 1–7." Pages 103–20 in *The Book of Leviticus: Composition and Reception*. Edited by R. Rendtorff and R. A. Kugler. Supplements to Vetus Testamentum 93. Leiden: E. J. Brill, 2003.

Masetti-Rouault, Maria Grazia. "Le roi, la fête et le sacrifice dans les inscriptions Royales assyriennes jusqu'au VIIIe siècle Av. J.-C." Pages 67–95 in *Fêtes et Festivités*. Cahiers Kubaba 4:1. Paris: L'Harmattan, 2002.

Maul, Stefan M. "Der assyrische König—Hüter der Weltordnung." Pages 201–14 in *Priests and Officials in the Ancient Near East: Papers of the Second Colloquium on the Ancient Near East—The City and its Life Held at the Middle Eastern Culture Center in Japan (Mitaka, Tokyo), March 22-24, 1996*. Edited by K. Watanabe. Heidelberg: Winter, 1999.

___. "Die Frühjahrsfeierlichkeiten in Aššur." Pages 389–420 in *Wisdom, Gods and Literature: Studies in Assyriology in Honour of W.G. Lambert*. Edited by A. R. George and I. L. Finkel. Winona Lakes, Ind.: Eisenbrauns, 2000.

Mayes, Andrew D. H. *Deuteronomy*. New Century Bible. London: Marshall, Morgan & Scott, 1979.

___. "On Describing the Purpose of Deuteronomy." *Journal for the Study of the Old Testament* 58 (1993): 13–33.

Mcbride, S. Dean, Jr. "Polity of the Covenant People: The Book of Deuteronomy." Pages 62–77 in *A Song of Power and the Power of Song: Essays on the Book of Deuteronomy*. Edited by D. L. Christensen. Winona Lake, Ind.: Eisenbrauns, 1993. Reprinted from *Interpretation* 41 (1987); 229–44.

___. "The Yoke of the Kingdom: An Exposition of Deuteronomy 6:4–5." *Interpretation* 27 (1973): 273–306.

McCarthy, Carmel. *Biblia Hebraica Quinta, Fascicle 5: Deuteronomy*. Edited by A. Schenker et al. Stuttgart: Deutsche Bibelgesellschaft, 2007.

McCarthy, Dennis J. "The Symbolism of Blood and Sacrifice." *Journal of Biblical Literature* 88 (1969): 166–76.

___. "Further Notes on the Symbolism of Blood and Sacrifice." *Journal of Biblical Literature* 92 (1973): 205–10.

McCarter, P. Kyle Jr. *I Samuel: A New Translation With Introduction, Notes & Commentary*. Anchor Bible 8. Garden City, N.Y.: Doubleday, 1980.

___. *Textual Criticism: Recovering the Text of the Hebrew Bible*. Guides to Biblical Scholarship. Old Testament Guides. Philadelphia: Fortress, 1986.

McConville, J. Gordon. *Deuteronomy*. Apollos Old Testament Commentary 5. Leicester, England: Apollos and Downers Grove, Ill.: InterVarsity Press, 2002.

___. "Deuteronomy's Unification of Passover and Massôt: A Response to Bernard M. Levinson." *Journal of Biblical Literature*, 119/1 (2000): 47–58.

___. "King and Messiah in Deuteronomy and the Deuteronomistic History." Pages 271–95 in *King and Messiah in Israel and the Ancient Near East: Proceedings of the Oxford Old Testament Seminar*. Journal for the Study of the Old Testament Supplement Series 270. Edited by J. Day. Sheffield: Sheffield University Press, 1998.

___. *Law and Theology in Deuteronomy*. Journal for the Study of the Old Testament Supplement Series 33. Sheffield: JSOT Press, 1984.

___ and J. G. Millar. *Time and Place in Deuteronomy*. Journal for the Study of the Old Testament Supplement Series 179. Sheffield: JSOT Press, 1994.

McIntosh, William Alex, *Sociologies of Food and Nutrition*. New York: Plenum, 1996.

McNamara, Martin. *Targum Neofiti 1: Deuteronomy With Apparatus and Notes*. Aramaic Bible 5A. Collegeville, Minn.: Liturgical Press, 1997.

Mennell, Stephen. *The Sociology of Food : Eating, Diet, and Culture*. London: Sage, 1992.

Menzel, Brigitte. *Assyrische Tempel*. Volume 1. Rome: Biblical Institute Press, 1981.

Merendino, Rosario Pius. *Das deuteronomische Gesetz: Eine literarkritische, gattungs- und überlieferungsgeschichtliche Untersuchung zu Dt 12–26*. Bonner biblische Beiträge 31. Bonn: Hanstein, 1969.

Merlo, Paolo and Paolo Xella. "The Ugaritic Cultic Texts. 1: The Rituals." Pages 287–304 in *Handbook of Ugaritic Studies*. Handbuch der Orientalistik 39. Edited by W. G. E. Watson and N. Wyatt; Leiden: E. J. Brill, 1999.

Merrill, Eugene H. *Deuteronomy*. New Application Commentary. Nashville: Broadman & Holman, 1994.

Meyers, Carol. *Discovering Eve: Ancient Israelite Women in Context*. New York: Oxford University Press, 1988.

Milano, Lucio. "Food and Diet in Pre-Classical Syria," Pages 201–71 in *Production and Consumption in the Ancient Near East*. Edited by C. Zaccagnini. Budapest: University of Budapest, 1989.

___. "Food and Identity in Mesopotamia." Pages 243–56 in *Food and Identity in the Ancient World*. History of the Ancient Near East Studies 9. Edited by Cristiano Grottanelli and Lucio Milano. Padua: Sargon, 2004.

Milgrom, Jacob. "Biblical Diet Laws as Ethical System." *Interpretation* 17 (1963): 288–301.

___. "The Alleged 'Demythologization and Secularization' in Deuteronomy." Review of Moshe Weinfeld *Deuteronomy and the Deuteronomic School*. *Israel Exploratory Journal* 23 (1973): 156–61.

___. *Leviticus: A New Translation With Introduction and Commentary*. Anchor Bible 3–3B. New York: Doubleday, 1991–2001.

___. "Profane slaughter and a formulaic key to the composition of Deuteronomy." *Hebrew Union College Annual* 47 (1976): 1–17.

___. "A Prolegomenon to Leviticus 17:11." *Journal of Biblical Literature* 90 (1971): 149–56.

Miller, Patrick D., Jr. "Animal Names as Designations in Ugaritic and Hebrew." *Ugarit-Forschungen* 2 (1970): 177–86.

___. "Constitution or Instruction? The Purpose of Deuteronomy." Pages 253–68 in *The Way of the Lord: Essays in Old Testament Theology*. Tübingen: Mohr Siebeck, 2004. Reprint of "Constitution or Instruction? The Purpose of Deuteronomy" in *Constituting the Community: Studies on the Polity of Ancient Israel in Honor of S. Dean McBride, Jr.* Edited by S. Tuell and J. Strong. Winona Lake, Ind.: Eisenbrauns, 2004.

___. *Deuteronomy*. Interpretation. Louisville: Westminster John Knox, 1991.

___. *The Religion of Ancient Israel*. Louisville: Westminster John Knox, 2000.

Minette de Tillesse, Gaëtan. "TU & VOUS das le Deutéronome." Pages 156–63 in *Liebe und Gebot: Studien zum Deuteronomium*. Edited by R. G. Kratz and H. Spieckermann. Forschungen zur Religion und Literatur des Alten und Neuen Testaments 190. Göttingen: Vandenhoeck und Ruprecht, 2000.

Minette de Tillesse, Georges. "Sections 'tu' et sections 'vous' dans le Deutéronome," *Vetus Testamentum* 12 (1962): 29–87.

Miracle, Preston and Nicky Milner, eds. *Consuming Passions and Patterns of Consumption*. Cambridge: McDonald Institute for Archaeological Research, 2002.

Montanari, Massimo. *Food is Culture*. Translated by A. Sonnenfeld. New York: Columbia University Press, 2006.

Moor, Johannes C. de, *New Year With Canaanites and Israelites*. 2 Volumes. Kampen: Kok, 1972.

___. *Seasonal Pattern of the Ugaritic Myth of Baʿlu According to the Version of Ilimilku*. Alter Orient und Altes Testament 16. Kevelaer, Butzon & Bercker, 1971.

___. "Ugaritic Lexicographical Notes I." *Ugarit-Forschungen* 18 (1986): 258–61.

___ and Paul Sanders, "An Ugaritic Expiation Ritual and its Old Testament Parallels." *Ugarit-Forschungen* 23 (1991): 283–300.

Moran, William L. *The Amarna Letters*. Baltimore: Johns Hopkins, 1992.

Morrow, William S. "The Paradox of Deuteronomy 13: A Post-Colonial Reading." Pages 227–39 in *"Gerechtigkeit und Recht zu üben" (Gen. 18:19): Studien zur altorientalischen und biblischen Rechtsgeschichte, zur Religionsgeschichte Israels und zur Religionssoziologie*. Edited by R. Achenbach and M. Arneth. Beihefte zur Zeitschrift für Altorientalische und Biblische Rechtsgeschichte 13. Wiesbaden: Harrassowitz, 2009.

___. Review of Christoph Koch, *Vertrag, Treueid und Bund: Studien zur Rezeption des altorientalischen Vertragrechts im Deuteronomium und zur Ausbildung der Bundestheologie im Alten Testament*. *Journal of Hebrew Scriptures* 10 (2010). Cited 2 February, 2011. Online: http://www.arts.ualberta.ca/JHS/reviews/reviews_new/review466.htm.

___. *Scribing the Center: Organization and Redaction in Deuteronomy 14:1-17:13*. Society of Biblical Literature Monograph Series 49. Atlanta: Scholars, 1995.

___. "'To Set the Name' in the Deuteronomic Centralization Formula: A Case of Cultural Hybridity." *Journal of Semitic Studies* 55 (2010): 365–83.

Mowinckel, Sigmund. *Psalmsstudien*. Volume 2. Kristiania: J. Dybwad, 1921–24.

Mullen, E. Theodore, Jr. *Narrative History and Ethnic Boundaries: the Deuteronomistic Historian and the Creation of Israelite National Identity.* Atlanta: Scholars Press, 1993.

Müller, Karl F. *Das assyrische Ritual: Teil I: Texte zum assyrische Königsritual.* Mitteilungen der vorderasiatische-ägyptischen Gesellschaft 41:3. Leipzig: Hinrichs 1937.

Na'aman, Nadav. "The Debated Historicity of Hezekiah's Reform in Light of Historical and Archaeological Research." Pages 274–90 in *Ancient Israel's History and Historiography: The First Temple Period.* Vol. 3 of *Collected Essays*; Winona Lake, Ind.: Eisenbrauns, 2005. Repr. from *Zeitschrift für alttestamentliche Wissenschaft* 107 (1995): 179–95.

___. "The Distribution of Messages in the Kingdom of Judah in Light of the Lachish Ostraca." *Vetus Testamentum* 53 (2003): 169–80.

___. "The Law of the Altar in Deuteronomy and the Cultic Site Near Shechem." Pages 141–61 in *Rethinking the Foundations: Historiography in the Ancient World and in the Bible* Edited by S. L. McKenzie and T. Römer. Beihefte zur Zeitschrift für die alttestamentliche Wissenschaft 294. Berlin: de Gruyter, 2001. Repr. in *Ancient Israel's History and Historiography: The First Temple Period.* Vol. 3 of *Collected Essays*. Winona Lake: Eisenbrauns, 2006.

___. "Hezekiah and the Kings of Assyria." Pages 98–117 in *Ancient Israel and Its Neighbors: Interaction and Counteraction.* Vol. 1 of *Collected Essays*. Winona Lake, Ind.: Eisenbrauns, 2005. Repr. from *Tel Aviv* 21 (1994): 235–54

Nelson, Richard D. *Deuteronomy.* Old Testament Library. Louisville: Westminster John Knox, 2002.

___. "A Response to Thomas Römer, *The So-called Deuteronomistic History*." Pages 5–14 in "In Conversation with Thomas Römer, *The So-Called Deuteronomistic History: a Sociological, Historical and Literary Introduction* (London: T. & T. Clark, 2005)." In *The Journal of Hebrew Scriptures* 9/17 (2009) Edited by R. F. Person, Jr. Cited 7 December, 2009. Online: http://www.arts. ualberta. ca /JHS/ Articles/article_119.pdf.

Nemet-Nejat, Karen Rhea. *Daily Life in Ancient Mesopotamia.* Peabody, Mass.: Hendrickson, 2002.

Neusner, Jacob. *Sifre to Deuteronomy : an Analytical Translation.* 2 vols. Brown Judaic studies 98, 101. Atlanta: Scholars Press, 1987.

Nicholson, Ernest W. "Covenant in a Century of Study Since Wellhausen." Pages 78–93 in *A Song of Power and the Power of Song: Essays on the Book of Deuteronomy.* Edited by D. L. Christensen. Winona Lake, Ind.: Eisenbrauns, 1993. Reprinted from *Crisis in Perspectives*. Old Testament Studies 24. Leiden: E. J. Brill, 1986. Pages 54-69.

___. *Deuteronomy and Tradition.* Oxford: Blackwell, 1967.

___. "Traditum and traditio: the case of Deuteronomy 17: 14-20." Pages 46–62 in in *Scriptural Exegesis: The Shapes of Culture and the Religious Imagination: Essays in Honour of Michael Fishbane.* Edited by D. A. Green and L. S. Lieber. Oxford: Oxford University Press, 2009.

Niditch, Susan. *Oral World and Written Word: Ancient Israelite Literature.* Library of Ancient
    Israel. Louisville: Westminster John Knox, 1996.
Nielsen, Eduard. *Deuteronomium.* Handkommentar zum Alten Testament I/6. Tübingen:
    Mohr, 1995.
Nihan, Christophe. "The Holiness Code Between D and P: Some Comments on the Func-
    tion and Significance of Leviticus 17–26 in the Composition of the Torah." Pages 81–
    122 in *Das Deuteronomium zwischen Pentateuch und deuteronomistischem Geschichtswerk.*
    Edited by E. Otto and R. Achenbach. Forschungen zur Religion und Literatur des
    Alten und Neuen Testaments 206. Göttingen: Vandenhoeck & Ruprecht, 2004.
___. "The Laws About Clean and Unclean Animals in Leviticus and Deuteronomy."
    Paper presented at "The Pentateuch: International Perspectives on Current Re-
    search,", Zurich, 12 January, 2010.
Noth, Martin. *Exodus.* Translated by J. S. Bowden. Old Testament Library. Philadelphia:
    Westminster, 1962.

O'Connor. David. "The Social and Economic Organization of Ancient Egyptian Temples."
    Pages 319–29 in *Civilizations of the Ancient Near East.* Volume 1. Edited by J. Sasson.
    New York: Scribner, 1995.
Olmo Lete, Gregorio del. *Canaanite Religion According to the Liturgical Texts of Ugarit.*
    Translated by W. G. E. Watson. Bethesda, Md.: CDL, 1999.
___ and Joaquín Sanmartín, *A Dictionary of the Ugaritic Language in the Alphabetic Tradi-
    tion.* 2d, revised edition. 2 vols. Translated and Edited by W. G. E. Watson.
    Handbuch der Orientalistik 67. Leiden: E. J. Brill, 2004.
Olson, Dennis t. "How Does Deuteronomy Do Theology? Literary Juxtaposition and
    Paradox in the New Moab Covenant in Deuteronomy 29–32." Pages 201–13 in *God
    So Near.* Winona Lake, Ind.: Eisenbrauns, 2003.
___. *Numbers.* Interpretation. Louisville: John Knox, 1996.
___. Review of Moshe Weinfeld, *Deuteronomy 1-11: A New Translation with Introduction
    and Commentary. Journal of Biblical Literature* 112 (1993): 326–29.
Ornan, Tallay. "The Godlike Semblance of a King: The Case of Sennacherib's Rock Re-
    liefs." Pages 161–78 in *Ancient Near Eastern Art in Context* Edited by M. H. Feldman
    and J. Cheng; Leiden, E. J. Brill, 2007.
Osumi, Yuichi. *Die Komposition des Bundesbuches Exodus 20,22b–23,33.* Orbus Biblicus et
    Orientalis 105. Freiburg, Switz.: Universitätsverlag and Göttingen: Vandenhoeck &
    Ruprecht, 1991.
Otto, Eckart. *Das Deuteronomium: politische Theologie und Rechtsreform in Juda und Assyrien.*
    Beihefte zur Zeitschrift für die alttestamentliche Wissenschaft 284. Berlin: de
    Gruyter, 1999.
___. *Gottes Recht als Menschenrecht: Rechts- und literaturhistorische Studien zum Deutero-
    nomium.* Beihefte zur Zeitschrift für altorientalische Und biblische Rechtsgeschichte
    2; Wiesbaden: Harrassowitz, 2002.

___. "Die post-deuteronomistische Levitisierung des Deuteronomiums: Zu einem Buch von Ulrich Dahmen." *Zeitschrift für altorientalische und biblische Rechtsgeschichte* 5 (1999) 277-84.

___. "The Pre-exilic Deuteronomy as a Revision of the Covenant Code." Pages 112–22 in idem, *Kontinuum und Proprium: Studien zur Sozial- und Rechtsgeschichte des Alten Orients und des Alten Testaments.* Orientalia Biblica et Chrstiana 8. Wiesbaden: Harrassowitz, 1996 Revised paper from 1993 SBL Annual Meeting in Washington D.C.

___. "Von der Programmschrift einer Rechtsreform zum Verfassungsentwurf des Neuen Israel: Die Stellung des Deuteronomiums in der Rechtsgeschichte Israels." Pages 93–104 in *Bundesdokument und Gesetz: Studien zum Deuteronomium.* Edited by G. Braulik. Freiburg: Herder, 1995.

___. *Wandel der Rechtsbegründungen in der Gesellschaftsgeschichte des antiken Israel: eine Rechtsgeschichte des "Bundesbuches" Ex XX 22–XXIII 13.* Studia Biblica 3. Leiden: E. J. Brill, 1988.

Overholt, Thomas W. *Cultural Anthropology and the Old Testament.* Guides to biblical scholarship, Minneapolis: Augsburg Fortress, 1996.

Pakkala, Juha. "The Date of the Oldest Edition of Deuteronomy." *Zeitschrift für die Alttestamentliche Wissenschaft.* 121 (2009): 388–401.

___. "Der literar- und religionsgeschichtliche Ort von Deuteronomium 13." Pages 125–37 in *Die deuteronomistischen Geschichtswerke: Redaktions- und religionsgeschichtliche Perspektiven zur "Deuteronomismus"-Diskussion in Tora und Vorderen Propheten.* Edited by M. Witte et al. Beihefte zur Zeitschrift für die alttestamentliche Wissenschaft 365, Berlin: de Gruyter, 2006.

___. "Why the Cult Reforms in Judah Probably Did not Happen." Pages 201–35 in *One God - One Cult - One Nation: Archaeological and Biblical Perspectives.* Edited by R. G. Kratz and H. Spieckermann. Beihefte zur Zeitschrift für die alttestamentliche Wissenschaft 405. Berlin: de Gruyter, 2010.

Pardee, Dennis. "A New Aramaic Inscription from Zincirli." *Bulletin of the American Schools of Oriental Research* 356 (2009): 51–71.

___. *Ritual and Cult at Ugarit.* Writings from the Ancient World 10. Atlanta: Scholars, 2002.

___. "The Structure of RS 1.002." Pages 1181–95 in *Semitic Studies in Honor of Wolf Leslau: On the Occasion of his Eighty-Fifth Birthday, November 14th, 1991.* Volume 2. Edited by A. S. Kaye. Wiesbaden: Harrassowitz, 1991.

___. *Les Textes Rituels.* vol. 12:1–2 of *Ras Shamra-Ougarit;* Paris: Editions Recherche sur les civilizations, 2000.

Parker, Simon B. "Aqhat." Pages 51–80 in *Ugaritic Narrative Poetry.* Writings from the Ancient World 9. Atlanta: Scholars Press, 1997.

___, ed. *Ugaritic Narrative Poetry.* Writings from the Ancient World 9. Atlanta: Scholars Press, 1997.

Parpola, Simo. "The Leftovers of God and King: On the Distribution of Meat at the Assyrian and Achaemenid Imperial Courts." Pages 281–312 in *Food and Identity in the Ancient Word*. Edited by C. Grottanelli and L. Milano. History of the Ancient Near East
Studies 9. Padua: Sargon, 2004.

___ and Kazuko Watanabe, eds., *Neo-Assyrian Treaties and Loyalty Oaths*. State Archives
of Assyria 2. Helsinki: Helsinki University Press, 1988.

Parrot, André. *Arts of Assyria*. Translated by S. Gilbert and J. Emmons. New York:
Golden, 1961.

Paul, Shalom. *Studies in the Book of the Covenant in the Light of Cuneiform and Biblical Law*
Vetus Testamentum Supplement 18. Leiden: E. J. Brill, 1970.

Payne, Sabastian. "Kill-Off Patterns in Sheep and Goats: The Mandibles From Aşvan
Kale." *Anatolian Studies* 23 (1973): 281–303.

Payne Smith, J. (Mrs. Margoliouth), editor. *A Compendious Syriac Dictionary*. Founded
upon the *Thesaurus Syriacus* by R. Payne Smith. Winona Lakes, Ind.: Eisenbrauns,
1998.

Peckham, Brian. "The Composition of Deuteronomy 5–11. Pages 217–40 in *The Word Shall
Go Forth*. Edited by C. L. Meyers and M. O'Connor. ASOR special volume series 1.
Winona Lakes, Ind.: Eisenbrauns, 1983

Pedersen, Johannes. *Israel: Its Life and Culture*. 2 vols. South Florida Studies in the History
of Judaism 29. Atlanta: Scholars Press, 1991 [1926].

Pentiuc, Eugen J. "West Semitic Terms in Akkadian Texts From Emar." *Journal of Near
Eastern Studies* 58:2 (1999): 81–96.

___. *West Semitic Vocabulary in the Akkadian texts from Emar*. Harvard Semitic Studies 49.
Winona Lake, Ind.: Eisenbrauns, 2001.

Perlitt, Lothar. *Bundestheologie im Alten Testament* Wissenschaftliche Monographien zum
Alten und Neuen Testament 36. Neukirchen-Vluyn: Neukirchner, 1969.

Peshiṭta Institute, *The Old Testament in Syriac, According to the Peshiṭta Version*. Volume
1:2:1: Leviticus-Joshua. Vetus Testamentum Syriace iuxta simplicem Syrorum ver-
sionem. Leiden : E. J. Brill, 1991.

Pieper, Josef. *In Tune With the World: A Theory of Festivity*. Translated by R. and C.
Winston. South Bend, Ind.: St. Augustine's Press, 1999.

Pinnock, Frances "Considerations on the «Banquet Theme» in the Figurative Art of
Mesopotamia and Syria." Pages 15–26 in *Drinking in Ancient Societies: History and
Culture of Drinks in the Ancient Near East*. Edited by L. Milano. History of Ancient
Near East Studies 6. Padua: Sargon, 1994.

Pitard, Wayne T. "A New Edition of the 'Rāpi'uma' Texts: KTU 1.20–22." *Bulletin of the
American Schools of Oriental Research* 285 (1992): 33–77.

___. "The *RPUM* Texts." Pages 259–69 in *Handbook of Ugaritic Studies*. Handbuch der
Orientalistik 39. Ed. W. G. E. Watson and N. Wyatt. Leiden: E. J. Brill, 1999.

Pittman, Holly. "The White Obelisk and the Problem of Historical Narrative in the Art of
Assyria." *The Art Bulletin* 78 (1996): 334–55.

Pollock, Susan. "Feast, Funerals, and Fast Food in Early Mesopotamian States." Pages 17–38 in *The Archaeology and Politics of Food and Feasting in Early States and Empires*. Edited by T. L. Bray. New York: Kluwer Academic/Plenum, 2003.

Pongratz-Leisten, Beate. *Ina Šulmi Īrub: Die kulttopographische und ideologische Programmatik der* akītu-*Prozession in Babylonien und Assyrien im 1. Jahrtausend v. Chrs.* Baghdader Forschungen 16. Mainz: von Zabern, 1994.

___. "The Interplay of Military Strategy and Cultic Practice in Assyrian Politics." Pages 245–52 in *Assyria 1995: Proceedings of the 10th Anniversary Symposium of the Neo-Assyrian Text Corpus Project Helsinki, September 7-11, 1995*. Edited by S. Parpola and R. M. Whiting. Helsinki: University of Helsinki, 1997.

___. "Neujahr(sfest). B" *Reallexikon der Assyriologie*. 9: 294–98.

___. "Translating Universalism into Cultic Omnipresence in Assyria and Babaylonia in the 7th and 6th Century BCE." Paper presented at the "Reconsidering the Concept of 'Revolutionary Monotheism.'" Princeton, N.J., 11 February, 2007.

Pope, Marvin. H. *Probative Pontificating in Ugaritic and Biblical Literature: Collected Essays*. Edited by M. S. Smith. Ugaritisch-biblische Literatur 10. Münster: Ugarit-Verlag, 1994.

Pressler, Carolyn. *The View of Women Found in the Deuteronomic Family Laws*. Beihefte zur Zeitschrift für die alttestamentliche Wissenschaft 216. Berlin: de Gruyter, 1993.

Preuss, Horst D. *Deuteronomium*. Erträge der Forschung 164. Darmstadt: Wissenschaftliche Buchgesellschaft, 1982.

Pritchard, James B. *The Ancient Near East in Pictures Relating to the Old Testament*. 2. Edition with Supplement. Princeton: Princeton University Press, 1969.

Propp, William H.C. *Exodus 1–18*. Anchor Bible 2. New York: Doubleday, 1998.

Prosic, Tamara. *The Development and Symbolism of Passover until 70 CE*. Journal for the Study of the Old Testament: Supplement Series 414. London: T & T Clark International, 2004.

Quaegebeur, Jan, ed. *Ritual and Sacrifice in the Ancient Near East*: *Proceedings of the International Conference Organized by the Katholieke Universiteit Leuven from the 17th to the 20th of April 1991*. Orientalia Lovaniensia analecta 55. Leuven: Peeters, 1993.

Rad, Gerhard von. *Das fünfte Buch Mose: Deuteronomium*. Das Alt Testament Deutsch 8. Göttingen: Vandenhoeck & Ruprecht, 1964.

___. *Studies in Deuteronomy*. Translated by D. Stalker. London: SCM Press, 1961. Translation from *Deuteronomium-studien*. Forschungen zur Religion und Literatur des Alten und Neuen Testaments, Neue Folge 40. Göttingen: Vandenhoeck & Ruprecht, 1947.

___. "The Form Critical Problem of the Hexateuch." Pages 1–78 in *The Problem of the Hexateuch and Other Essays*. Translated by E. W. Trueman Dickens; Edinburgh: Oliver & Boyd Ltd.,1966. Reprinted London: SCM Press, 1984. Translation from "Das formgeschichtliche Problem des Hexateuchs." Pages 9–86 in idem, *Gesammelte Studien zum Alten Testament* Theologische Bücherei 8. Munich: Kaiser, 1958.

Radner, Karen. "Assyrische *ṭuppr adê* als Vorbild für Deuteronomium." Pages 351–78 in *Die deuteronomistischen Geschichtswerke: Redaktions- und religionsgeschichtliche Perspektiven zur "Deuteronomismus"-Diskussion in Tora und Vorderen Propheten*. Edited by M. Witte et al. Beihefte zur Zeitschrift für die alttestamentliche Wissenschaft 365. Berlin: de Gruyter, 2006.

___. Review of Holloway, Steven W., *Aššur Is King! Aššur Is King! Religion in the Exercise of Power in the Neo-Assyrian Empire. Journal of the Economic and Social History of the Orient* 46/2: Aspects of Warfare in Premodern Southeast Asia (2003): 226–230.

Rainey, Anson F. "Institutions: Family, Civil, and Military." Pages 93–98 in *Ras Shamra Parallels: The Texts from Ugarit and the Hebrew Bible*. Vol. 2. Edited by L. R. Fisher. Analecta Orientalia 50. Rome: Pontifical Bible Institute, 1975.

Rahlfs, Alfred. *Septuaginta, Id est Vetus testamentum graece iuxta LXX interpretes*. Stuttgart: Deutsche Bibel Gesellschaft, 1979.

Ramírez Kidd, José E. *Alterity and Identity in Israel: Th גּר in the Old Testament*. Beihefte zur Zeitschrif für die alttestamentliche Wissenschaft 283. Berlin: Walter de Gruyter, 1999.

Redford, Donald B., ed. *The Oxford Encyclopedia of Ancient Egypt*. 3 Volumes. Oxford: Oxford University Press, 2001.

___. "Studies in the Relations between Palestine and Egypt during the First Millennium B.C.: The Taxations System of Solomon." in *Studies in the Ancient Palestinian World*. Edited by J. W. Wevers and D. B. Redford. Toronto: University of Toronto Press, 1972.

Reindl, Joseph. *Das Angesicht Gottes im Sprachgebrauch des Alten Testaments*. Erfurter theologische Studien 25. Leipzig: St. Benno-Verlag, 1970.

Reinhartz, Adele. "Reflections on Table Fellowship and Community Identity." *Semeia 86* (1999): 227–33.

Rendtorff, Rolf. "Die Entwicklung des altisraelitischen Festkalenders." Pages 185–204 in *Das Fest und das Heilige: religiöse Kontrapunkte zur Alltagswelt*. Edited by J. Assman and T. Sundermeier. Gütersloh: Gütersloher Verlaghaus, 1991.

Reuter, Eleanore. *Kultzentralisation: Entstehung und Theologie von Dtn 12*. Bonner biblische Beiträge 87. Frankfurt am Main: Hain, 1993.

Richter, Sandra. L. *The Deuteronomistic History and the Name Theology:* lešakken šemô šām *in the Bible and the Ancient Near East*. Beihefte zur Zeitschrift für die alttestamentliche Wissenschaft 318. Berlin: de Gruyter, 2003.

Ricoeur, Paul. *Lectures in Ideology and Utopia*. Edited by George H. Taylor. New York: Columbia University Press, 1986.

___. *The Rule of Metaphor: Multi-disciplinary Studies of the Creation of Meaning in Language.* Translated by R. Czerny, K. McLaughlin and J. Costello. University of Toronto Romance Series 37. Toronto: University of Toronto Press, 1977.

Robbins, Jill. "Sacrifice." Pages 285–97 in *Critical Terms for Religious Studies.* Edited by Mark C. Taylor. Chicago: University of Chicago Press, 1998.

Roberts, J. J. M. *The Bible and the Ancient Near East.* Winona Lake, Ind.: Eisenbrauns, 2002.

Robertson, John F. "The Social and Economic Organization of Ancient Mesopotamian Temples," Pages 443–54 in *Civilizations of the Ancient Near East.* Volume 1. Edited by J. Sasson. New York: Scribner, 1995.

Rofé, Alexander. *Deuteronomy: Issues and Interpretation.* London: T & T Clark, 2002.

Rogerson, John W. *Anthropology and the Old Testament.* Growing Points in Theology; Oxford: Basil Blackwell, 1978.

Römer, Thomas. "Cult Centralization in Deuteronomy 12: Between Deuteronomistic History and Pentateuch." Pages 168–180 in *Das Deuteronomium zwischen Pentateuch un Deuteronomistichem Geschichtswerk.* Edited by E. Otto and R. Achenbach. Forschungen zur Religion und Literatur des Alten und Neuen Testaments 206. Göttingen: Vandenhoeck & Ruprecht, 2004.

___. *The So-called Deuteronomistic History: a Sociological, Historical and Literary Introduction.* London: T & T Clark, 2007.

Rose, Martin. *5. Mose Teilband 1:5. Mose 12–25: Einführung und Gesetze.* Zürcher Bibelkommentare 5,1. Zurich: Theologischer Verlag Zürich, 1994.

___. *5. Mose Teilband 2: 5. Mose 1–11 und 26–34: Rahmenstücke zum Gesetzeskorpus.* Zürcher Bibelkommentare 5:2. Zurich: Theologischer Verlag Zürich, 1994.

___. *Der Ausschliesslichkeitsanspruch Jahwes: deuteronomische Schultheologie und die Volksfrömmigkeit in der späten Königszeit.* Beiträge zur Wissenschaft vom Alten und Neuen Testament 6/6. Stuttgart: Kohlhammer, 1975.

Rosen, Baruch. "Subsistence Economy of Stratum II." Pages 156–85 in *'Izbet Ṣarṭah: an Early Iron Age site near Rosh Ha'ayin, Israel.* Edited by I. Finkelstein. Oxford: B.A.R., 1986.

Rost, Leonard. "Das kleine Geschichtliche Credo." Pages11–25 in *Das kleine Credo und andere Studien zum Alten Testament.* Heidelberg: Quelle und Meyer, 1965.

___. *Studien zum Opfer im Alten Israel.* Beiträge zur Wissenschaft vom Alten und Neuen Testament 6/13. Stuttgart: Kohlhammer, 1981.

Rüterswörden, Udo. *Das Buch Deuteronomium.* Neuer Stuttgarter Kommentar, Altes Testament 4. Stuttgart: Verlag Katholisches Bibelwerk, 2006.

___. "Das Deuteronomium im Licht epigraphischer Zeugnisse." Pages 241–56 in *Sprachen—Bilder—Klänge: Dimensionen der Theologie im Alten Testament und in seinem Umfeld.* Edited by C. Karrer-Grube et al. Alter Orient und Altes Testament 359. Munster: Ugarit-Verlag, 2009.

___. "Deuteronomium 12,20–28 und Leviticus 17." Pages 217–26 in *Gerechtigkeit und Recht zu üben" (Gen. 18:19): Studien zur altorientalischen und biblischen Rechtsgeschichte, zur Religionsgeschichte Israels und zur Religionssoziologie.* Edited by R. Achenbach and M. Arneth. Beihefte zur Zeitschrift für Altorientalische and Biblische Rechtsgeschichte, 13. Wiesbaden: Harrassowitz, 2009.

Ruwe, Andreas. *"Heiligkeitsgesetz" und „Priesterschrift": Literaturgeschichtliche und rechts-systematische Untersuchungen zu Leviticus 17,1–26,2.* Forschung zum Alten Testament 26. Tübingen: Mohr Siebeck, 1999.

Sakenfeld, Katharine Doob, ed. *The New Interpreter's Dictionary of the Bible.* 5 Volumes. Nashville: Abingdon Press, 2006-2009.

Said, Edward. *Orientalism.* London: Routledge & Kegan Paul, 1978.

Sancini-Weerdenburg, Heleen. "Persian Food: Stereotypes and Political Identity." Pages 286–302 in *Food in Antiquity.* Edited by J. Wilkens, D. Harvey and M. Dobson. Exeter: University of Exeter, 1995.

Sanders, Seth. *The Invention of Hebrew.* Champagne, Ill.: University of Illinois Press, 2009.

Sasson, Jack M. "The Calendar and Festivals of Mari During the Reign of Zimli-Lim." Pages 119–41 in *Studies in Honor of Tom B. Jones.* Edited by M. A. Powell, Jr. and R. H. Sack. Alter Orient und Altes Testament 203. Kevelaer: Butzon und Bercker and Neukirchen-Vluyn: Neukirchener, 1979.

___, ed. *Civilizations of the Ancient Near East.* 4 Volumes. New York: Scribner, 1995.

___. "The King's Table: Food and Fealty in Old Babylonian Mari." Pages 179–215 in *Food and Identity in the Ancient Word.* Edited by C. Grottanelli and L. Milano. History of the Ancient Near East Studies 9. Padua: Sargon, 2004.

Schab, Frank R. and William S. Cain, "Memory for Odors." Pages 223–24 in *The Human Sense of Smell.* Edited by D. G. Laing, et al. Berlin: Springer-Verlag, 1991.

Schaper, Joachim. *Priester und Leviten im achämenidischen Juda: Studien zur Kult- und Sozialgeschichte Israels in persischer Zeit.* Forschungen zum Alten Testament 31. Tübingen: Mohr Siebeck, 2000.

___. "Schriftauslegung und Schriftwerdung im alten Israel: Eine vergleichende Exegese von Ex 20,24–26 und Dtn 12,13–19." *Zeitschrift für altorientalische und biblische Rechtsgeschichte* 5 (1999): 111–132.

Schmandt-Besserat, Denise. "Feasting in the Ancient Near East." Pages 391–403 in *Feasts: Archaeological and Ethnographic Perspectives on Food, Politics, and Power.* Edited by M. Dietler and B. Hayden. Washington D.C.: Smithsonian Institution Press, 2001.

Schmid, Hans H. *Der Sogenannte Jahwist: Beobachtungen und Fragen zur Pentateuch-forschung.* Zurich: Theologischer Verlag Zürich, 1976.

Schmid, Konrad. " Das Deuteronomium innerhalb der 'deuteronomistischen Geschichts-werke' in Gen-2Kön: Pages 193–211 in *Das Deuteronomium zwischen Pentateuch und deuteronomistischem Geschichtswerk.* Edited by E. Otto and R. Achenbach. For-schungen zur Religion und Literatur des Alten und Neuen Testaments 206. Gött-ingen: Vandenhoek & Ruprecht: 2004.

___. *Erzväter und Exodus: Untersuchungen zur doppelten Begründung der Ursprünge Israels innerhalb der Geschichtsbücher des Alten Testaments.* Wissenschaftliche Monographien zum Alten und Neuen Testament 81; Neukirchen-Vluyn: Neukirchner, 1999.

___. "Hatte Wellhausen recht? Das Problem der literarhistorischen Anfänge des Deuteronomismus in den Königebüchern." Pages 23–47 in *Die deuteronomistischen Geschichtswerke: Redaktions- und religionsgeschichtliche Perspektiven zur Deuteronomismusdiskussion in Tora und Vorderen Propheten.* Edited by M. Witte et al. Beihefte zur Zeitschrift für die alttestamentliche Wissenschaft 365, Berlin: de Gruyter, 2006.

___. *Literaturgeschichte des Alten Testaments: Eine Einführung.* Darmstadt: WBG, 2008.

Schmidt, Brian B. *Israel's Beneficient Dead: Ancestor Cult and Necromancy in Ancient Israelite Religion and Tradition.* Forschungen zum Alten Testament 11. Tübingen: Mohr, 1994.

Schmitt, Eleanore. *Das Essen in der Bibel: literaturethnologische Aspekte des Alltäglichen.* Studien zur Kulturanthropologie 2. Münster: Lit, 1994.

Schniedewind, William. *How the Bible Became a Book: the Textualization of Ancient Israel.* Cambridge: Cambridge University Press, 2004.

Schwartz, Baruch J. "The Priestly Account of the Theophany and Lawgiving at Sinai." Pages 103–34 in *Texts, Temples, and Traditions: A Tribute to Menahem Haran.* Edited by M. V. Fox, et al. Winona Lake, Ind.: Eisenbrauns, 1996.

Schwemer, Daniel. *Die Wettergottgestalten Mesopotamiens und Nordsyriens im Zeitalter der Keilschriftkulturen: Materialien und Studien nach den schriftlichen Quellen.* Wiesbaden: Harrassowitz, 2001.

Schwienhorst-Schönberger. *Das Bundesbuch (Ex 20,22–23,33): Studien zu seiner Entstehung und Theologie.* Beihefte zur Zeitschrift für die alttestamentliche Wissenschaft 188. Berlin: de Gruyter, 1990.

Scurlock, Joann. "Animals in Ancient Mesopotamian Religion." Pages 361–388 in *A History of the Animal World in the Ancient Near East.* Edited by B. J. Collins. Handbuch der Orientalistik 64. Leiden: E. J. Brill, 2002.

___. "Animal Sacrifice in Ancient Mesopotamian Religion." Pages 389–404 in *A History of the Animal World in the Ancient Near East.* Edited by B. J. Collins. Handbuch der Orientalistik 64. Leiden: E. J. Brill, 2002.

Seebass, Horst. "Vorschlag zur Vereinfachung literarischer Analysen im dtn Gesetz," *Biblische Notizen* 58 (1991): 83–98.

Seitz, Gottfried. *Redaktionsgeschichtliche Studien zum Deuteronomium.* Beiträge zur Wissenschaft vom Alten und Neuen Testament 93. Stuttgart: Kohlhammer, 1971.

Seow, C. L. *Myth, Drama, and the Politics of David's Dance.* Harvard Semitic Monographs 44. Atlanta: Scholars Press, 1989.

Sharon, Diane M. *Patterns of Destiny: Narrative Structures of Foundation and Doom in the Hebrew Bible.* Winona Lake, Ind.: Eisenbrauns, 2002.

Simpson, William Kelly, ed., *The Literature of Ancient Egypt: An Anthology of Stories, Instructions, Stelae, Autobiographies, and Poetry.* 3d. Edition. New Haven: Yale University Press, 2003.

Singer, Ithamar. "A Political History of Ugarit." Pages 603–733 in *Handbook of Ugaritic Studies*. Edited by W. G. E. Watson and N. Wyatt. Handbuch der Orientalistik 39. Leiden: E. J. Brill, 1999.

Skolnik, Fred, ed. *Encyclopaedia Judaica*. 2d. ed. 22 Volumes. Detroit: Thomson/Gale, 2007.

Smith, Mark. S. "The Baal Cycle." Pages 81–176 in *Ugaritic Narrative Poetry*. Edited by S. B. Parker. Writings from the Ancient World 9. Atlanta: Scholars Press, 1997.

___. "The Death of 'Dying and Rising Gods' in the Biblical World." *Scandinavian Journal of the Old Testament* 12/2 (1998): 257–313.

___. *The Early History of God: Yahweh and the Other Deities in Ancient Israel*. San Francisco: Harper & Row, 1990.

___. *God in Translation*. Forschungen zum Alten Testament 57. Tübingen: Mohr Siebeck, 2008.

___. "Interpreting the Baal Cycle." *Ugarit-Forschungen* 18 (1986): 313–339.

___ and Wayne T. Pitard, *The Ugaritic Baal Cycle, Vol II: Introduction with Text, Translation and Commentary of KTU/CAT 1.3-1.4*. Leiden: E. J. Brill, 2009.

Smith, R. Payne. *A Compendious Syriac Dictionary*. Edited by J. Payne Smith. Eugene, Or.: Wipf and Stock, 1999.

Smith, William Robertson. *The Religion of the Semites*. 2nd ed. London: Black, 1907.

Soden, Wolfram von. *Akkadisches Handwörterbuch*. 3 Volumes. Wiesbaden: Harrassowitz, 1965–81.

Soler, Jean. "The Semiotics of Food in the Bible." Pages 126–38 in *Food and Drink in History: Selections from the Annales Economies, Societes, Civilisations, vol 5*. Edited by R. Forster and O. Ranum. Translated by E. Forster and P. M. Ranum. Baltimore: Johns Hopkins University, 1979.

Soden, Wolfram van. *Akkadisches Handwörtebuch*. 3 Volumes.

Sommers, Ben. "Dating Pentateuchal Texts and the Perils of Pseudo-Historicism." Paper presented at "The Pentateuch: International Perspectives on Current Research," Zurich, 12 January, 2010.

Sparks, Kenneth. *Ethnicity and Identity in Ancient Israel: Prolegomena to the Study of Ethnic Sentiments and Their Expression in the Hebrew Bible*. Winona Lake, Ind.: Eisenbrauns, 1998.

Sperber, Alexander. *The Bible in Aramaic: Based on Old Manuscripts and Printed Texts*. Volume 1. Leiden: E. J. Brill, 1959.

Spieckermann, Hermann. *Juda unter Assur in der Sargonidenzeit*. Forschungen zur Religion und Literatur des Alten und Neuen Testaments 129. Göttingen: Vandenhoeck & Ruprecht, 1982.

Stackert, Jeffrey. *Rewriting the Torah: Literary Revision in Deuteronomy and the Holiness Legislation*. Forschung zum Alten Testament 52. Tübingen: Mohr Siebeck, 2007.

Stager, Lawrence E. "Archaeology of the Family." *Bulletin of the American Schools of Oriental Research* 260 (1985): 1–35.

Stavrakopoulou, Francesca. *Land of Our Fathers: the Roles of Ancestor Veneration in Biblical Land Claims.* Library of Hebrew Bible/Old Testament Studies 473. London: T & T Clark, 2010.

Steinberg, Naomi, "The Deuteronomic Law Code and The Politics of State Centralization." Pages 365–75 in *The Bible and Liberation: Political and Social Hermeneutics.* Edited by N. K. Gottwald and R. A. Horsley. Maryknoll, N.Y.: Orbis, 1993.

Stern, Ephraim. *Archaeology of the Land of the Bible, Volume 2: The Assyrian, Babylonian, and Persian periods, 732-332 BCE.* New York: Doubleday, 2001.

Stevenson, Richard J. and Robert A. Boakes, "A Mnemonic Theory of Odor Perception." *Psychological Review* 110:2 (1993): 340–64.

Steuernagel, Carl. *Das Deuteronomium. Handkommentar* I.3,1. Rev. ed. Göttingen: Vandenhoeck & Ruprecht, 1923.

Steymans, Hans Ulrich. *Deuteronomium 28 und die* adê *zur Thronfolgeregelung Asarhaddons: Segen und Fluch im Alten Orient und in Israel.* Orbis Biblicus et Orientalis 145. Freiburg, Switz.: Universitätsverlag and Göttingen: Vandenhoeck & Ruprecht, 1995.

___. "Die literarische und historische Bedeutung der Thronfolgevereidigungen Asarhaddons." Pages 331–49 in *Die deuteronomistischen Geschichtswerke: Redaktions- und religionsgeschichtliche Perspektiven zur "Deuteronomismus"-Diskussion in Tora und Vorderen Propheten.* Edited by M. Witte et al. Beihefte zur Zeitschrift für die alttestamentliche Wissenschaft 365. Berlin: de Gruyter, 2006.

___. "Die Opfer im Buch Deuteronomium." *Bibel und Kirche* 49 (1994): 26–31.

Stoddart, D. Michael. "Human Odour Culture: a Zoological Perspective." Pages 3–17 in *Perfumery: The Psychology and Biology of Fragrance.* Edited by S. Van Toller and G. H. Dodd. London: Champman & Hall, 1988.

Stohlmann, Stephen C. "The Judaean Exile After 701 b.c.e." Pages 147–75 in *Scripture in Context II: More Essays on the Comparative Method.* Edited by W. W. Hallo, J. C. Moyer, and L. G. Perdue. Winona Lake, Ind.: Eisenbrauns, 1983.

Strommenger, Eva. *Fünf Jahrtausende Mesopotamien.* Munich: Hirmer, 1962.

Struble Eudora J. and Virginia Rimmer Hermann. "An Eternal Feast at Sam'al: The New Iron Age Mortuary Stele from Zincirli in Context." *Bulletin of the American Schools of Oriental Research* 356 (2009): 15–49.

Stulman, Louis. "Encroachment in Deuteronomy: An Analysis of the Social World of the D Code." *Journal of Biblical Literature* 109 (1990): 613–32.

Sutton, David E. *Remembrance of Repasts: An Anthropology of Food and Memory.* Oxford: Berg, 2001.

Tal, Abraham. *The Samaritan Pentateuch: Edited according to MS 6 (C) of the Shekhem Synagogue Tel-Aviv*: Tel-Aviv University, The Chaim Rosenberg School for Jewish Studies, 1994.

Talmon, Shemaryahu. "The 'Comparative Method' in Biblical Interpretation—Principles and Problems." Pages 320–56 in *Vetus Testamentum Supplement* 29 (1977): 320–56. Reprinted as pages 381–419 in *Essential Papers on Israel and the Ancient Near East*. Edited by F. E. Greenspahn. New York: New York University Press, 1991.

Teissier, Beatrice. *Ancient Near Eastern Cylinder Seals From the Marcopoli Collection*. Berkeley: University of California, 1984.

Tigay, Jeffrey H. *Deuteronomy = [Devarim]: the Traditional Hebrew Text With the New JPS Translation / Commentary*. Philadelphia: Jewish Publication Society, 1996.

Tilley, Christopher, ed. *Reading Material Culture: Structuralism, Hermeneutics, and Poststructuralism*. Oxford: Blackwell, 1990.

Tov, Emanuel. *Hebrew Bible, Greek Bible, and Qumran: Collected Essays*. Texts and Studies in Ancient Judaism 121. Tübingen: Mohr Siebeck, 2008.

___. *Textual Criticism of the Hebrew Bible*. Rev. ed. Minneapolis: Augsburg, 2001.

Toorn, Karel van der. "The Babylonian New Year Festival: New Insights From the Cuneiform Texts and Their Bearing on Old Testament Study." Pages 331–44 in *Congress Volume Leuven, 1989*. Edited by J. A. Emerton. Leiden: E. J. Brill, 1991.

___. *Family Religion in Babylonia, Syria and Israel: Continuity and Change in the Forms of Religious Life*. Leiden: E. J. Brill, 1996.

___. *Scribal Culture and the Making of the Bible*. Cambridge, Mass: Harvard University Press, 2007.

Tropper, Josef. "Ugaritic Grammar." Pages 105–110 in *Handbook of Ugaritic Studies*. Handbuch der Orientalistik 39. Edited by W. G. E. Wyatt and N. Wyatt. Leiden: E. J. Brill, 1999.

___. *Ugaritisch: Kurzgefasste Grammatik mit Übungstexten und Glossar*. Elementa Linguarum Orientis 1. Münster: Ugarit-Verlag, 2002.

___. *Ugaritische Grammatik*. Alter Orient und Altes Testament 273; Münster: Ugarit-Verlag, 2000.

Tsumura, David Toshio. "Kings and Cults in Ancient Ugarit." Pages 215–38 in *Priests and Officials in the Ancient Near East: Papers of the Second Colloquium on the Ancient Near East—The City and its Life Held at the Middle Eastern Culture Center in Japan (Mitaka, Tokyo), March 22-24, 1996*. Edited by K. Watanabe. Heidelberg: Winter, 1999.

Turner, Victor. *Dramas, Fields, and Metaphors: Symbolic Action in Human Society*. Ithaca, N.Y.: Cornell University Press, 1974.

___. *The Ritual Process: Structure and Anti-Structure*. New York: de Gruyter, 1995 [1966].

Uehlinger, Christoph. "Cult, Ritual and Monotheism: Considering the Rise of Judahite/Samarian Monotheism in Practical Terms." Paper presented at the "Reconsidering the Concept of 'Revolutionary Monotheism.'" Princeton, N.J., 11 February, 2007.

___. "Figurative Policy, Propaganda und Prophetie." Pages 297–349 in *Congress Volume, Cambridge 1995*. Edited by J. A. Emerton. Supplement to Vetus Testamentum 66. Leiden: E. J. Brill, 1997.

___. "Gab es eine joschijanische Kultreform? Plädoyer für ein begründetes Minimum." Pages 57–89 in *Jeremia und die »deuteronomistische Bewegung«*. Edited by W. Groß. Bonner biblische Beiträge 98. Winheim: Beltz Athenäum, 1995.

Van Buren, Elizabeth Douglas. *The Fauna of Ancient Mesopotamia as Represented in Art*. Analecta orientalia 18. Rome: Pontifical Bible Institute, 1939.

Van Seters, John. *Abraham in History and Tradition*. New Haven, Conn.: Yale University, 1975.

___. "Cultic Laws in the Covenant Code and Their Relationship to Deuteronomy and the Holiness Code." Pages 319–34 in *Studies in the Book of Exodus: Redaction—Reception—Interpretation*. Edited by M. Vervenne. Bibliotheca ephemeridum theologicarum Lovaniensium Leuven: Leuven University, 1996.

___. *A Law Book For the Diaspora*. Oxford: Oxford University Press, 2003.

Veijola, Timo. "Bundestheologisches Redaktion im Deuteronomium." Pages 242–76 in *Deuteronomium und seine Querbeziehungen*. Edited by T. Veijola. Schriften der Finnischen Exegetischen Gesellschaft 62. Helsinki: Finnische Exegetische Gesellschaft and Göttingen: Vandenhoeck & Ruprecht, 1996.

___. *Das 5. Buch Mose: Deuteronomium: Kapitel 1,1–16,17*. Das Alt Testament Deutsch 8,1. Göttingen: Vandenhoeck & Ruprecht, 2004.

Vantisphout, H. L. J. "The Banquet Scene in the Mesopotamian Debate Poems." Pages 9–22 in *Banquets D'Orient*. Edited by R. Gyselen. Res Orientales IV. Bures Saint-Yves: Group pour l'Etude de la Civilisation du Moyen-Orient, 1992.

Vera Chamaza, Galo W. *Die Omnipotez Aššurs: Entwicklungen in der Aššur-Theologie unter der Sargoniden Sargon II., Sanherib und Asarhaddon*. Alter Orient und Altes Testament 295. Münster: Ugarit-Verlag, 2002.

Vervenne, Marc. "Current Tendencies and Developments in the Study of the Book of Exodus." Pages 47–54 in *Studies in the Book of Exodus: Redaction—Reception—Interpretation*. Edited by M. Vervenne. Leuven: Leuven University Press, 1996.

Vogt, Peter T. *Deuteronomic Theology and the Significance of Torah: A Reappraisal*. Winona Lake, Ind.: Eisenbrauns, 2006.

Volgger, David. *Israel wird feiern: Untersuchung zu den Gesetztexten in Exodus bis Deuteronomium*. Arbeiten zu Text und Sprache im alten Testament 73. St. Ottilien, Germany: EOS, 2002.

Wagenaar, Jan. "Passover and the First Day of the Festival of Unleavened Bread." *Vetus Testamentum* 54 (2004): 253–54.

Wagner, Volkmar. *Profanität und Sakralisierung im Alten Testament*. Beihefte zur Zeitschrift für die alttestamentliche Wissenschaft 351. Berlin: de Gruyter, 2005

Waltke, Bruce K. and Michael P. O'Connor. *An Introduction to Biblical Hebrew Syntax*. Winona Lake, Ind.: Eisenbrauns, 1990.

Wapnish, Paula. "Archaeozoology: The Integration of Faunal Data with Biblical Archaeology." Pages 426–42 in *Biblical Archaeology Today, 1990: Proceedings of the Second International Congress on Biblical Archaeology*. Edited by A. Biran and J. Aviram. Jerusalem: Israel Exploration Society, 1993.

___. "Is *ṣēnī ana lā māni* an Accurate Description or a Royal Boast?" Pages 285–96 in *Retrieving the Past: Essays on Archaeological Research and Methodology in Honor of Gus W. Van Beek*. Edited by J. D. Seger. Winona Lake, Ind.: Eisenbrauns, 1996.

Watanabe, Kazuko. *Die adê-Vereidigung Anlässlich der Thronfolgeregelung Asarhaddons*. Baghdader Mitteilungen Beiheft 3; Berlin: Mann, 1987.

Watson, Wilfred G. E. "Wonderful Wine (KTU 1.22 I 17–20)." *Ugarit-Forschungen* 31 (1999): 777–84.

Watts, James W. *Ritual and Rhetoric in Leviticus: From Sacrifice to Scripture*. Cambridge: Cambridge University Press, 2007.

Weinfeld, Moshe. *Deuteronomy 1–11: A New Translation with Introduction and Commentary*. Anchor Bible 5. New York: Doubleday, 1991.

___. *Deuteronomy and the Deuteronomistic School*. Oxford: Clarendon, 1972.

___. "The Emergence of the Deuteronomic Movement: The Historical Antecedents." Pages 76–98 in *Das Deuteronomium: Entstehung, Gestalt und Botschaft*. Edited by N. Lohfink. Bibliotheca ephemeridum theologicarum lovaniensium 68. Leuven: Leuven University Press, 1985.

___. *The Place of the Law in the Religion of Ancient Israel*. Leiden: E. J. Brill, 2004.

___. "Reply to J. Milgrom." *Israel Exploration Journal* 23 (1973): 230–33.

Wenham, Gordon J. "Deuteronomy and the Central Sanctuary." Pages 94–108 in *A Song of Power and the Power of Song: Essays on the Book of Deuteronomy*. Edited by D. L. Christensen. Winona Lake, Ind.: Eisenbrauns, 1993. Reprinted from *Tyndale Bulletin* 22 (1971): 103–18.

Wellhausen, Julius. *Prolegomena to the History of Ancient Israel: With a Reprint of the Article, Israel, From the Encyclopedia Britannica*. Preface by W. Robertson Smith. Cleveland: Meridian Books, 1965.

Wevers, John W. *Deuteronomium*. Septuaginta: Vetus Testamentum Graecum. Auctoritate Academiea Scientiarum Gottingensis editum. Volume III, 2. Göttingen: Vandenhoeck & Ruprecht, 1977.

___. *Notes on the Greek text of Deuteronomy*. Septuagint and Cognate Studies Series 39. Atlanta: Scholars, 1995.

___. *Text History of the Greek Deuteronomy*. Mitteilungen des Septuaginta-Unternehmens 13 / Abhandlungen der Akademie der Wissenschaften zu Göttingen. Philologisch-Historische Klasse 3/106. Göttingen: Vandenhoeck & Ruprecht, 1978.

Whit, William C. *Food and Society: A Sociological Approach*. Dix Hills, N.Y.: General Hall, 1995.

Wilber, Donald N. *Persepolis: The Archaeology of Parsa, Seat of the Persian Kings*. Rev. ed. Princeton: Darwin, 1989.

Willi-Plein, Ina. *Opfer und Kult im alttestamentlichen Israel: Textbefragungen und Zwischenergebnisse.* Stuttgarter Bibelstudien 153. Stuttgart: Katholische Bibelwerk, 1993.

Willis, Timothy M. *The Elders of the City: A Study of the Elders-Laws in Deuteronomy.* Society of Biblical Literature Monograph Series 55. Atlanta: SBL, 2001.

Wilson, Ian. *Out of the Midst of the Fire: Divine Presence in Deuteronomy.* Society of Biblical Literature Dissertation Series 151. Atlanta: Scholars, 1995.

Wilson, Robert R. "Deuteronomy, Ethnicity, and Reform." Pages 107–23 in *Constituting the Community: Studies on the Polity of Ancient Israel in Honor of S. Dean McBride, Jr.* Edited by J. T. Strong and S. S. Tuell. Winona Lake, Ind.: Eisenbrauns, 1995.

Winegardner, Mark, ed. *We Are What We Ate: 24 Memories of Food.* San Diego: Harcourt Brace, 1998.

Winter, Irene J. "Art *in* Empire: The Royal Image and the Visual Dimensions of Assyrian Ideology." Pages 359–81 in *Assyria 1995: Proceedings of the 10th Anniversary Symposium of the Neo-Assyrian Text Corpus Project Helsinki, September 7-11, 1995.* Edited by S. Parpola and R. M. Whiting. Helsinki: University of Helsinki, 1997.

___. "The King and the Cup: Iconography of the Royal Presentation Scene on the Ur III Seals." Pages 253–68 in *Insight Through Images: Studies in Honor of Edith Porada.* Edited by M. Kelly-Beccellati, P. Matthiae, and M. Van Loon. Bibliotheca Mesopotamica 21. Malibu, Calif.: Undena Publications, 1986.

Wood, Roy C. *The Sociology of the Meal.* Edinburgh: Edinburgh University Press, 1995

Wright, Christopher J. H. *Deuteronomy.* New International Biblical Commentary. Peabody, Mass.: Hendrickson, 1996.

Wright, David P. *Ritual in Narrative: the Dynamics of Feasting, Mourning, and Retaliation Rites in the Ugaritic Tale of Aqhat.* Winona Lake, Ind.: Eisenbrauns, 2001.

Yu, Suee-Yan. "Tithes and Firstlings in Deuteronomy." Ph.D. diss., Union Theological Seminary in Virginia, 1997.

Zahn, Molly. "Reexamining Empirical Models: The Case of Exodus 13." Pages 36–55 in *Das Deuteronomium zwischen Pentateuch und Deuteronomistischem Geschichtswerk.* Edited by E. Otto and R. Achenbach. Forschungen zur Religion und Literatur des Alten und Neuen Testaments 206. Göttingen. Vandenhoeck & Ruprecht, 2004.

Zgoll, Annette, "Königslauf und Götterrat: Struktur und Deutung des babylonischen Neujahrsfests." Pages 11–80 in *Festtraditionen in Israel und im Alten Orient.* Edited by E. Blum and R. Lux. Veröffentlichungen der Wissenschaftlichen Gesellschaft für Theologie 28. Gütersloh: Gütersloher Verlagshaus, 2006.

Index

Biblical Texts

Extra Biblical Texts

West Semitic

KAI 11	152
KAI 200–202	24, 29, 31
TAD A4.10	18
TAD A4.7	18
TAD A4.8	18
Arad 5:10–12	222
Azitawadda	133, 185
Samaria Ostraca	76, 230

Ugaritic

CTU 1.1–1.6	55, 69, 133, 168, 173–83, 205, 209, 222, 243
CTU 1.3.I.02–22	171
CTU 1.3.I.2–27	174–75
CTU 1.3.I.9	221
CTU 1.3.II.36–37	174
CTU 1.3.III–IV	174
CTU 1.3.IV.40–46	170
CTU 1.4.III.10–16	177
CTU 1.4.III.14–22	206
CTU 1.4.III.17–22	148
CTU 1.4.III.33–44	174
CTU 1.4.IV.33–38	174
CTU 1.4.VI.38–49	171
CTU 1.4.VI.38–59	174, 176
CTU 1.4.VI.40–59	185
CTU 1.4.VI.44–47	177
CTU 1.4.VI.46	145
CTU 1.4.VI.47–52	176
CTU 1.4.VI.51–52	176
CTU 1.5–1.6	174
CTU 1.6.II.30–35	183
CTU 1.14–1.16	168–69
CTU 1.14.II.27	176

CTU 1.16.I.39–41	221
CTU 1.16.VI.17–21	170
CTU 1.17	170–72
1.17–1.19	168–70, 180, 202
CTU 1.17.V.16	176
CTU 1.17.VI.30	221
CTU 1.20	182–83
1.20–1.22	169–73, 180, 205, 243
CTU 1.20.I.12–14	176
CTU 1.20.II.06–7	170
CTU 1.22.I.12–20	171
CTU 1.22.I.22–26	169
CTU 1.22.II.20–26	170
CTU 1.23	24, 180
CTU 1.40	68, 135, 149–56, 203, 242
CTU 1.41	148, 164, 182
CTU 1.41.10	176
CTU 1.43.2	221
CTU 1.54	149
CTU 1.84	149
CTU 1.87	148, 182
CTU 1.91	148–49, 185
CTU 1.106:18–28	149
CTU 1.114	154, 172–74, 177, 202, 205
CTU 1.114.1–2	173
CTU 1.114.1–4	172
CTU 1.119	23, 153–54, 243
CTU 1.119.32–33	249
CTU 1.121	149
CTU 1.122	149
PRU III.10.044	223
PRU III.16.153	223
PRU V.11	223
Ug 5.iii.6	149

Iconography